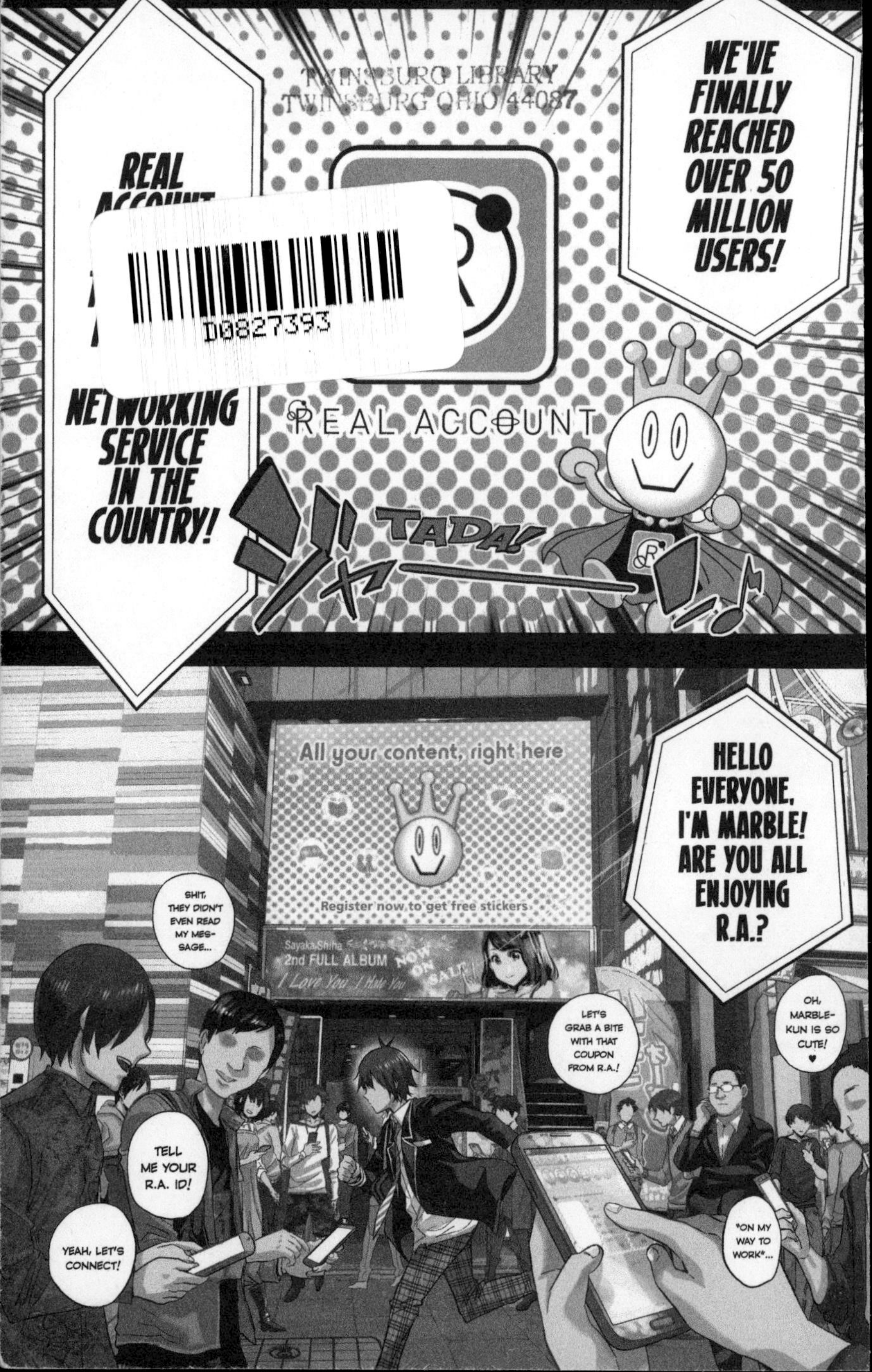
WE'VE FINALLY REACHED OVER 50 MILLION USERS!
REAL
NETWORKING SERVICE IN THE COUNTRY!
REAL ACCOUNT
TADA!
HELLO EVERYONE, I'M MARBLE! ARE YOU ALL ENJOYING R.A.?
OH, MARBLE-KUN IS SO CUTE! ♥
ON MY WAY TO WORK...
LET'S GRAB A BITE WITH THAT COUPON FROM R.A.!
All your content, right here
Register now to get free stickers
Sayaka Shiina 2nd FULL ALBUM NOW ON SALE!
I Love You, I Hate You
SHIT, THEY DIDN'T EVEN READ MY MESSAGE...
TELL ME YOUR R.A. ID!
YEAH, LET'S CONNECT!

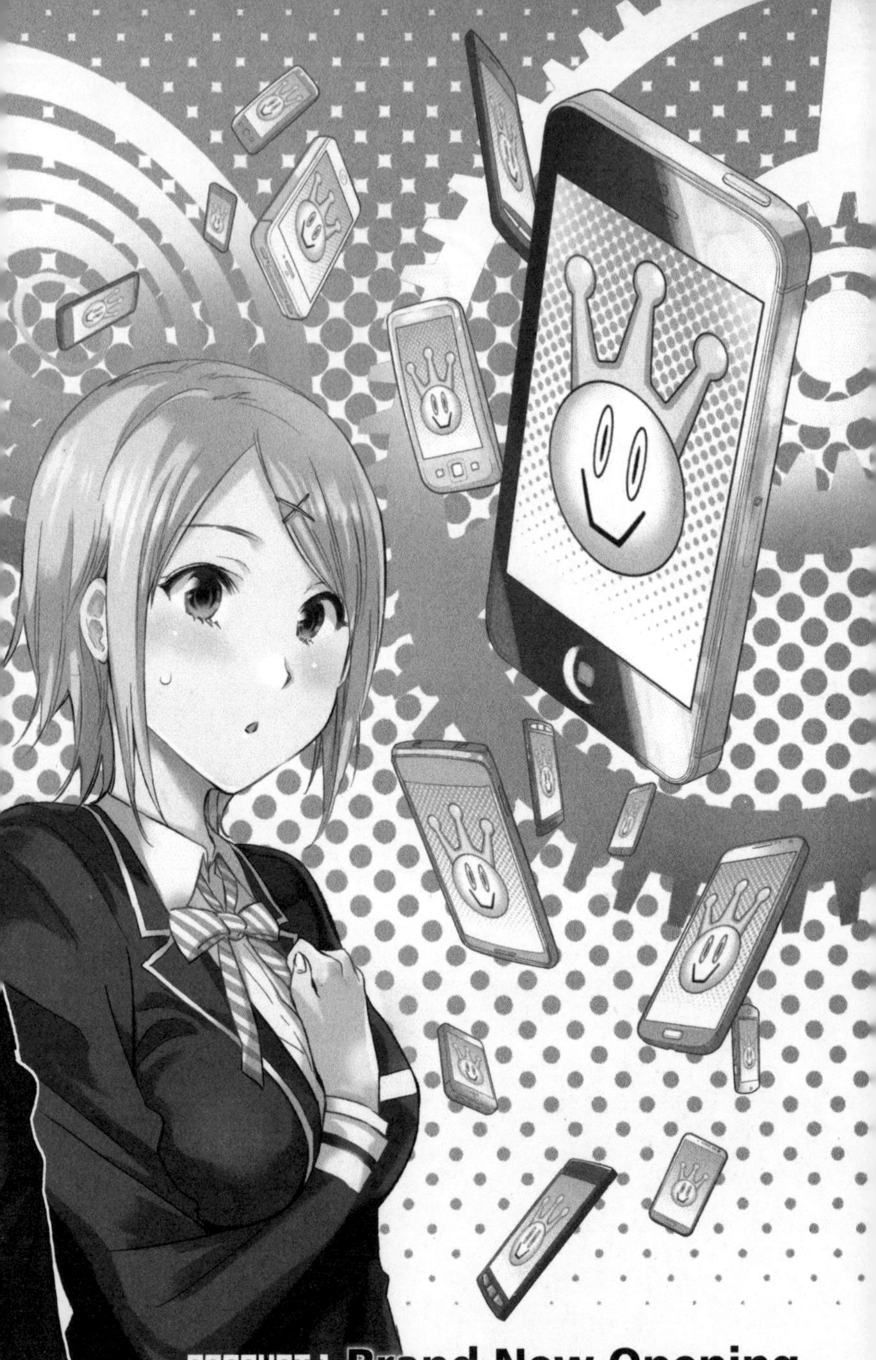

ACCOUNT 1 Brand New Opening

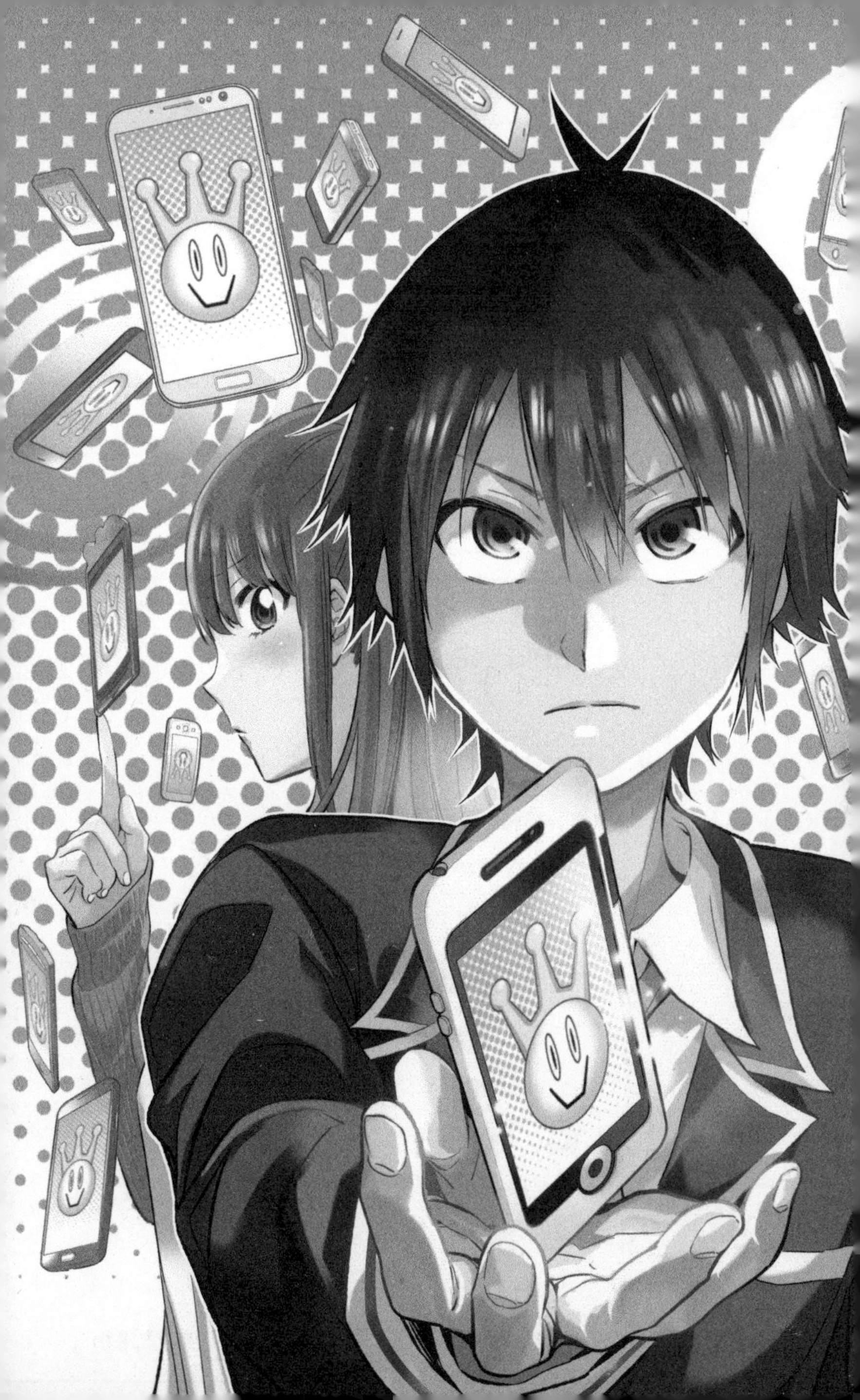

CONTENTS

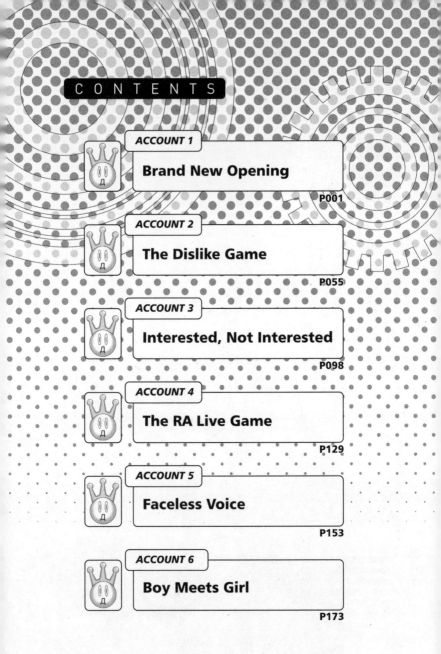

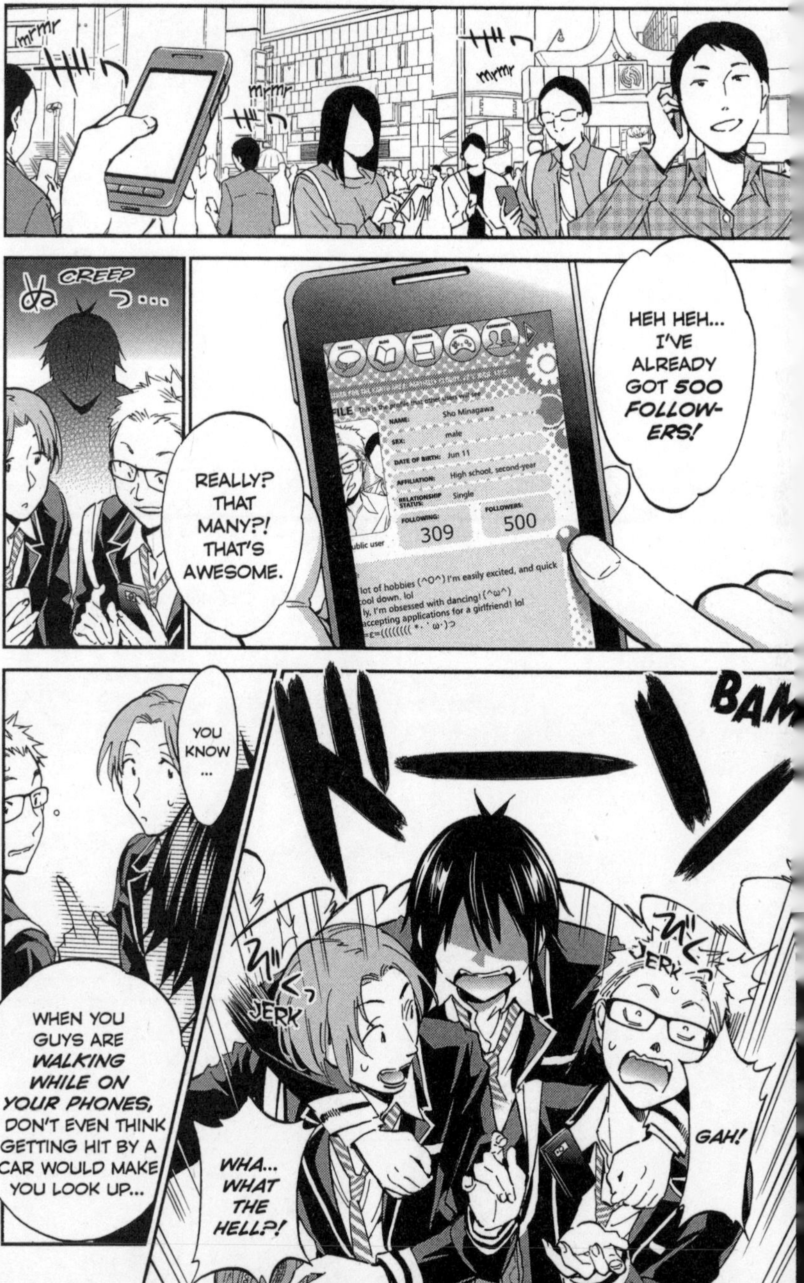
mrmr
mrmr
mrmr
HEH HEH... I'VE ALREADY GOT 500 FOLLOWERS!
NAME: Sho Minagawa
SEX: male
DATE OF BIRTH: Jun 11
AFFILIATION: High school, second-year
RELATIONSHIP STATUS: Single
FOLLOWING: 309
FOLLOWERS: 500
REALLY? THAT MANY?! THAT'S AWESOME.
CREEP...
BAM
JERK
GAH!
JERK
WHA... WHAT THE HELL?!
YOU KNOW...
WHEN YOU GUYS ARE WALKING WHILE ON YOUR PHONES, I DON'T EVEN THINK GETTING HIT BY A CAR WOULD MAKE YOU LOOK UP...

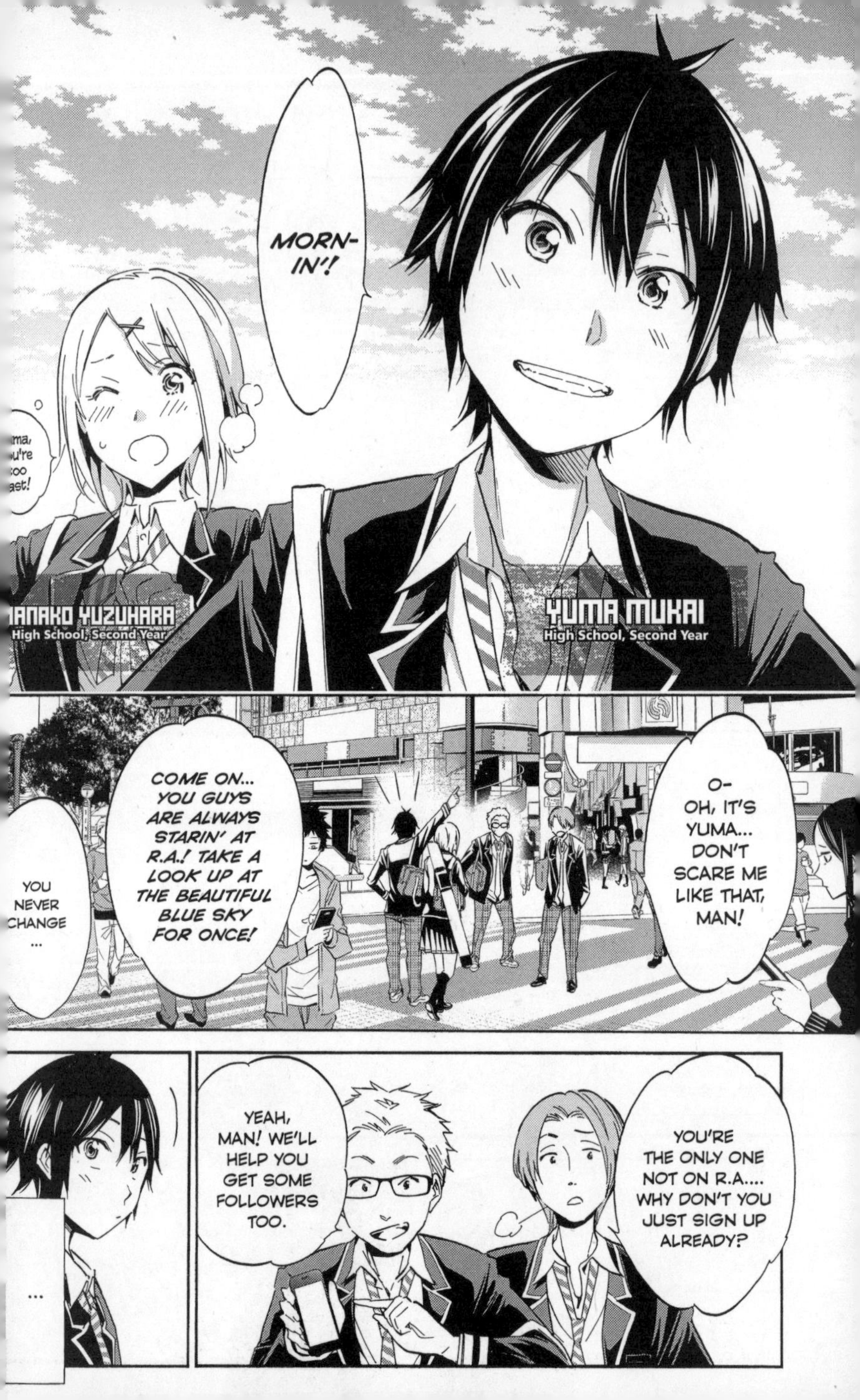
YUMA MUKAI
High School, Second Year
MORN-IN'!
ANAKO YUZUHARA
High School, Second Year
O- OH, IT'S YUMA... DON'T SCARE ME LIKE THAT, MAN!
COME ON... YOU GUYS ARE ALWAYS STARIN' AT R.A.! TAKE A LOOK UP AT THE BEAUTIFUL BLUE SKY FOR ONCE!
YOU NEVER CHANGE ...
YOU'RE THE ONLY ONE NOT ON R.A.... WHY DON'T YOU JUST SIGN UP ALREADY?
YEAH, MAN! WE'LL HELP YOU GET SOME FOLLOWERS TOO.
...

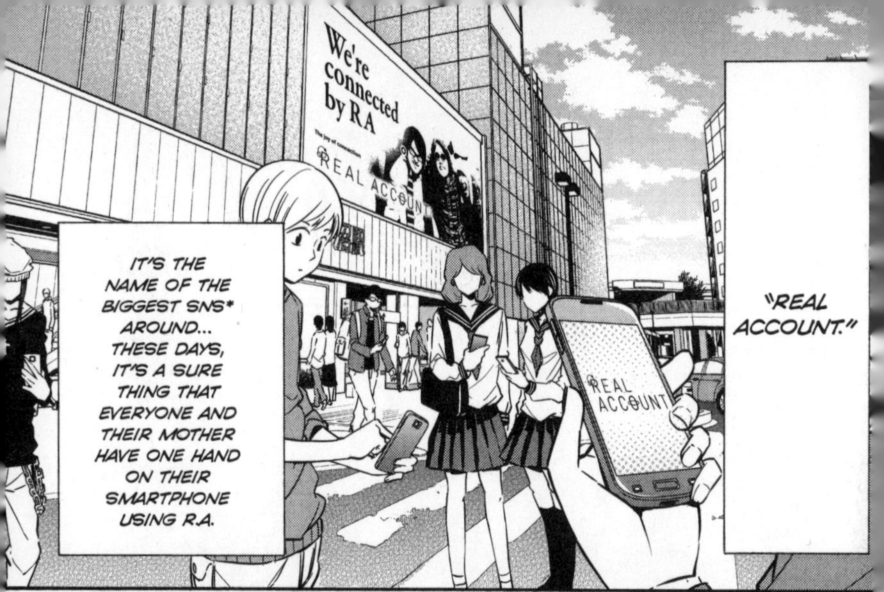
We're connected by RA
The joy of connection
REAL ACCOUNT
"REAL ACCOUNT."
IT'S THE NAME OF THE BIGGEST SNS* AROUND... THESE DAYS, IT'S A SURE THING THAT EVERYONE AND THEIR MOTHER HAVE ONE HAND ON THEIR SMARTPHONE USING R.A.
REAL ACCOUNT

SNS (Social Networking Service): A general term for a community-style website that promotes and supports connections between people.

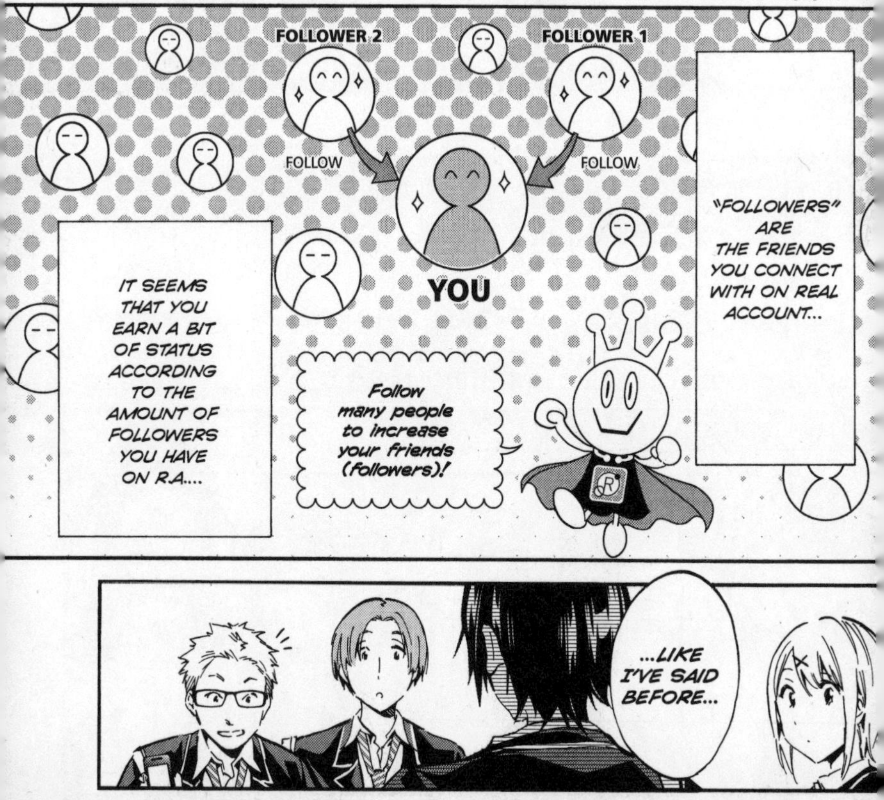
"FOLLOWERS" ARE THE FRIENDS YOU CONNECT WITH ON REAL ACCOUNT...
FOLLOWER 1
FOLLOWER 2
FOLLOW
FOLLOW
YOU
Follow many people to increase your friends (followers)!
IT SEEMS THAT YOU EARN A BIT OF STATUS ACCORDING TO THE AMOUNT OF FOLLOWERS YOU HAVE ON R.A....
...LIKE I'VE SAID BEFORE...

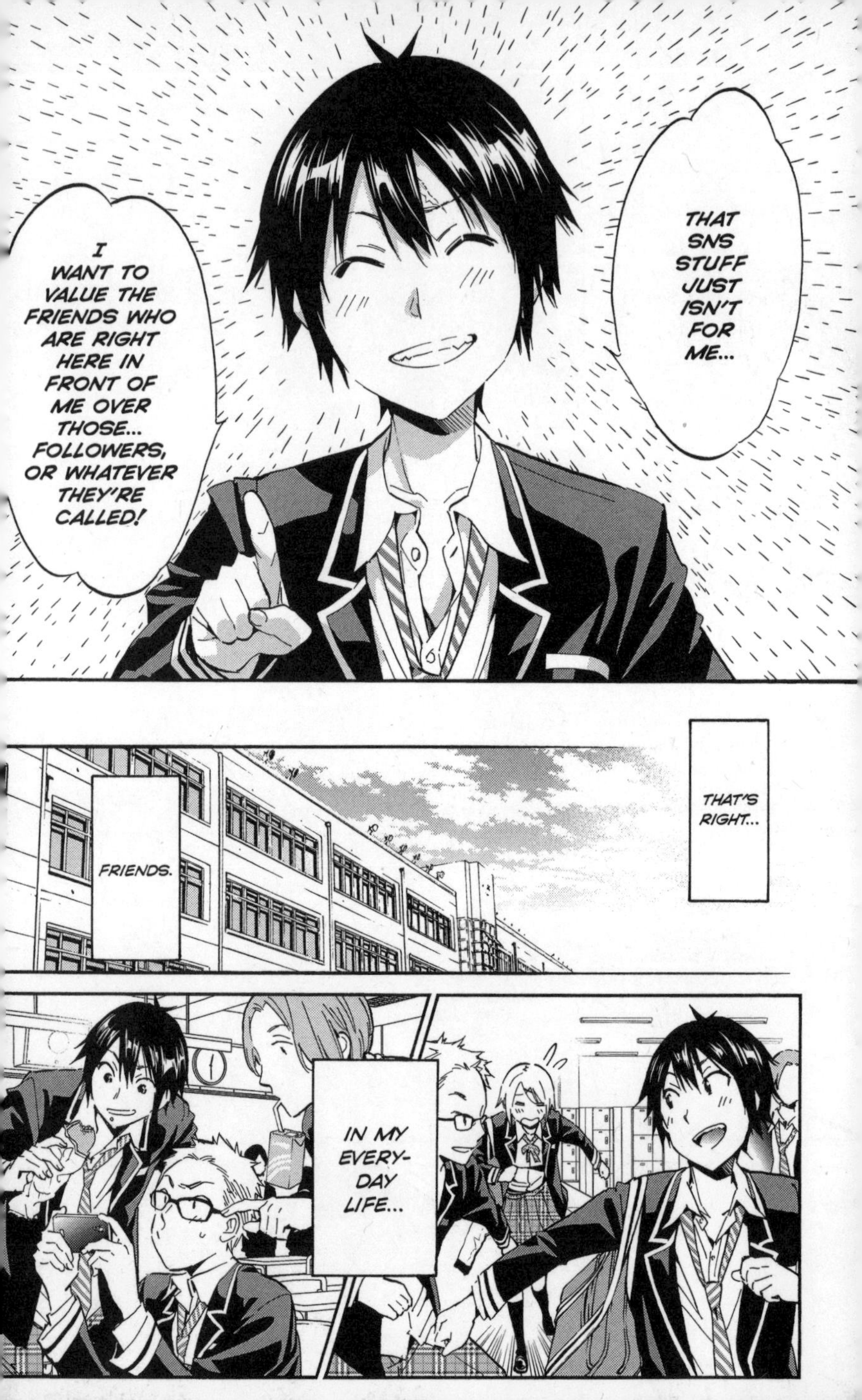
THAT SNS STUFF JUST ISN'T FOR ME...
I WANT TO VALUE THE FRIENDS WHO ARE RIGHT HERE IN FRONT OF ME OVER THOSE... FOLLOWERS, OR WHATEVER THEY'RE CALLED!
THAT'S RIGHT...
FRIENDS.
IN MY EVERY-DAY LIFE...

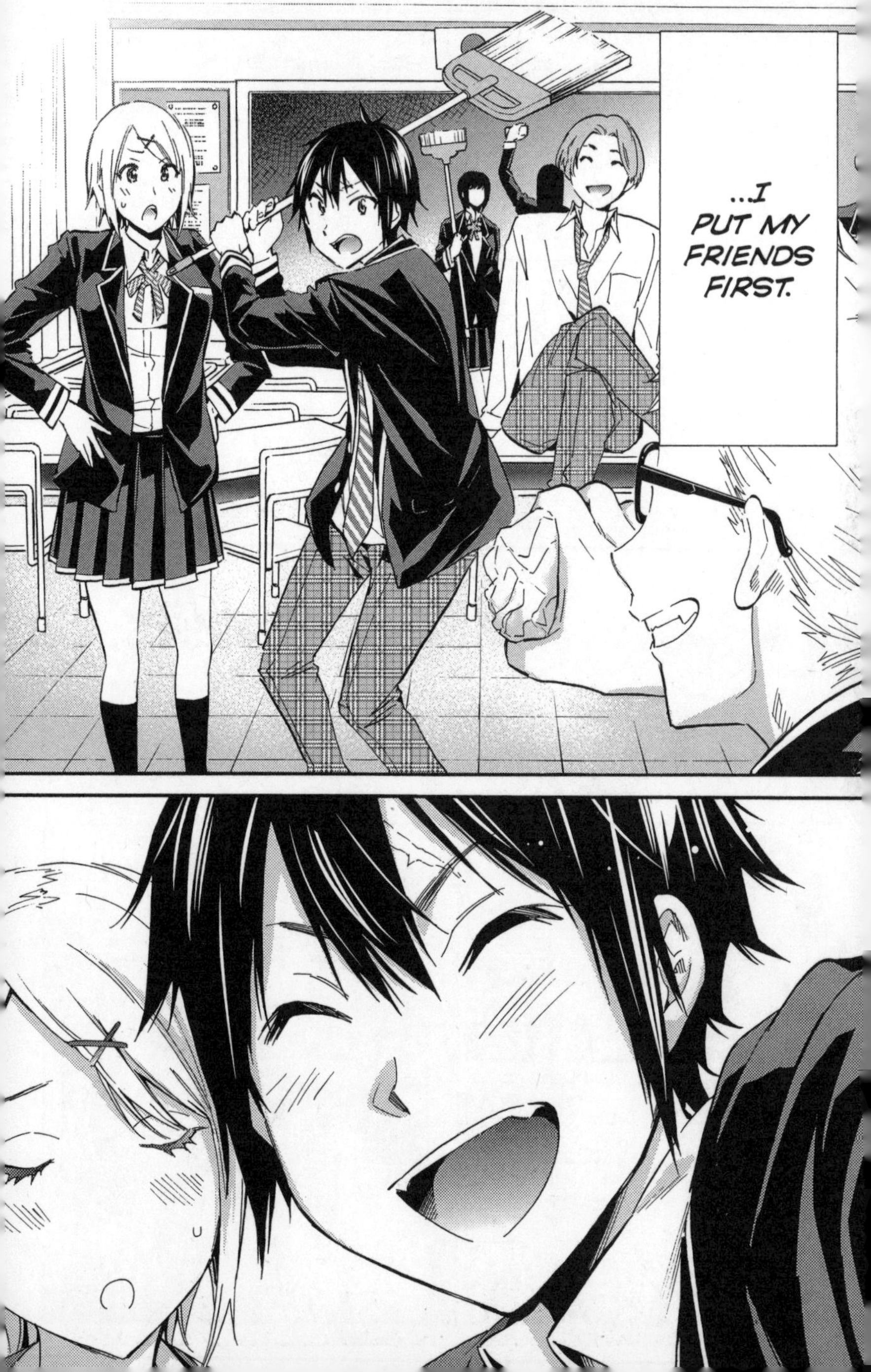
...I PUT MY FRIENDS FIRST.

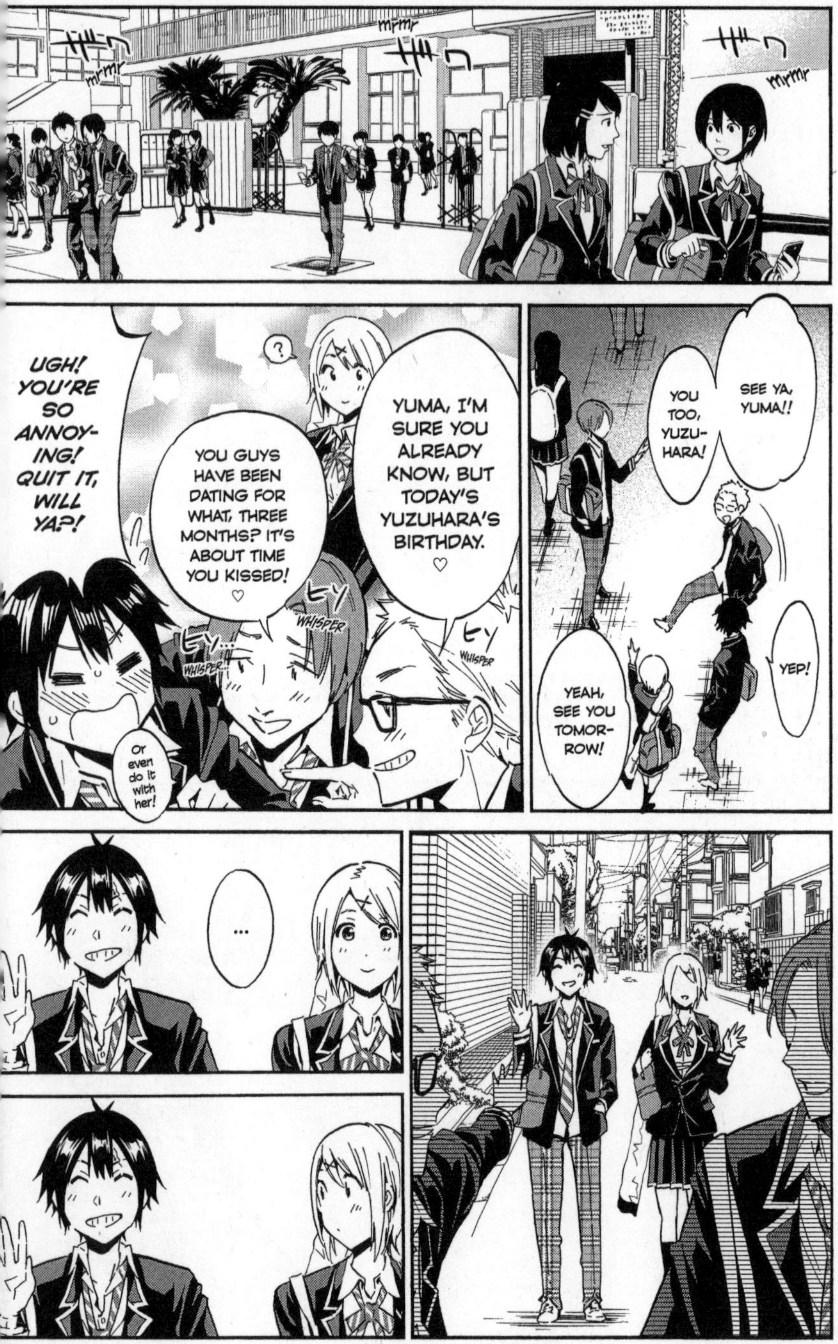
mrmr
mrmr
mrmr
SEE YA, YUMA!!
YOU TOO, YUZUHARA!
YEP!
YEAH, SEE YOU TOMORROW!
YUMA, I'M SURE YOU ALREADY KNOW, BUT TODAY'S YUZUHARA'S BIRTHDAY. ♡
WHISPER
?
YOU GUYS HAVE BEEN DATING FOR WHAT, THREE MONTHS? IT'S ABOUT TIME YOU KISSED! ♡
WHISPER
WHISPER...
UGH! YOU'RE SO ANNOYING! QUIT IT, WILL YA?!
Or even do it with her!
...

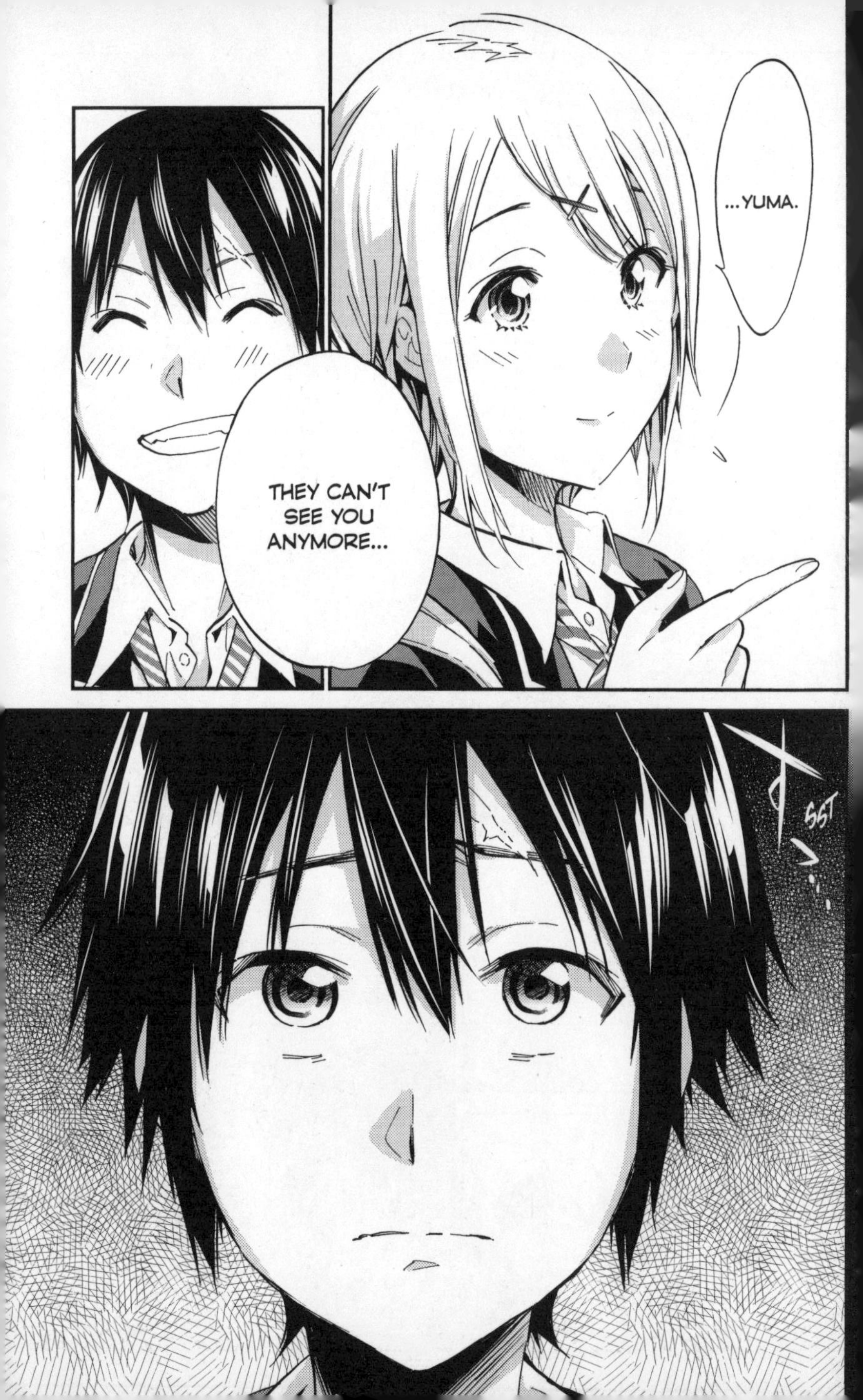
...YUMA.
THEY CAN'T SEE YOU ANYMORE...
SST

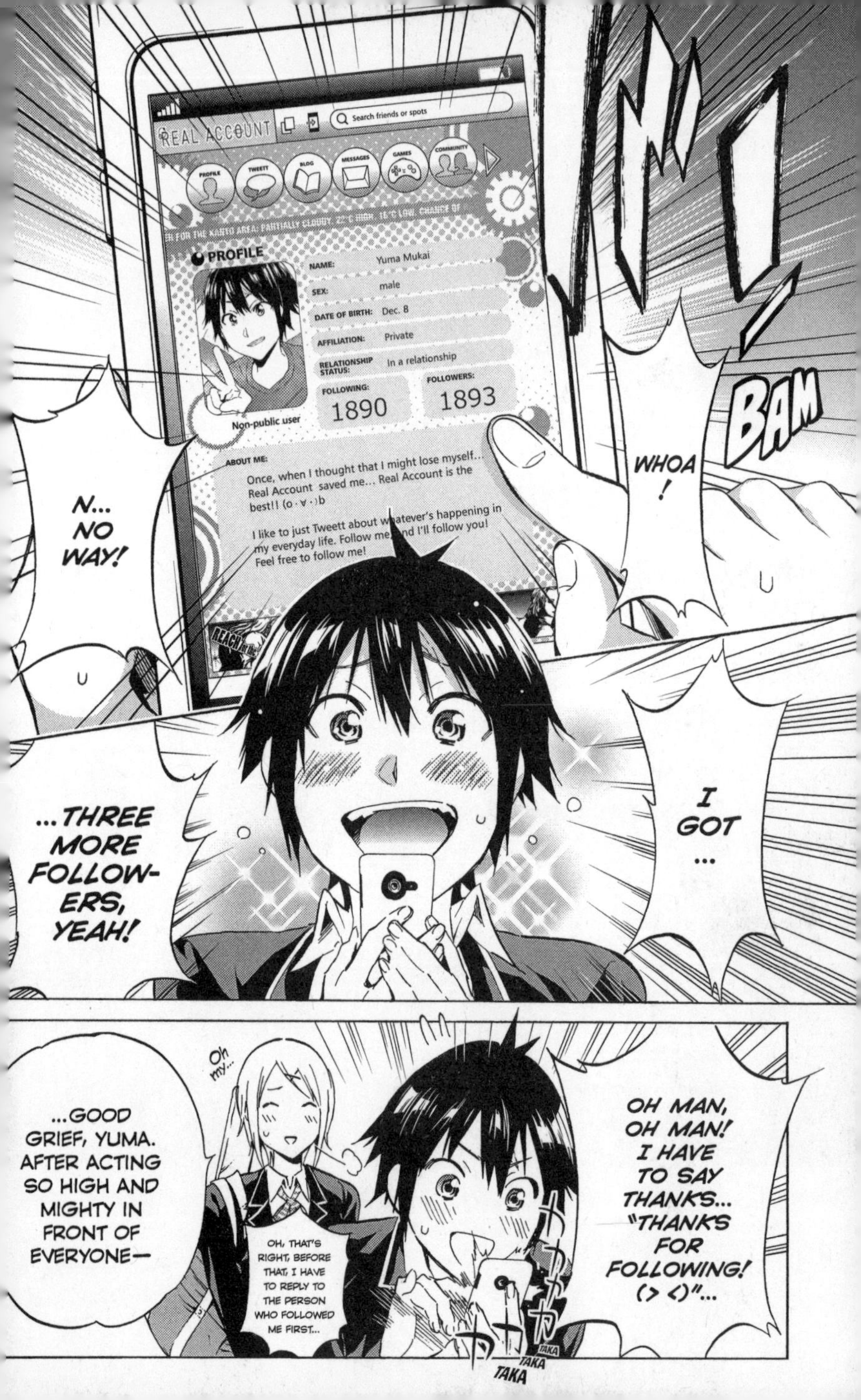
BAM
WHOA!
REAL ACCOUNT
Search friends or spots
PROFILE
TWEETT
BLOG
MESSAGES
GAMES
COMMUNITY
PROFILE
NAME: Yuma Mukai
SEX: male
DATE OF BIRTH: Dec. 8
AFFILIATION: Private
RELATIONSHIP STATUS: In a relationship
FOLLOWING: 1890
FOLLOWERS: 1893
Non-public user
ABOUT ME:
Once, when I thought that I might lose myself... Real Account saved me... Real Account is the best!! (o·∀·)b
I like to just Tweett about whatever's happening in my everyday life. Follow me and I'll follow you! Feel free to follow me!
N... NO WAY!
I GOT...
...THREE MORE FOLLOWERS, YEAH!
OH MAN, OH MAN! I HAVE TO SAY THANKS... "THANKS FOR FOLLOWING! (> <)"...
TAKA TAKA TAKA
OH, THAT'S RIGHT, BEFORE THAT, I HAVE TO REPLY TO THE PERSON WHO FOLLOWED ME FIRST...
Oh my...
...GOOD GRIEF, YUMA. AFTER ACTING SO HIGH AND MIGHTY IN FRONT OF EVERYONE—

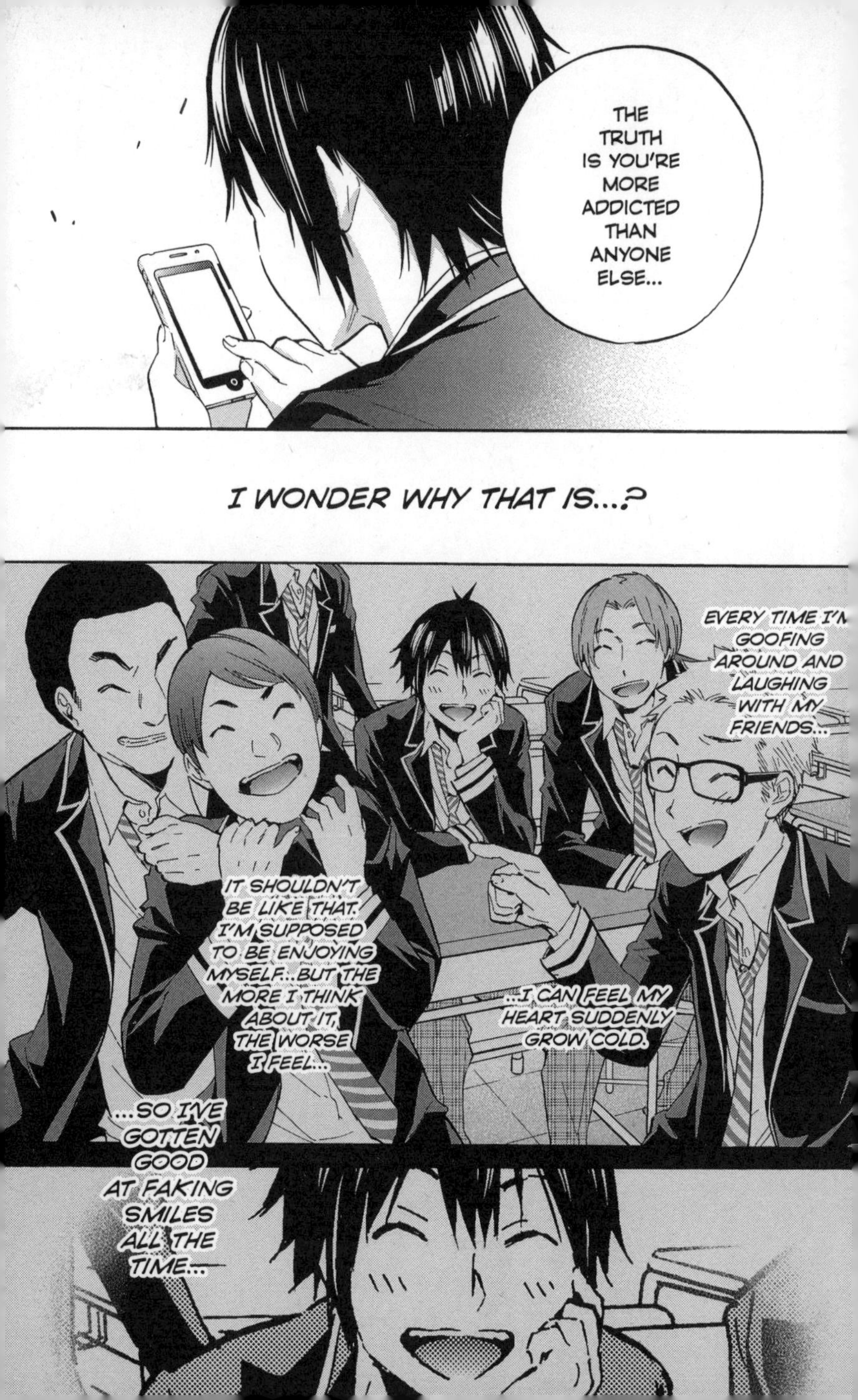
THE TRUTH IS YOU'RE MORE ADDICTED THAN ANYONE ELSE...
I WONDER WHY THAT IS...?
EVERY TIME I'M GOOFING AROUND AND LAUGHING WITH MY FRIENDS...
...I CAN FEEL MY HEART SUDDENLY GROW COLD.
IT SHOULDN'T BE LIKE THAT. I'M SUPPOSED TO BE ENJOYING MYSELF...BUT THE MORE I THINK ABOUT IT, THE WORSE I FEEL...
...SO I'VE GOTTEN GOOD AT FAKING SMILES ALL THE TIME...

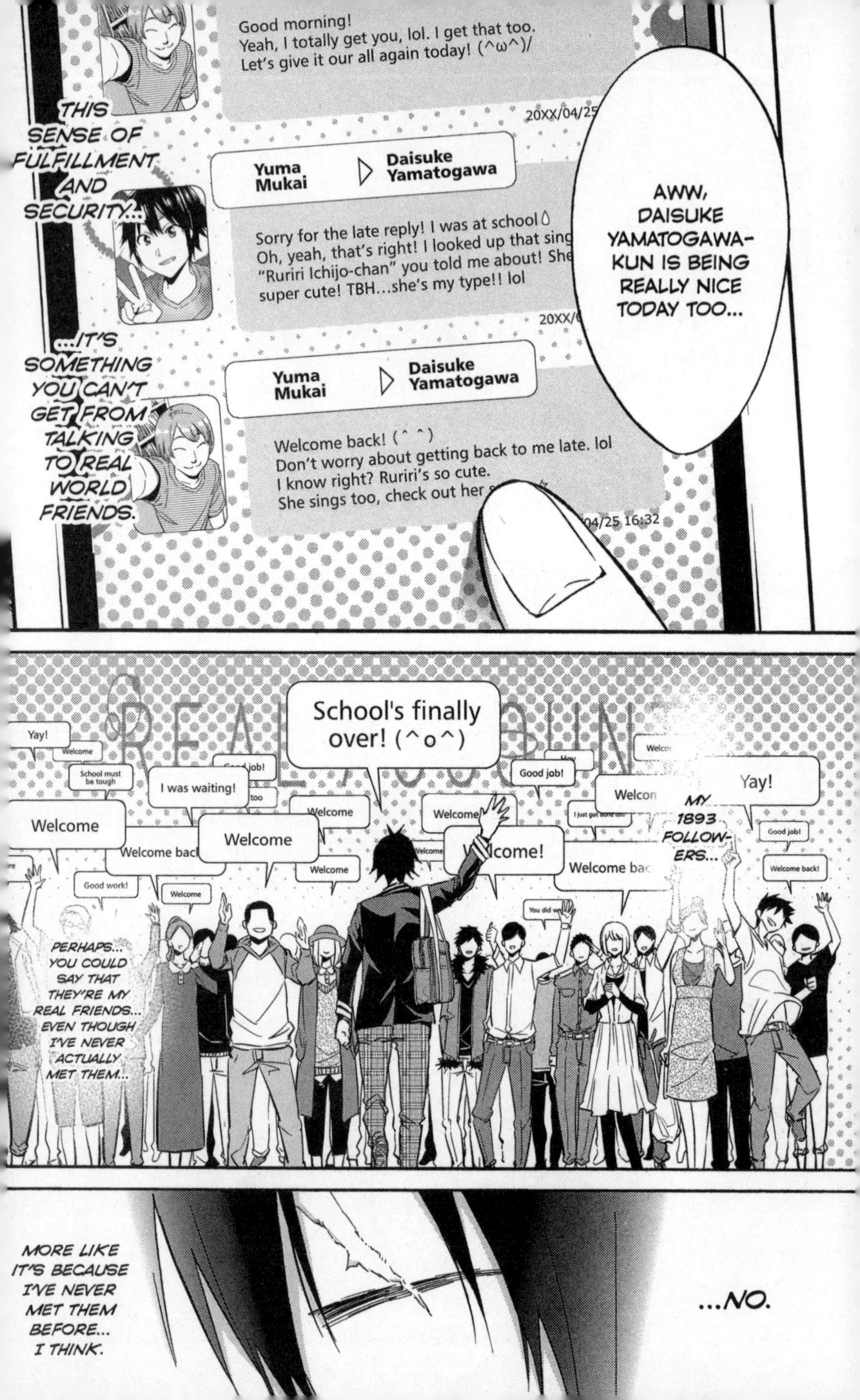
AWW, DAISUKE YAMATOGAWA-KUN IS BEING REALLY NICE TODAY TOO...
Good morning!
Yeah, I totally get you, lol. I get that too.
Let's give it our all again today! (^ω^)/
20XX/04/25
Yuma Mukai ▷ Daisuke Yamatogawa
Sorry for the late reply! I was at school
Oh, yeah, that's right! I looked up that sing
"Ruriri Ichijo-chan" you told me about! She
super cute! TBH...she's my type!! lol
20XX/0
Yuma Mukai ▷ Daisuke Yamatogawa
Welcome back! (^ ^)
Don't worry about getting back to me late. lol
I know right? Ruriri's so cute.
She sings too, check out her
04/25 16:32
THIS SENSE OF FULFILLMENT AND SECURITY...
...IT'S SOMETHING YOU CAN'T GET FROM TALKING TO REAL WORLD FRIENDS.
Yay!
Good job!
Welcome back!
MY 1893 FOLLOW-ERS...
Good job!
Welcome bac
Welcon
Welcome!
School's finally over! (^o^)
Welcome
Welcome
Welcome
I was waiting!
Good job!
Welcome
Welcome back
Welcome
Good work!
School must be tough
Welcome
Yay!
PERHAPS... YOU COULD SAY THAT THEY'RE MY REAL FRIENDS... EVEN THOUGH I'VE NEVER ACTUALLY MET THEM...
...NO.
MORE LIKE IT'S BECAUSE I'VE NEVER MET THEM BEFORE... I THINK.

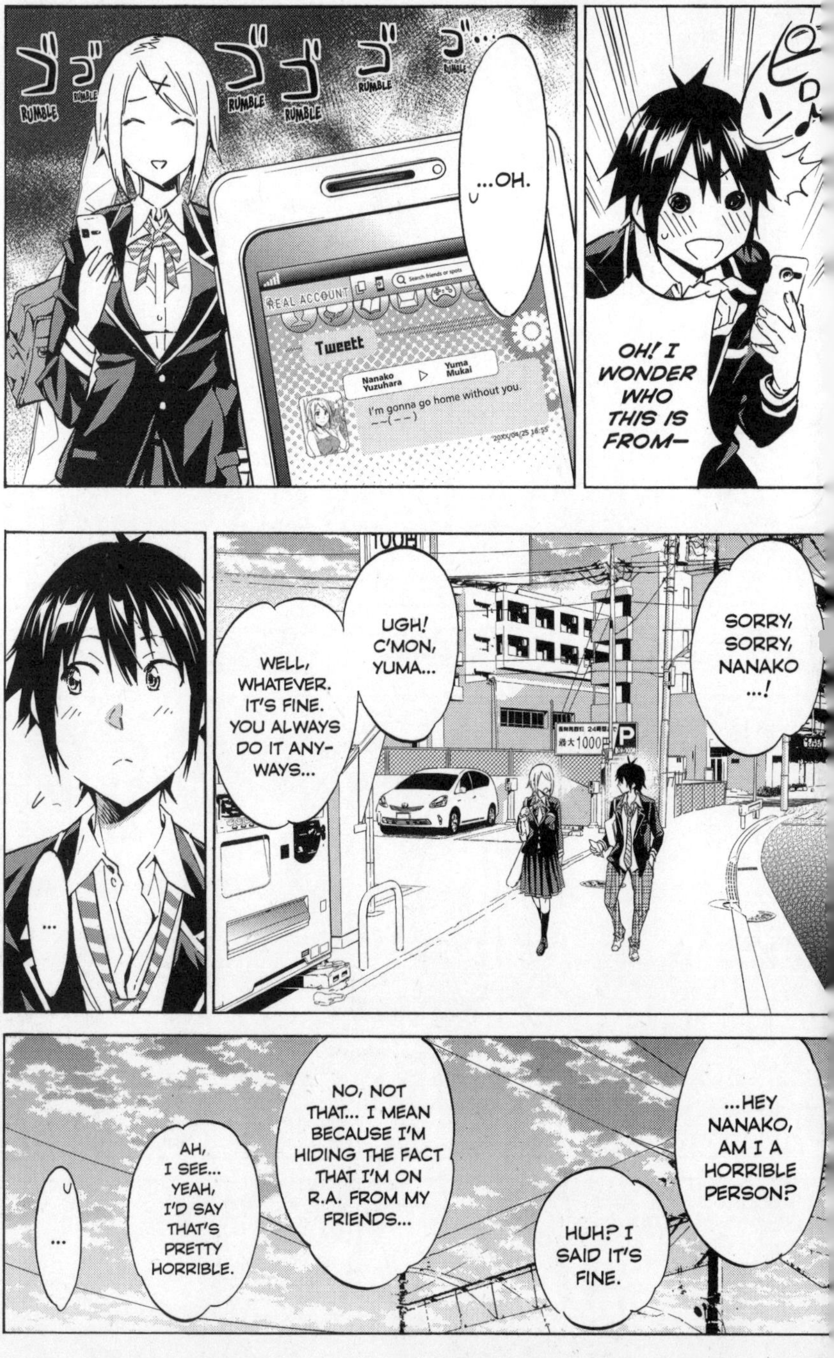
OH! I WONDER WHO THIS IS FROM—
RUMBLE
RUMBLE
RUMBLE
RUMBLE
RUMBLE
RUMBLE
...OH.
REAL ACCOUNT
Tweett
Nanako Yuzuhara
Yuma Mukai
I'm gonna go home without you. ~~(－－)
SORRY, SORRY, NANAKO ...!
UGH! C'MON, YUMA...
WELL, WHATEVER. IT'S FINE. YOU ALWAYS DO IT ANY-WAYS...
...
...HEY NANAKO, AM I A HORRIBLE PERSON?
HUH? I SAID IT'S FINE.
NO, NOT THAT... I MEAN BECAUSE I'M HIDING THE FACT THAT I'M ON R.A. FROM MY FRIENDS...
AH, I SEE... YEAH, I'D SAY THAT'S PRETTY HORRIBLE.
...

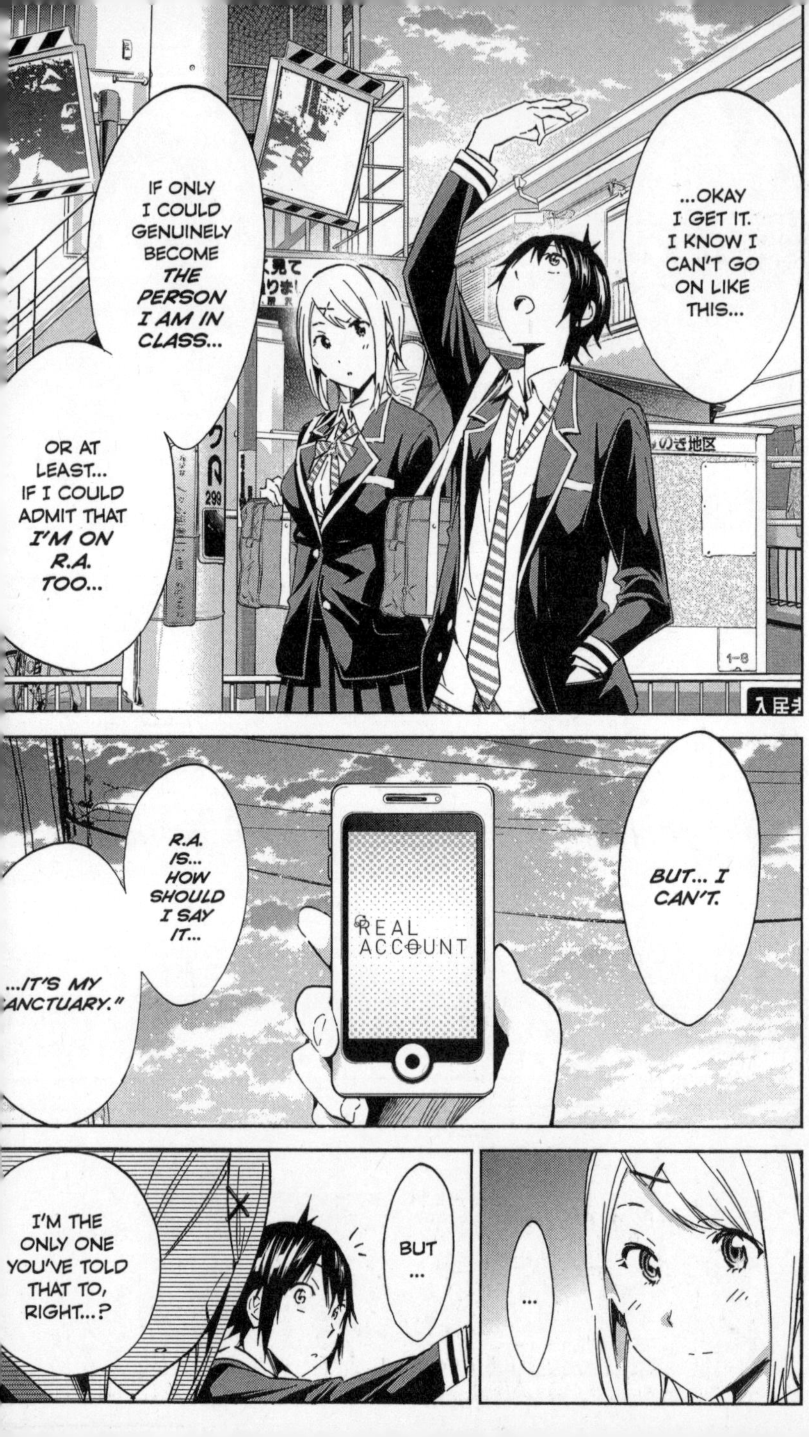
...OKAY I GET IT. I KNOW I CAN'T GO ON LIKE THIS...
IF ONLY I COULD GENUINELY BECOME THE PERSON I AM IN CLASS...
OR AT LEAST... IF I COULD ADMIT THAT I'M ON R.A. TOO...
BUT... I CAN'T.
REAL ACCOUNT
R.A. IS... HOW SHOULD I SAY IT...
...IT'S MY ANCTUARY."
...
BUT ...
I'M THE ONLY ONE YOU'VE TOLD THAT TO, RIGHT...?

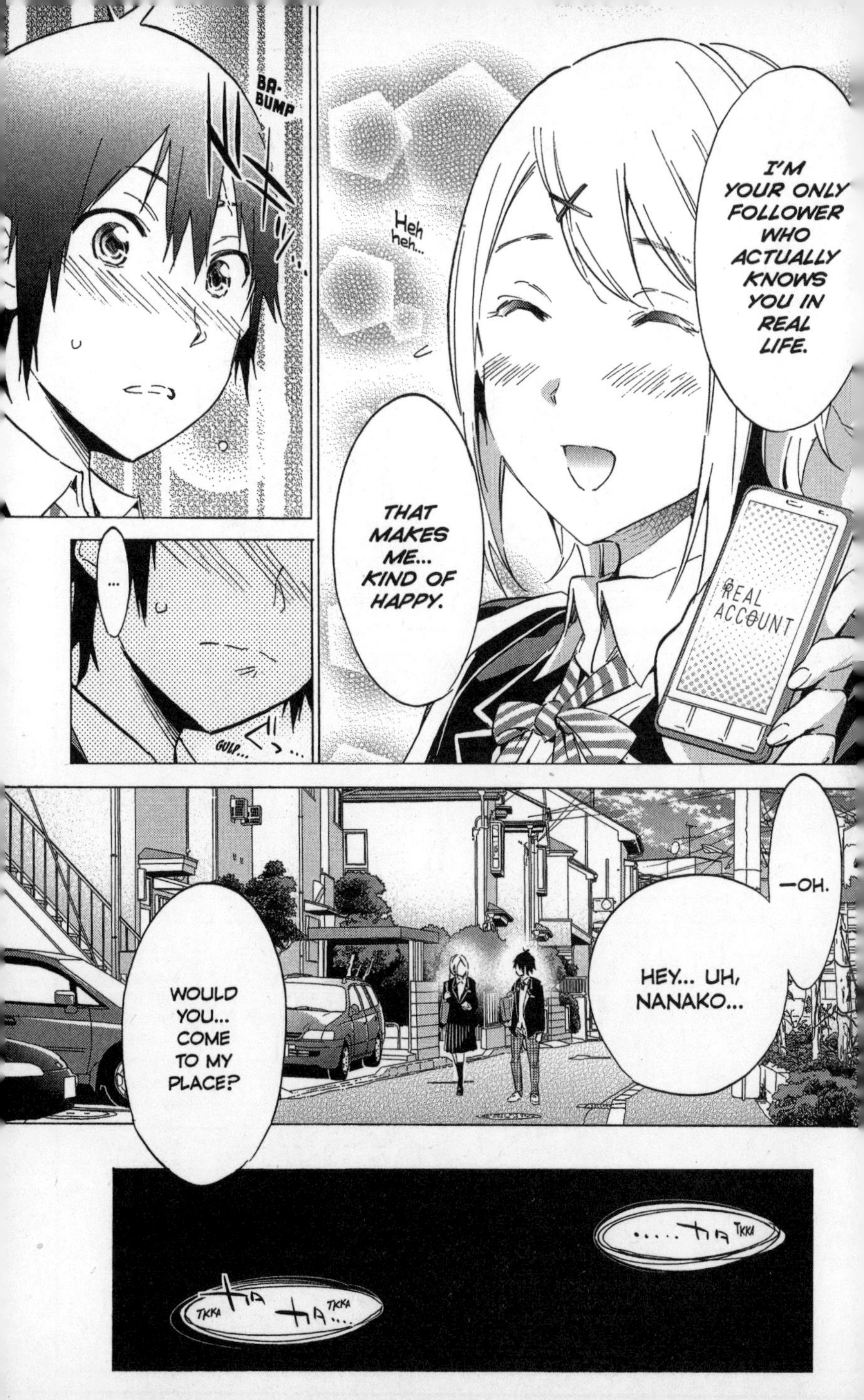
I'M YOUR ONLY FOLLOWER WHO ACTUALLY KNOWS YOU IN REAL LIFE.
Heh heh...
THAT MAKES ME... KIND OF HAPPY.
REAL ACCOUNT
BA-BUMP
...
GULP...
—OH.
HEY... UH, NANAKO...
WOULD YOU... COME TO MY PLACE?
TKKA
TKKA
TKKA

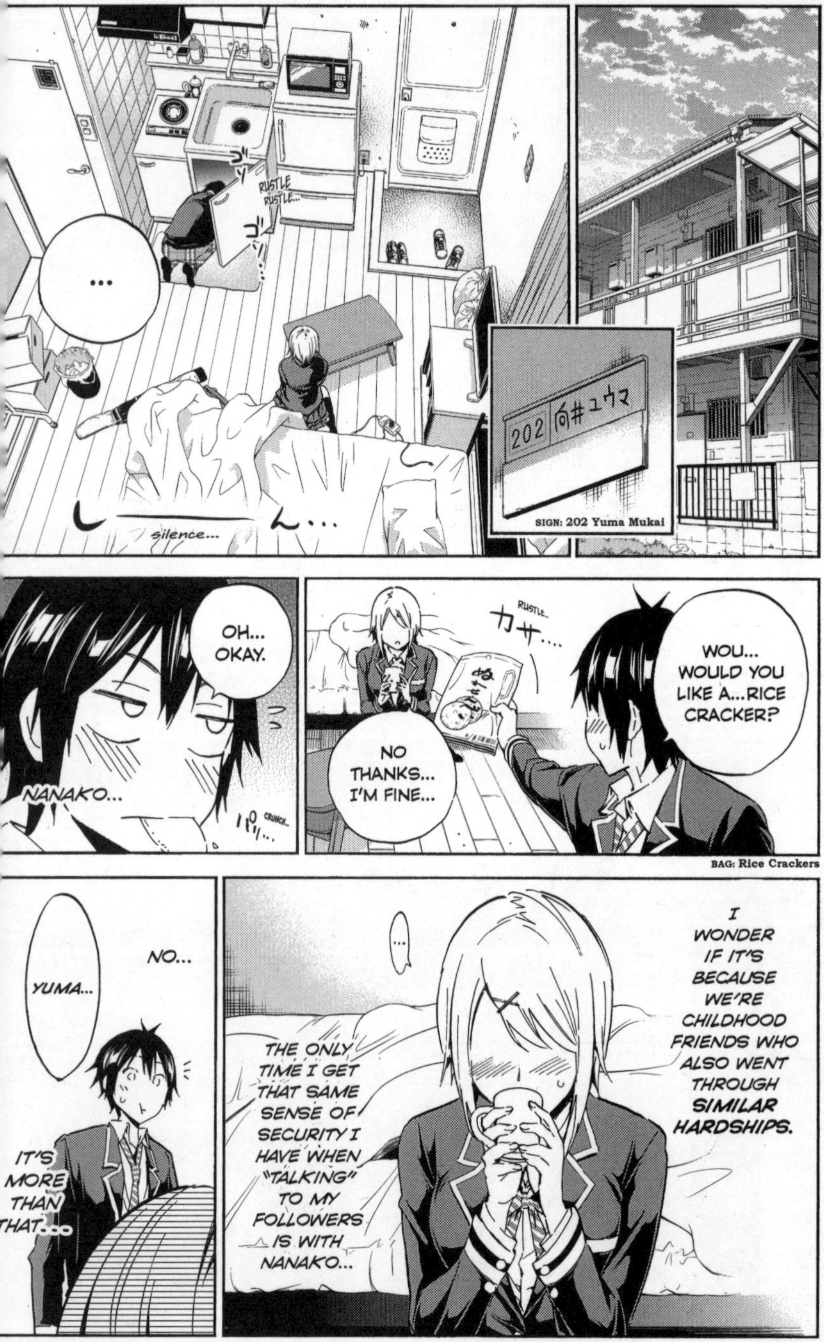
202 向井ユウマ
SIGN: 202 Yuma Mukai
RUSTLE RUSTLE...
...
silence...
カサ...
RUSTLE
WOU... WOULD YOU LIKE A...RICE CRACKER?
NO THANKS... I'M FINE...
BAG: Rice Crackers
OH... OKAY.
NANAKO...
CRUNCH
I WONDER IF IT'S BECAUSE WE'RE CHILDHOOD FRIENDS WHO ALSO WENT THROUGH SIMILAR HARDSHIPS.
...
THE ONLY TIME I GET THAT SAME SENSE OF SECURITY I HAVE WHEN "TALKING" TO MY FOLLOWERS IS WITH NANAKO...
NO...
YUMA...
IT'S MORE THAN THAT...

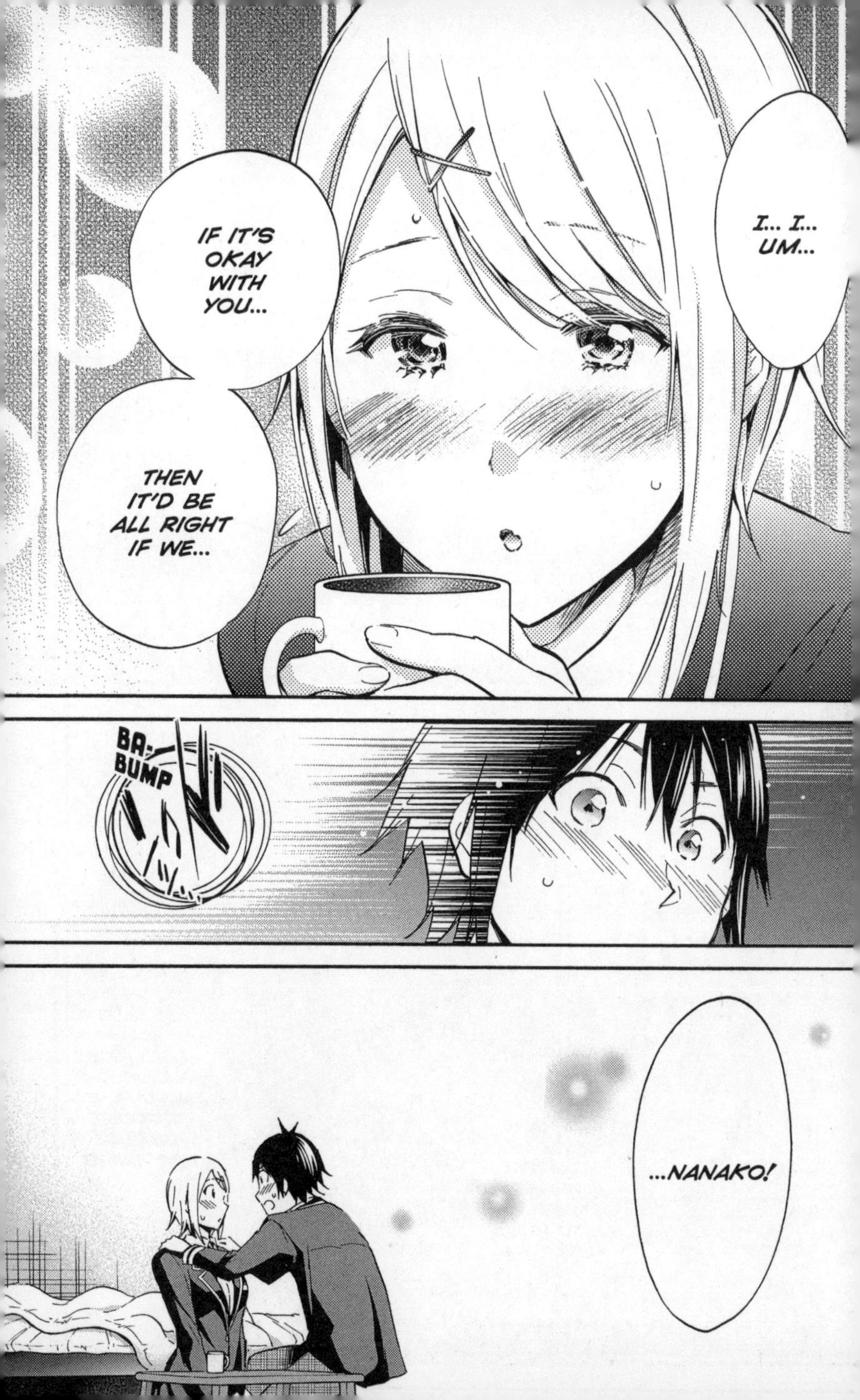
I... I... UM...
IF IT'S OKAY WITH YOU...
THEN IT'D BE ALL RIGHT IF WE...
BA-BUMP
...NANAKO!

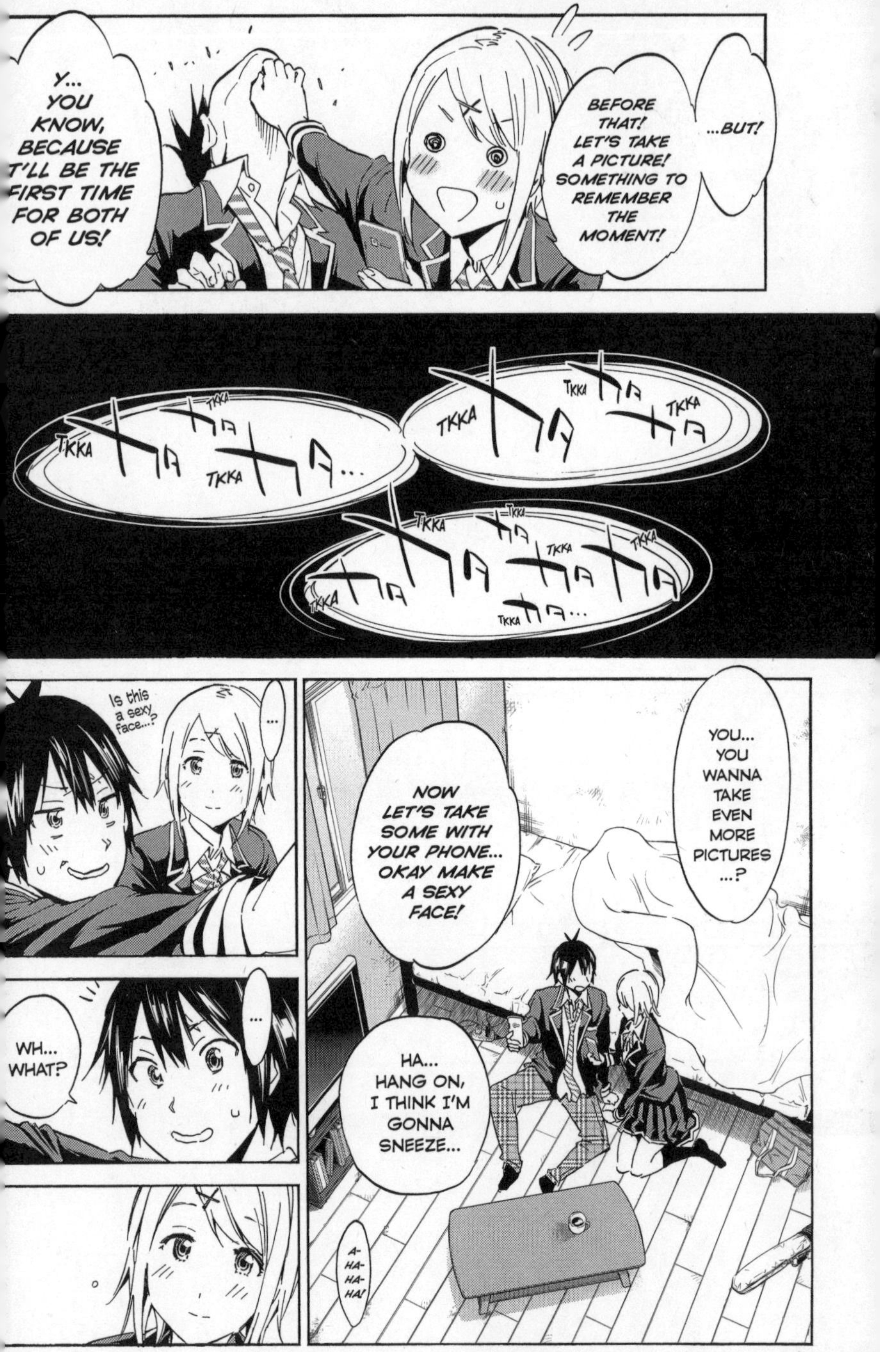
...BUT!
BEFORE THAT! LET'S TAKE A PICTURE! SOMETHING TO REMEMBER THE MOMENT!
Y... YOU KNOW, BECAUSE T'LL BE THE FIRST TIME FOR BOTH OF US!
TKKA HA TKKA HA TKKA HA
TKKA HA TKKA HA TKKA HA...
TKKA HA TKKA HA TKKA HA TKKA HA TKKA HA TKKA HA...
YOU... YOU WANNA TAKE EVEN MORE PICTURES ...?
NOW LET'S TAKE SOME WITH YOUR PHONE... OKAY MAKE A SEXY FACE!
HA... HANG ON, I THINK I'M GONNA SNEEZE...
A-HA-HA-HA!
...
Is this a sexy face...?
...
WH... WHAT?

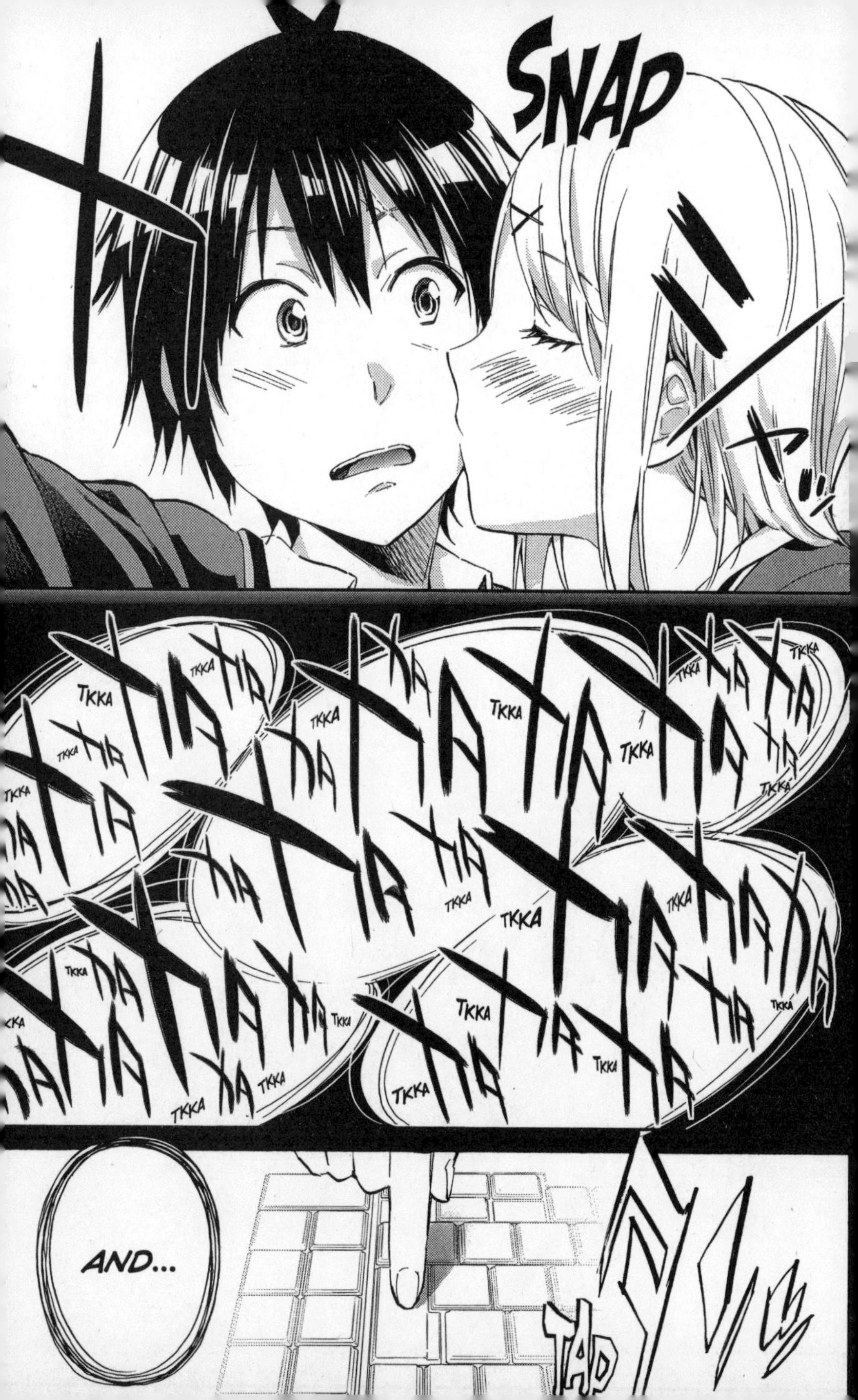
SNAP
TKKA TKKA TKKA TKKA TKKA TKKA TKKA TKKA TKKA TKKA TKKA TKKA TKKA TKKA TKKA TKKA TKKA TKKA TKKA TKKA TKKA TKKA TKKA
TAP
AND...

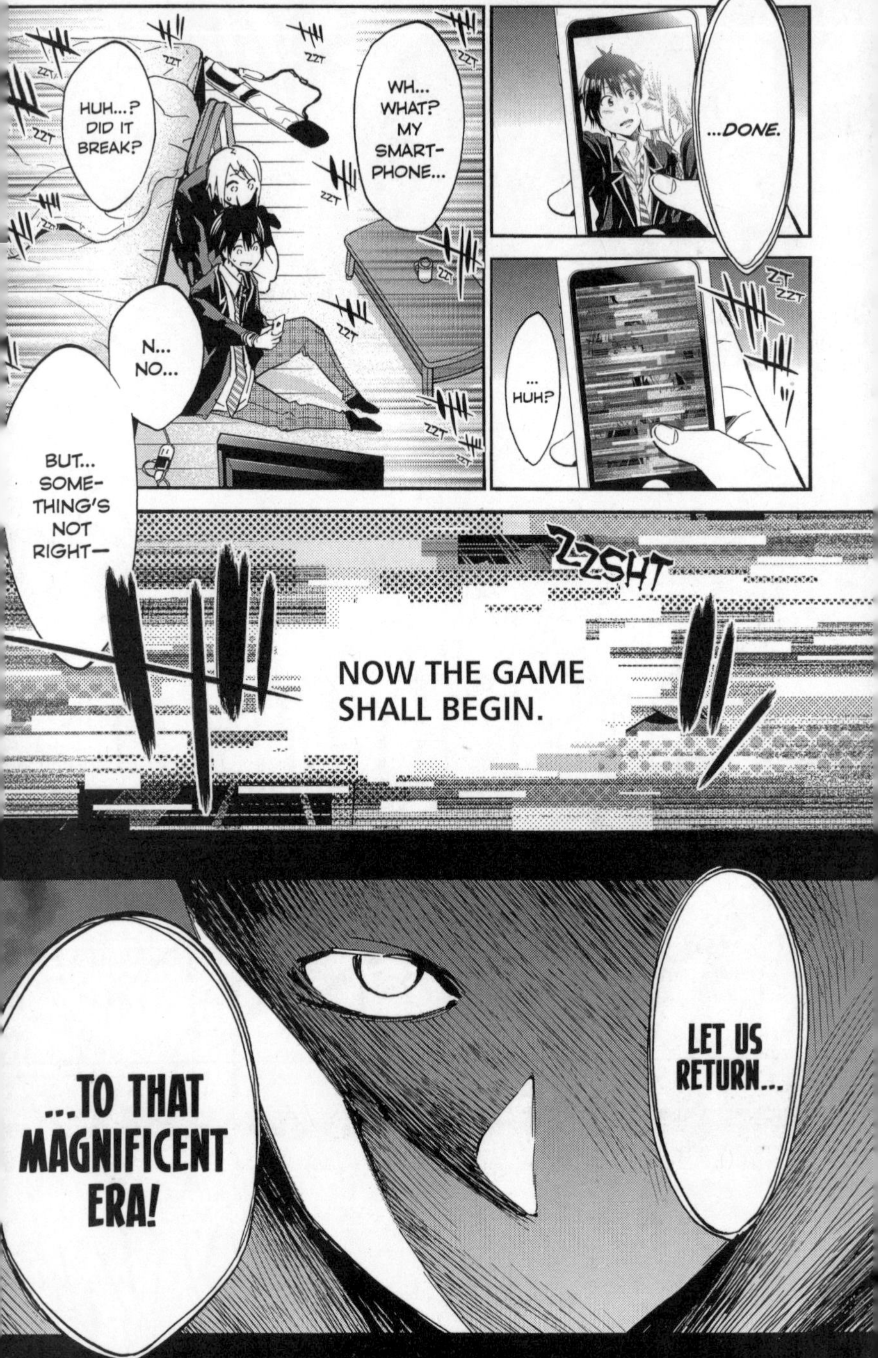
...DONE.
ZZT ZZT
... HUH?
WH... WHAT? MY SMART-PHONE...
ZZT
HUH...? DID IT BREAK?
N... NO...
BUT... SOME-THING'S NOT RIGHT—
ZZSHT
NOW THE GAME SHALL BEGIN.
LET US RETURN...
...TO THAT MAGNIFICENT ERA!

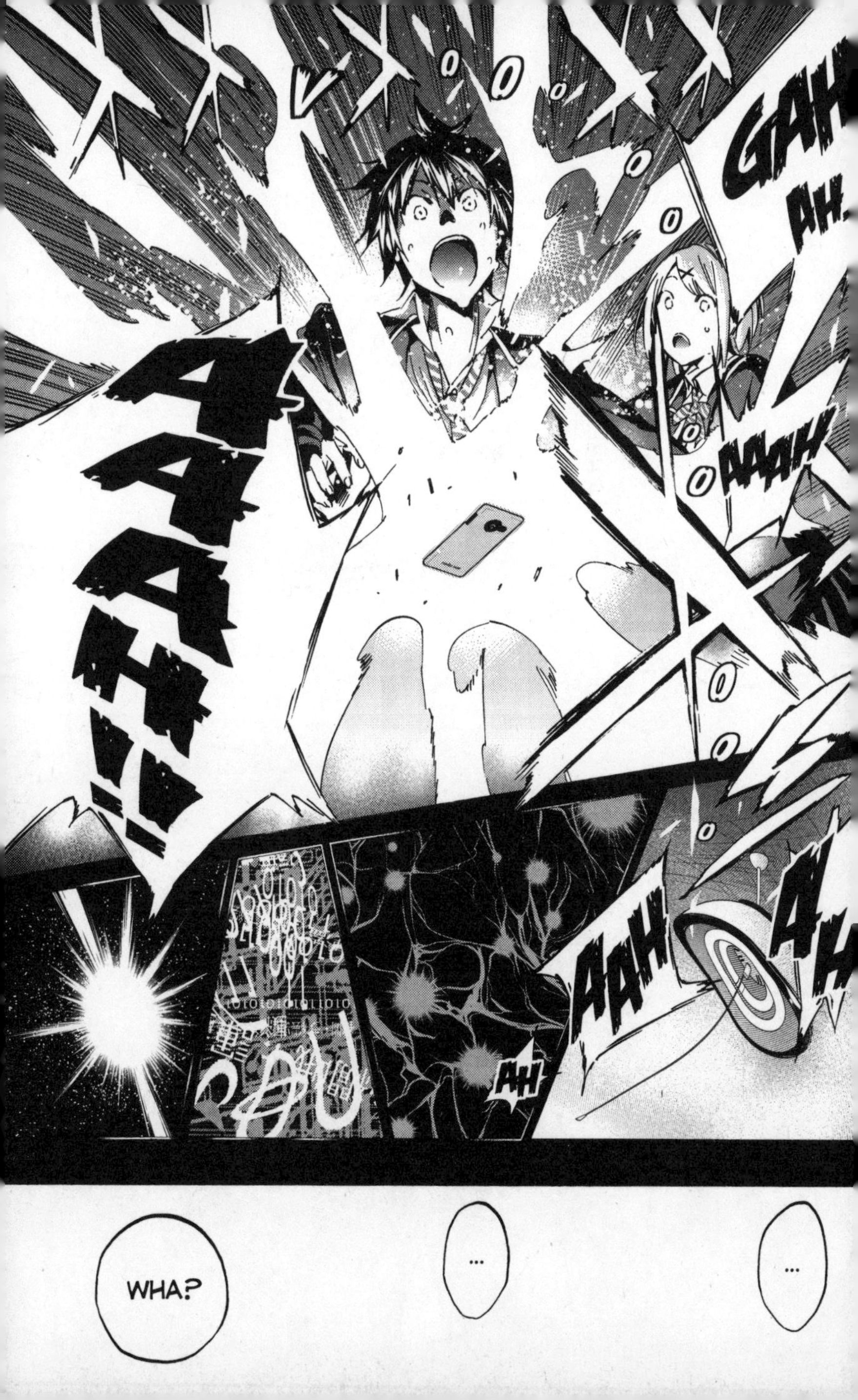
GAH
AH...
AAAAH!!
AAAH!!
AH
AAH
AH
...
...
WHA?

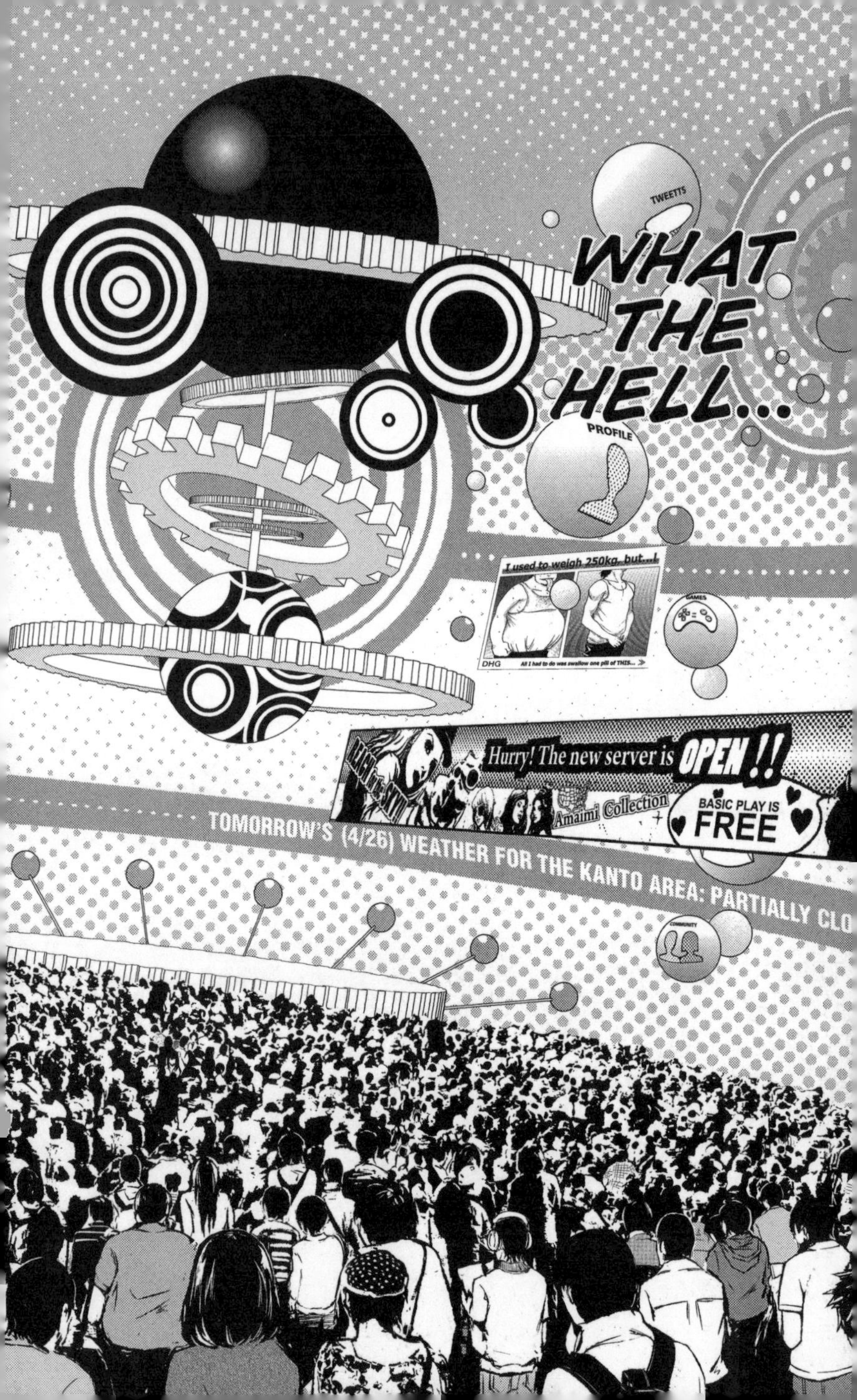
WHAT THE HELL...
TWEETTS
PROFILE
I used to weigh 250kg, but...!
DHG
All I had to do was swallow one pill of THIS...
GAMES
Hurry! The new server is OPEN!!
Amaimi Collection
BASIC PLAY IS FREE
TOMORROW'S (4/26) WEATHER FOR THE KANTO AREA: PARTIALLY CLO
COMMUNITY

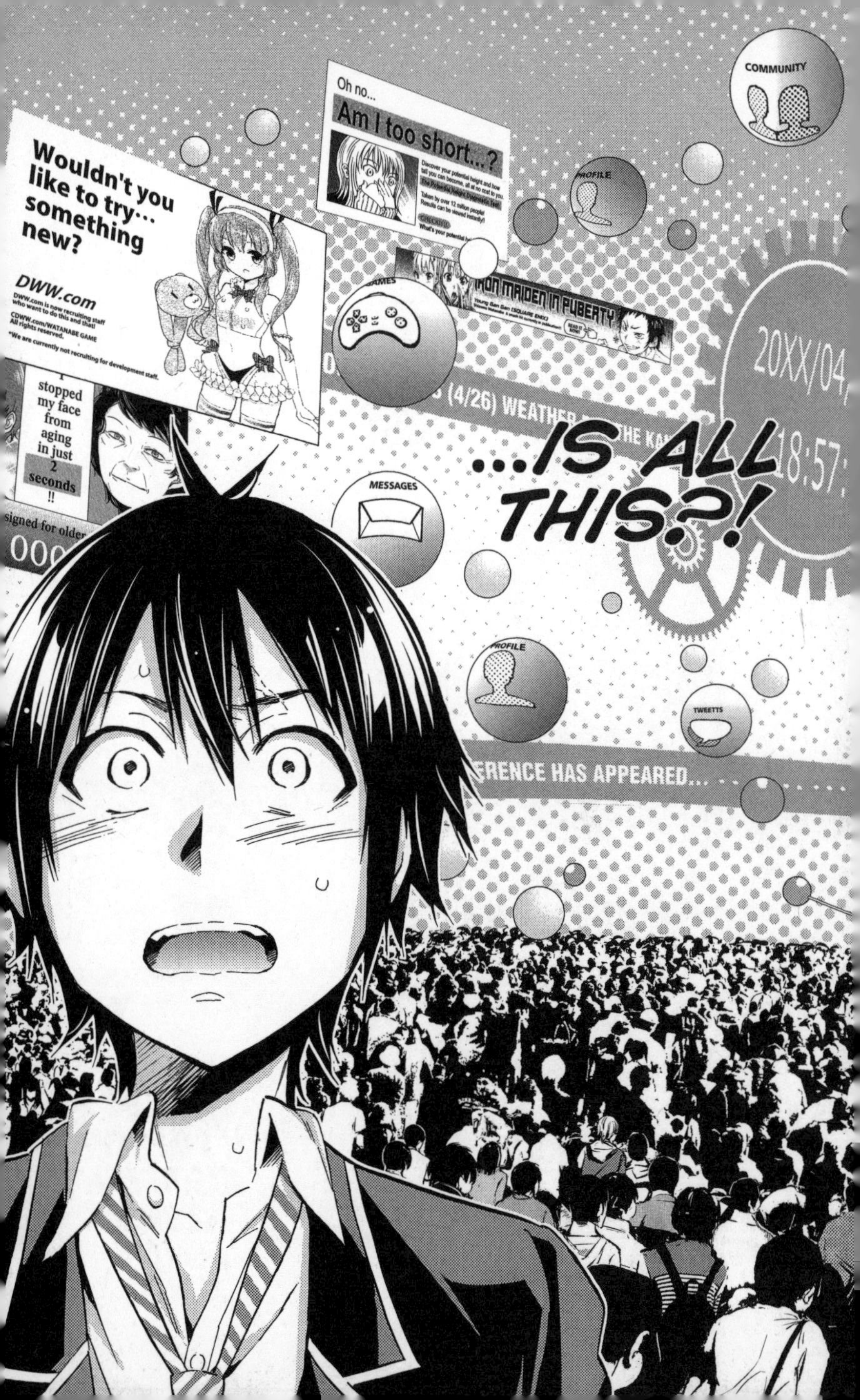
Oh no...
Am I too short...?
Discover your potential height and how tall you can become, all at no cost to you.
The Potential Height Diagnostic Test
Taken by over 12 million people! Results can be viewed instantly!
CHECK!!!
COMMUNITY
PROFILE
Wouldn't you like to try… something new?
DWW.com
DWW.com is now recruiting staff who want to do this and that!
CDWW.com/WATANABE GAME All rights reserved.
*We are currently not recruiting for development staff.
GAMES
IRON MAIDEN IN PUBERTY
20XX/04/
(4/26) WEATHER
THE KA
I stopped my face from aging in just 2 seconds !!
signed for older
...IS ALL THIS?!
18:57:
MESSAGES
PROFILE
TWEETTS
ERENCE HAS APPEARED...

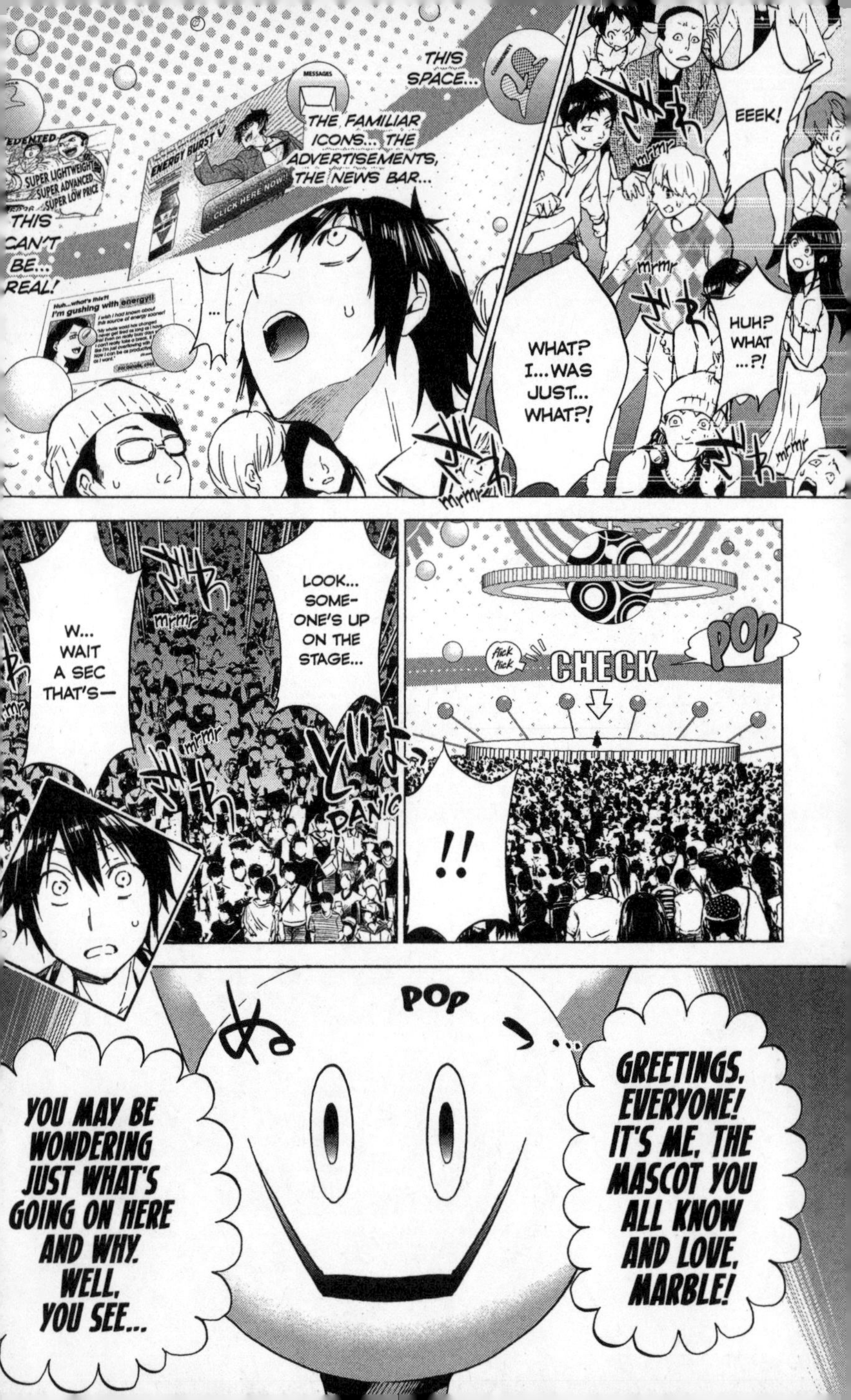
EEEK!
mrmr
HUH? WHAT ...?!
WHAT? I...WAS JUST... WHAT?!
mrmr
THIS SPACE...
MESSAGES
THE FAMILIAR ICONS... THE ADVERTISEMENTS, THE NEWS BAR...
ENERGY BURST V
CLICK HERE NOW!
SUPER LIGHTWEIGHT
SUPER ADVANCED
SUPER LOW PRICE
THIS CAN'T BE... REAL!
Huh...what's this?! I'm gushing with energy!!
...
POP
flick flick
CHECK
!!
LOOK... SOME-ONE'S UP ON THE STAGE...
mrmr
W... WAIT A SEC THAT'S—
PANIC
POP
GREETINGS, EVERYONE! IT'S ME, THE MASCOT YOU ALL KNOW AND LOVE, MARBLE!
YOU MAY BE WONDERING JUST WHAT'S GOING ON HERE AND WHY. WELL, YOU SEE...

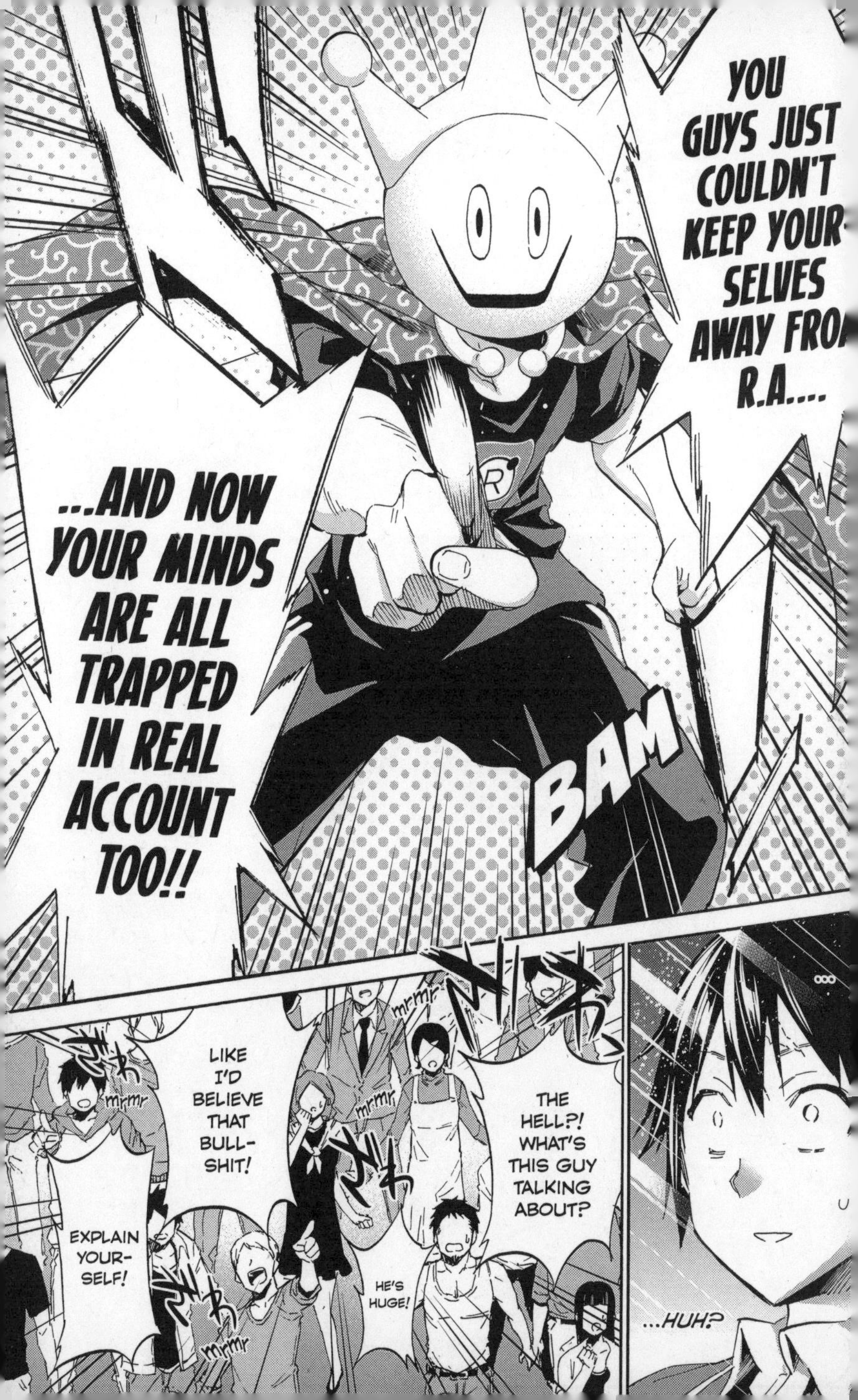
YOU GUYS JUST COULDN'T KEEP YOURSELVES AWAY FROM R.A....
...AND NOW YOUR MINDS ARE ALL TRAPPED IN REAL ACCOUNT TOO!!
BAM
...HUH?
mrmr
THE HELL?! WHAT'S THIS GUY TALKING ABOUT?
mrmr
LIKE I'D BELIEVE THAT BULL-SHIT!
mrmr
HE'S HUGE!
EXPLAIN YOUR-SELF!
mrmr

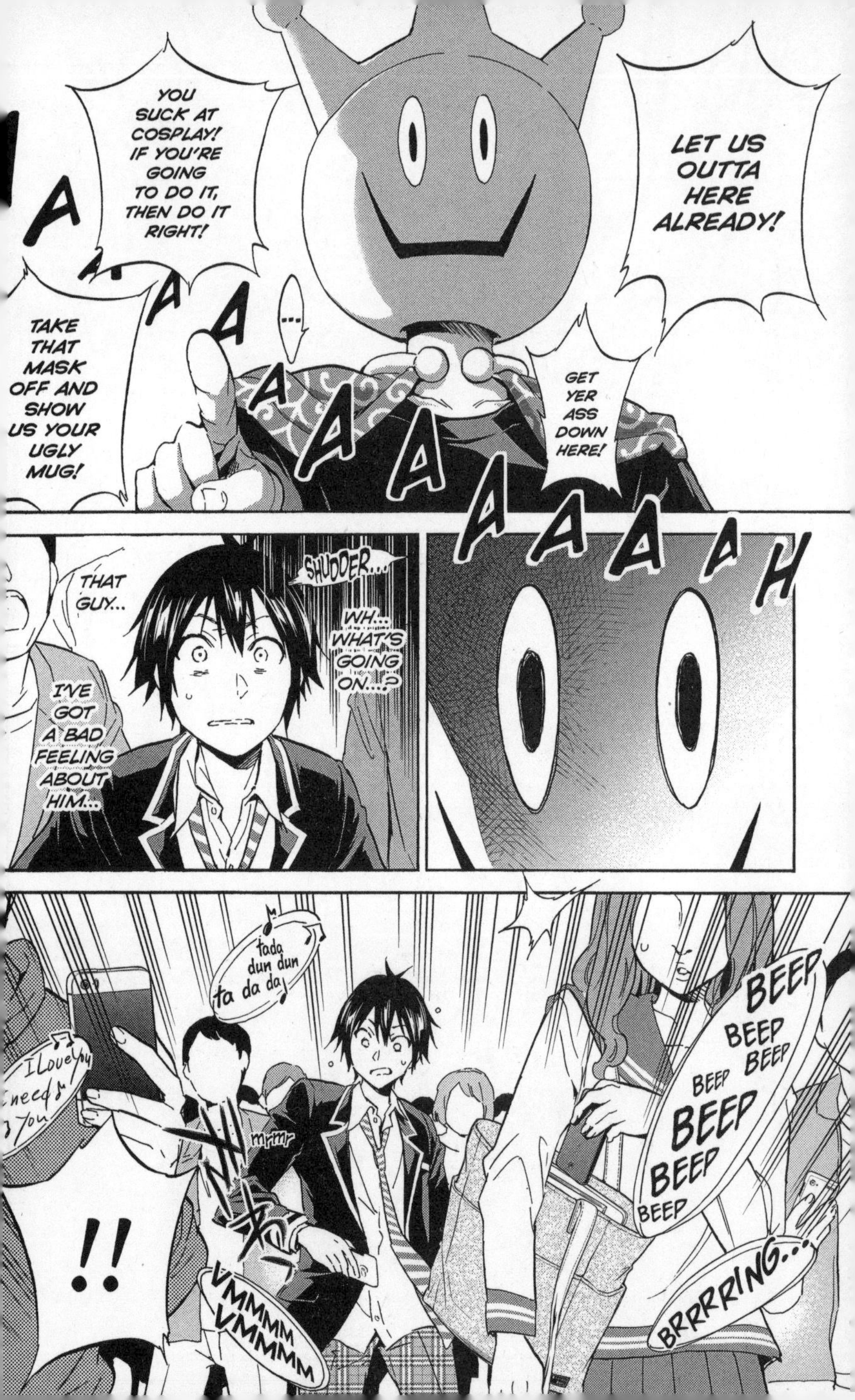
LET US OUTTA HERE ALREADY!
GET YER ASS DOWN HERE!
...
YOU SUCK AT COSPLAY! IF YOU'RE GOING TO DO IT, THEN DO IT RIGHT!
TAKE THAT MASK OFF AND SHOW US YOUR UGLY MUG!
AAAAAAAAAAAAAH
SHUDDER...
WH... WHAT'S GOING ON...?
THAT GUY...
I'VE GOT A BAD FEELING ABOUT HIM...
BEEP BEEP BEEP BEEP BEEP BEEP BEEP
BRRRING...
tada dun dun ta da da
VMMMM VMMMM
mrmr
I Love you I need you
!!

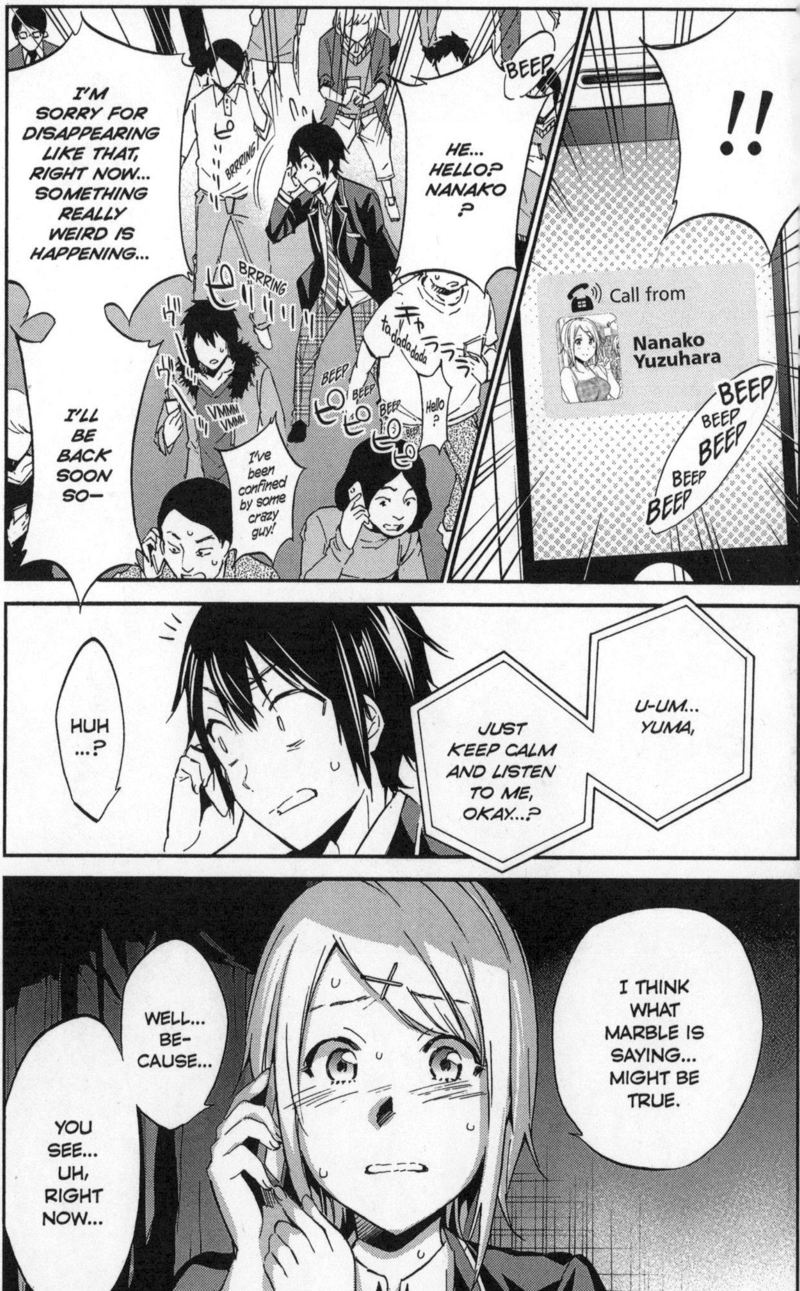
!!
BEEP
Call from
Nanako Yuzuhara
BEEP BEEP BEEP BEEP BEEP
HE... HELLO? NANAKO?
BRRRING
BRRRING
BEEP
BEEP
BEEP
BEEP
ta-dadadada
Hello?
VMMM VMMM
I've been confined by some crazy guy!
I'M SORRY FOR DISAPPEARING LIKE THAT, RIGHT NOW... SOMETHING REALLY WEIRD IS HAPPENING...
I'LL BE BACK SOON SO—
U-UM... YUMA,
JUST KEEP CALM AND LISTEN TO ME, OKAY...?
HUH ...?
I THINK WHAT MARBLE IS SAYING... MIGHT BE TRUE.
WELL... BE-CAUSE...
YOU SEE... UH, RIGHT NOW...

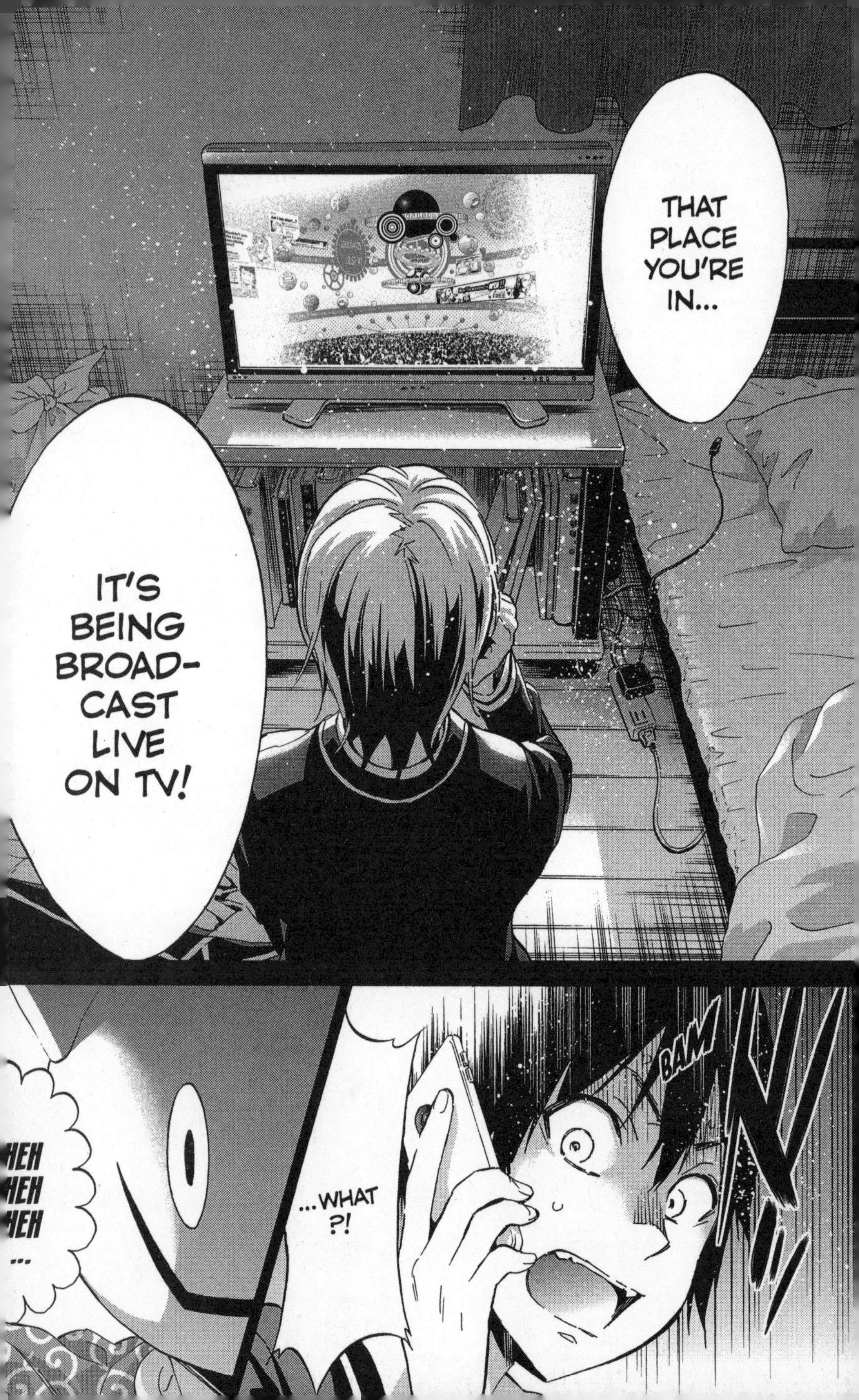
THAT PLACE YOU'RE IN...
IT'S BEING BROAD-CAST LIVE ON TV!
BAM
...WHAT ?!
HEH HEH HEH ...

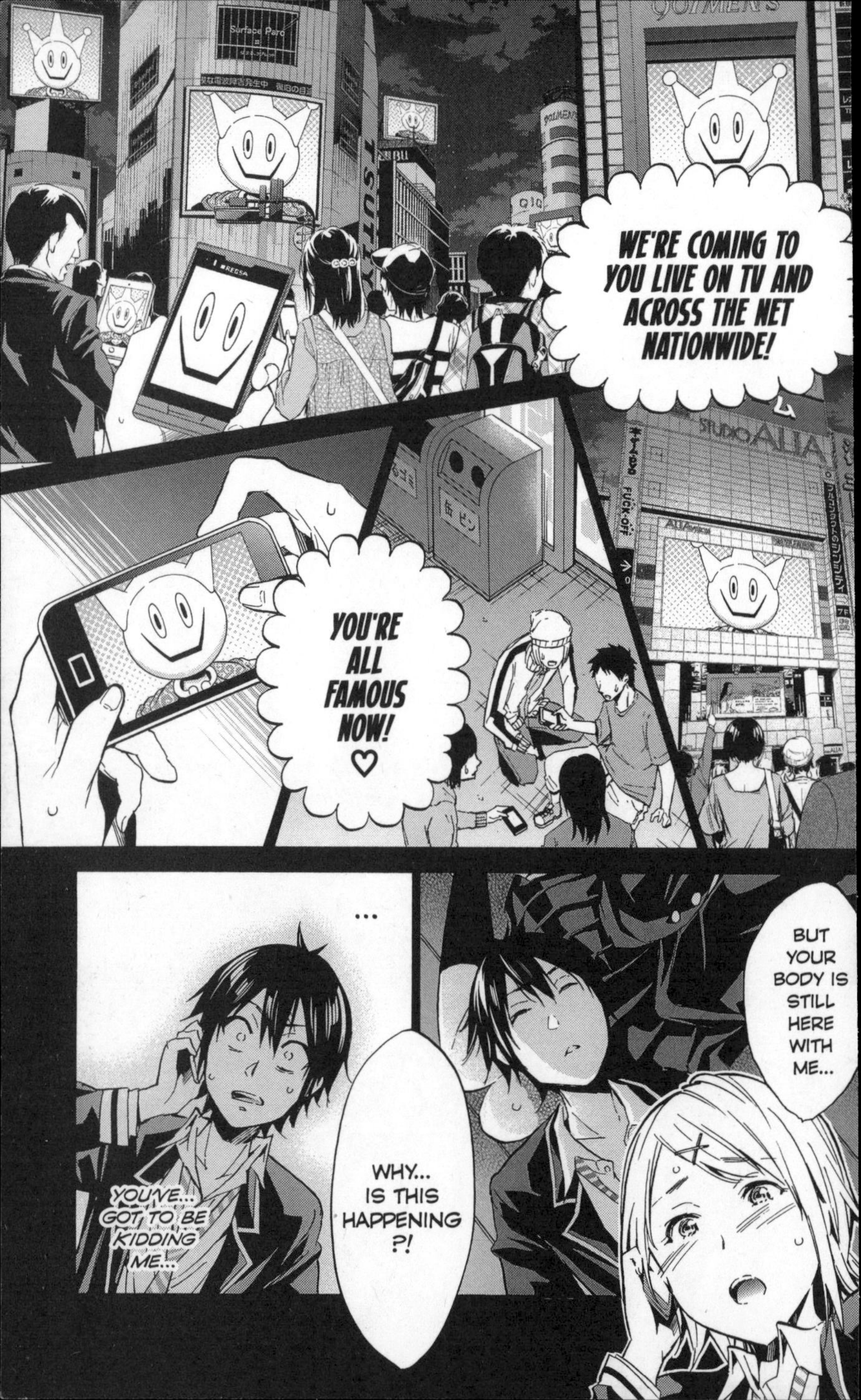
WE'RE COMING TO YOU LIVE ON TV AND ACROSS THE NET NATIONWIDE!
YOU'RE ALL FAMOUS NOW! ♡
BUT YOUR BODY IS STILL HERE WITH ME...
...
WHY... IS THIS HAPPENING?!
YOU'VE... GOT TO BE KIDDING ME...

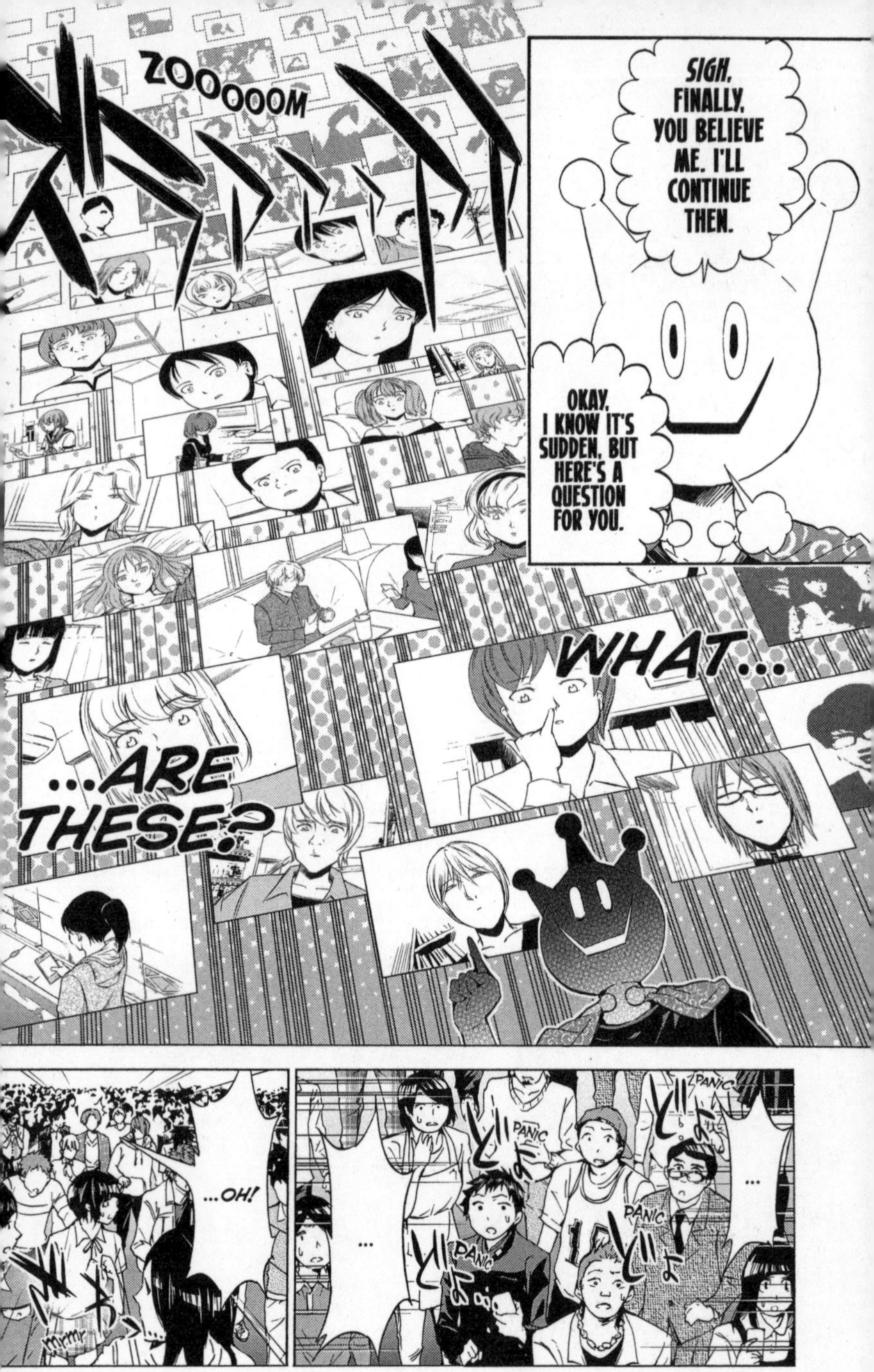
SIGH. FINALLY, YOU BELIEVE ME. I'LL CONTINUE THEN.
OKAY, I KNOW IT'S SUDDEN, BUT HERE'S A QUESTION FOR YOU.
ZOOOOOM
WHAT...
...ARE THESE?
PANIC
PANIC
...
PANIC
PANIC
...
...OH!
mrmr

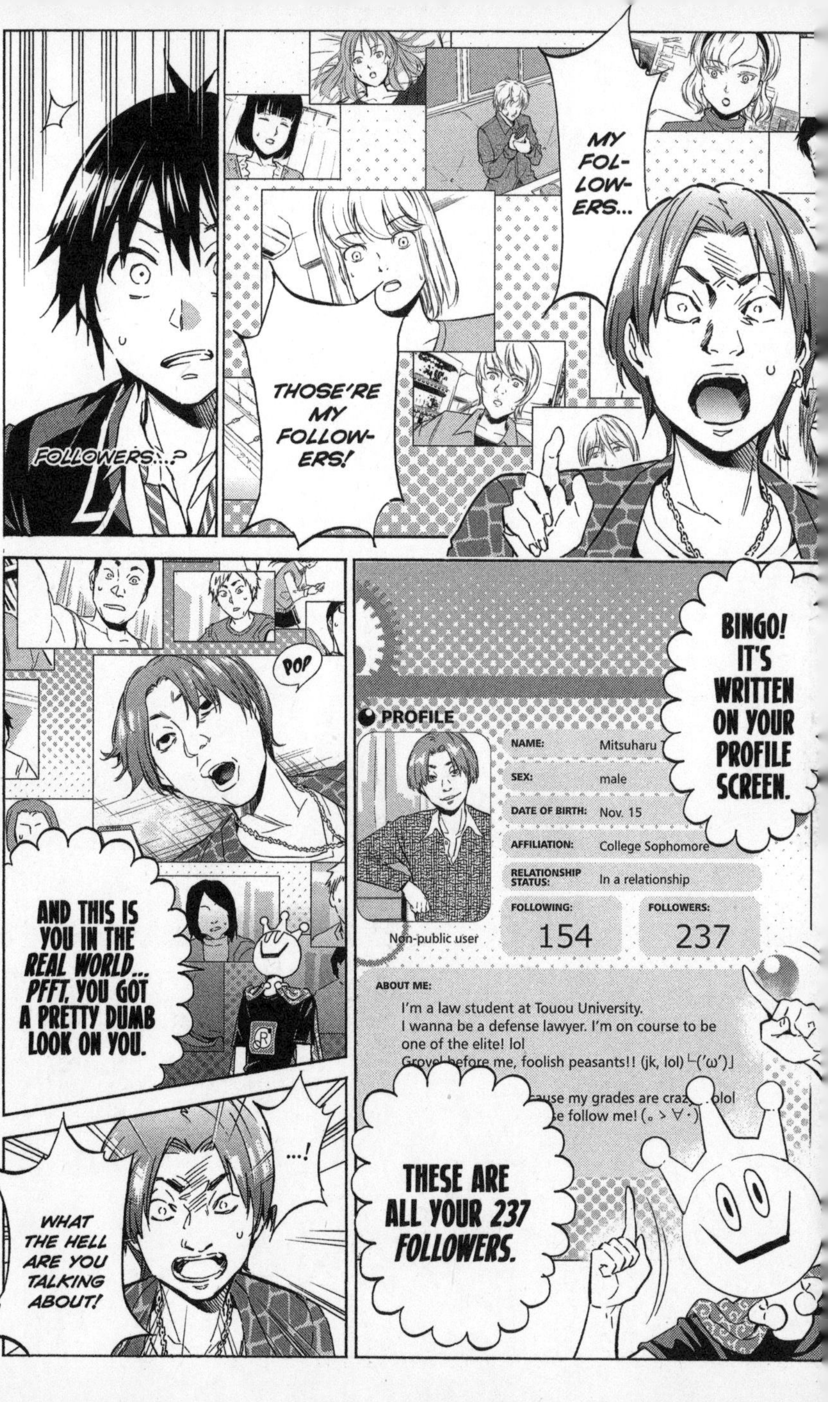
MY FOL-LOW-ERS...
THOSE'RE MY FOLLOW-ERS!
FOLLOWERS...?
BINGO! IT'S WRITTEN ON YOUR PROFILE SCREEN.
PROFILE
NAME: Mitsuharu
SEX: male
DATE OF BIRTH: Nov. 15
AFFILIATION: College Sophomore
RELATIONSHIP STATUS: In a relationship
FOLLOWING: 154
FOLLOWERS: 237
Non-public user
ABOUT ME:
I'm a law student at Touou University.
I wanna be a defense lawyer. I'm on course to be one of the elite! lol
Grovel before me, foolish peasants!! (jk, lol) └('ω')┘
POP
AND THIS IS YOU IN THE REAL WORLD... PFFT, YOU GOT A PRETTY DUMB LOOK ON YOU.
THESE ARE ALL YOUR 237 FOLLOWERS.
...!
WHAT THE HELL ARE YOU TALKING ABOUT!

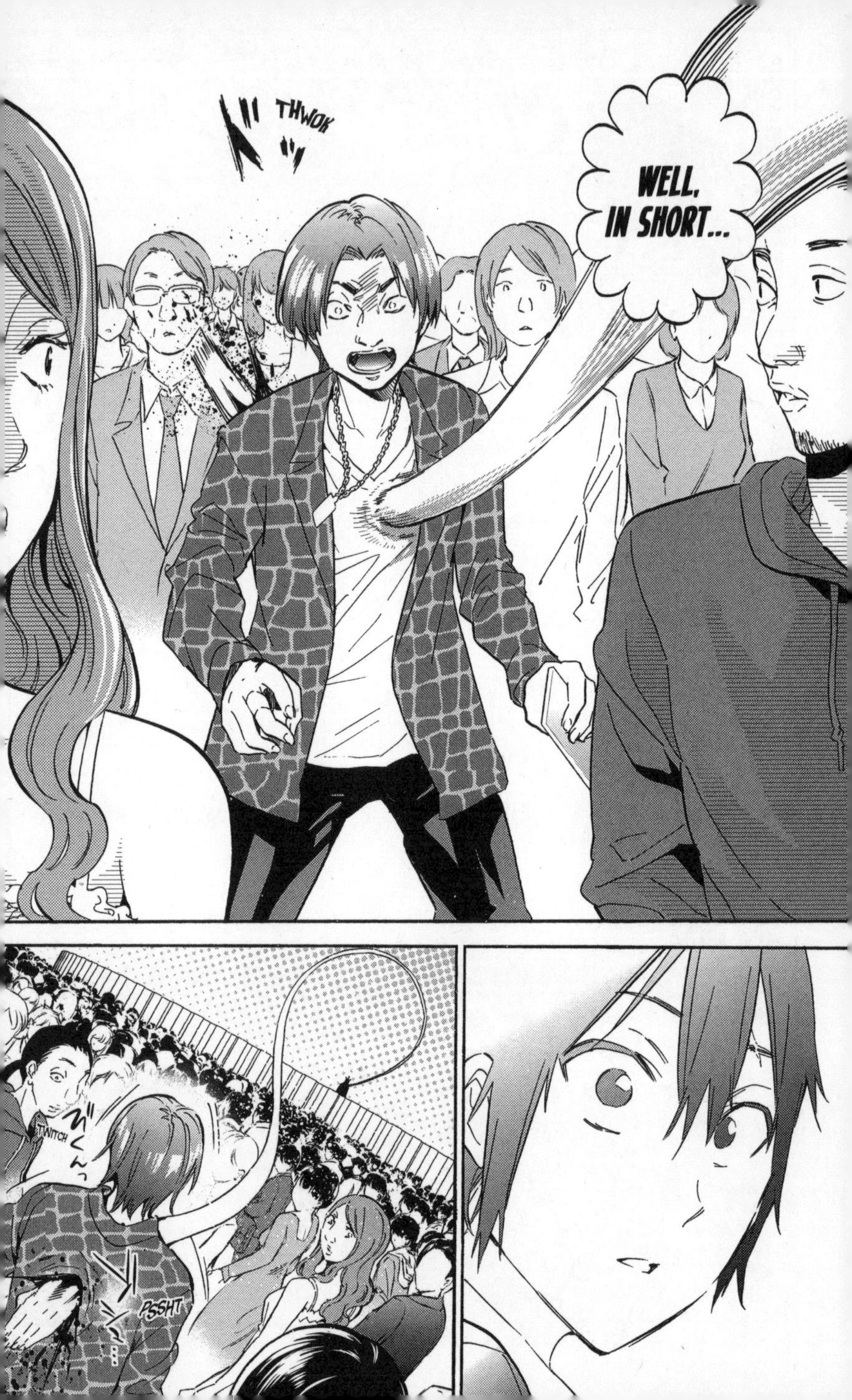
WELL, IN SHORT...
THWOK
TWITCH
PSSHT

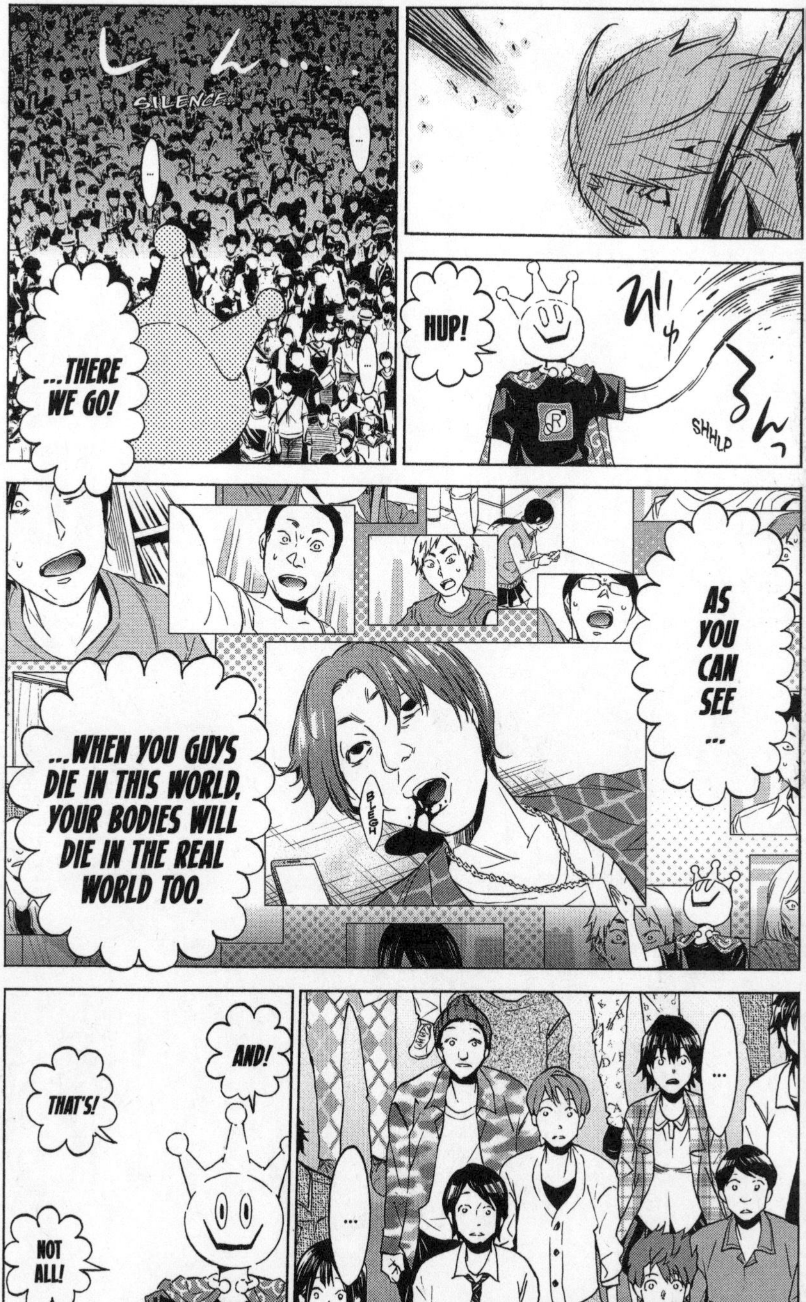
HUP!
SHHLP
しん…
SILENCE
...
...
...
...THERE WE GO!
AS YOU CAN SEE ...
...WHEN YOU GUYS DIE IN THIS WORLD, YOUR BODIES WILL DIE IN THE REAL WORLD TOO.
BLEGH
...
...
AND!
THAT'S!
NOT ALL!

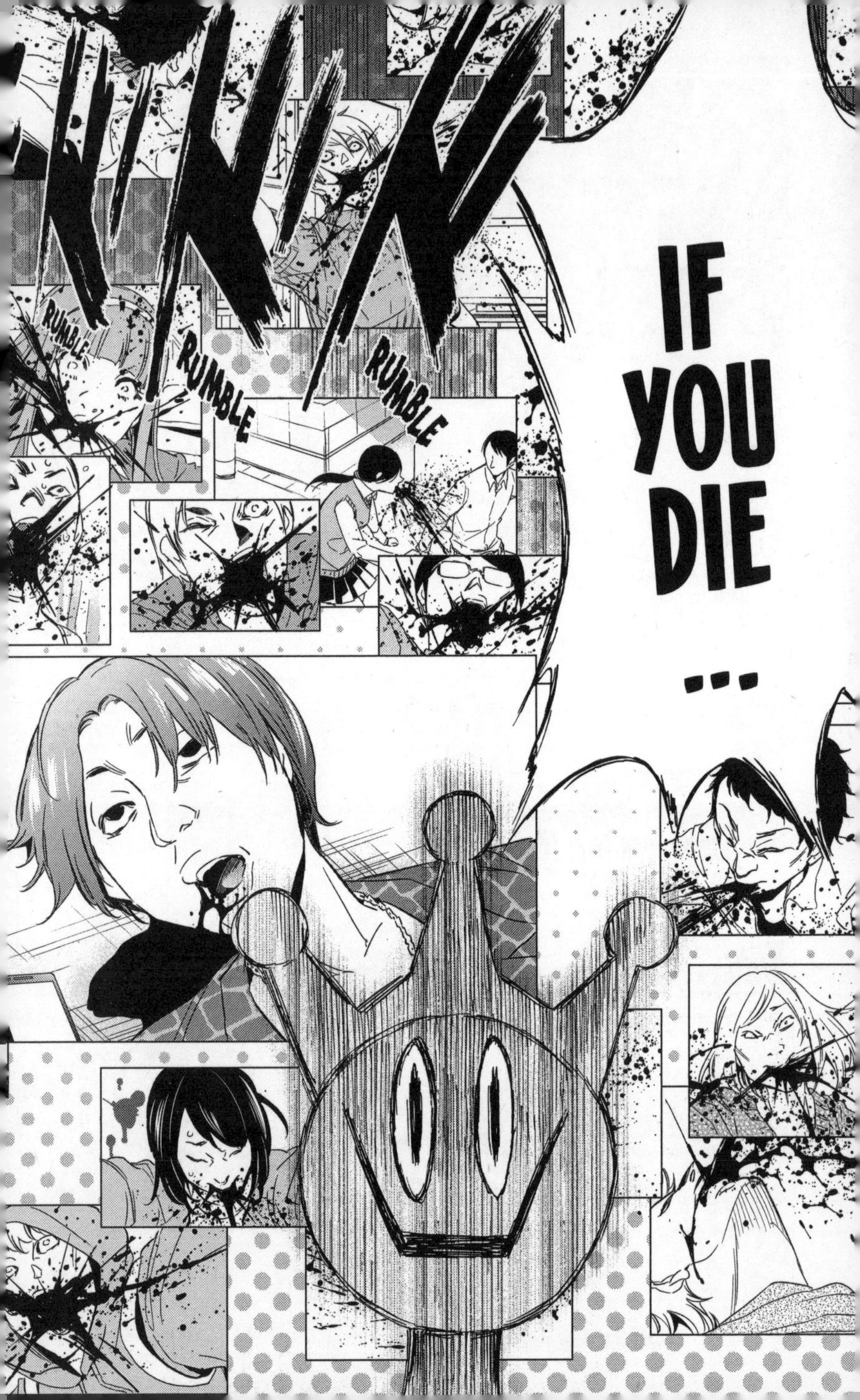
IF YOU DIE ...
RUMBLE
RUMBLE
RUMBLE

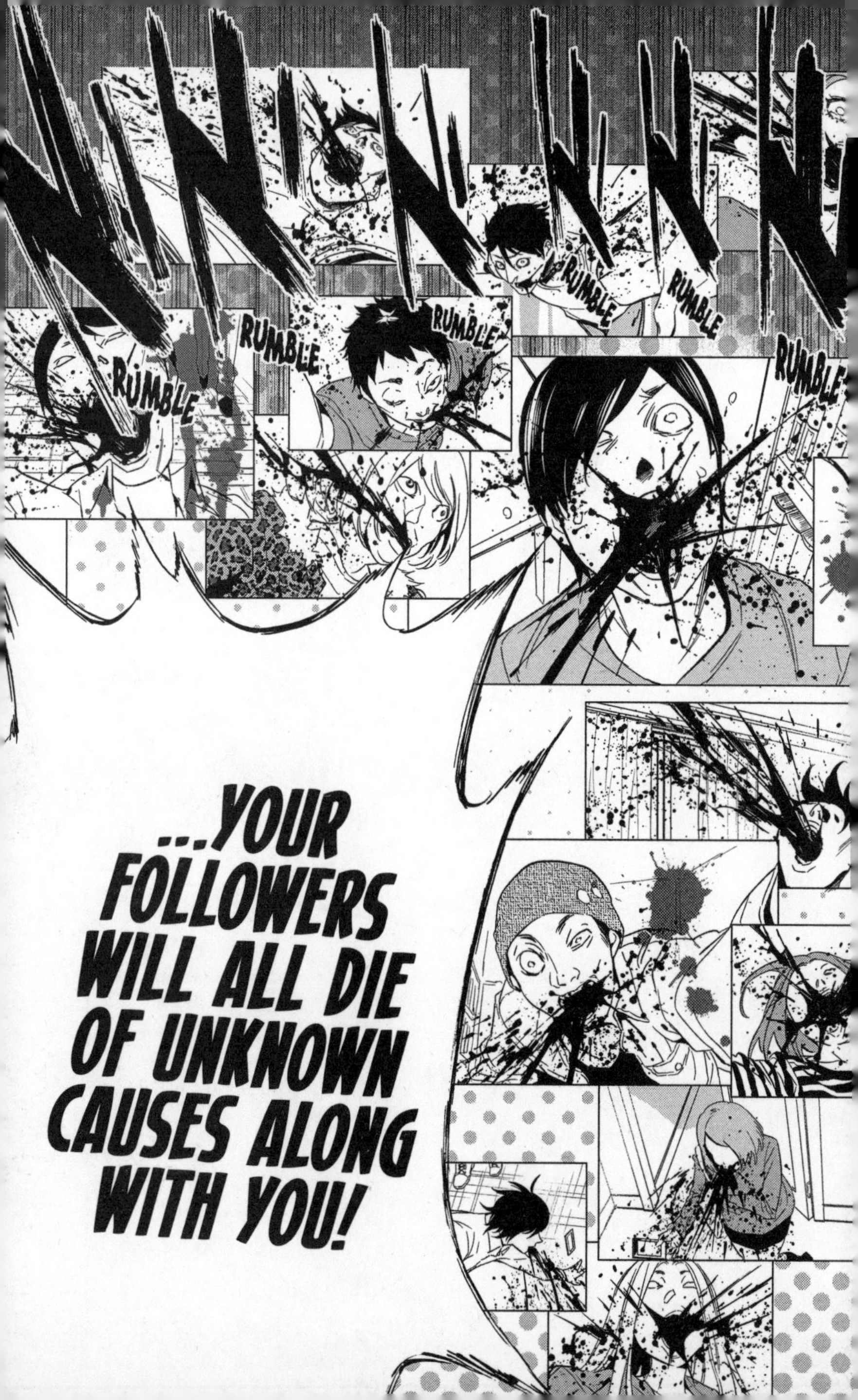
RUMBLE
RUMBLE
RUMBLE
RUMBLE
RUMBLE
RUMBLE
...YOUR FOLLOWERS WILL ALL DIE OF UNKNOWN CAUSES ALONG WITH YOU!

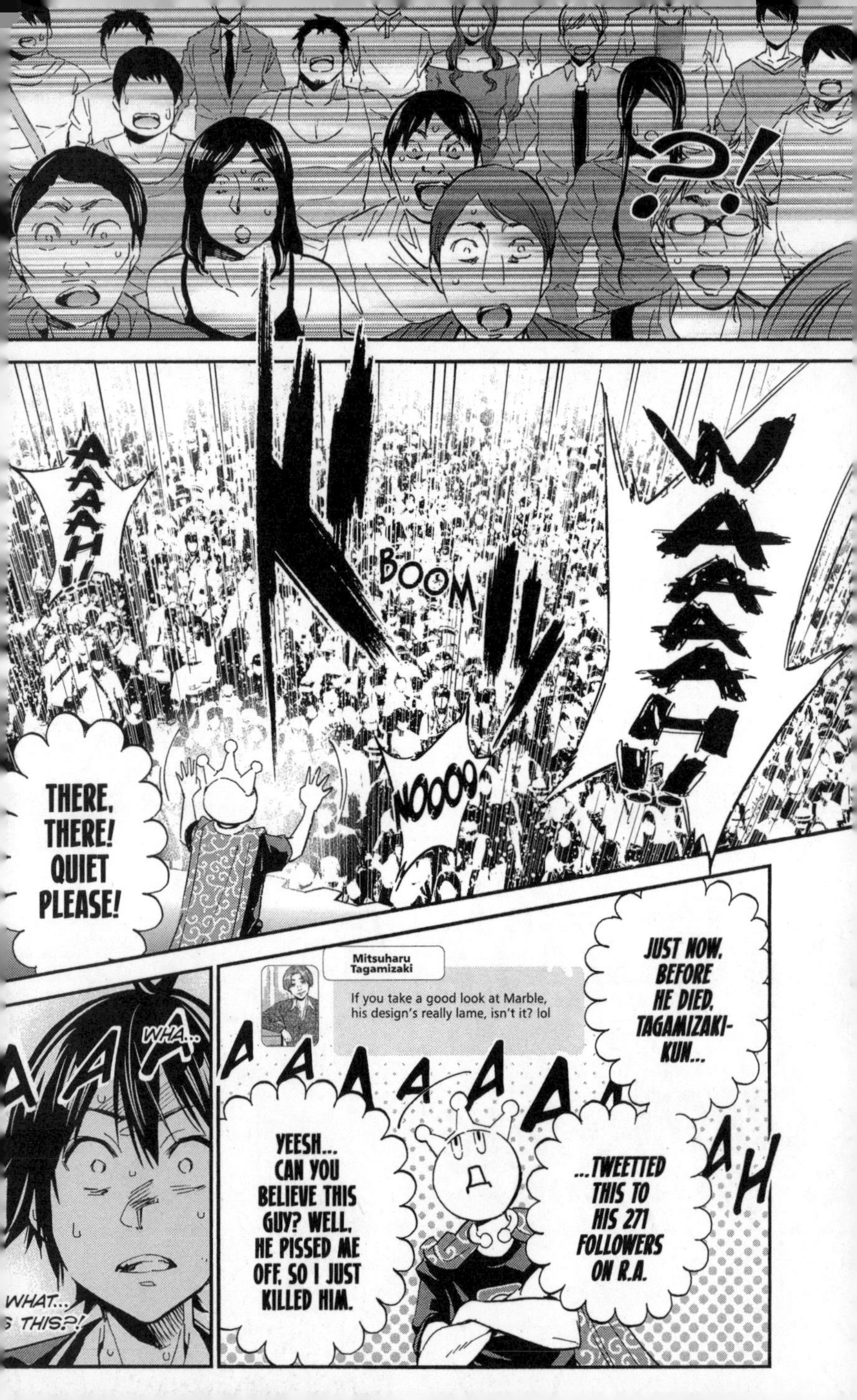
?!
WAAAAH!!
BOOM
NOOOO
AAAAH!!
THERE, THERE! QUIET PLEASE!
JUST NOW, BEFORE HE DIED, TAGAMIZAKI-KUN...
Mitsuharu Tagamizaki
If you take a good look at Marble, his design's really lame, isn't it? lol
...TWEETTED THIS TO HIS 271 FOLLOWERS ON R.A.
YEESH... CAN YOU BELIEVE THIS GUY? WELL, HE PISSED ME OFF, SO I JUST KILLED HIM.
AAAAAAAAH
WHA...
WHAT... S THIS?!

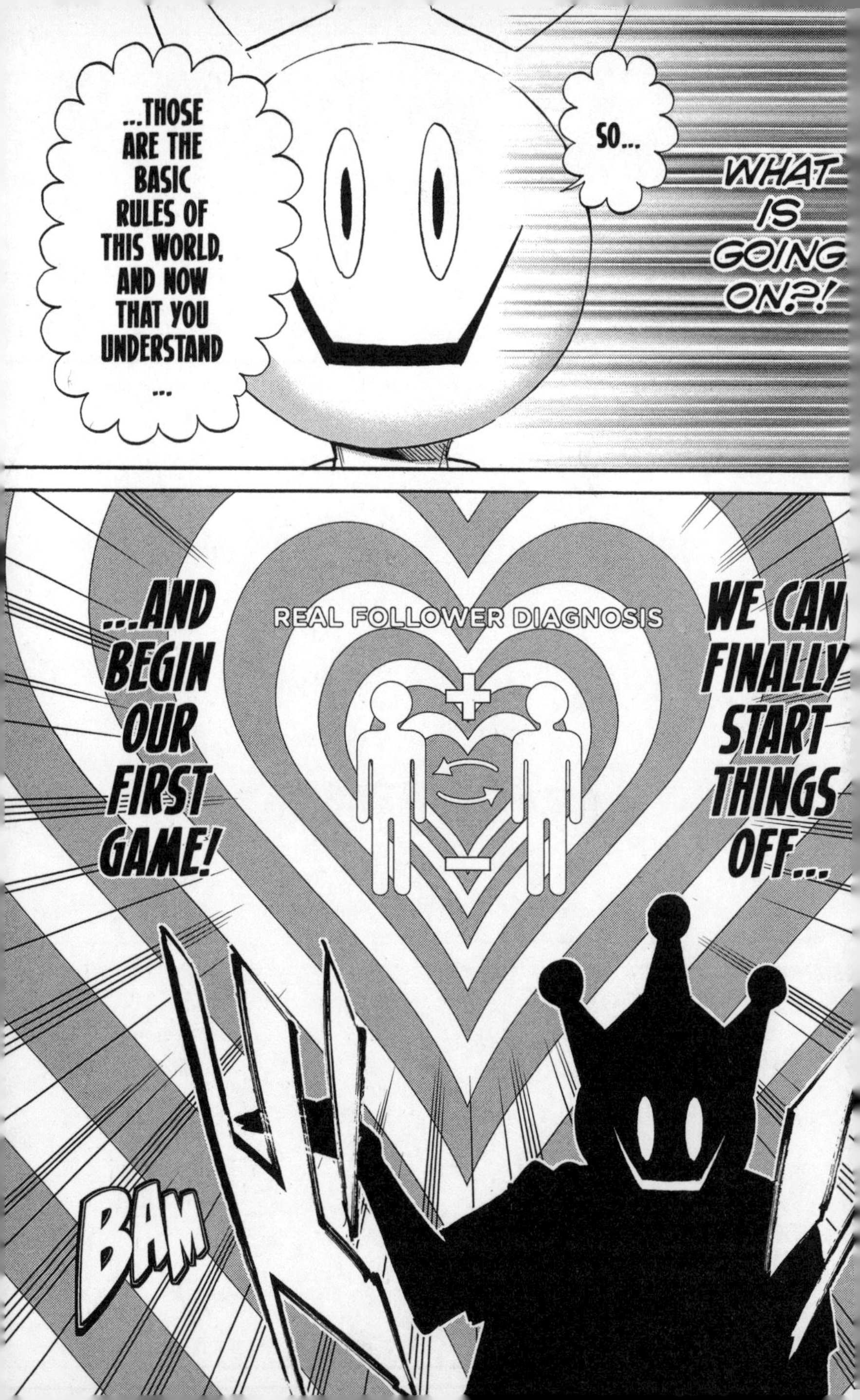
SO...
WHAT IS GOING ON?!
...THOSE ARE THE BASIC RULES OF THIS WORLD, AND NOW THAT YOU UNDERSTAND ...
WE CAN FINALLY START THINGS OFF...
REAL FOLLOWER DIAGNOSIS
...AND BEGIN OUR FIRST GAME!
BAM

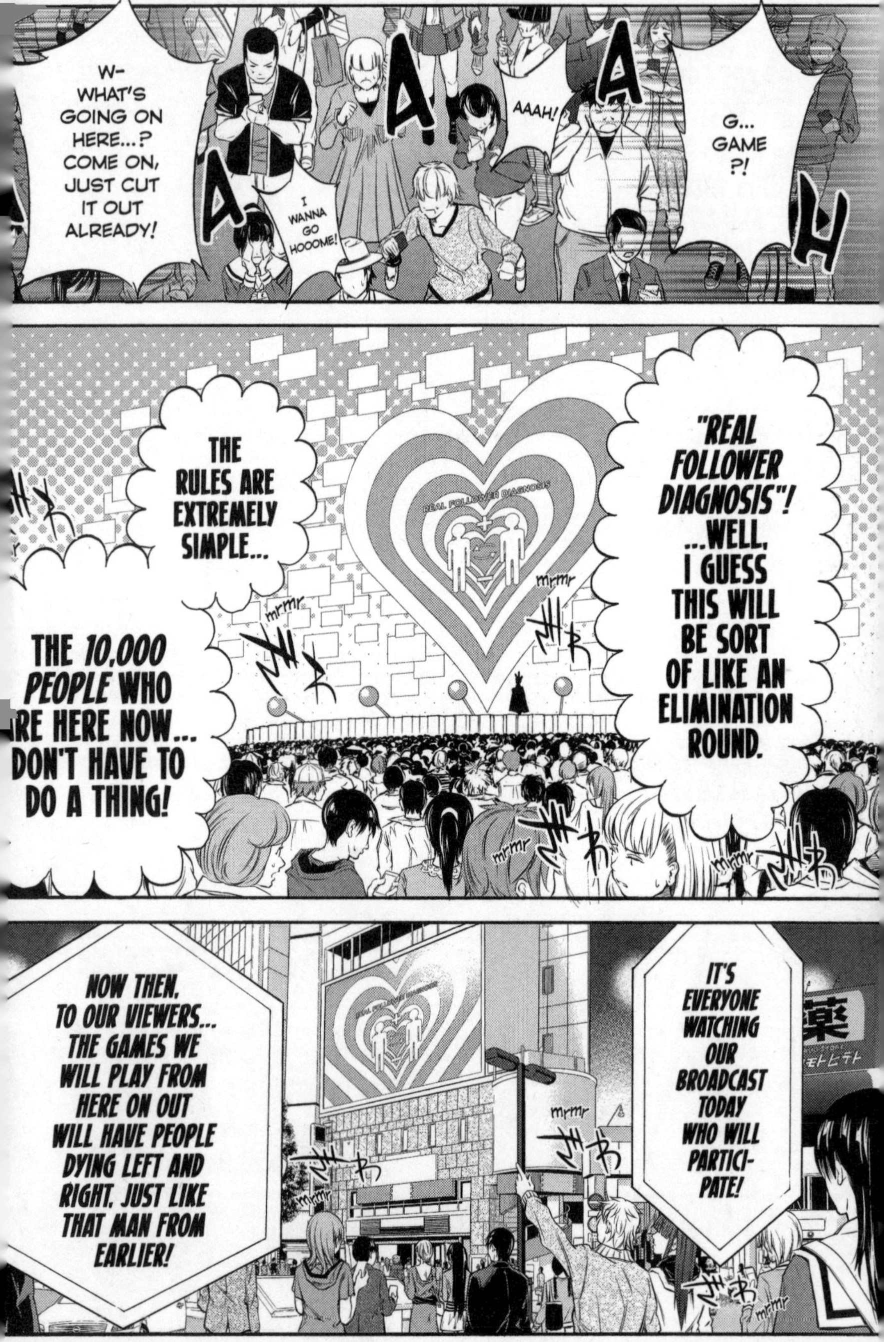
G... GAME?!
AAAAH
AAAH!
I WANNA GO HOOOME!
W- WHAT'S GOING ON HERE...? COME ON, JUST CUT IT OUT ALREADY!
"REAL FOLLOWER DIAGNOSIS"! ...WELL, I GUESS THIS WILL BE SORT OF LIKE AN ELIMINATION ROUND.
REAL FOLLOWER DIAGNOSIS
mrmr
THE RULES ARE EXTREMELY SIMPLE...
THE 10,000 PEOPLE WHO RE HERE NOW... DON'T HAVE TO DO A THING!
IT'S EVERYONE WATCHING OUR BROADCAST TODAY WHO WILL PARTICI-PATE!
薬
mrmr
NOW THEN, TO OUR VIEWERS... THE GAMES WE WILL PLAY FROM HERE ON OUT WILL HAVE PEOPLE DYING LEFT AND RIGHT. JUST LIKE THAT MAN FROM EARLIER!

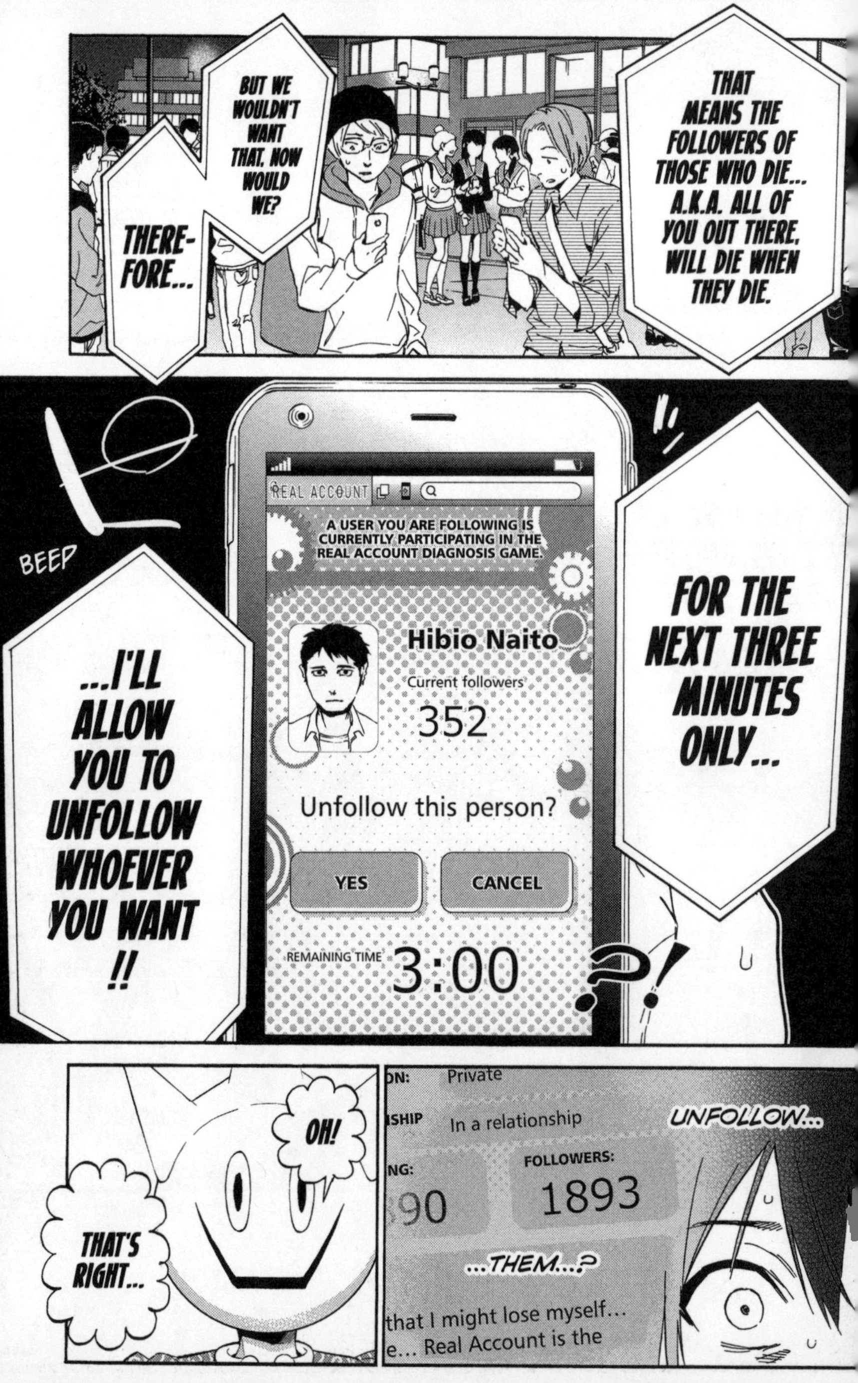
THAT MEANS THE FOLLOWERS OF THOSE WHO DIE... A.K.A. ALL OF YOU OUT THERE, WILL DIE WHEN THEY DIE.
BUT WE WOULDN'T WANT THAT, NOW WOULD WE?
THEREFORE...
FOR THE NEXT THREE MINUTES ONLY...
REAL ACCOUNT
A USER YOU ARE FOLLOWING IS CURRENTLY PARTICIPATING IN THE REAL ACCOUNT DIAGNOSIS GAME.
Hibio Naito
Current followers
352
Unfollow this person?
YES
CANCEL
REMAINING TIME
3:00
BEEP
...I'LL ALLOW YOU TO UNFOLLOW WHOEVER YOU WANT!!
UNFOLLOW...
ON: Private
ISHIP In a relationship
NG:
FOLLOWERS:
890
1893
...THEM...?
that I might lose myself...
e... Real Account is the
OH!
THAT'S RIGHT...

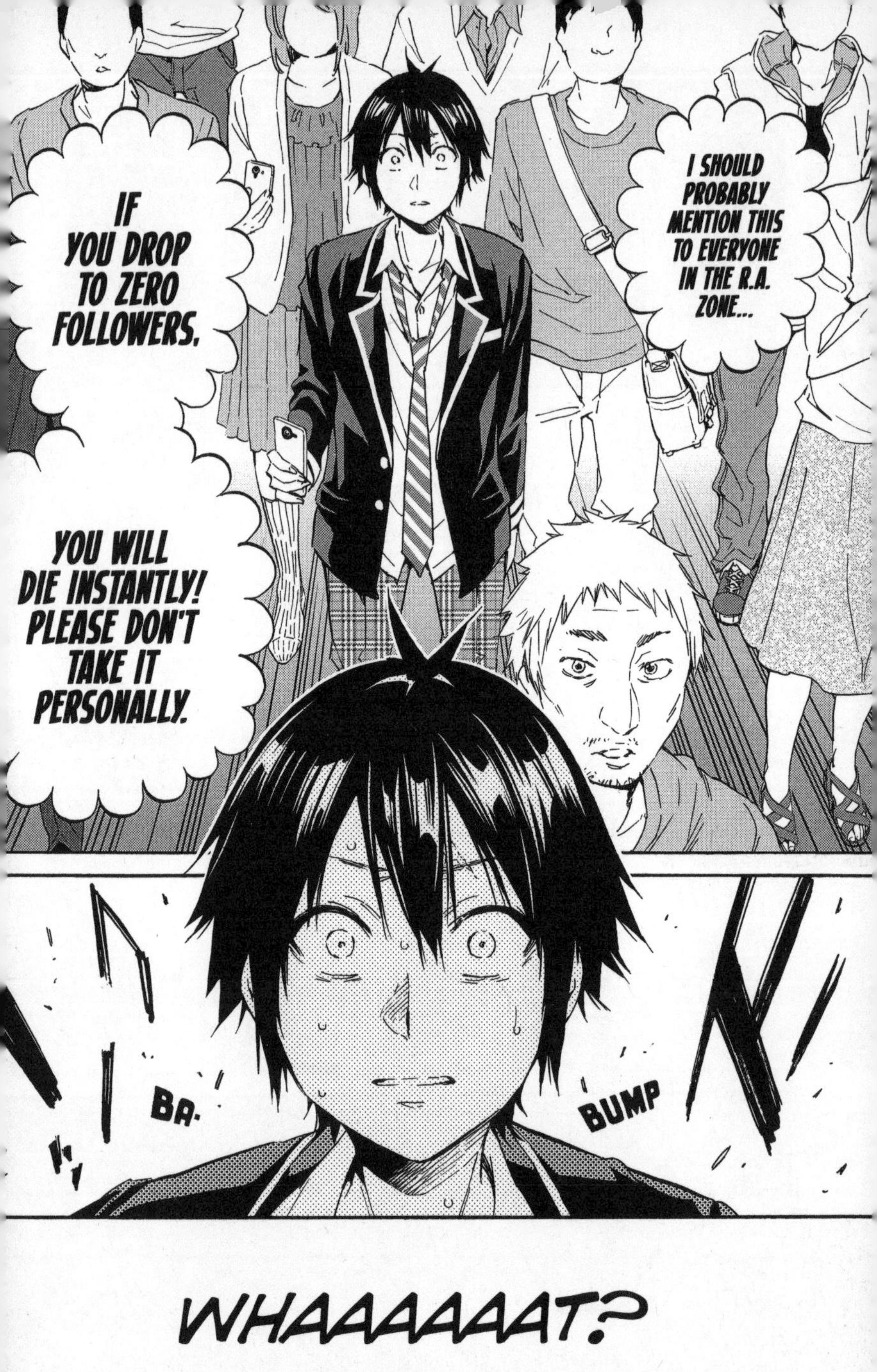
I SHOULD PROBABLY MENTION THIS TO EVERYONE IN THE R.A. ZONE...
IF YOU DROP TO ZERO FOLLOWERS.
YOU WILL DIE INSTANTLY! PLEASE DON'T TAKE IT PERSONALLY.
BA-
BUMP
WHAAAAAAT?

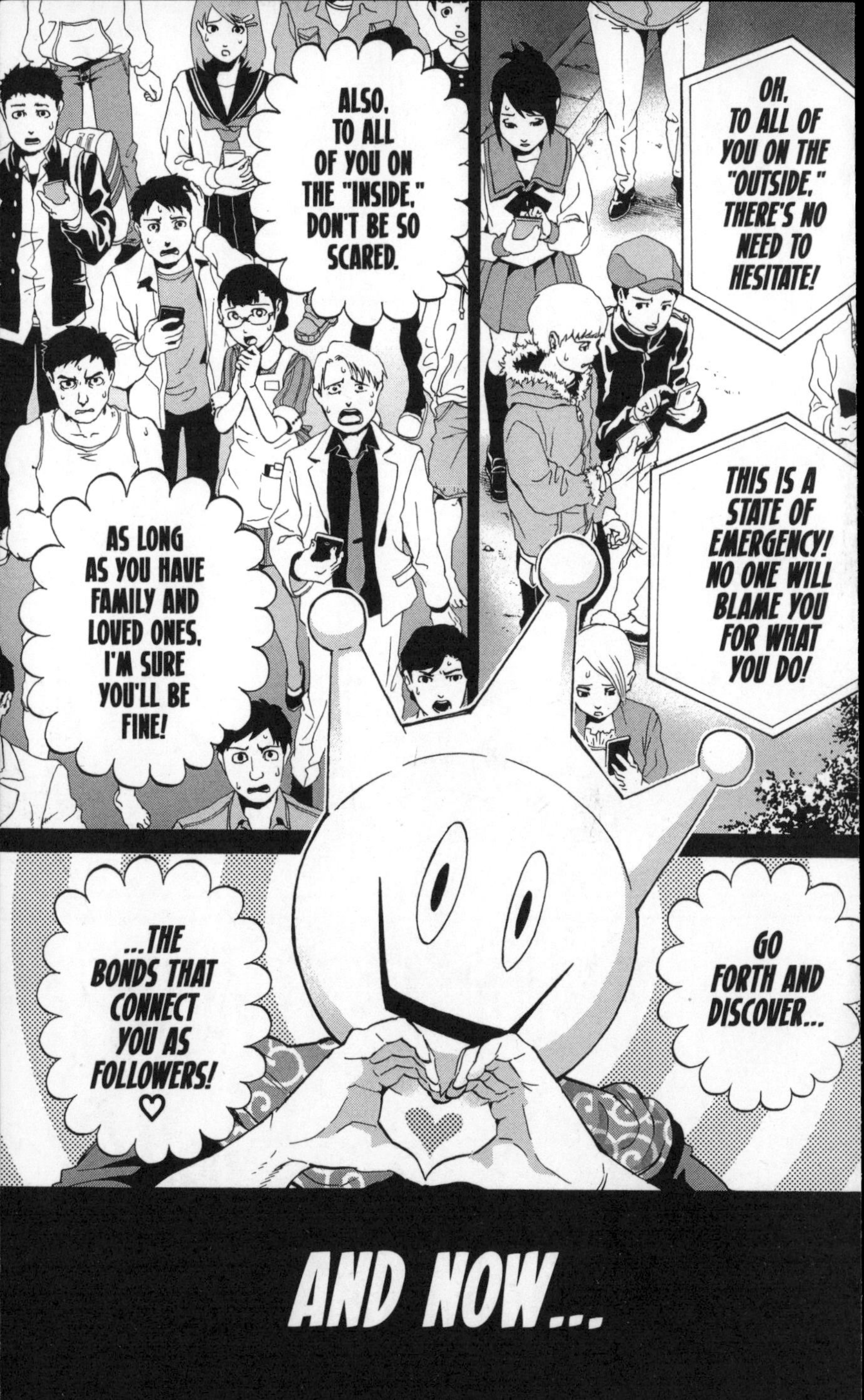
OH, TO ALL OF YOU ON THE "OUTSIDE," THERE'S NO NEED TO HESITATE!
THIS IS A STATE OF EMERGENCY! NO ONE WILL BLAME YOU FOR WHAT YOU DO!
ALSO, TO ALL OF YOU ON THE "INSIDE," DON'T BE SO SCARED.
AS LONG AS YOU HAVE FAMILY AND LOVED ONES, I'M SURE YOU'LL BE FINE!
GO FORTH AND DISCOVER...
...THE BONDS THAT CONNECT YOU AS FOLLOWERS! ♡
AND NOW...

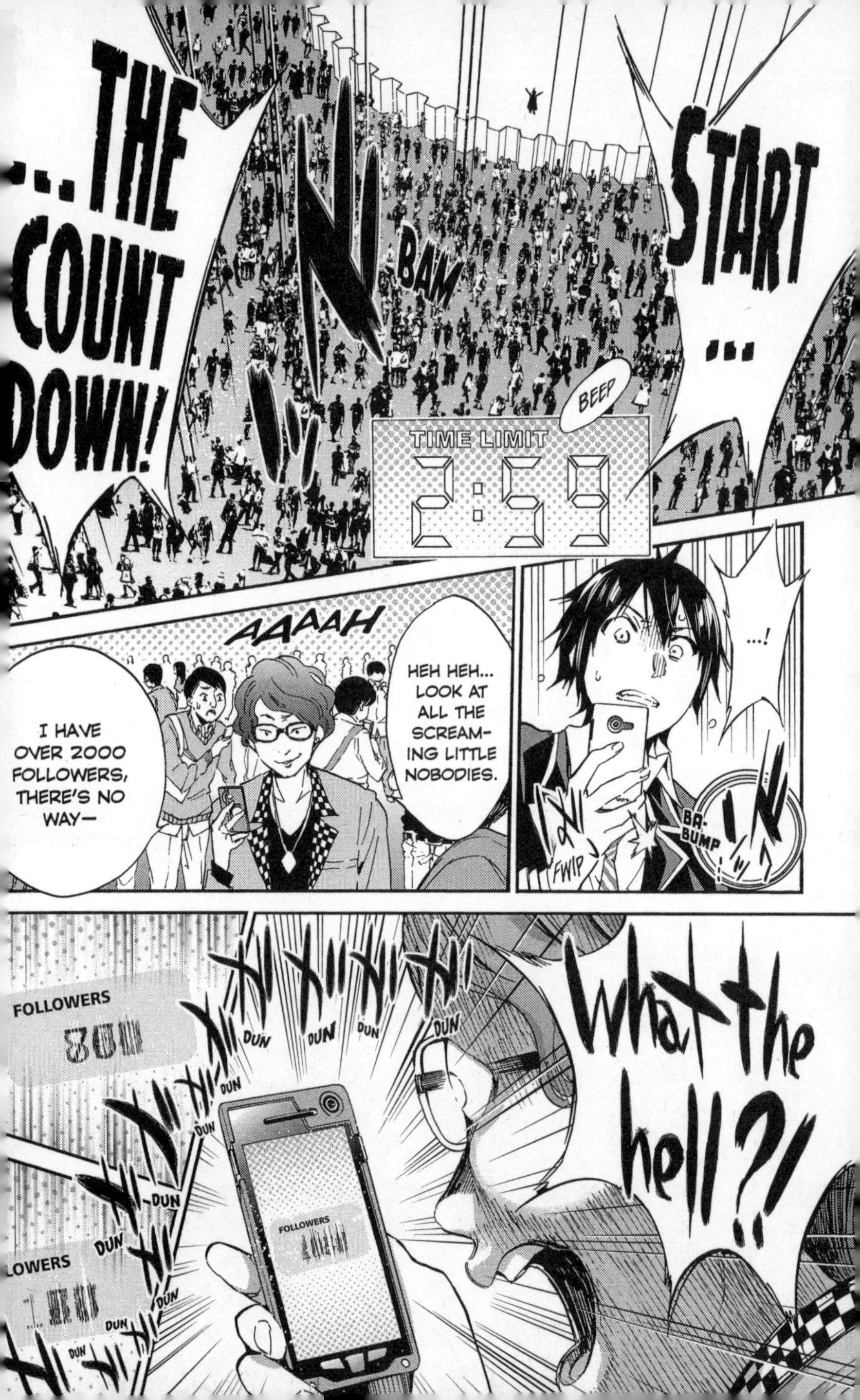
START...
BAM
BEEP
TIME LIMIT
2:59
...THE COUNT DOWN!
...!
BA-BUMP
FWIP
AAAAH
HEH HEH... LOOK AT ALL THE SCREAM-ING LITTLE NOBODIES.
I HAVE OVER 2000 FOLLOWERS, THERE'S NO WAY—
What the hell?!
DUN
DUN
DUN
DUN
DUN
DUN
-DUN
DUN
DUN
DUN
DUN
FOLLOWERS
FOLLOWERS
LOWERS

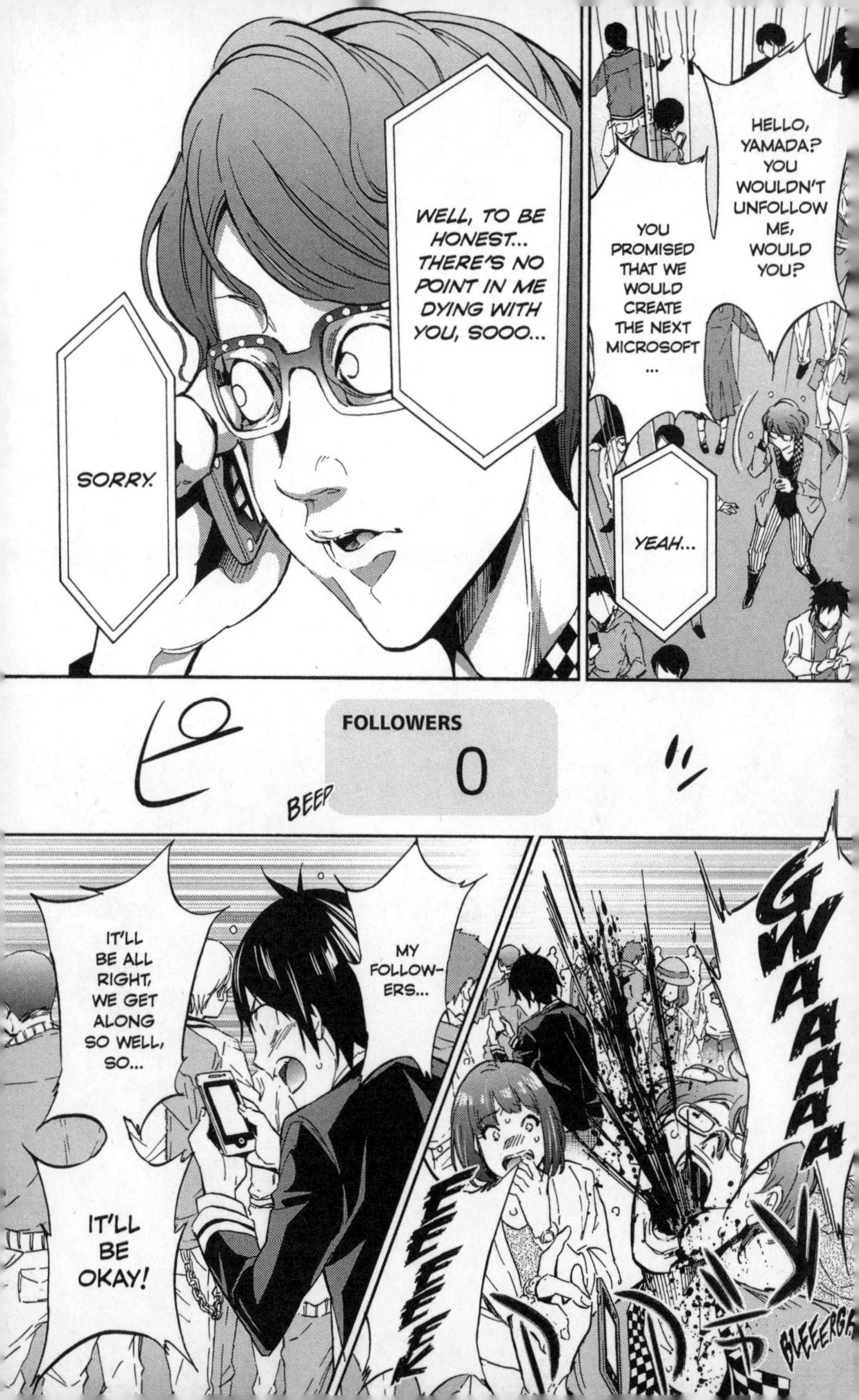
HELLO, YAMADA? YOU WOULDN'T UNFOLLOW ME, WOULD YOU?
YOU PROMISED THAT WE WOULD CREATE THE NEXT MICROSOFT ...
YEAH...
WELL, TO BE HONEST... THERE'S NO POINT IN ME DYING WITH YOU, SOOO...
SORRY.
FOLLOWERS
0
BEEP
GWAAAAAA
EEEEEK
BLEEERG
MY FOLLOW-ERS...
IT'LL BE ALL RIGHT, WE GET ALONG SO WELL, SO...
IT'LL BE OKAY!

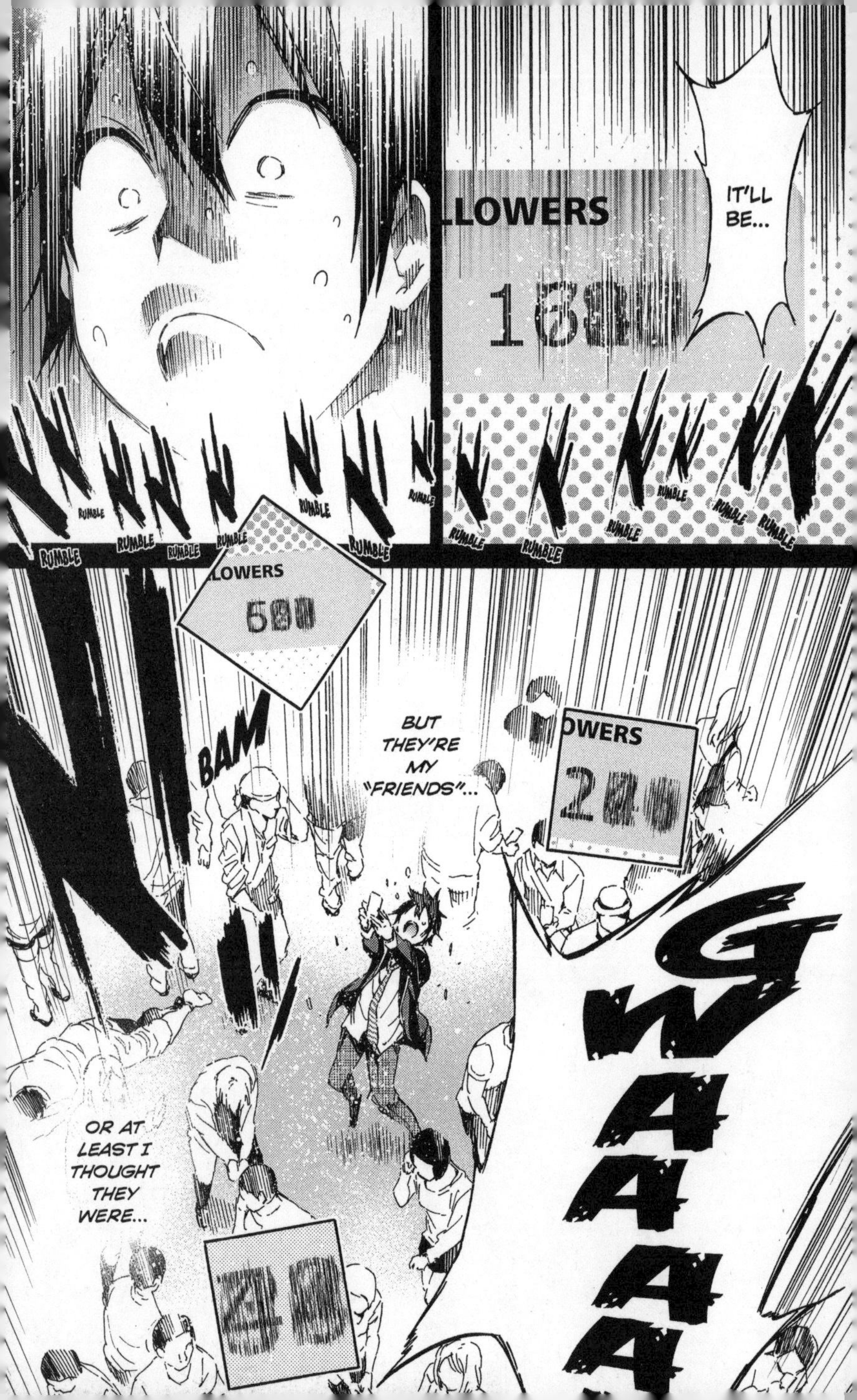
IT'LL BE...
LLOWERS
RUMBLE RUMBLE RUMBLE RUMBLE RUMBLE RUMBLE
RUMBLE RUMBLE RUMBLE RUMBLE RUMBLE RUMBLE RUMBLE RUMBLE
GWAAAAA
OWERS
BUT THEY'RE MY "FRIENDS"...
LOWERS
BAM
OR AT LEAST I THOUGHT THEY WERE...

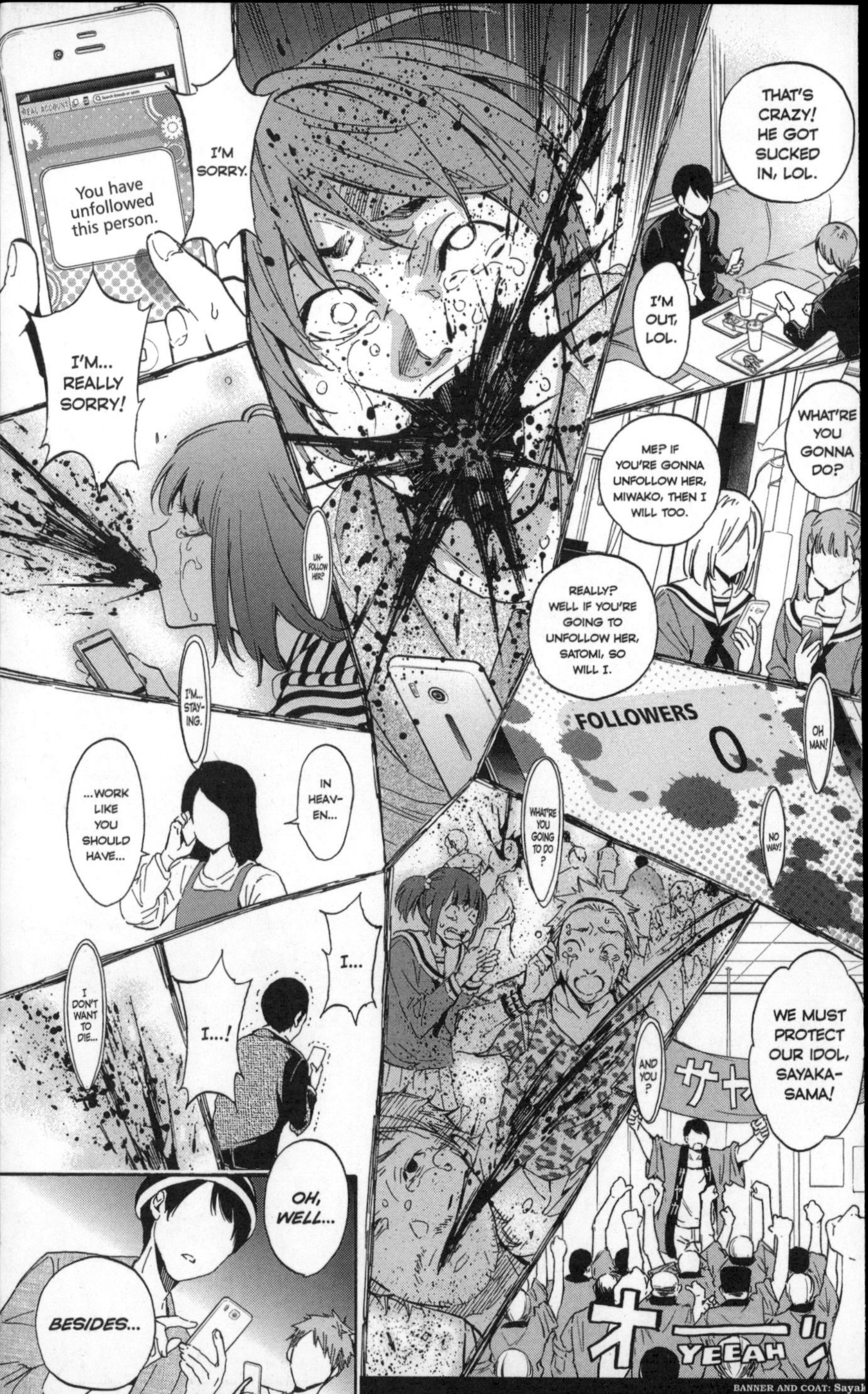
THAT'S CRAZY! HE GOT SUCKED IN, LOL.
I'M OUT, LOL.
REAL ACCOUNT
You have unfollowed this person.
I'M SORRY.
I'M... REALLY SORRY!
WHAT'RE YOU GONNA DO?
ME? IF YOU'RE GONNA UNFOLLOW HER, MIWAKO, THEN I WILL TOO.
REALLY? WELL IF YOU'RE GOING TO UNFOLLOW HER, SATOMI, SO WILL I.
UN-FOLLOW HER?
I'M... STAYING.
FOLLOWERS
0
OH MAN!
NO WAY!
WHAT'RE YOU GOING TO DO?
IN HEAV-EN...
...WORK LIKE YOU SHOULD HAVE...
WE MUST PROTECT OUR IDOL, SAYAKA-SAMA!
AND YOU?
オーーーー!!
YEEAH
I...
I...!
I DON'T WANT TO DIE...
OH, WELL...
BESIDES...

BANNER AND COAT: Sayak

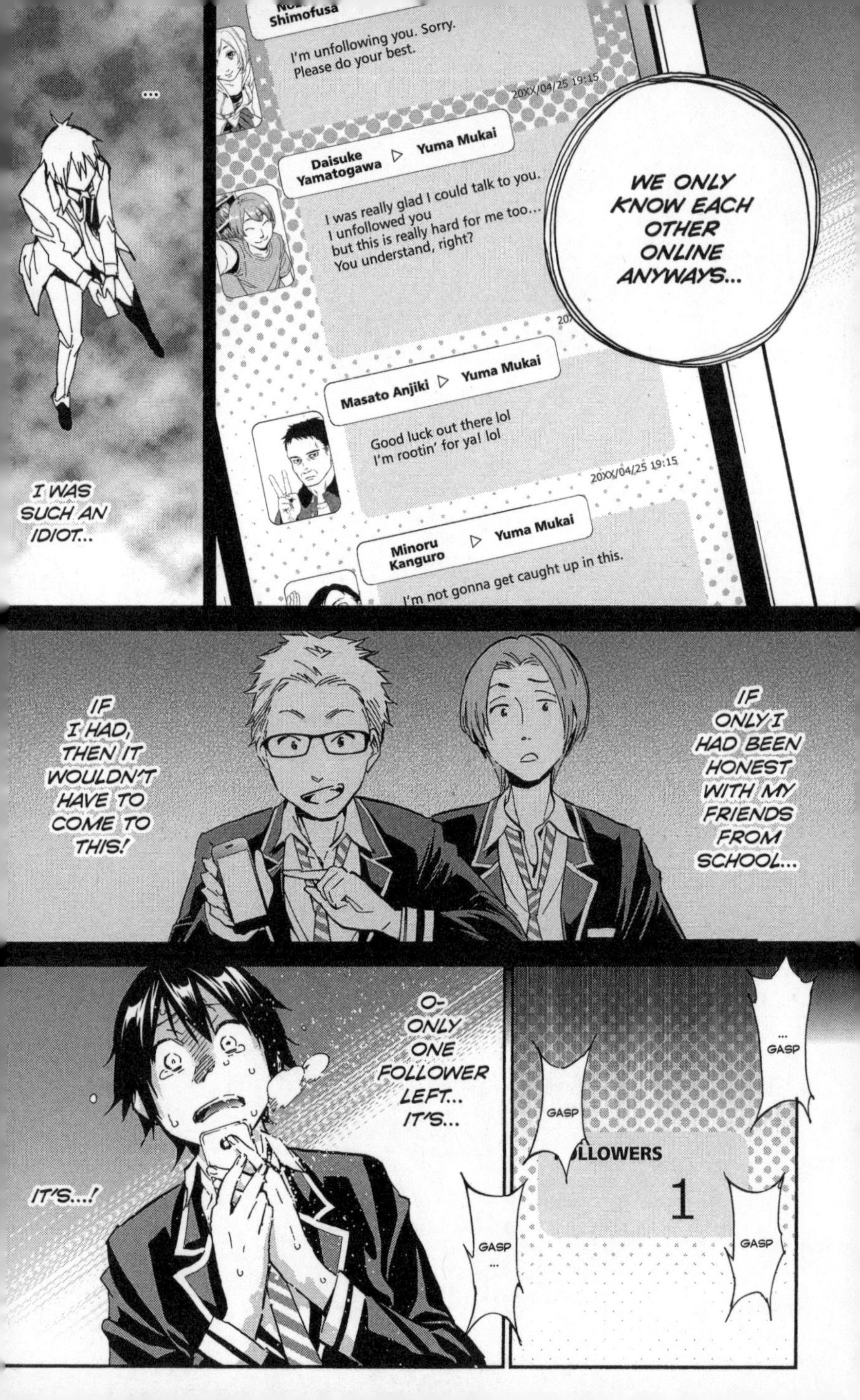

Shimofusa
I'm unfollowing you. Sorry.
Please do your best.
20XX/04/25 19:15
Daisuke Yamatogawa ▷ Yuma Mukai
I was really glad I could talk to you.
I unfollowed you
but this is really hard for me too...
You understand, right?
Masato Anjiki ▷ Yuma Mukai
Good luck out there lol
I'm rootin' for ya! lol
20XX/04/25 19:15
Minoru Kanguro ▷ Yuma Mukai
I'm not gonna get caught up in this.
WE ONLY KNOW EACH OTHER ONLINE ANYWAYS...
...
I WAS SUCH AN IDIOT...
IF ONLY I HAD BEEN HONEST WITH MY FRIENDS FROM SCHOOL...
IF I HAD, THEN IT WOULDN'T HAVE TO COME TO THIS!
... GASP
GASP
FOLLOWERS
1
GASP
GASP ...
O- ONLY ONE FOLLOWER LEFT... IT'S...
IT'S...!

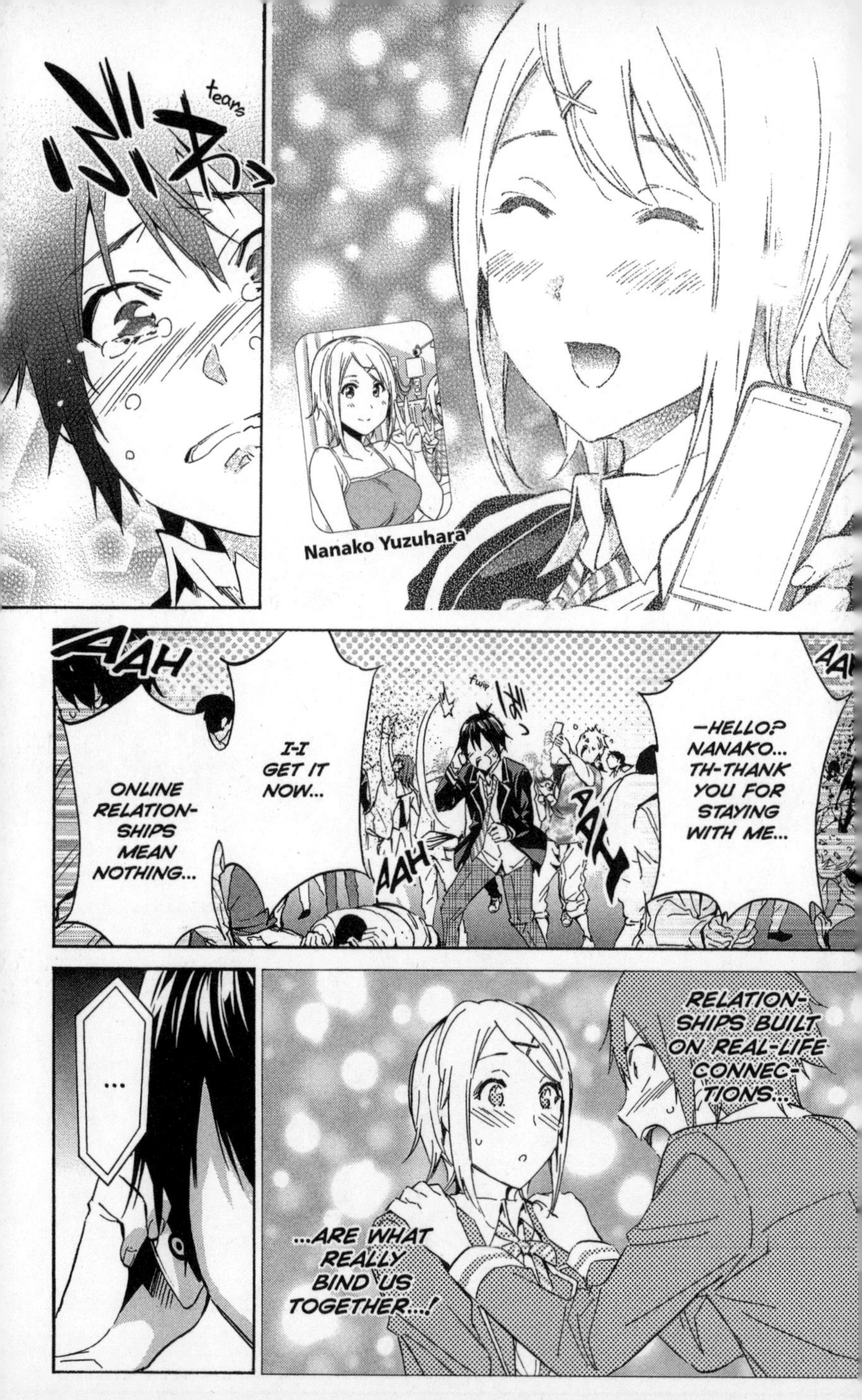
Nanako Yuzuhara
tears
AAH
—HELLO? NANAKO... TH-THANK YOU FOR STAYING WITH ME...
AAH
AAH
fwip
I-I GET IT NOW...
ONLINE RELATIONSHIPS MEAN NOTHING...
AAH
RELATIONSHIPS BUILT ON REAL-LIFE CONNECTIONS...
...ARE WHAT REALLY BIND US TOGETHER...!
...

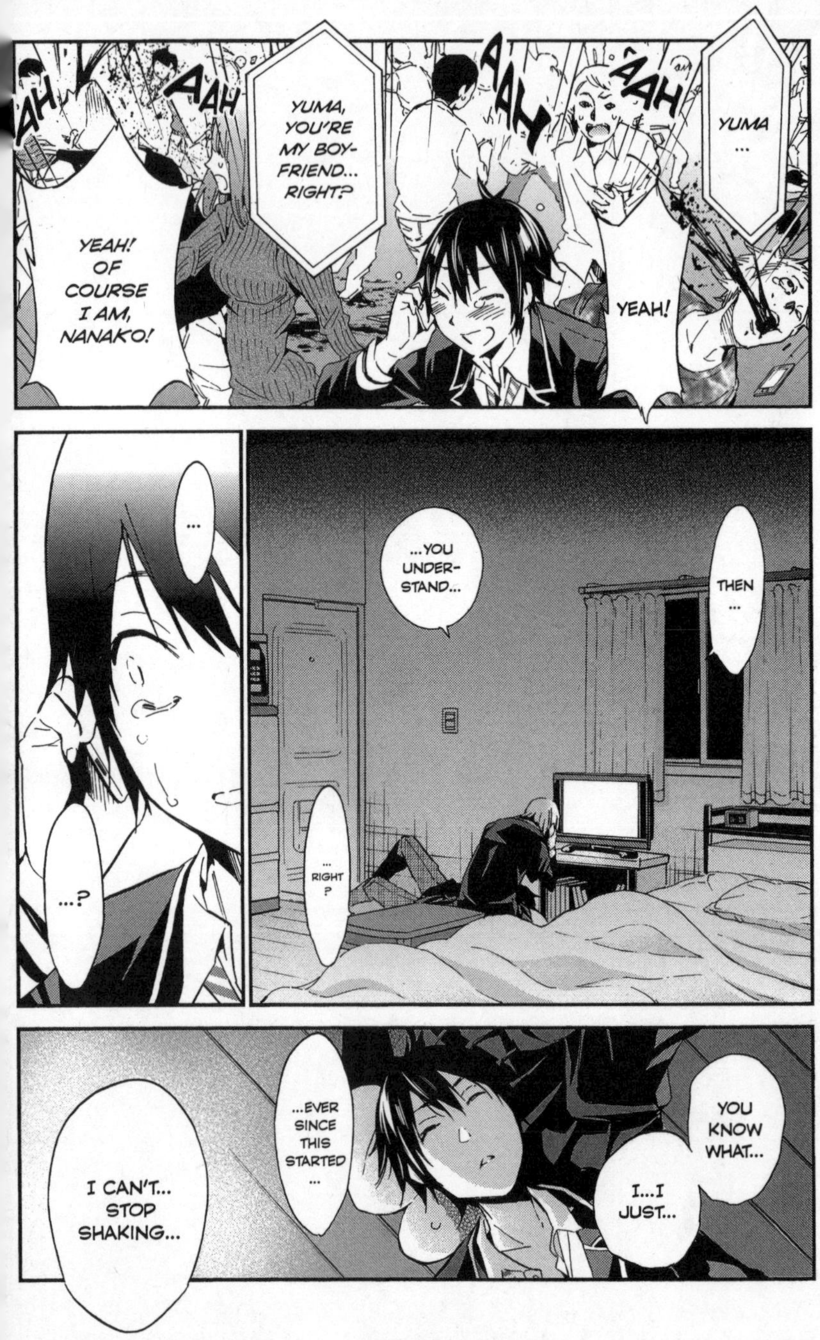
YUMA...
YEAH!
AAH
AAH
YUMA, YOU'RE MY BOY-FRIEND... RIGHT?
AAH
AH
YEAH! OF COURSE I AM, NANAKO!
THEN...
...YOU UNDER-STAND...
...RIGHT?
...
...?
YOU KNOW WHAT...
I...I JUST...
...EVER SINCE THIS STARTED...
I CAN'T... STOP SHAKING...

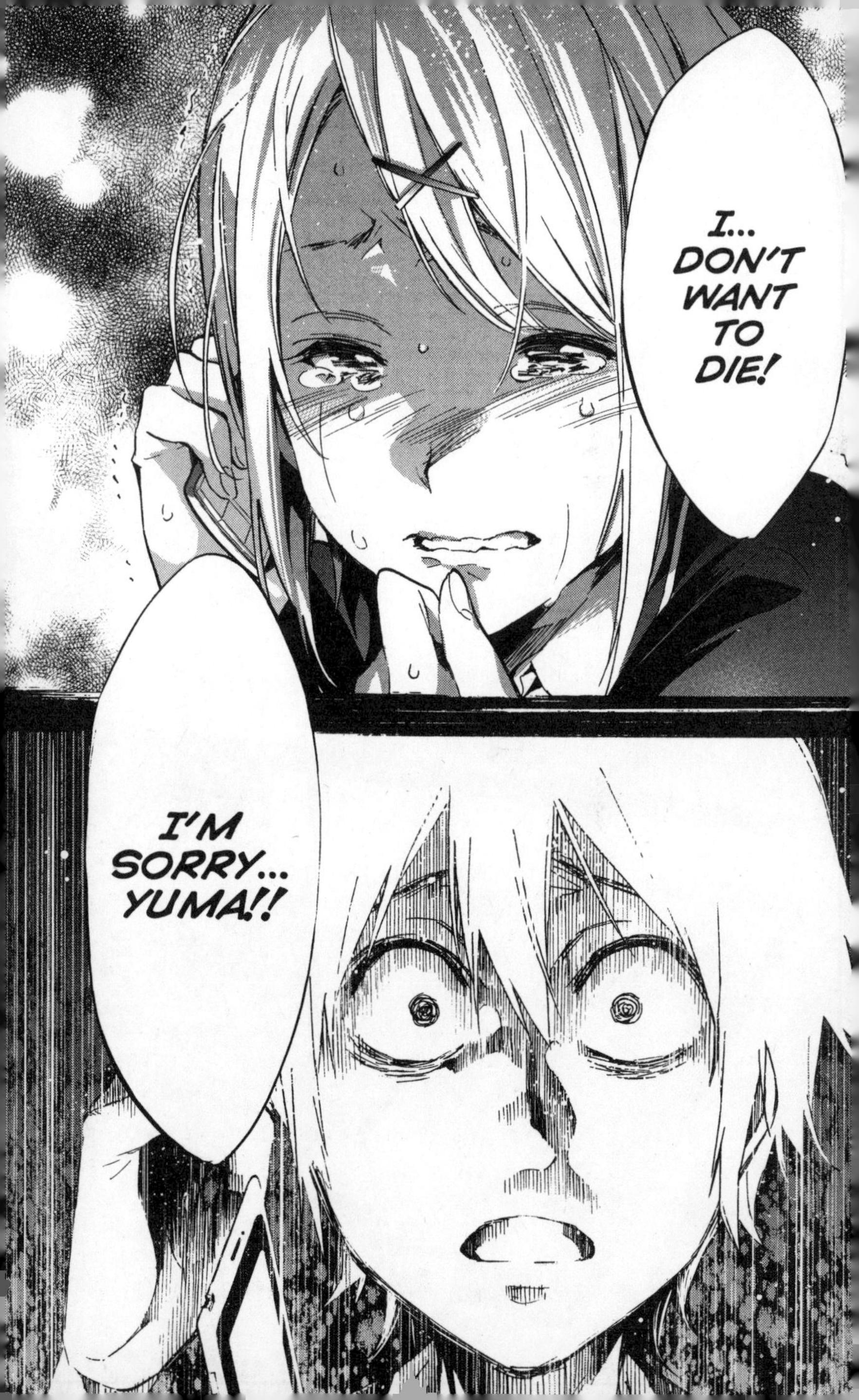
I... DON'T WANT TO DIE!
I'M SORRY... YUMA!!

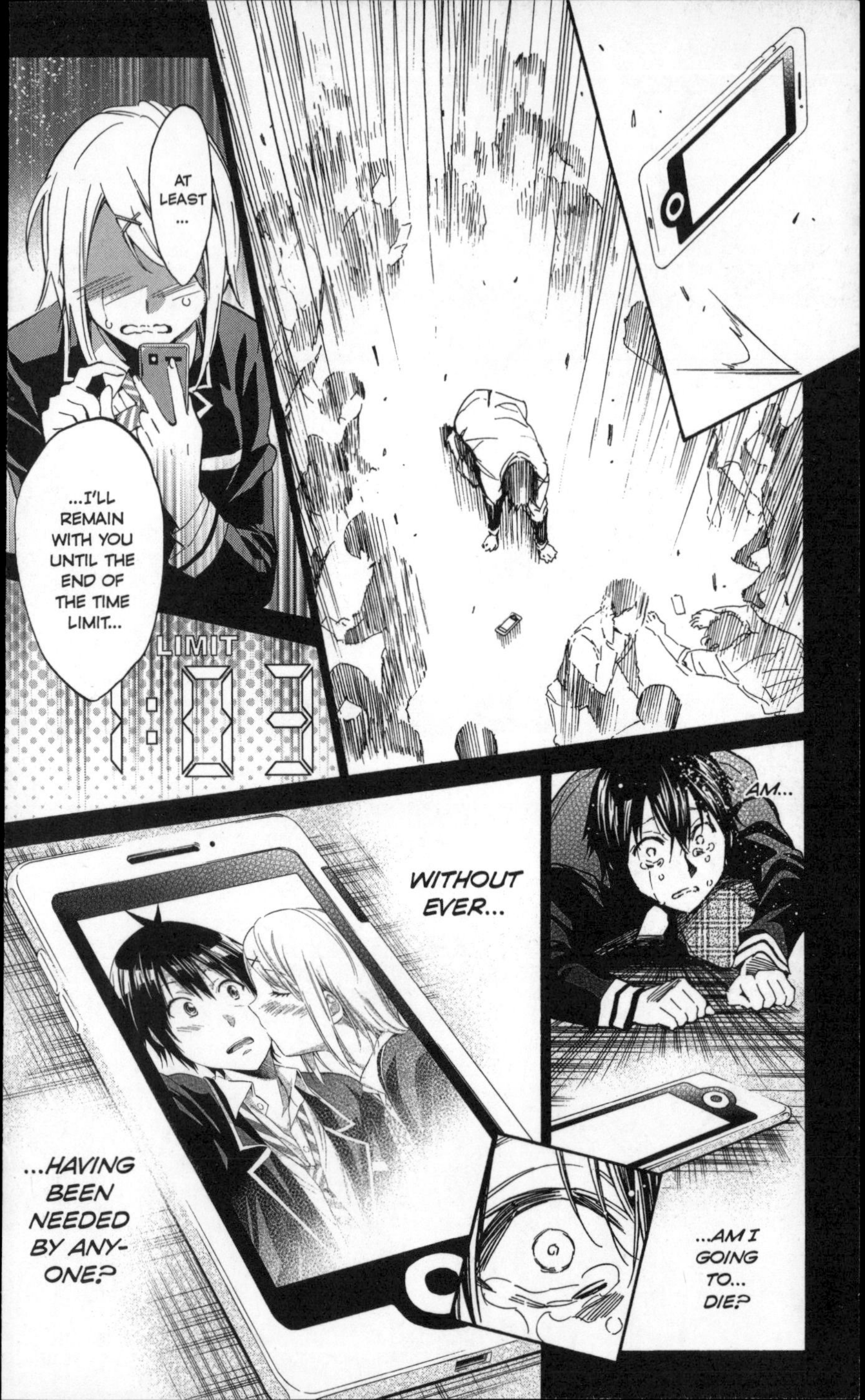
AT LEAST ...
...I'LL REMAIN WITH YOU UNTIL THE END OF THE TIME LIMIT...
LIMIT
AM...
...AM I GOING TO... DIE?
WITHOUT EVER...
...HAVING BEEN NEEDED BY ANY-ONE?

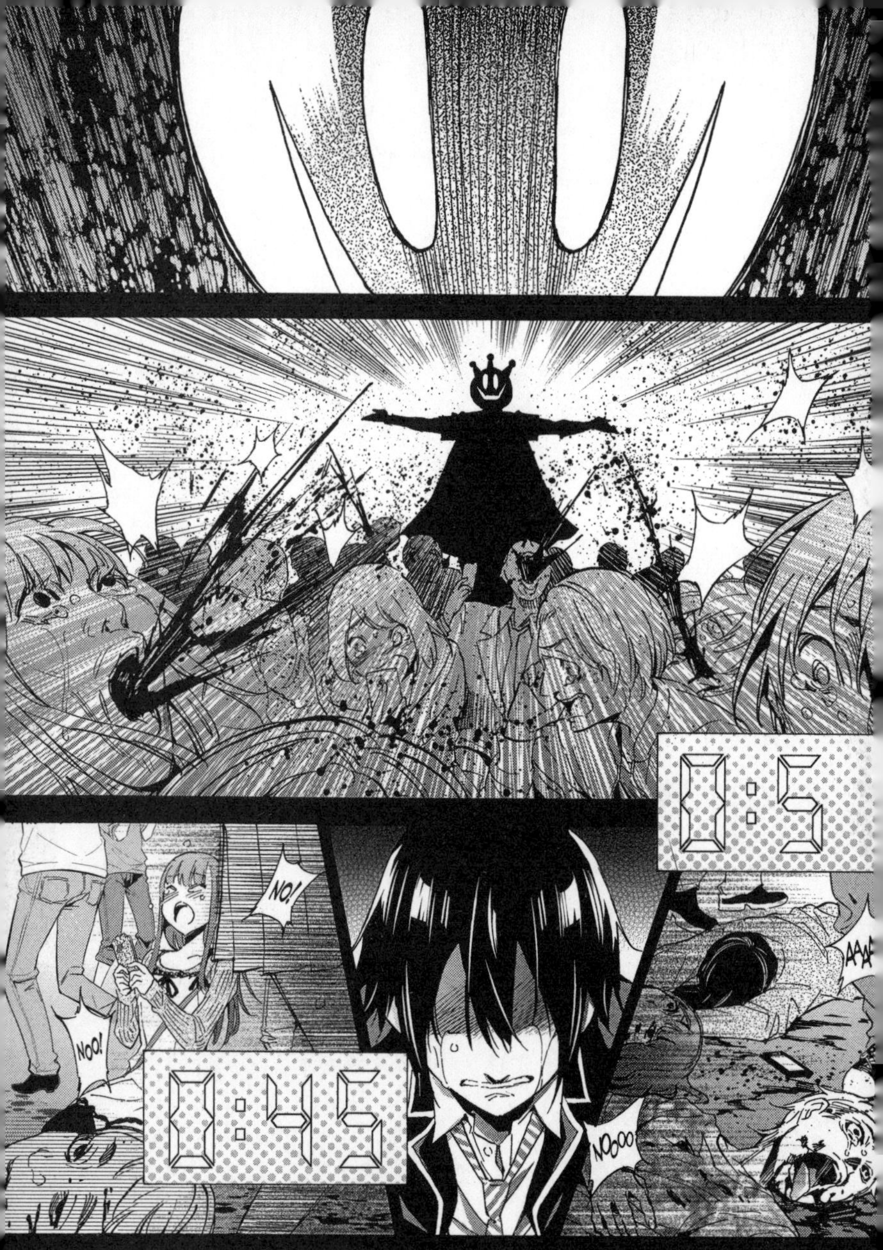
0:5
AAAA
NOOOO
NO!
NOO!
0:45

I CAN'T...

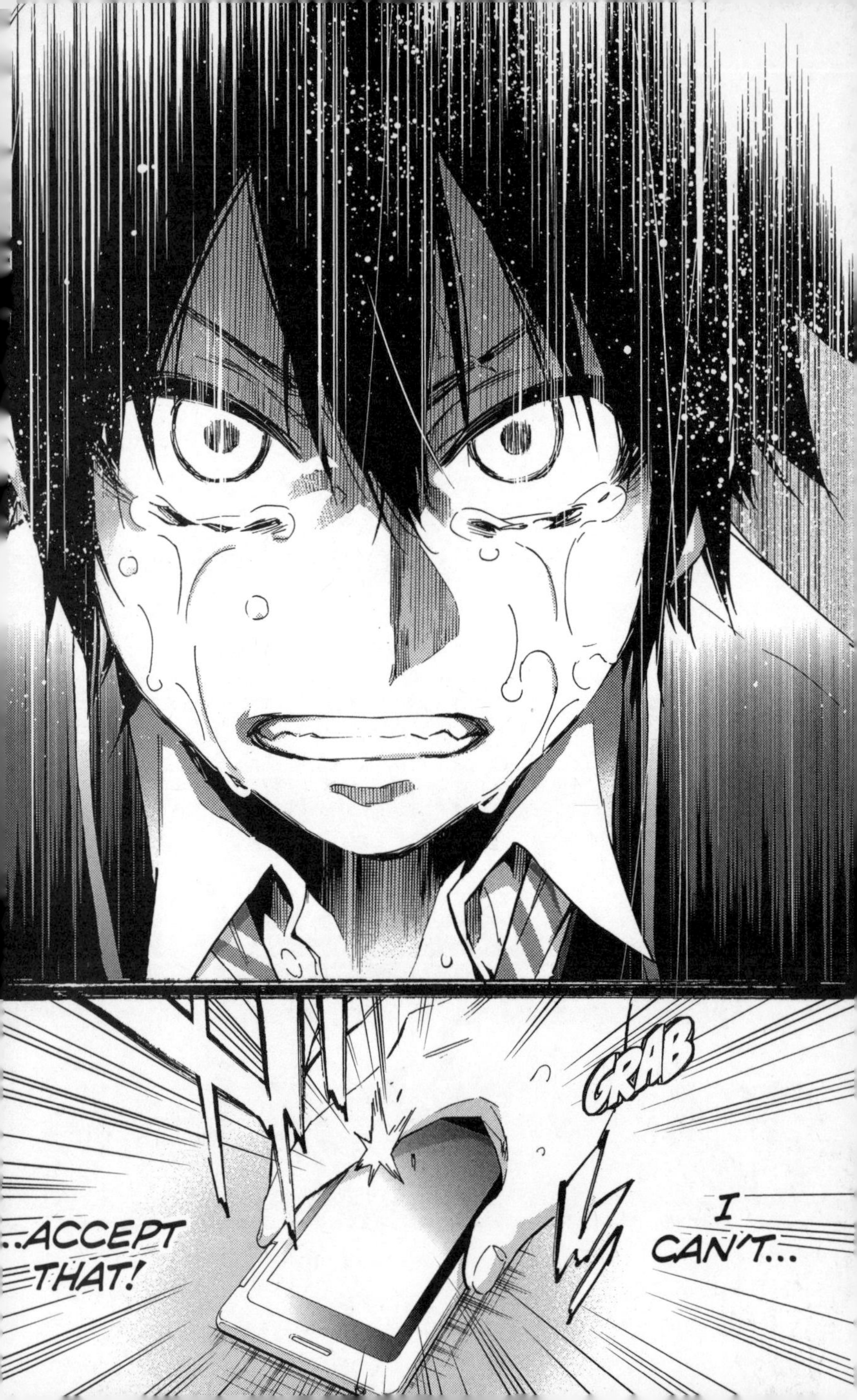
GRAB
I CAN'T...
..ACCEPT THAT!

ACCOUNT 2 The Dislike Game

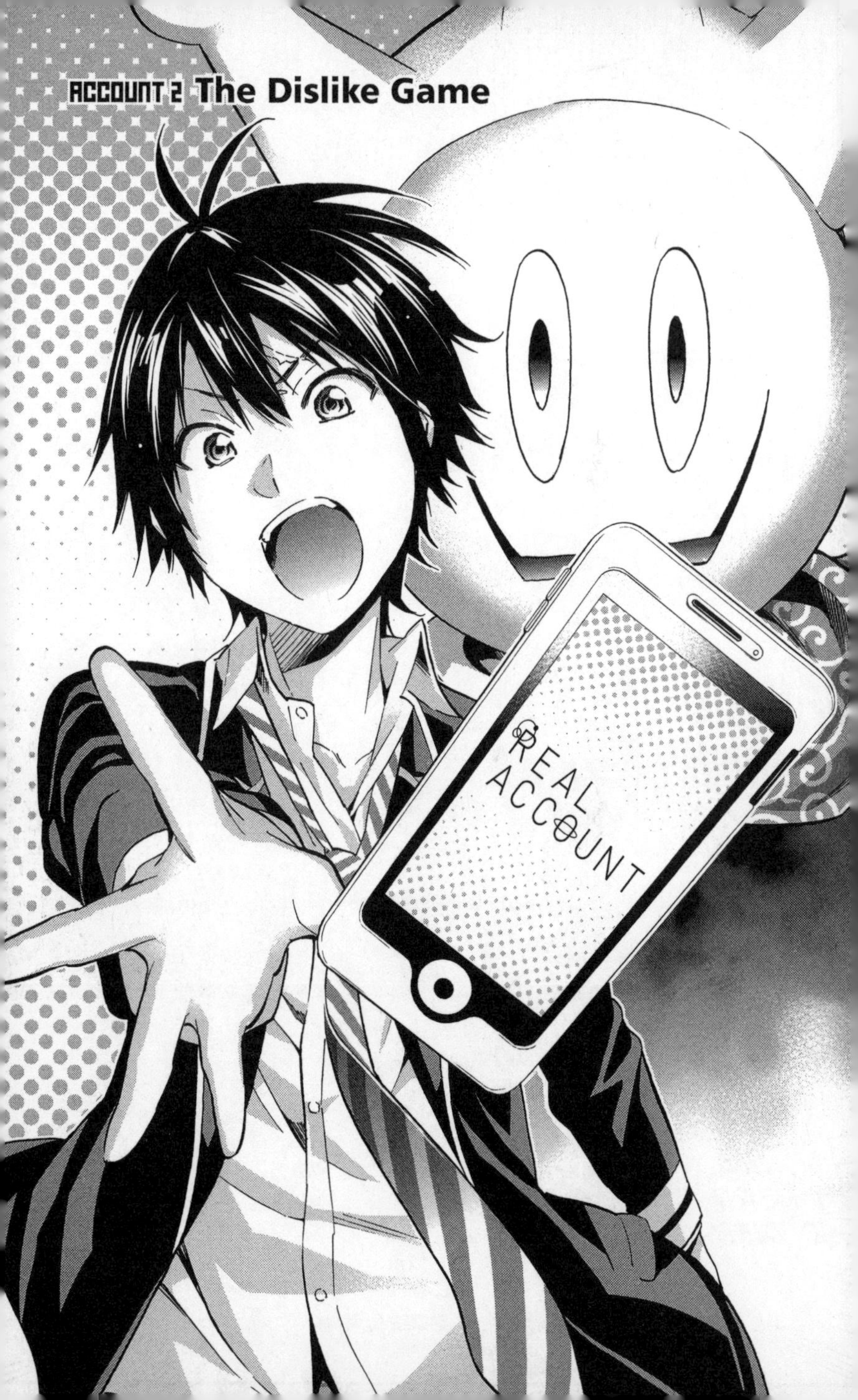
REAL ACCOUNT

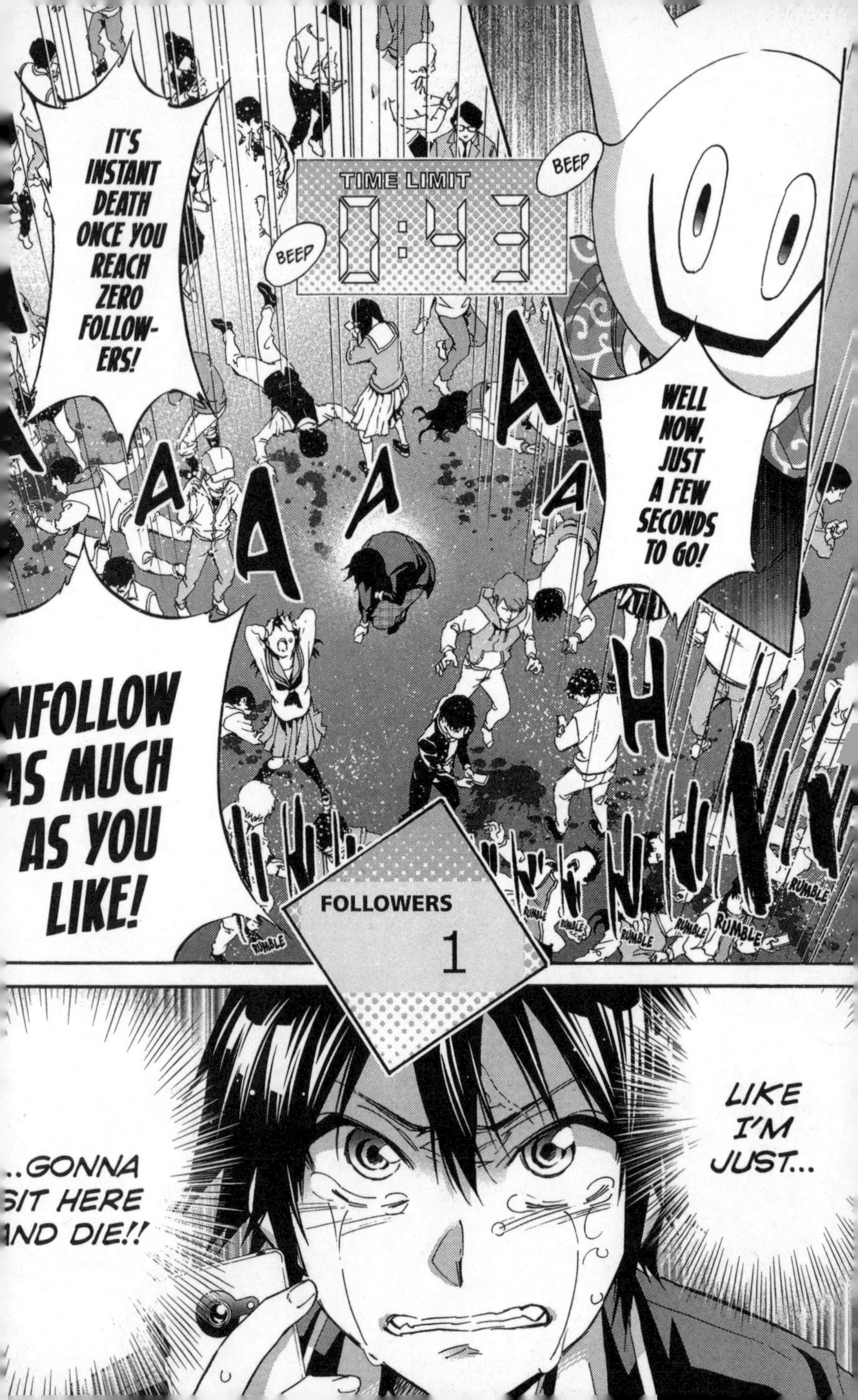
BEEP
TIME LIMIT 0:43
BEEP
WELL NOW, JUST A FEW SECONDS TO GO!
IT'S INSTANT DEATH ONCE YOU REACH ZERO FOLLOW-ERS!
AAAAAA
HNNNNNNNNN
NFOLLOW AS MUCH AS YOU LIKE!
RUMBLE
RUMBLE
RUMBLE
RUMBLE
RUMBLE
RUMBLE
RUMBLE
FOLLOWERS 1
LIKE I'M JUST...
..GONNA SIT HERE AND DIE!!

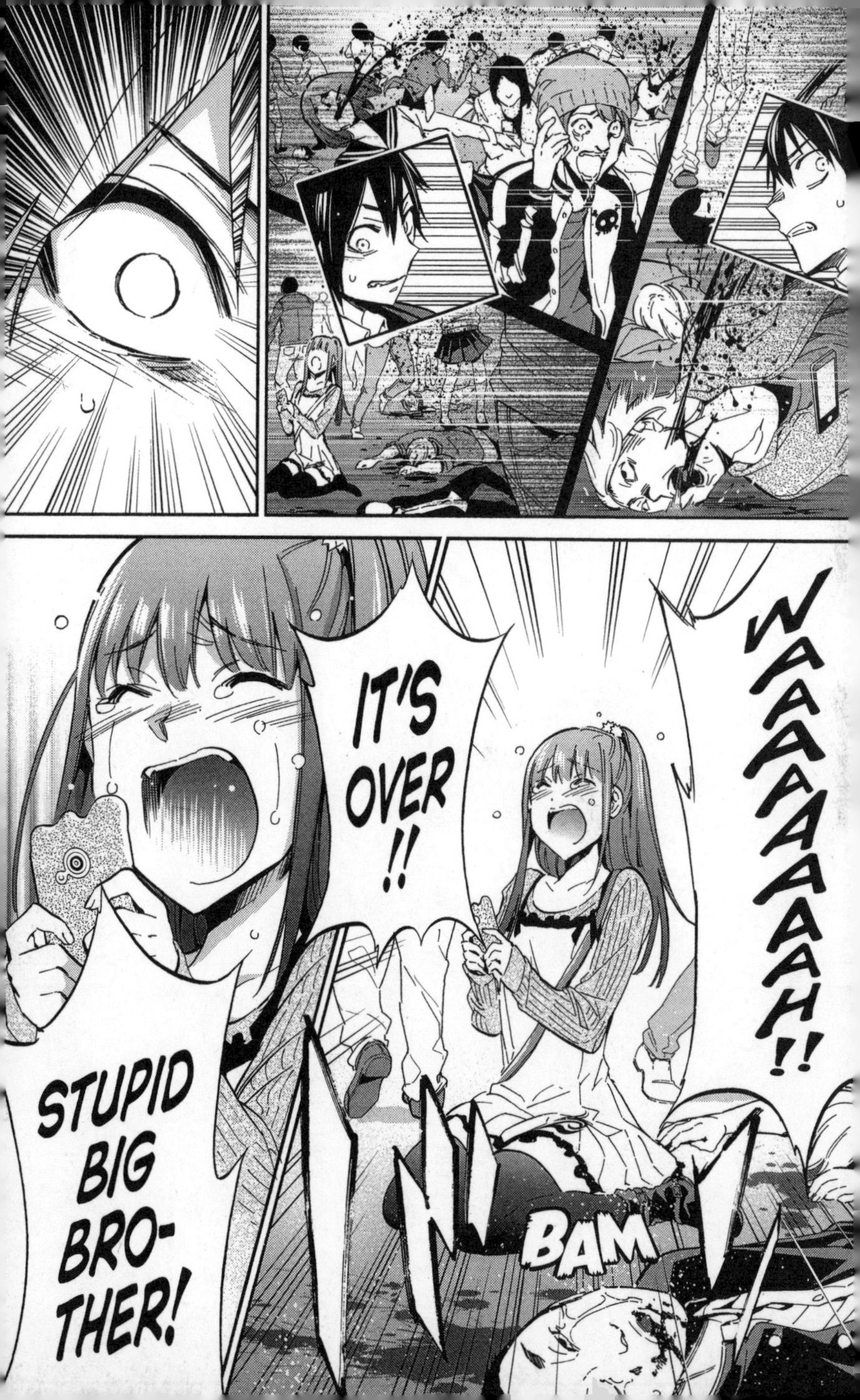

WAAAAAAAAH!!
IT'S OVER!!
STUPID BIG BRO-THER!
BAM

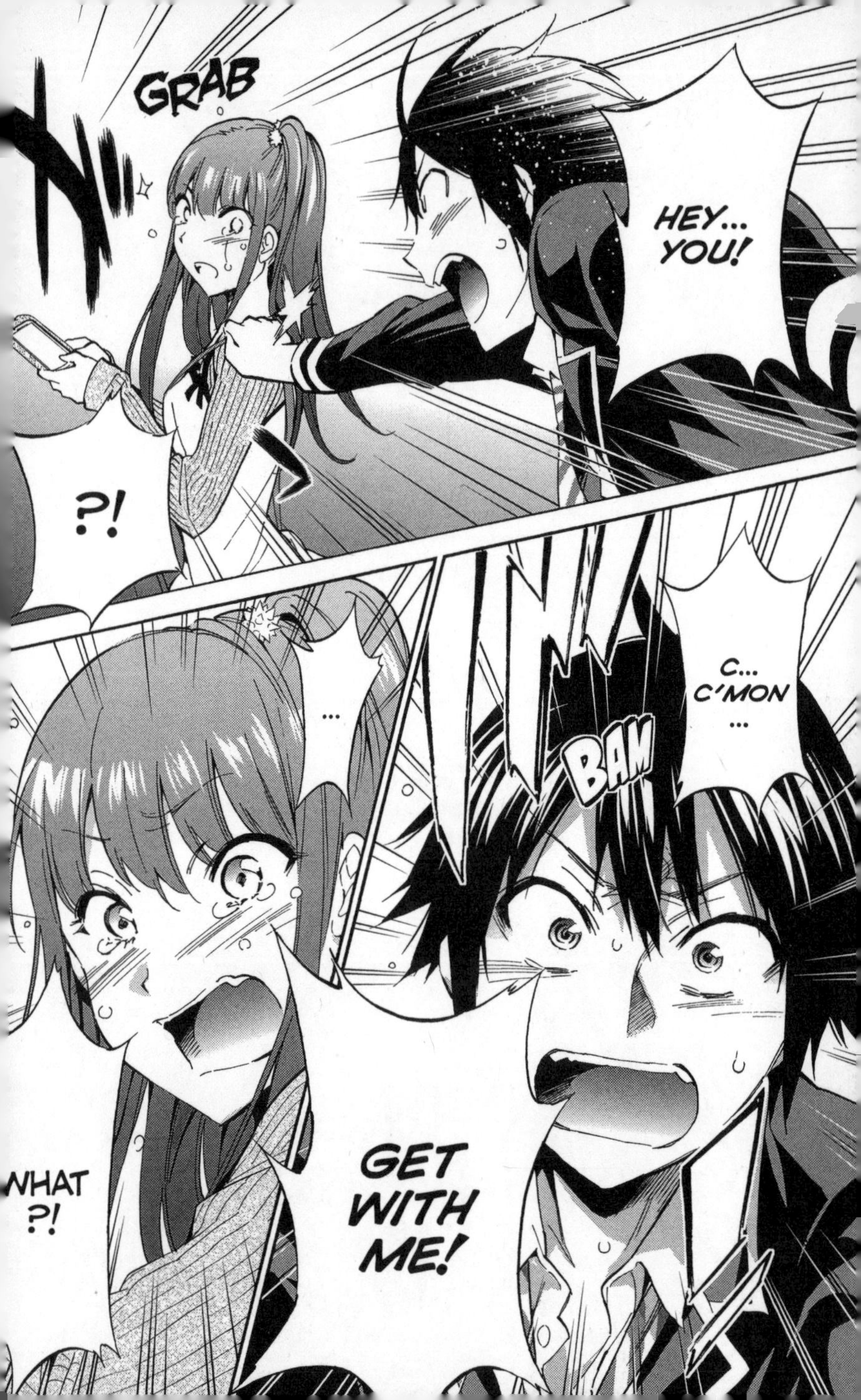
HEY... YOU!
GRAB
?!
C... C'MON ...
BAM
...
GET WITH ME!
NHAT ?!

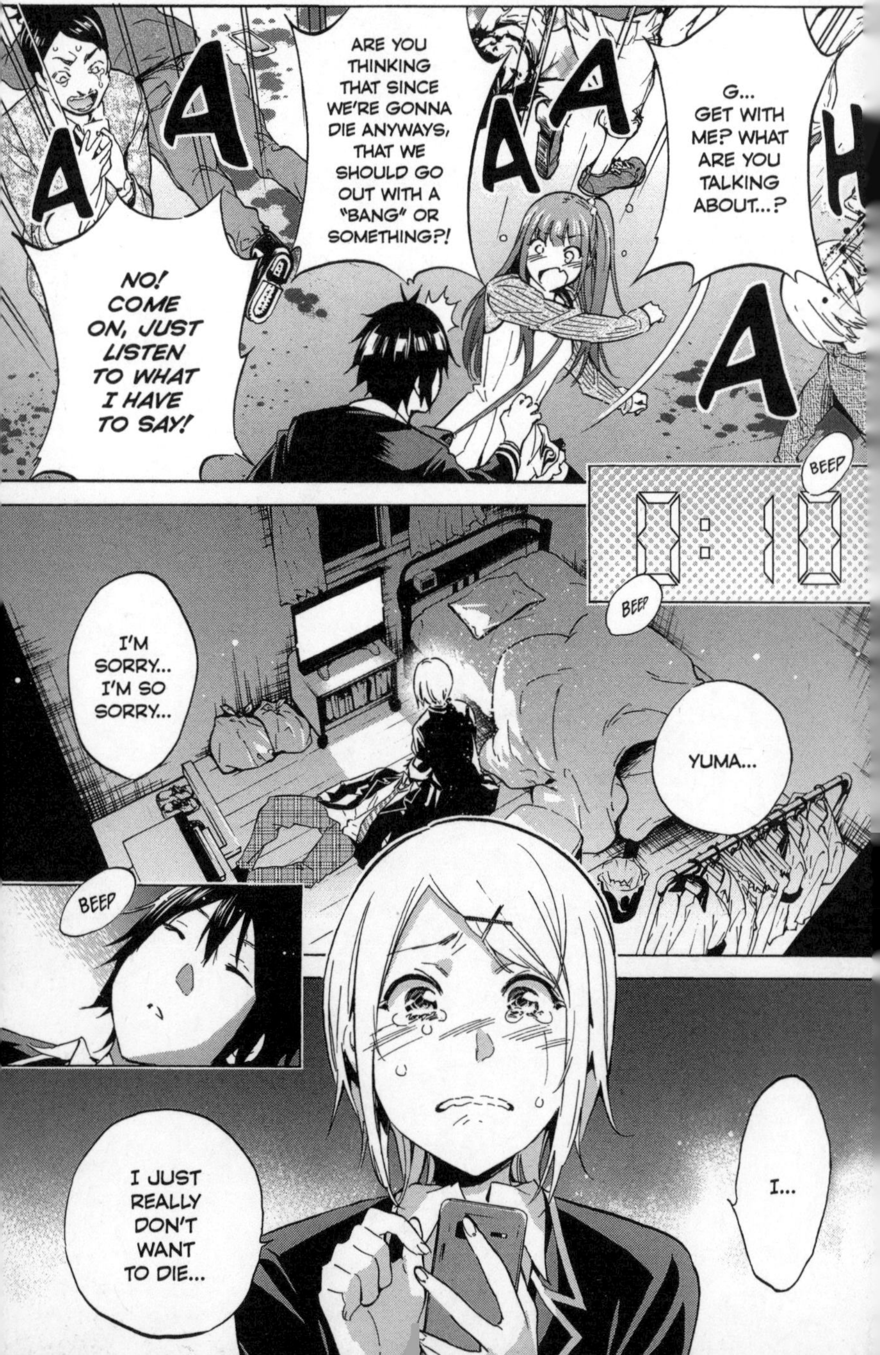
G... GET WITH ME? WHAT ARE YOU TALKING ABOUT...?
ARE YOU THINKING THAT SINCE WE'RE GONNA DIE ANYWAYS, THAT WE SHOULD GO OUT WITH A "BANG" OR SOMETHING?!
AAAAAH
NO! COME ON, JUST LISTEN TO WHAT I HAVE TO SAY!
BEEP
0:10
BEEP
YUMA...
I'M SORRY... I'M SO SORRY...
BEEP
I...
I JUST REALLY DON'T WANT TO DIE...

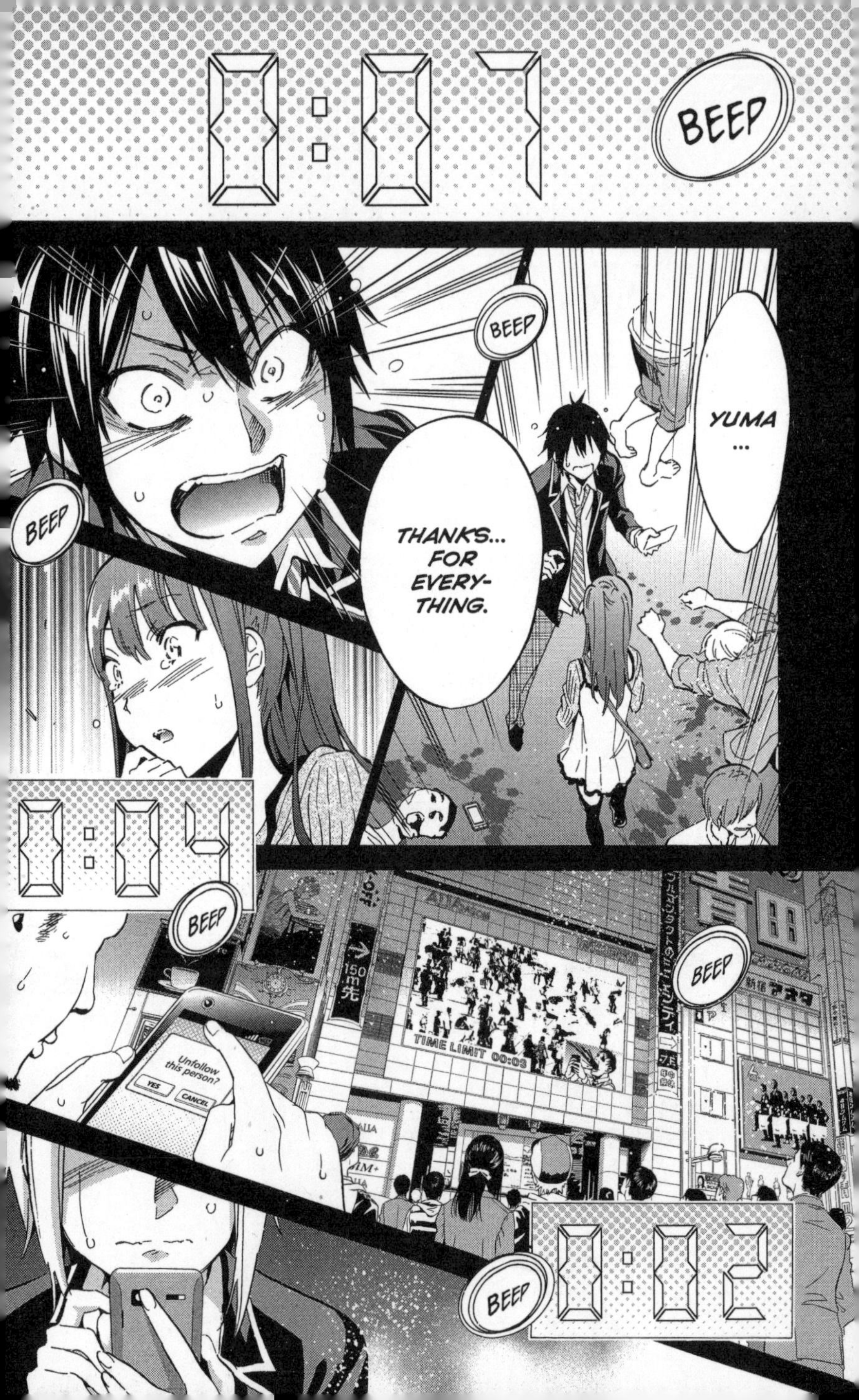
0:07
BEEP
YUMA ...
BEEP
THANKS... FOR EVERY-THING.
BEEP
0:04
BEEP
BEEP
TIME LIMIT 00:03
150m先
Unfollow this person?
YES
CANCEL
BEEP
0:02

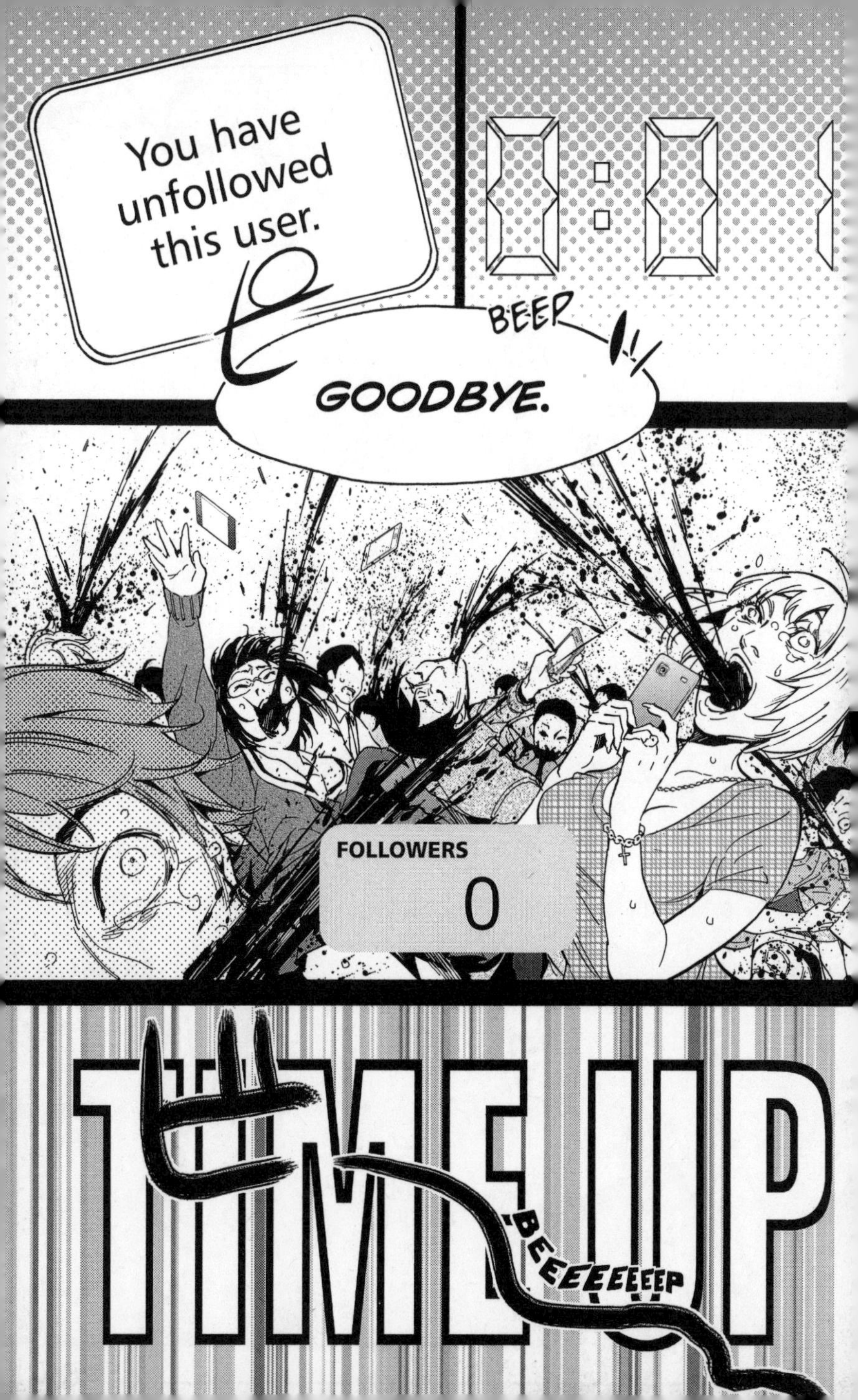
0:01
BEEP
You have unfollowed this user.
GOODBYE.
FOLLOWERS
0
TIME UP
BEEEEEEEP

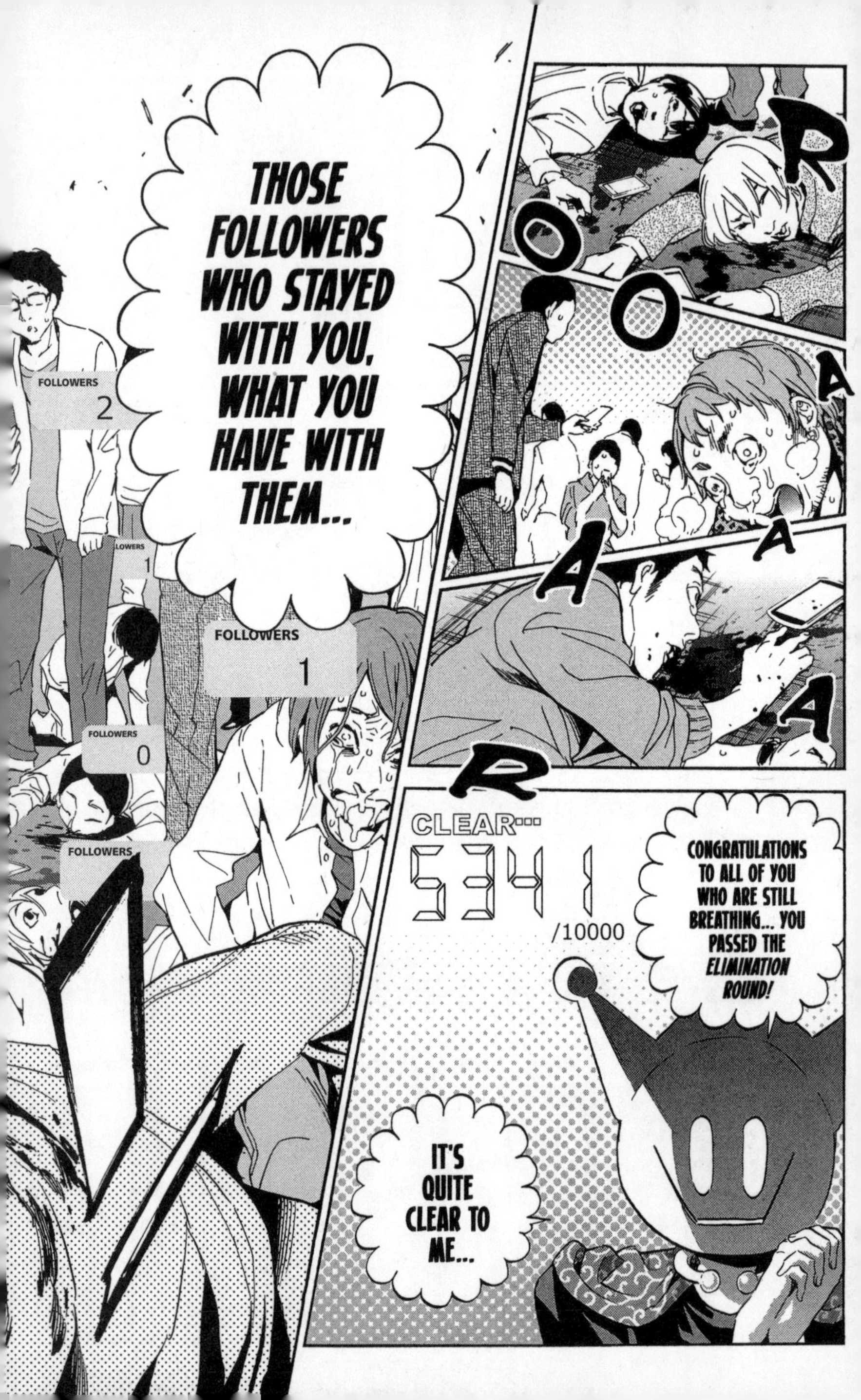
ROOAAAAR
CLEAR...
5341
/10000
CONGRATULATIONS TO ALL OF YOU WHO ARE STILL BREATHING... YOU PASSED THE *ELIMINATION ROUND!*
IT'S QUITE CLEAR TO ME...
FOLLOWERS 2
LOWERS 1
THOSE FOLLOWERS WHO STAYED WITH YOU, WHAT YOU HAVE WITH THEM...
FOLLOWERS 1
FOLLOWERS 0
FOLLOWERS

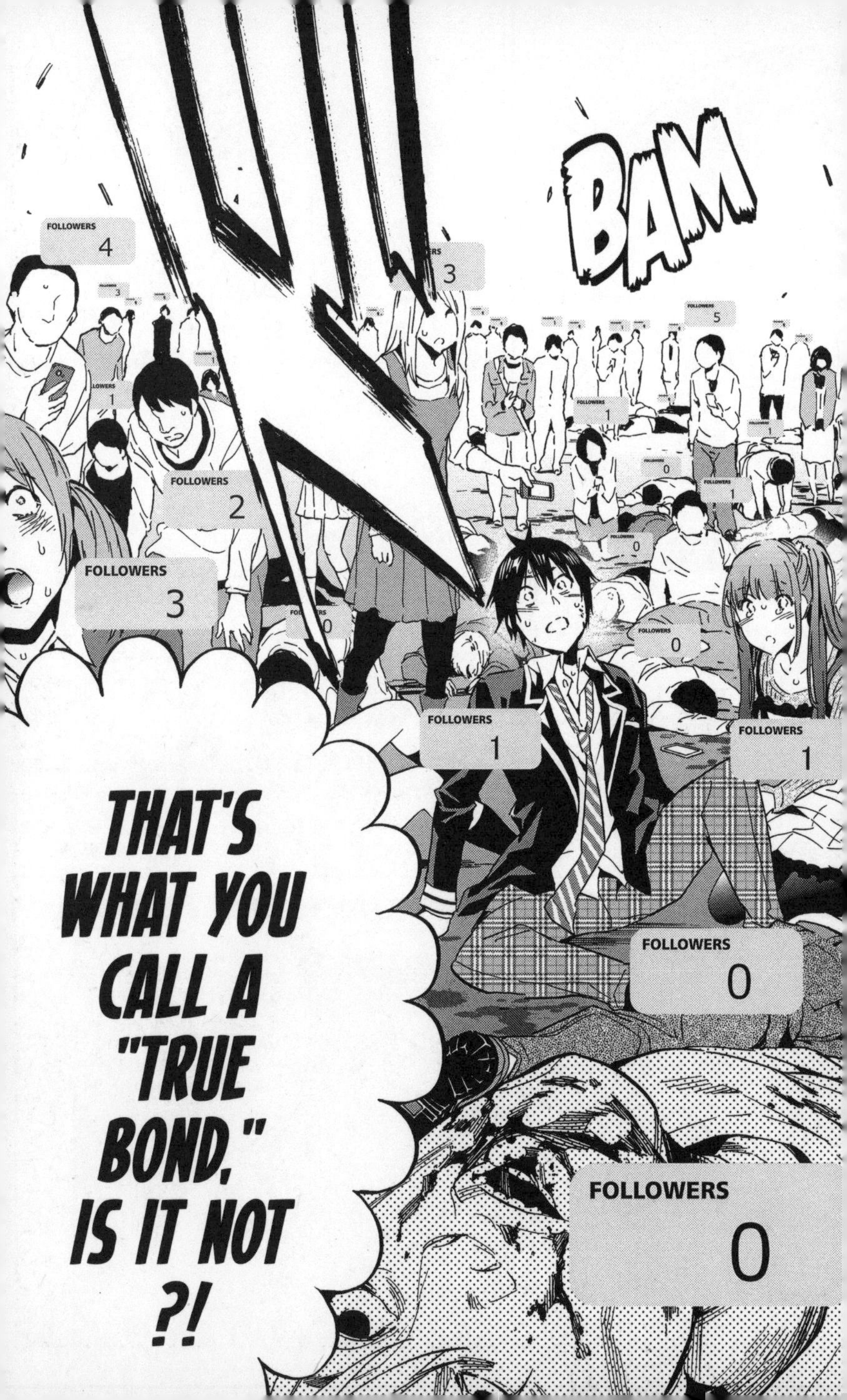
BAM
FOLLOWERS 5
FOLLOWERS 4
FOLLOWERS 1
FOLLOWERS 0
FOLLOWERS 1
FOLLOWERS 2
FOLLOWERS 0
FOLLOWERS 0
FOLLOWERS 3
FOLLOWERS 1
FOLLOWERS 1
FOLLOWERS 0
FOLLOWERS 0
THAT'S WHAT YOU CALL A "TRUE BOND," IS IT NOT ?!

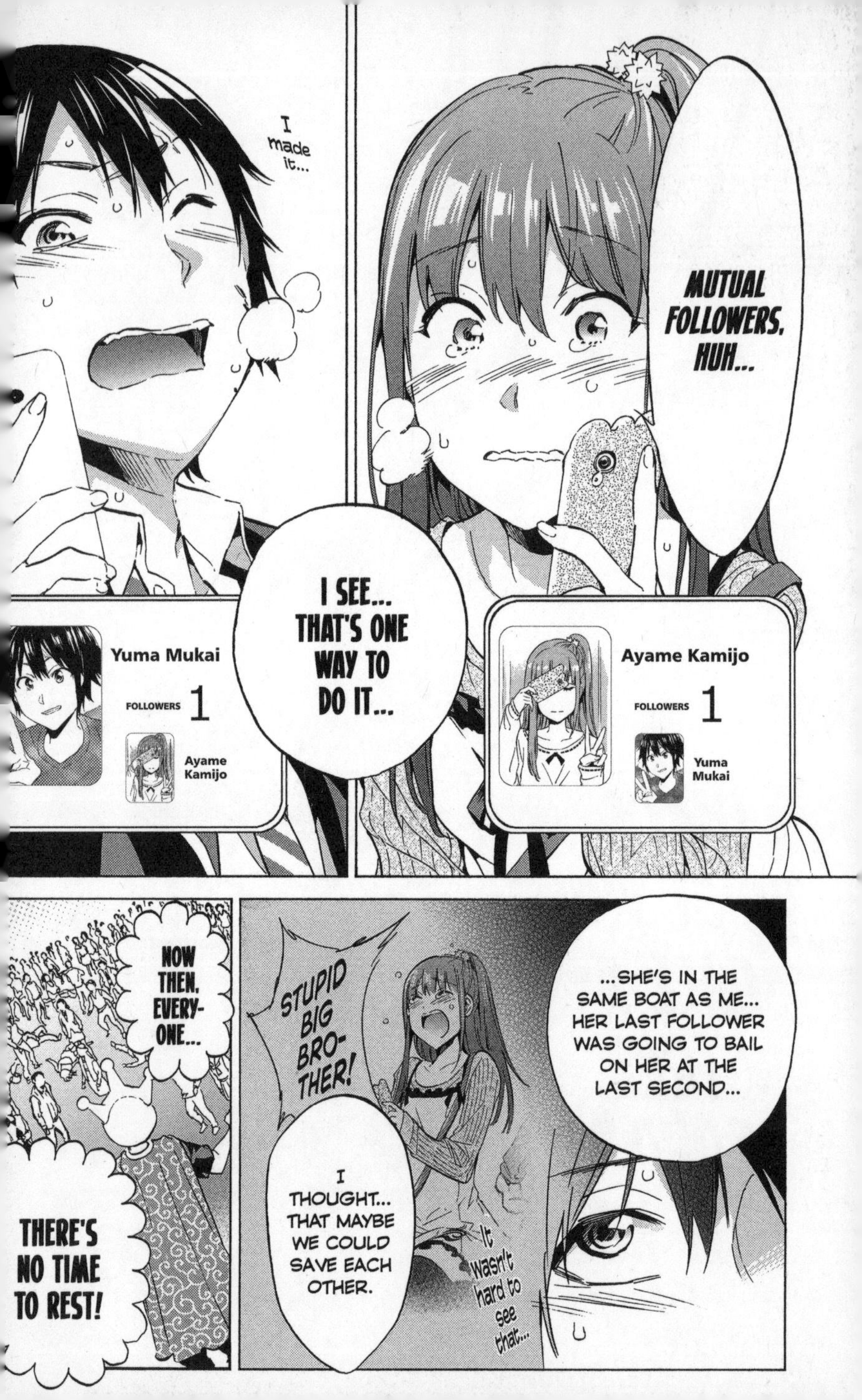
MUTUAL FOLLOWERS, HUH...
Ayame Kamijo
FOLLOWERS 1
Yuma Mukai
I SEE... THAT'S ONE WAY TO DO IT...
I made it...
Yuma Mukai
FOLLOWERS 1
Ayame Kamijo
...SHE'S IN THE SAME BOAT AS ME... HER LAST FOLLOWER WAS GOING TO BAIL ON HER AT THE LAST SECOND...
STUPID BIG BRO-THER!
It wasn't hard to see that...
I THOUGHT... THAT MAYBE WE COULD SAVE EACH OTHER.
NOW THEN, EVERY-ONE...
THERE'S NO TIME TO REST!

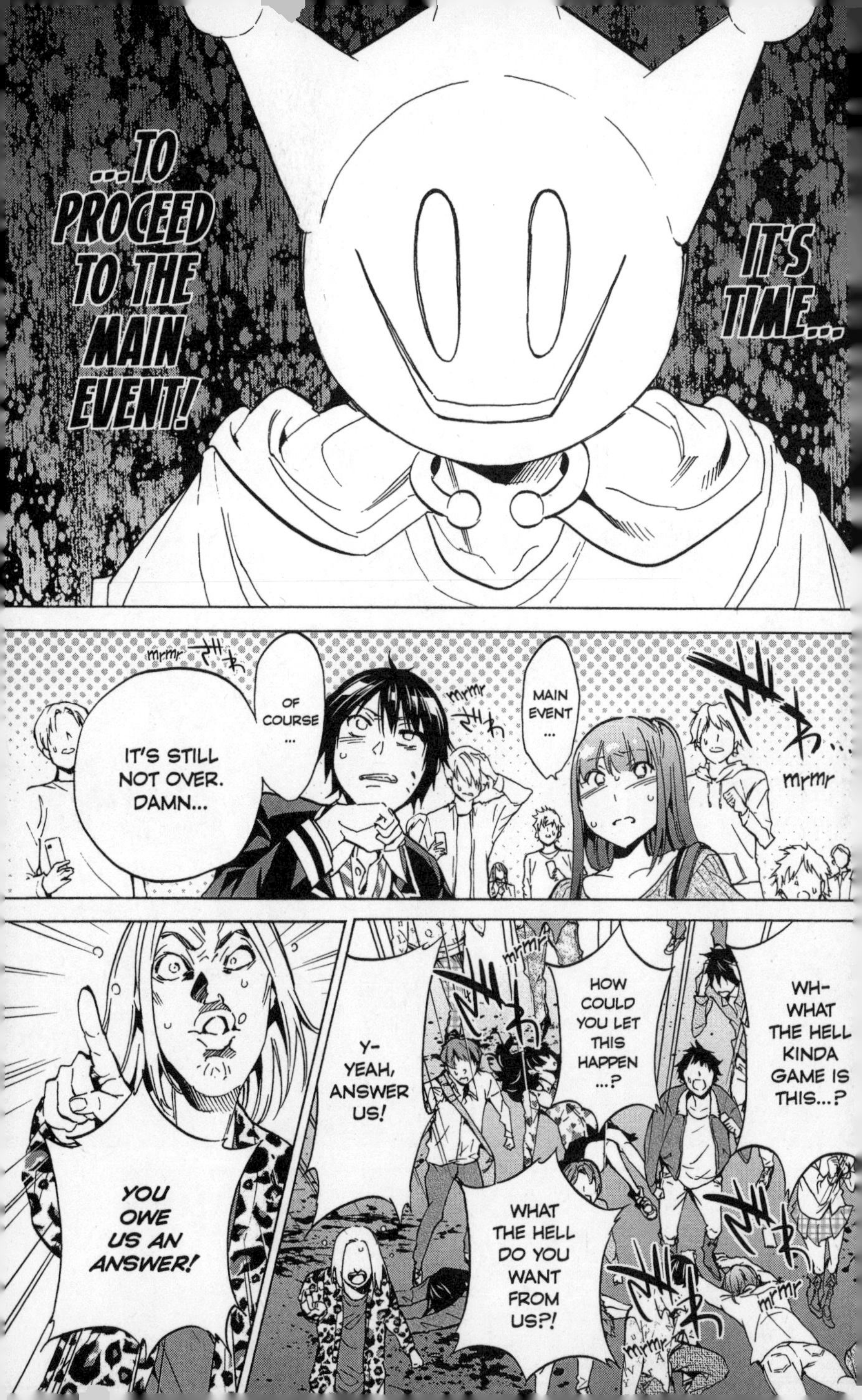
IT'S TIME...
...TO PROCEED TO THE MAIN EVENT!
mrmr
MAIN EVENT ...
mrmr
OF COURSE ...
mrmr
IT'S STILL NOT OVER. DAMN...
WH- WHAT THE HELL KINDA GAME IS THIS...?
HOW COULD YOU LET THIS HAPPEN ...?
mrmr
Y- YEAH, ANSWER US!
mrmr
WHAT THE HELL DO YOU WANT FROM US?!
YOU OWE US AN ANSWER!

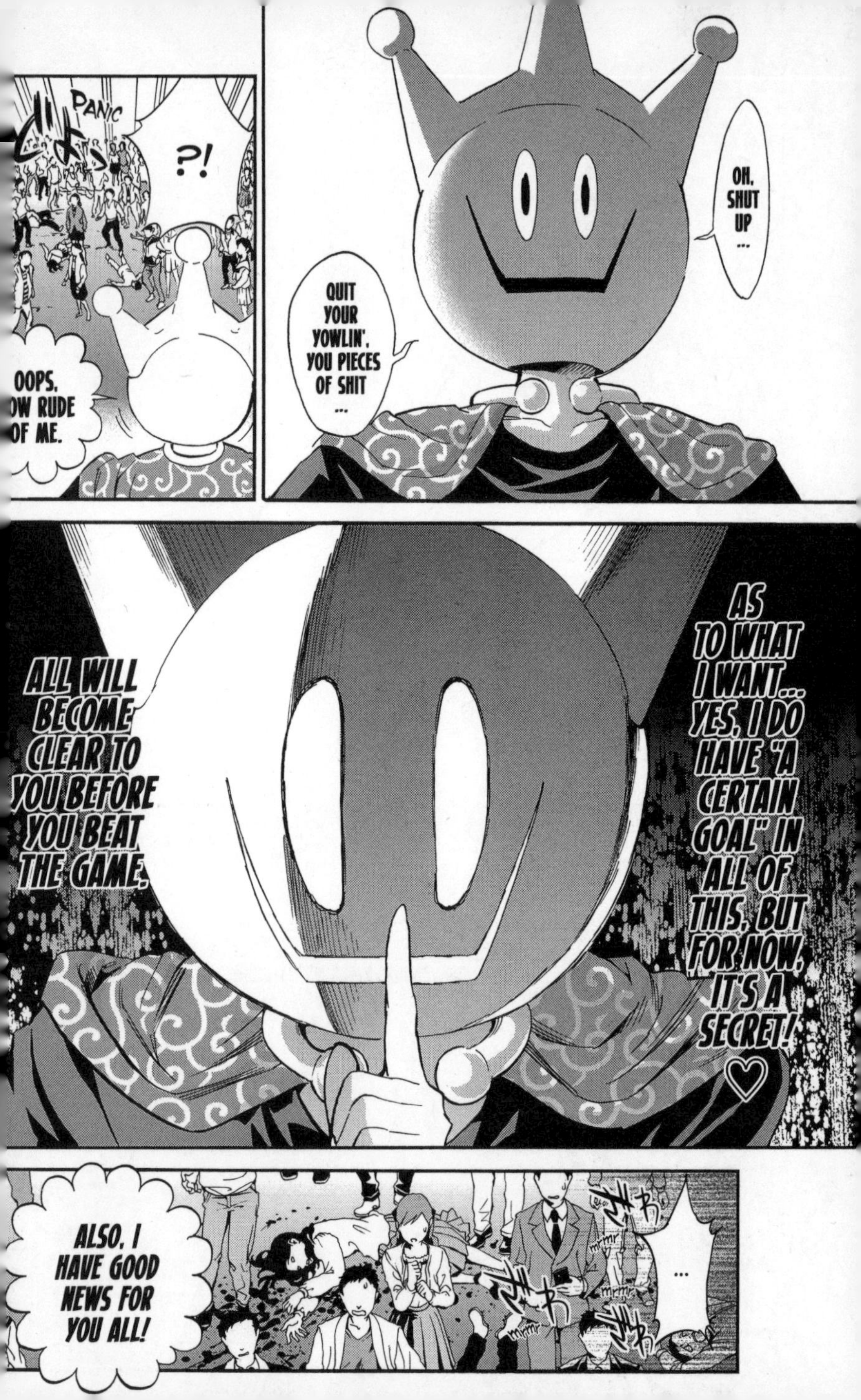
OH, SHUT UP ...
QUIT YOUR YOWLIN', YOU PIECES OF SHIT ...
PANIC
?!
OOPS. OW RUDE OF ME.
AS TO WHAT I WANT... YES, I DO HAVE "A CERTAIN GOAL" IN ALL OF THIS, BUT FOR NOW, IT'S A SECRET! ♡
ALL WILL BECOME CLEAR TO YOU BEFORE YOU BEAT THE GAME.
...
ALSO, I HAVE GOOD NEWS FOR YOU ALL!

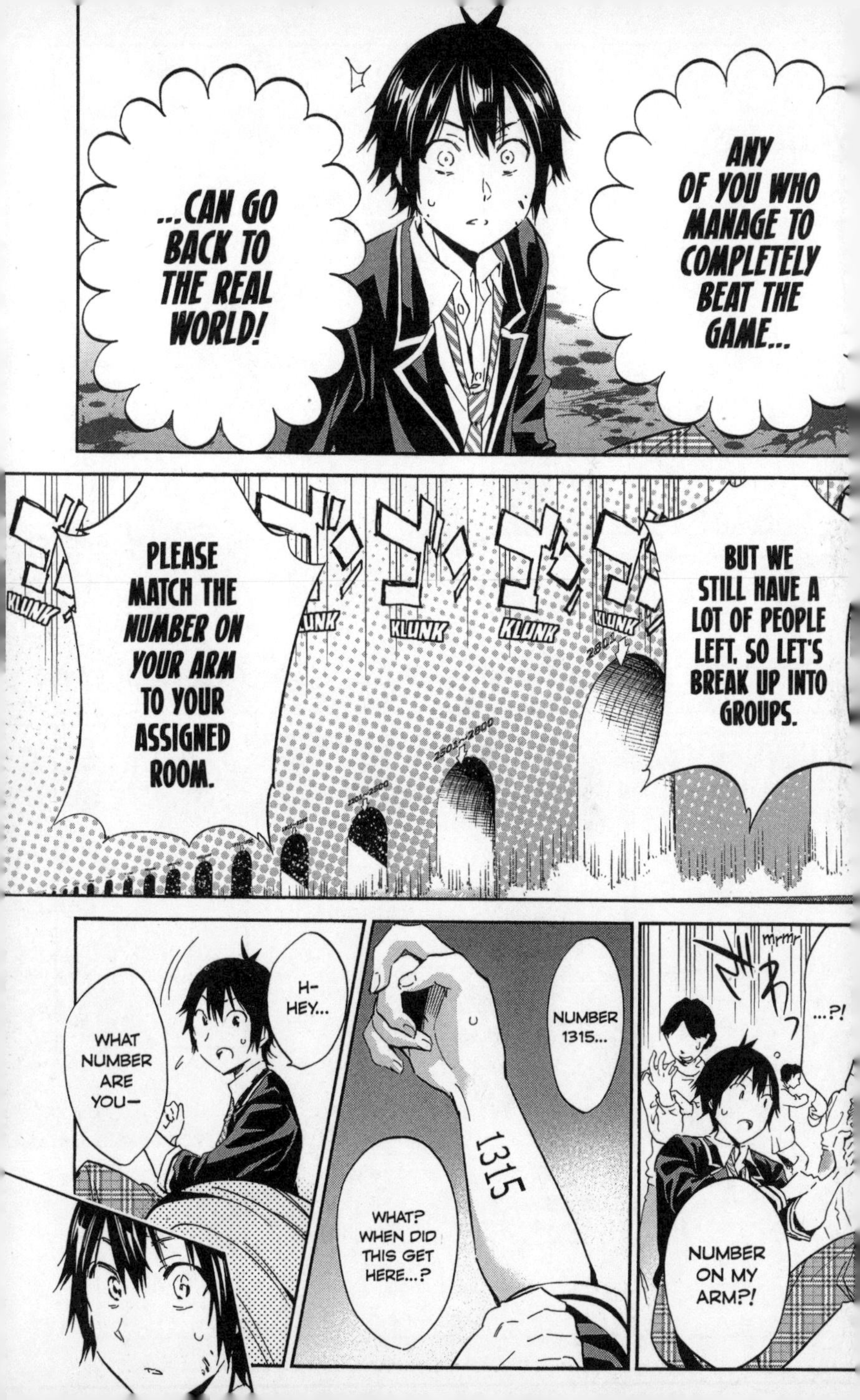
ANY OF YOU WHO MANAGE TO COMPLETELY BEAT THE GAME...
...CAN GO BACK TO THE REAL WORLD!
BUT WE STILL HAVE A LOT OF PEOPLE LEFT, SO LET'S BREAK UP INTO GROUPS.
KLUNK
KLUNK
KLUNK
KLUNK
KLUNK
PLEASE MATCH THE NUMBER ON YOUR ARM TO YOUR ASSIGNED ROOM.
mrmr
...?!
NUMBER ON MY ARM?!
NUMBER 1315...
1315
WHAT? WHEN DID THIS GET HERE...?
H-HEY...
WHAT NUMBER ARE YOU—

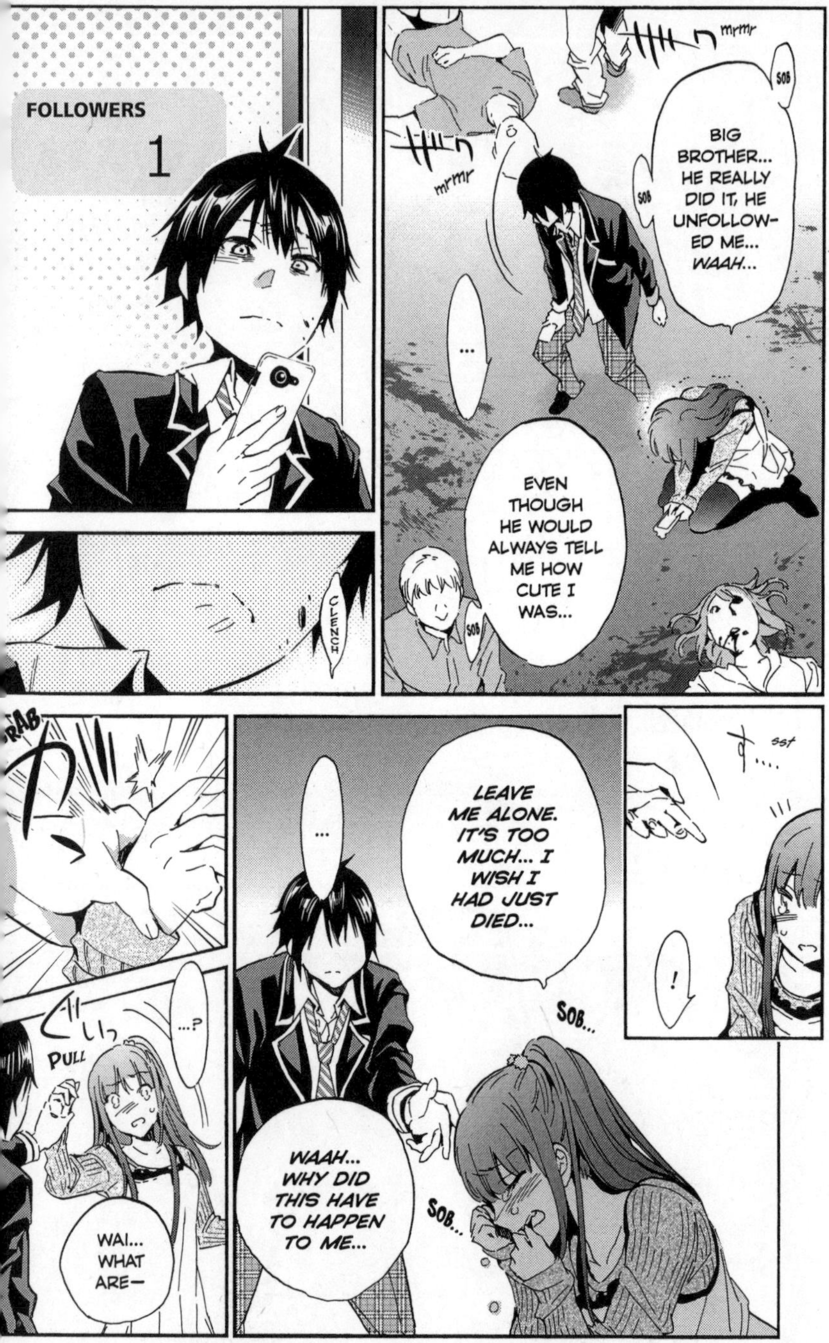
mrmr
SOB
BIG BROTHER... HE REALLY DID IT, HE UNFOLLOWED ME... WAAH...
SOB
mrmr
...
EVEN THOUGH HE WOULD ALWAYS TELL ME HOW CUTE I WAS...
SOB
FOLLOWERS
1
CLENCH
sst
!
...
LEAVE ME ALONE. IT'S TOO MUCH... I WISH I HAD JUST DIED...
SOB...
WAAH... WHY DID THIS HAVE TO HAPPEN TO ME...
SOB...
GRAB
PULL
...?
WAI... WHAT ARE—

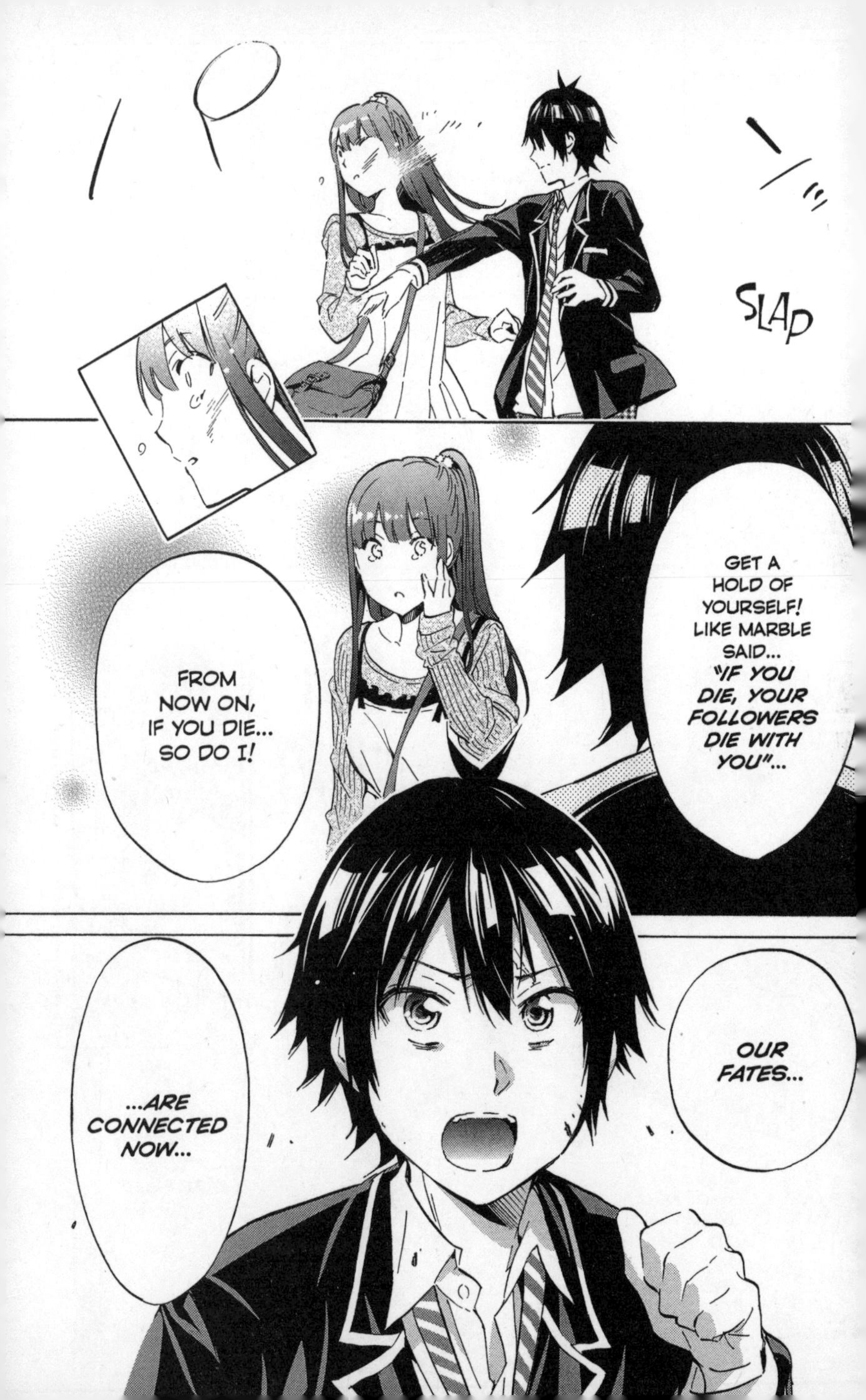
SLAP
GET A HOLD OF YOURSELF! LIKE MARBLE SAID... "IF YOU DIE, YOUR FOLLOWERS DIE WITH YOU"...
FROM NOW ON, IF YOU DIE... SO DO I!
OUR FATES...
...ARE CONNECTED NOW...

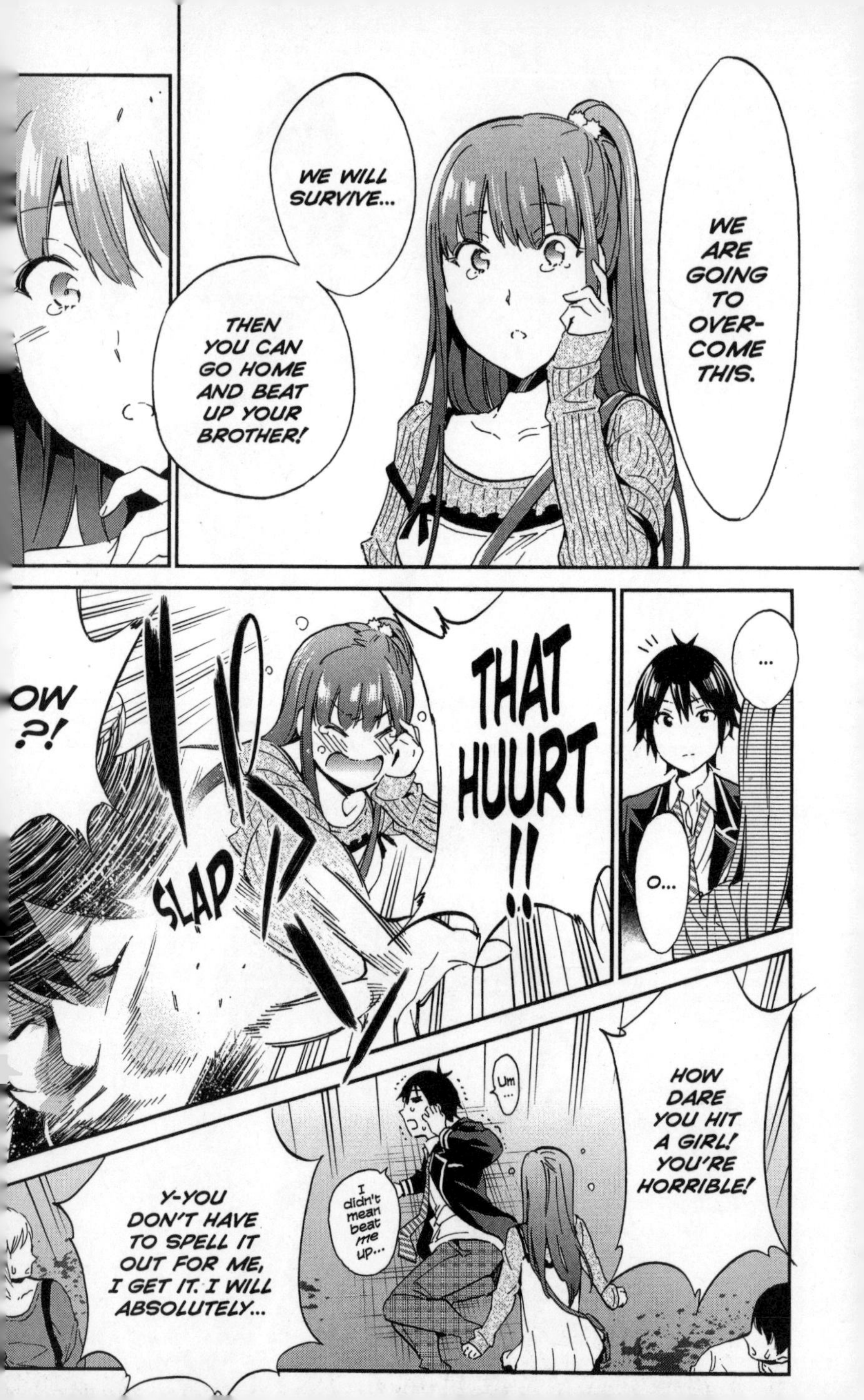
WE ARE GOING TO OVER-COME THIS.
WE WILL SURVIVE...
THEN YOU CAN GO HOME AND BEAT UP YOUR BROTHER!
...
O...
THAT HUURT !!
SLAP
OW ?!
HOW DARE YOU HIT A GIRL! YOU'RE HORRIBLE!
Um ...
I didn't mean beat me up...
Y-YOU DON'T HAVE TO SPELL IT OUT FOR ME, I GET IT. I WILL ABSOLUTELY...

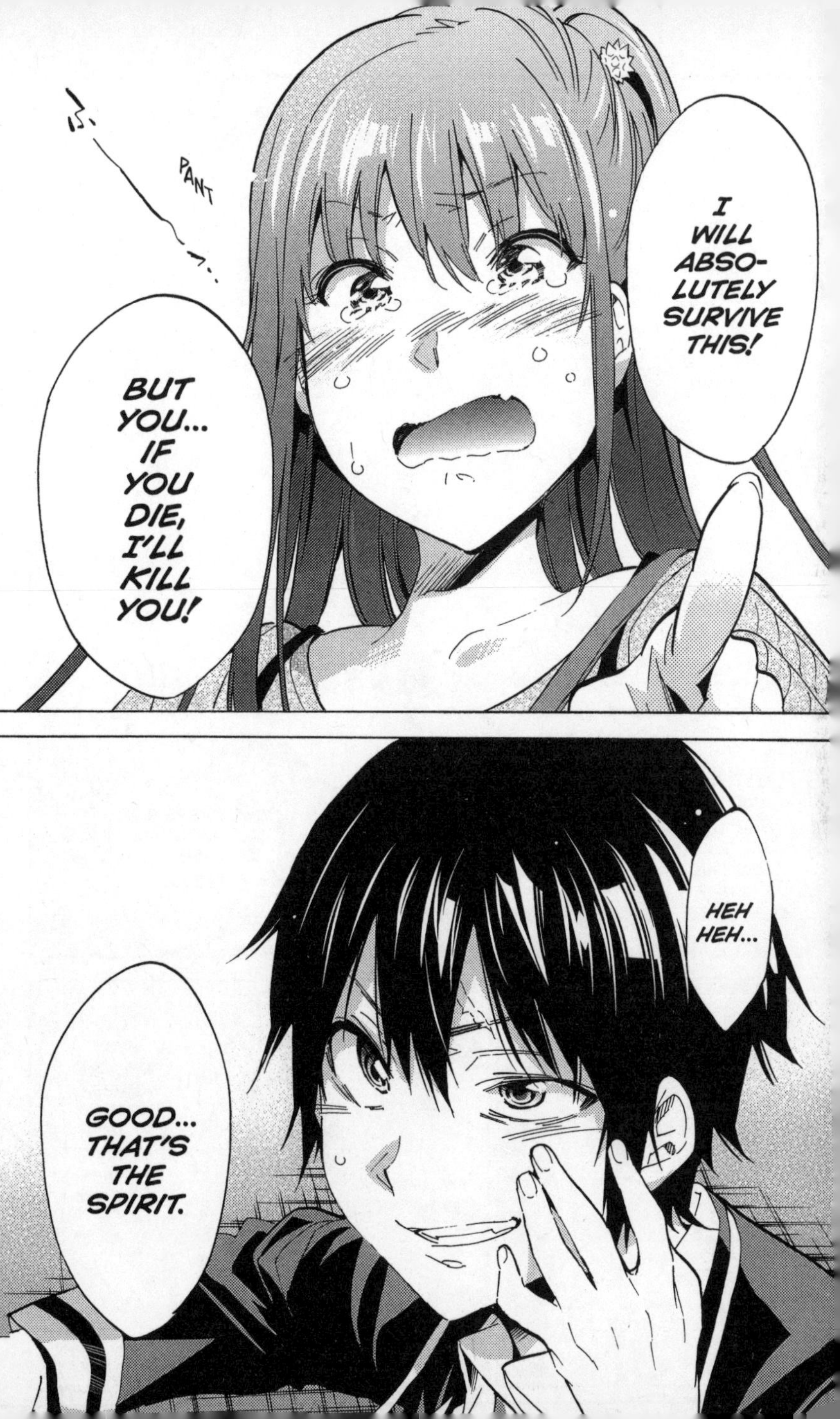
I WILL ABSOLUTELY SURVIVE THIS!
PANT
BUT YOU... IF YOU DIE, I'LL KILL YOU!
HEH HEH...
GOOD... THAT'S THE SPIRIT.

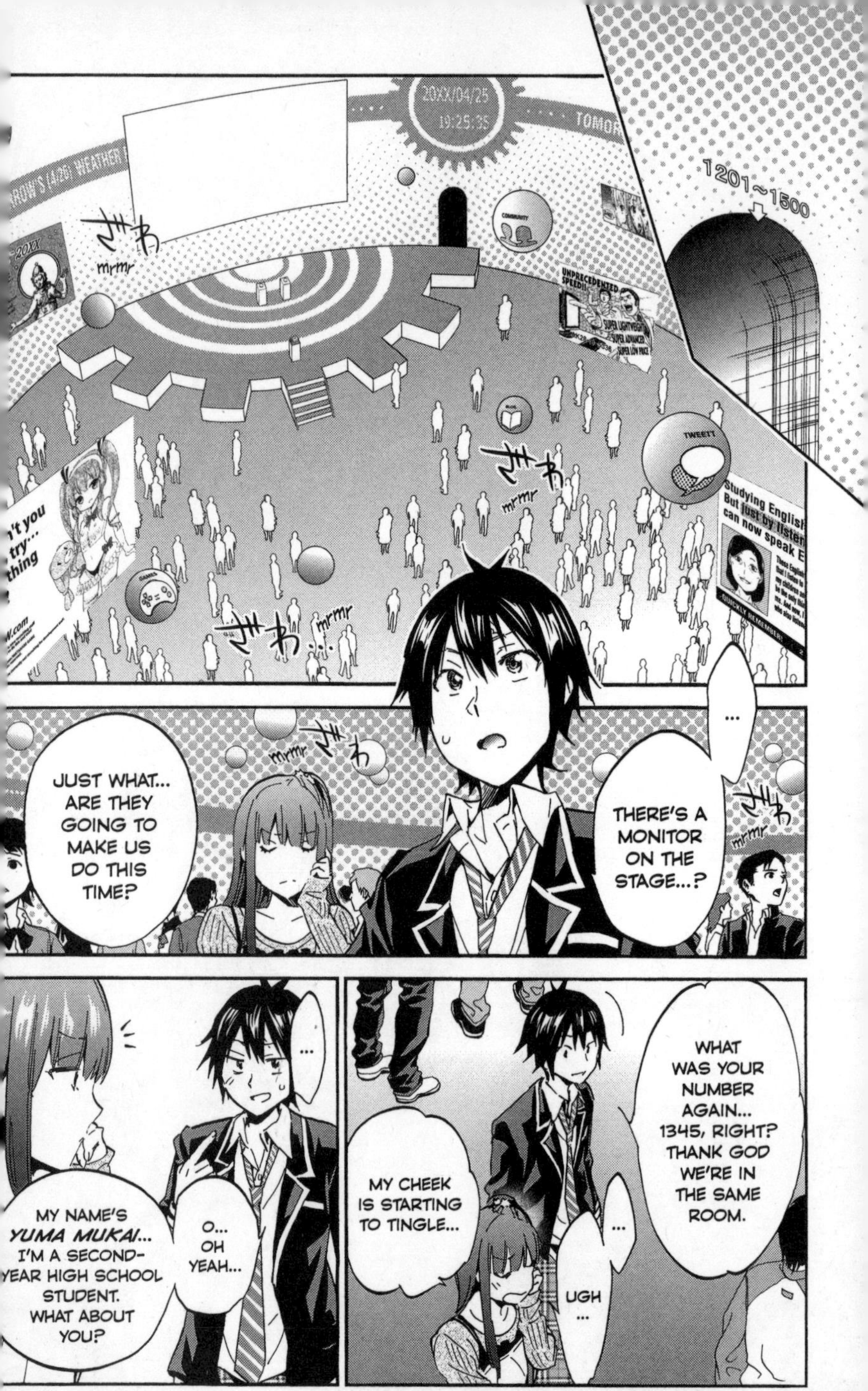
1201~1500
20XX/04/25
19:25:35
mrmr
UNPRECEDENTED SPEED!!
SUPER LIGHTWEIGHT
SUPER ADVANCED
SUPER LOW PRICE
mrmr
mrmr
...
THERE'S A MONITOR ON THE STAGE...?
mrmr
JUST WHAT... ARE THEY GOING TO MAKE US DO THIS TIME?
WHAT WAS YOUR NUMBER AGAIN... 1345, RIGHT? THANK GOD WE'RE IN THE SAME ROOM.
...
UGH...
MY CHEEK IS STARTING TO TINGLE...
...
O... OH YEAH...
MY NAME'S *YUMA MUKAI*... I'M A SECOND-YEAR HIGH SCHOOL STUDENT. WHAT ABOUT YOU?

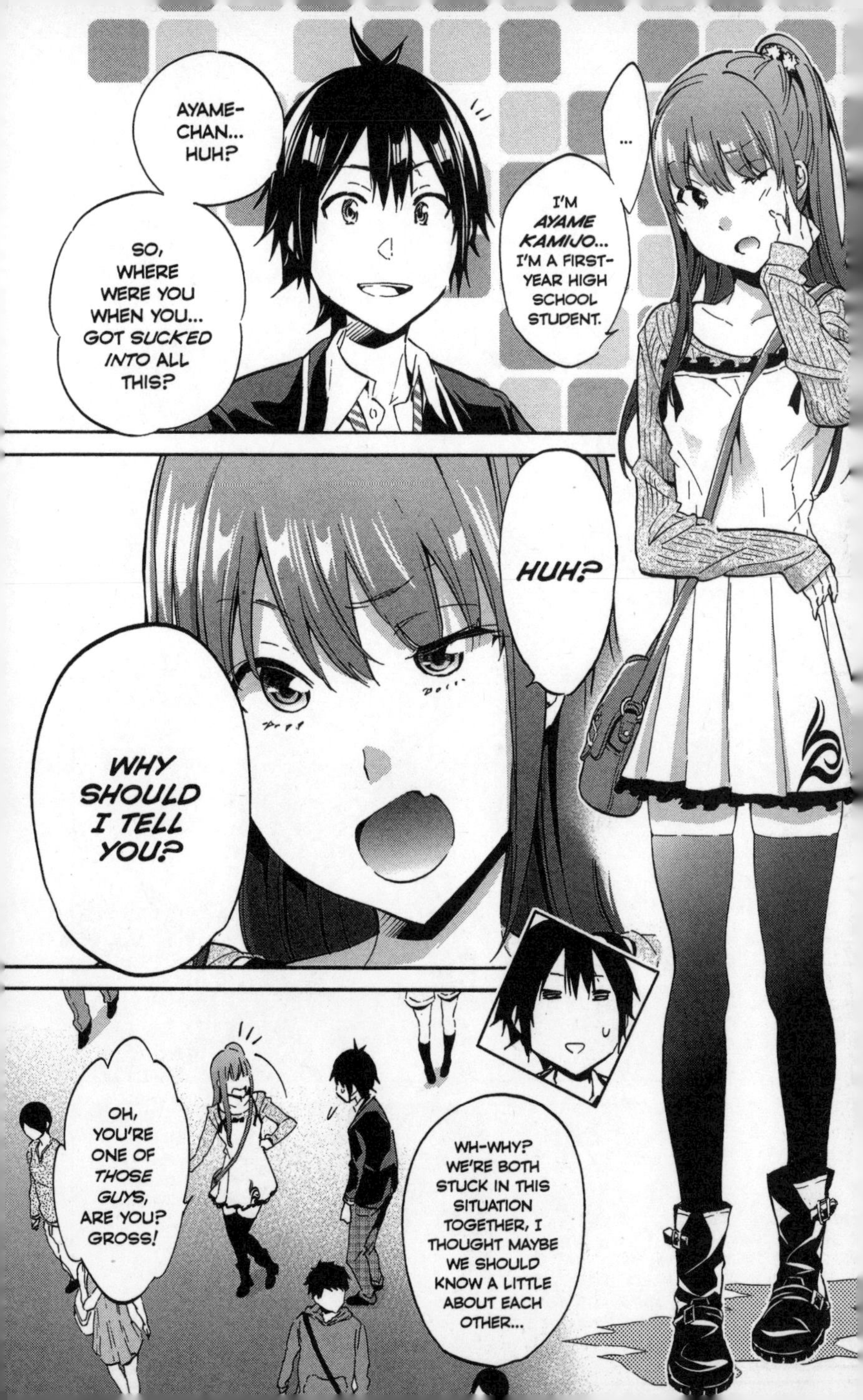
...
I'M AYAME KAMIJO... I'M A FIRST-YEAR HIGH SCHOOL STUDENT.
AYAME-CHAN... HUH?
SO, WHERE WERE YOU WHEN YOU... GOT SUCKED INTO ALL THIS?
HUH?
WHY SHOULD I TELL YOU?
WH-WHY? WE'RE BOTH STUCK IN THIS SITUATION TOGETHER, I THOUGHT MAYBE WE SHOULD KNOW A LITTLE ABOUT EACH OTHER...
OH, YOU'RE ONE OF THOSE GUYS, ARE YOU? GROSS!

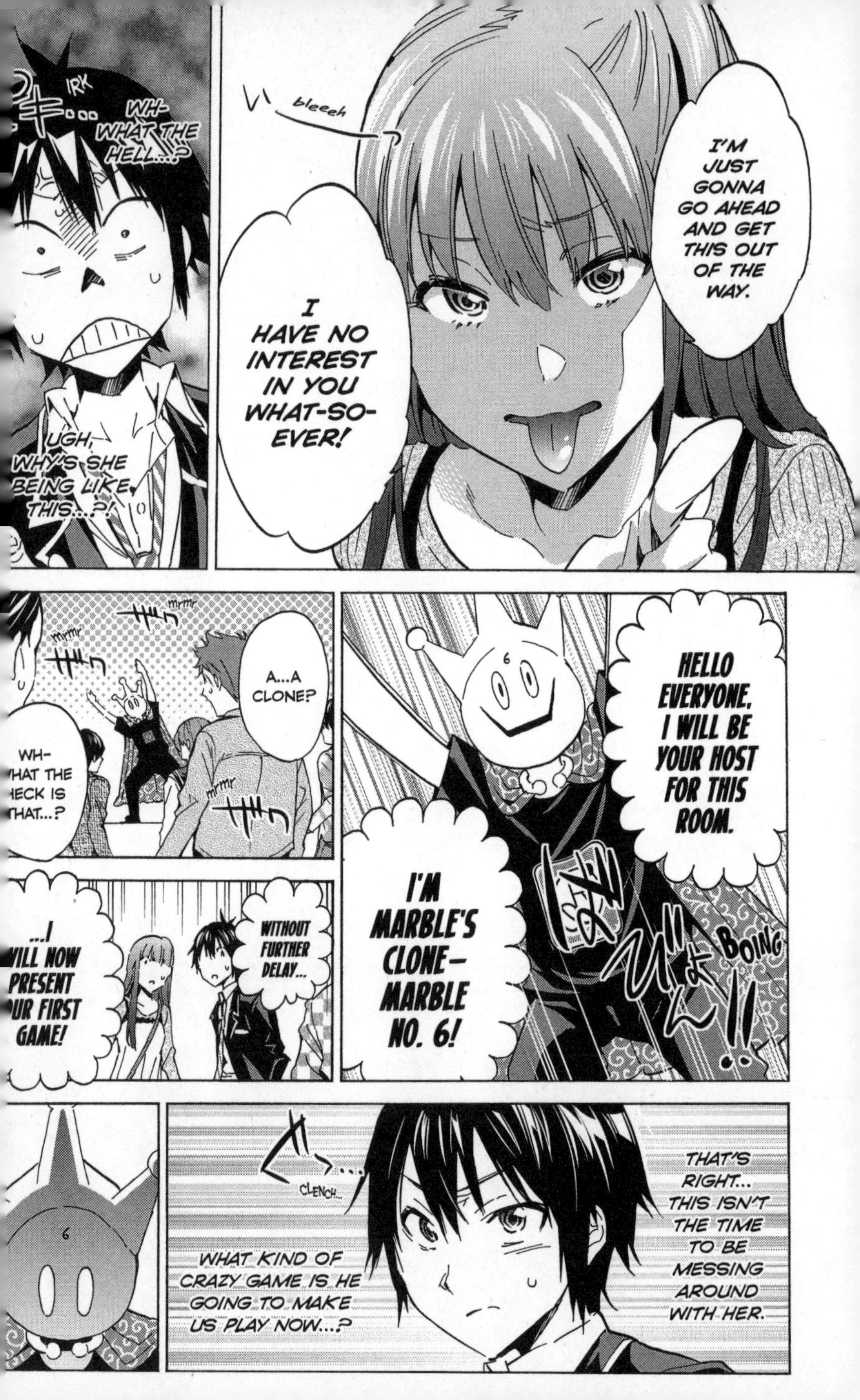
I'M JUST GONNA GO AHEAD AND GET THIS OUT OF THE WAY.
bleeeh
I HAVE NO INTEREST IN YOU WHAT-SO-EVER!
IRK
WH- WHAT THE HELL...!?
UGH, WHY'S SHE BEING LIKE THIS...?!
HELLO EVERYONE, I WILL BE YOUR HOST FOR THIS ROOM.
I'M MARBLE'S CLONE— MARBLE NO. 6!
BOING!!
A...A CLONE?
mrmr
mrmr
mrmr
WH- WHAT THE HECK IS THAT...?
WITHOUT FURTHER DELAY...
...I WILL NOW PRESENT OUR FIRST GAME!
THAT'S RIGHT... THIS ISN'T THE TIME TO BE MESSING AROUND WITH HER.
CLENCH...
WHAT KIND OF CRAZY GAME IS HE GOING TO MAKE US PLAY NOW...?

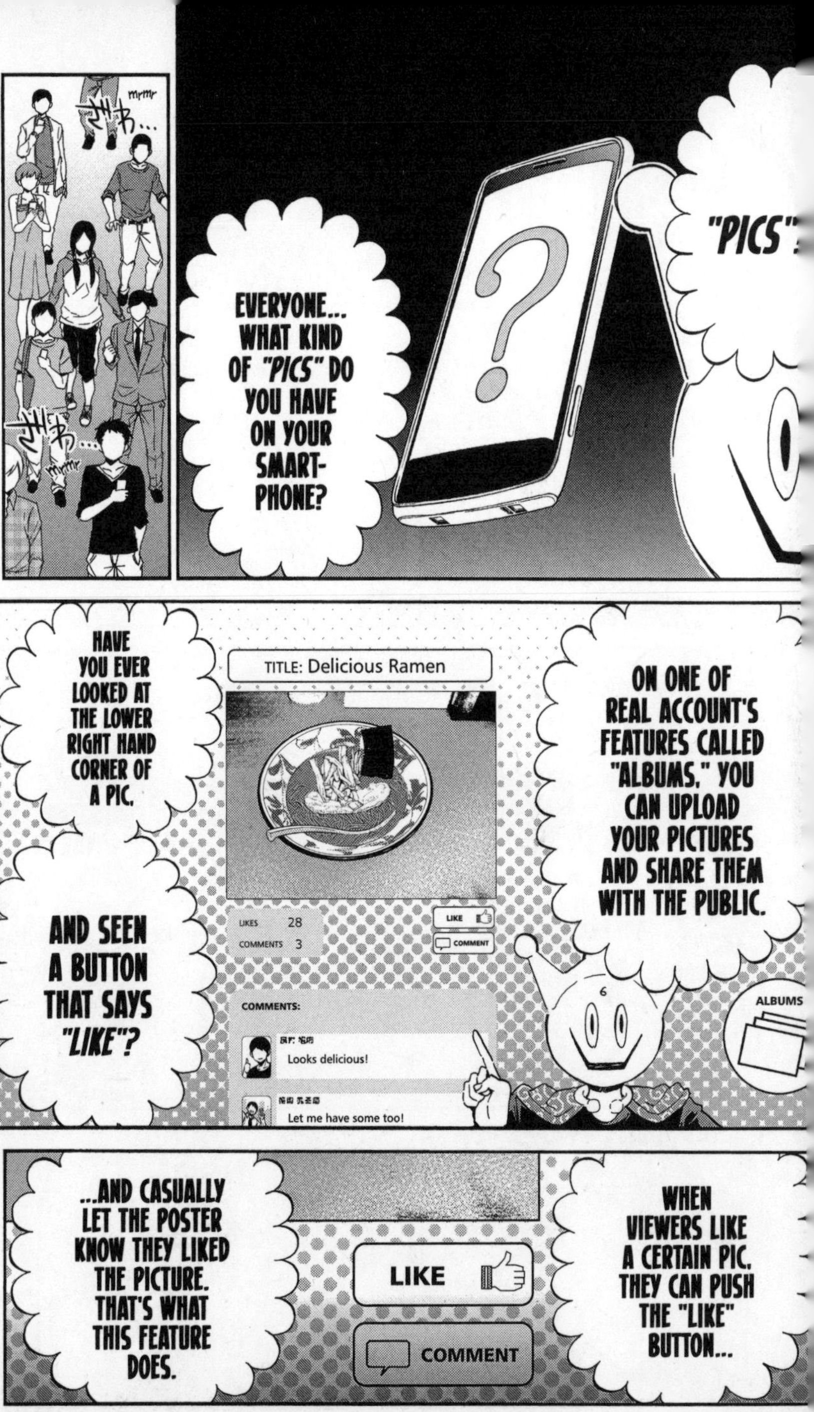
"PICS"
EVERYONE... WHAT KIND OF "PICS" DO YOU HAVE ON YOUR SMART-PHONE?
mrmr
ざわ...
ざわ...
mrmr
ON ONE OF REAL ACCOUNT'S FEATURES CALLED "ALBUMS," YOU CAN UPLOAD YOUR PICTURES AND SHARE THEM WITH THE PUBLIC.
ALBUMS
TITLE: Delicious Ramen
LIKES 28
COMMENTS 3
LIKE
COMMENT
COMMENTS:
Looks delicious!
Let me have some too!
HAVE YOU EVER LOOKED AT THE LOWER RIGHT HAND CORNER OF A PIC,
AND SEEN A BUTTON THAT SAYS "LIKE"?
WHEN VIEWERS LIKE A CERTAIN PIC, THEY CAN PUSH THE "LIKE" BUTTON...
LIKE
COMMENT
...AND CASUALLY LET THE POSTER KNOW THEY LIKED THE PICTURE. THAT'S WHAT THIS FEATURE DOES.

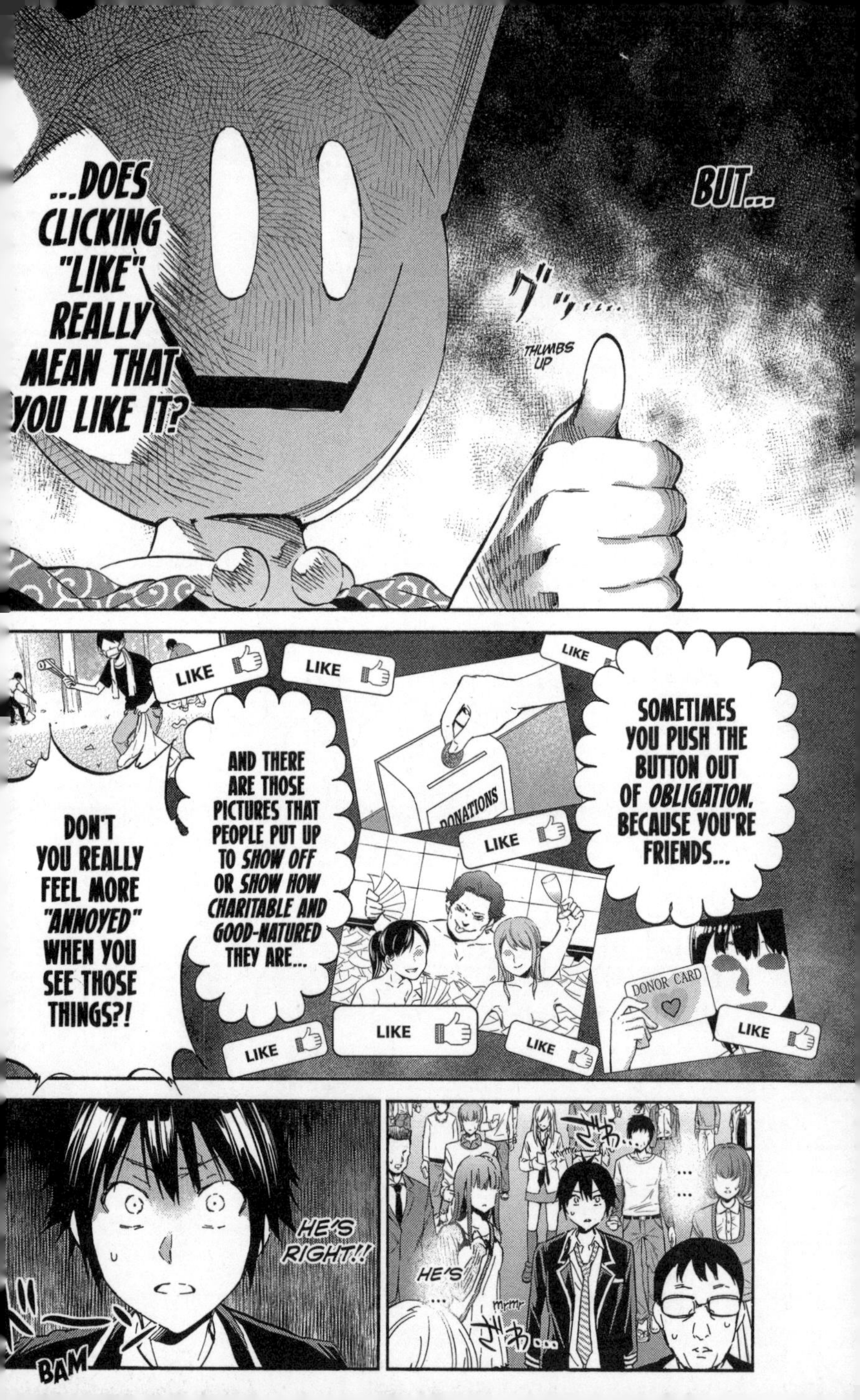

BUT...
グッ
THUMBS UP
...DOES CLICKING "LIKE" REALLY MEAN THAT YOU LIKE IT?
LIKE
SOMETIMES YOU PUSH THE BUTTON OUT OF *OBLIGATION*, BECAUSE YOU'RE FRIENDS...
LIKE
DONATIONS
LIKE
DONOR CARD
LIKE
LIKE
LIKE
AND THERE ARE THOSE PICTURES THAT PEOPLE PUT UP TO *SHOW OFF* OR *SHOW HOW CHARITABLE AND GOOD-NATURED* THEY ARE...
LIKE
LIKE
DON'T YOU REALLY FEEL MORE "ANNOYED" WHEN YOU SEE THOSE THINGS?!
ざわ...
mrmr
...
...
HE'S...
mrmr
ざわ...
HE'S RIGHT!!
BAM

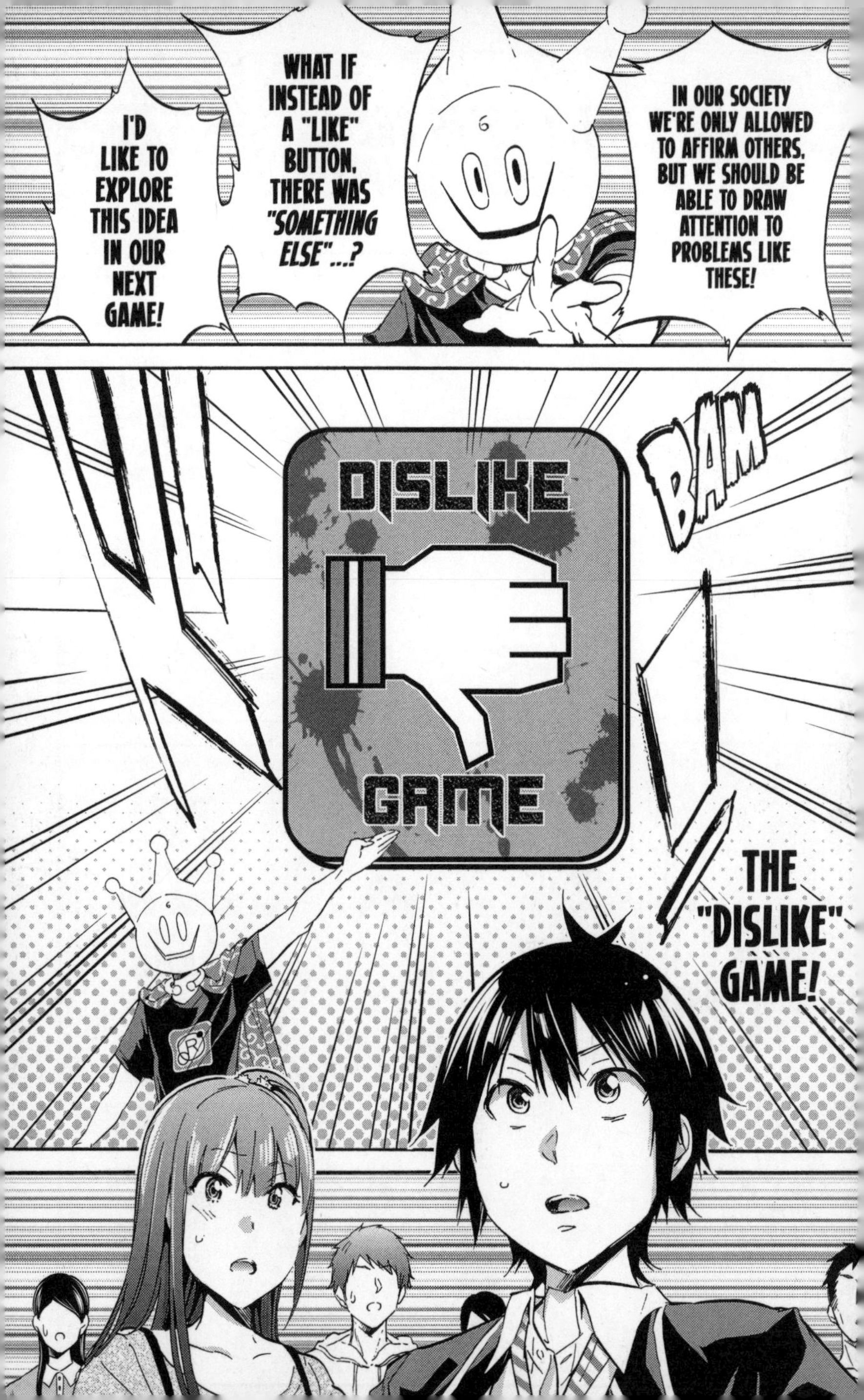
IN OUR SOCIETY WE'RE ONLY ALLOWED TO AFFIRM OTHERS, BUT WE SHOULD BE ABLE TO DRAW ATTENTION TO PROBLEMS LIKE THESE!
WHAT IF INSTEAD OF A "LIKE" BUTTON, THERE WAS *"SOMETHING ELSE"...?*
I'D LIKE TO EXPLORE THIS IDEA IN OUR NEXT GAME!
BAM
DISLIKE GAME
THE "DISLIKE" GAME!

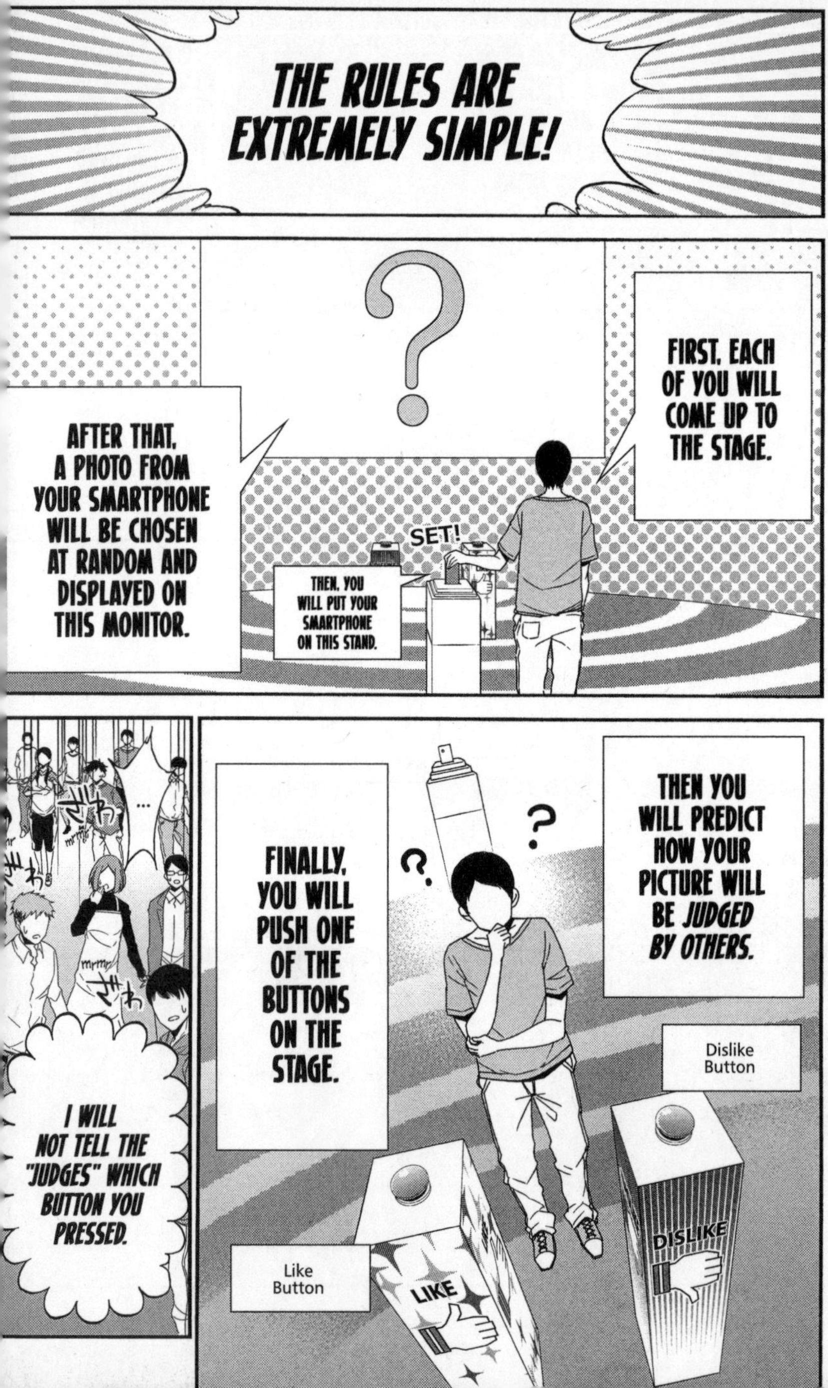
THE RULES ARE EXTREMELY SIMPLE!
FIRST, EACH OF YOU WILL COME UP TO THE STAGE.
SET!
THEN, YOU WILL PUT YOUR SMARTPHONE ON THIS STAND.
AFTER THAT, A PHOTO FROM YOUR SMARTPHONE WILL BE CHOSEN AT RANDOM AND DISPLAYED ON THIS MONITOR.
THEN YOU WILL PREDICT HOW YOUR PICTURE WILL BE *JUDGED BY OTHERS.*
Dislike Button
DISLIKE
FINALLY, YOU WILL PUSH ONE OF THE BUTTONS ON THE STAGE.
Like Button
LIKE
...
I WILL NOT TELL THE "JUDGES" WHICH BUTTON YOU PRESSED.

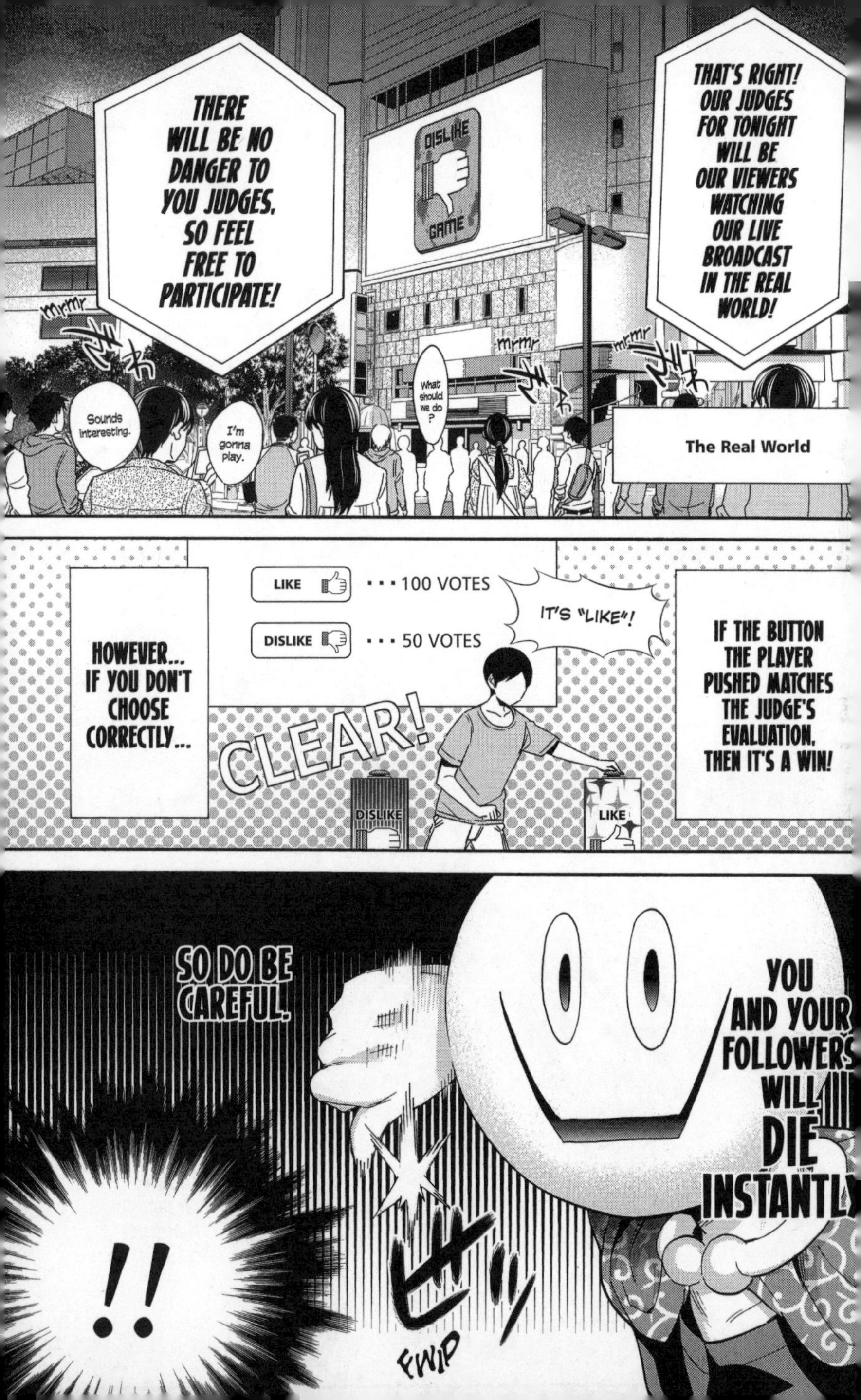
THAT'S RIGHT! OUR JUDGES FOR TONIGHT WILL BE OUR VIEWERS WATCHING OUR LIVE BROADCAST IN THE REAL WORLD!
The Real World
mrmr
mrmr
DISLIKE GAME
THERE WILL BE NO DANGER TO YOU JUDGES, SO FEEL FREE TO PARTICIPATE!
What should we do?
I'm gonna play.
Sounds interesting.
mrmr
IF THE BUTTON THE PLAYER PUSHED MATCHES THE JUDGE'S EVALUATION, THEN IT'S A WIN!
IT'S "LIKE"!
LIKE · · · 100 VOTES
DISLIKE · · · 50 VOTES
CLEAR!
LIKE
DISLIKE
HOWEVER... IF YOU DON'T CHOOSE CORRECTLY...
YOU AND YOUR FOLLOWERS WILL DIE INSTANTLY
SO DO BE CAREFUL.
FWIP
!!

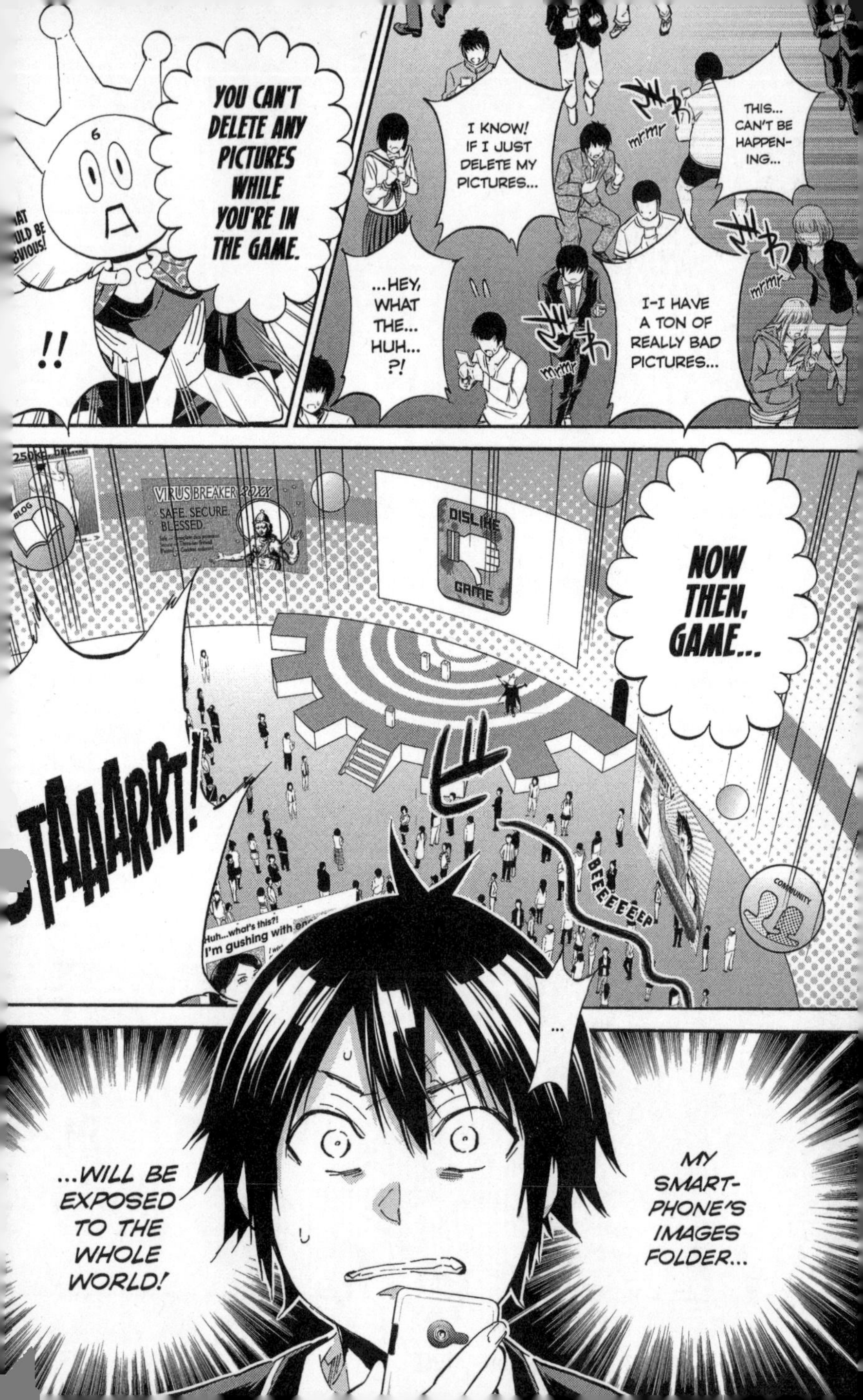
THIS... CAN'T BE HAPPEN-ING...
mrmr
I KNOW! IF I JUST DELETE MY PICTURES...
I-I HAVE A TON OF REALLY BAD PICTURES...
mrmr
mrmr
...HEY, WHAT THE... HUH...?!
YOU CAN'T DELETE ANY PICTURES WHILE YOU'RE IN THE GAME.
!!
NOW THEN, GAME...
VIRUS BREAKER 20XX
SAFE. SECURE. BLESSED.
DISLIKE GAME
BLOG
COMMUNITY
STAAARRT!
BEEEEEEEEP
...
MY SMART-PHONE'S IMAGES FOLDER...
...WILL BE EXPOSED TO THE WHOLE WORLD!

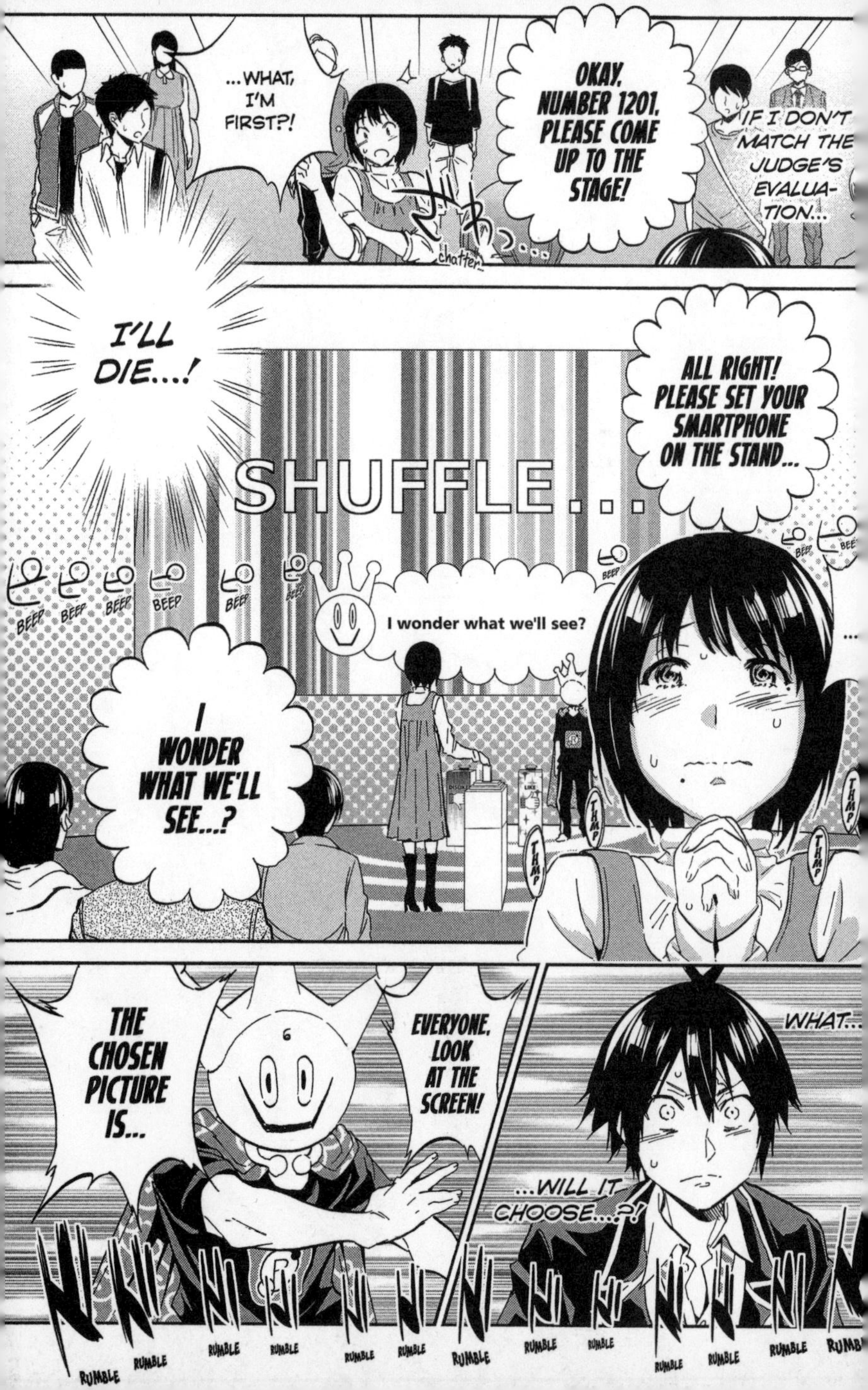
IF I DON'T MATCH THE JUDGE'S EVALUATION...
OKAY, NUMBER 1201, PLEASE COME UP TO THE STAGE!
...WHAT, I'M FIRST?!
chatter
I'LL DIE...!
ALL RIGHT! PLEASE SET YOUR SMARTPHONE ON THE STAND...
SHUFFLE...
BEEP BEEP
BEEP BEEP BEEP BEEP BEEP BEEP BEEP
I wonder what we'll see?
...
I WONDER WHAT WE'LL SEE...?
THMP THMP THMP THMP
WHAT...
...WILL IT CHOOSE...?!
EVERYONE, LOOK AT THE SCREEN!
THE CHOSEN PICTURE IS...
RUMBLE RUMBLE RUMBLE RUMBLE RUMBLE RUMBLE RUMBLE RUMBLE RUMBLE RUMBLE RUMBLE RUMBLE RUMBLE RUMBLE RUMBLE

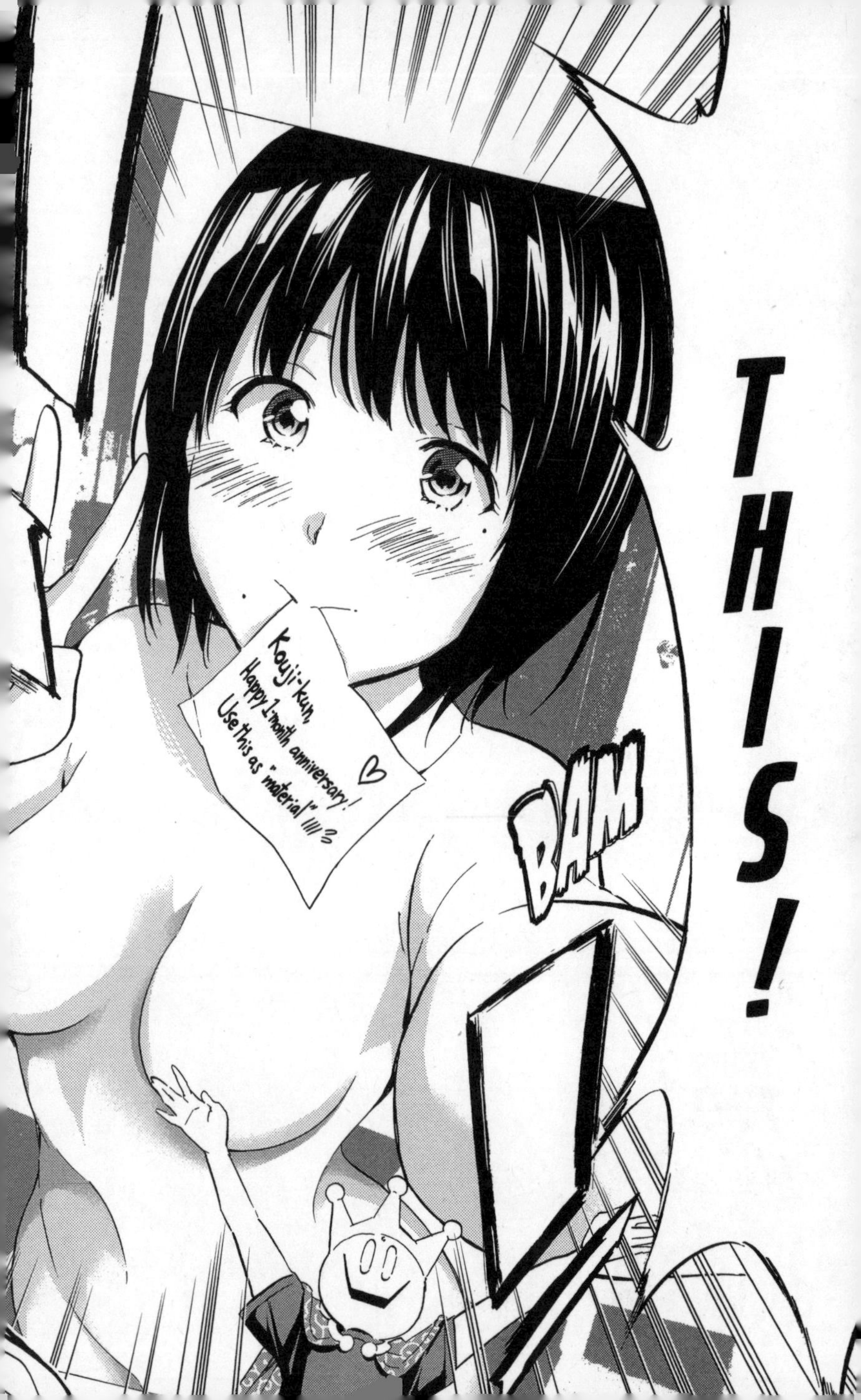
THIS!
BAM
Kouji-kun,
Happy 1-month anniversary! ♡
Use this as "material" ////

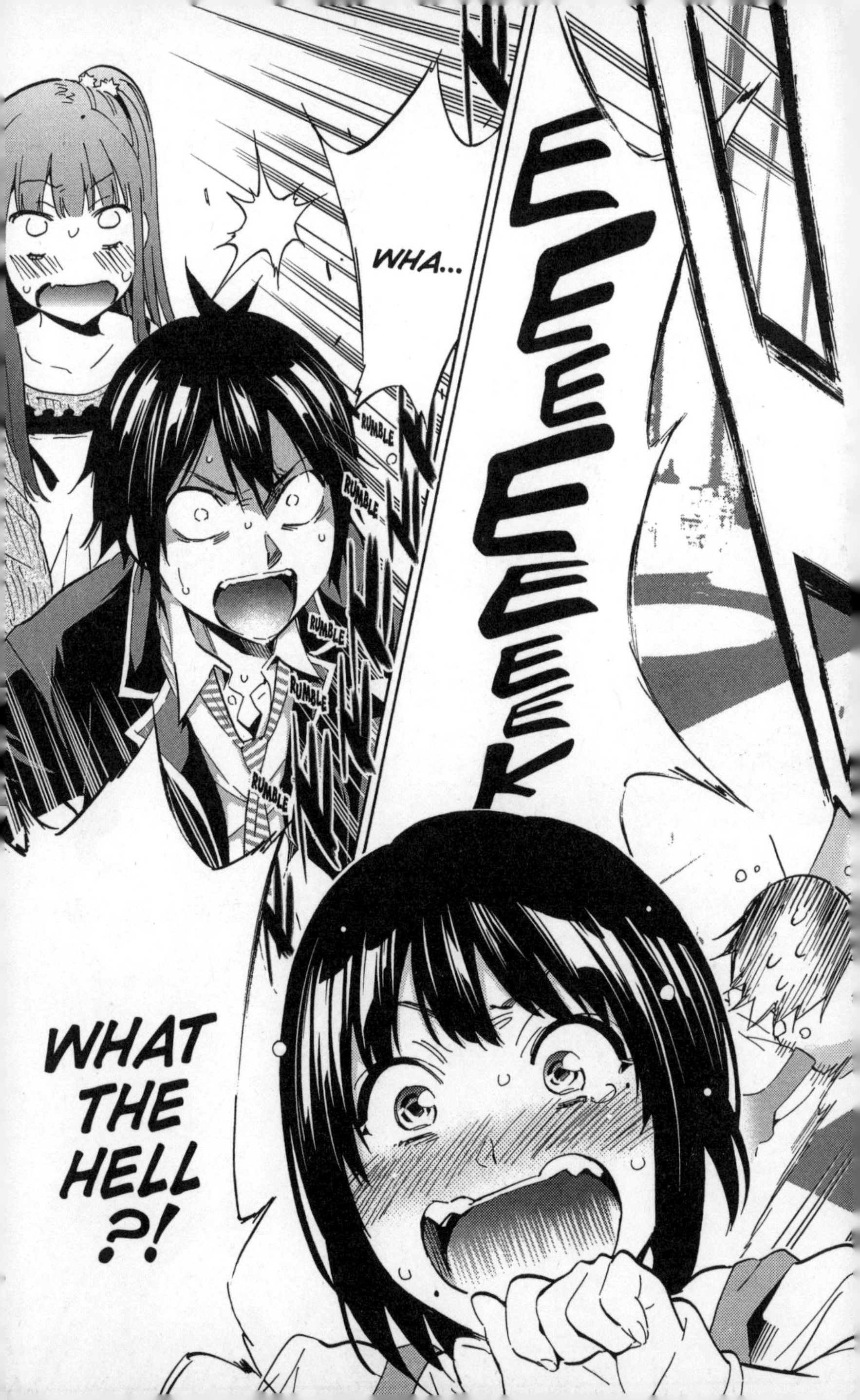
EEEEEEEK
WHA...
RUMBLE
RUMBLE
RUMBLE
RUMBLE
RUMBLE
WHAT THE HELL ?!

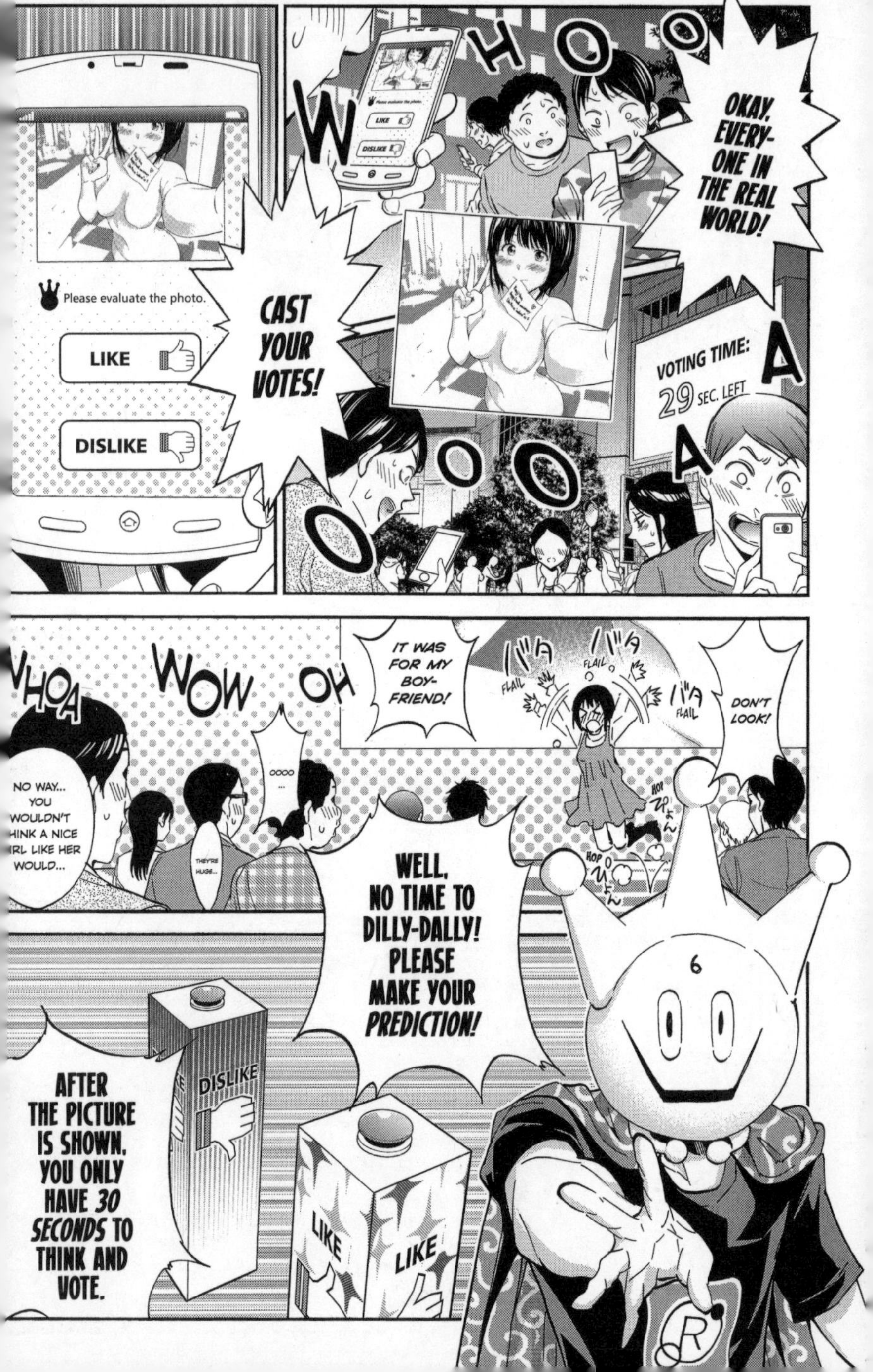
WHOOOO
OKAY, EVERYONE IN THE REAL WORLD!
VOTING TIME: 29 SEC. LEFT
AAA
OOOO
Please evaluate the photo.
LIKE
DISLIKE
CAST YOUR VOTES!
DON'T LOOK!
バタ FLAIL
バタ FLAIL
バタ FLAIL
IT WAS FOR MY BOY-FRIEND!
HOP ぴょん
HOP ぴょん
WHOA WOW OH
OOOO...
THEY'RE HUGE...
NO WAY... YOU WOULDN'T HINK A NICE IRL LIKE HER WOULD...
WELL, NO TIME TO DILLY-DALLY! PLEASE MAKE YOUR PREDICTION!
6
AFTER THE PICTURE IS SHOWN, YOU ONLY HAVE 30 SECONDS TO THINK AND VOTE.
DISLIKE
LIKE
LIKE

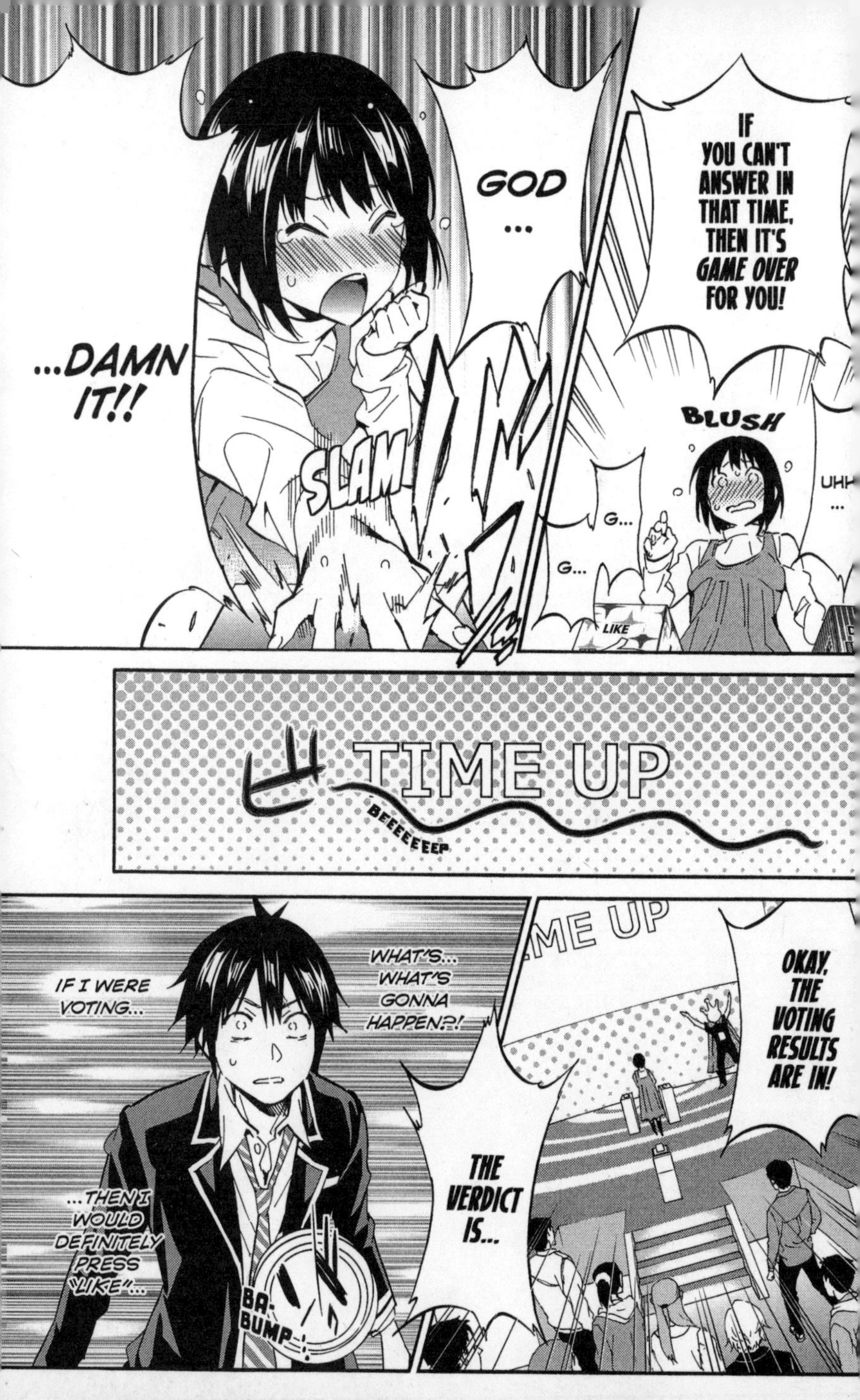
IF YOU CAN'T ANSWER IN THAT TIME, THEN IT'S GAME OVER FOR YOU!
BLUSH
UHH ...
G...
G...
LIKE
GOD ...
SLAM
...DAMN IT!!
ピ
TIME UP
BEEEEEEEP
ME UP
OKAY, THE VOTING RESULTS ARE IN!
THE VERDICT IS...
WHAT'S... WHAT'S GONNA HAPPEN?!
IF I WERE VOTING...
...THEN I WOULD DEFINITELY PRESS "LIKE"...
BA-BUMP

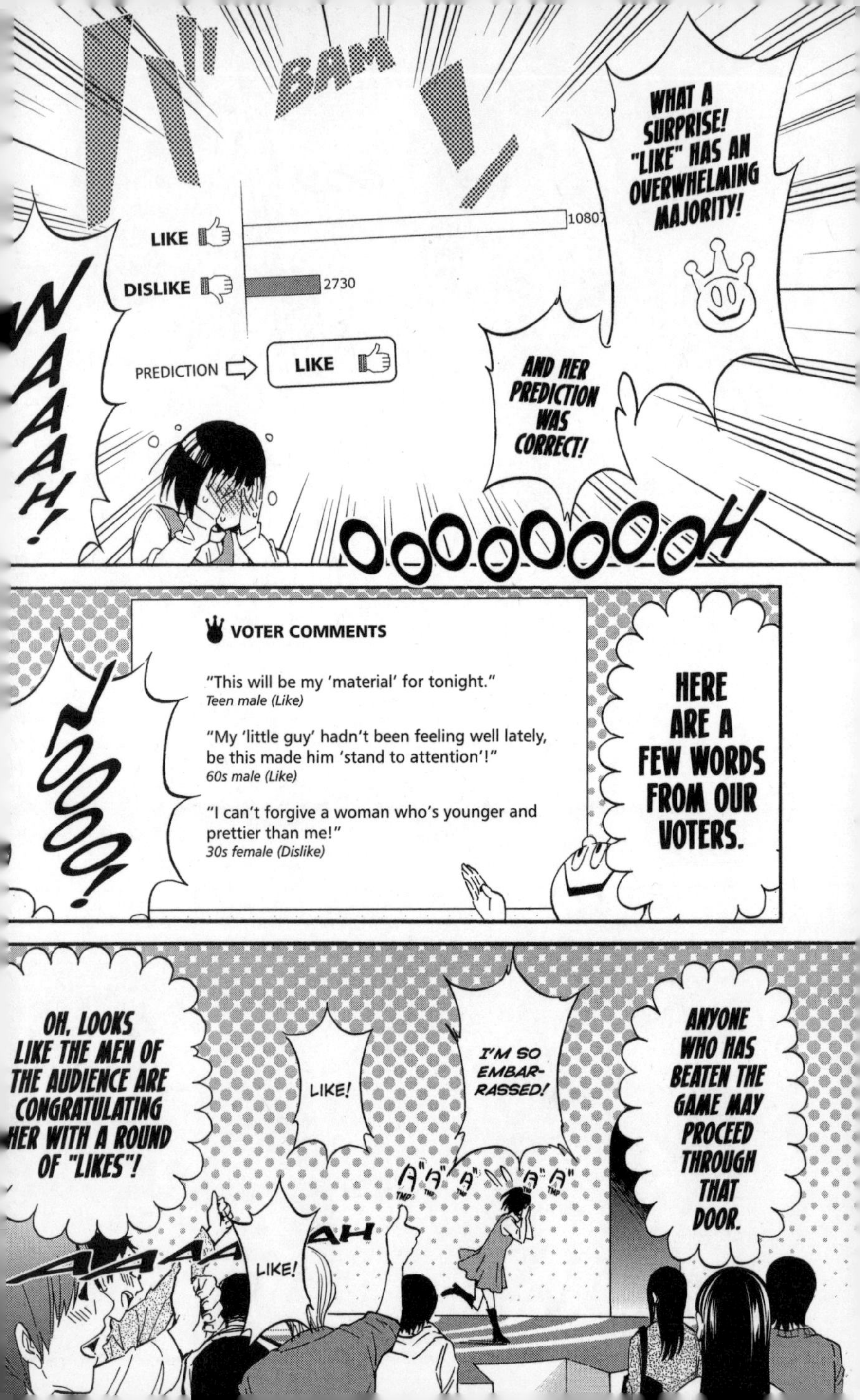
BAM
WHAT A SURPRISE! "LIKE" HAS AN OVERWHELMING MAJORITY!
LIKE 10807
DISLIKE 2730
PREDICTION LIKE
AND HER PREDICTION WAS CORRECT!
WAAAAH!
OOOOOOOOOH
HERE ARE A FEW WORDS FROM OUR VOTERS.
VOTER COMMENTS
"This will be my 'material' for tonight."
Teen male (Like)
"My 'little guy' hadn't been feeling well lately, be this made him 'stand to attention'!"
60s male (Like)
"I can't forgive a woman who's younger and prettier than me!"
30s female (Dislike)
NOOOO!
ANYONE WHO HAS BEATEN THE GAME MAY PROCEED THROUGH THAT DOOR.
I'M SO EMBARRASSED!
LIKE!
OH, LOOKS LIKE THE MEN OF THE AUDIENCE ARE CONGRATULATING HER WITH A ROUND OF "LIKES"!
AAAAAH
LIKE!

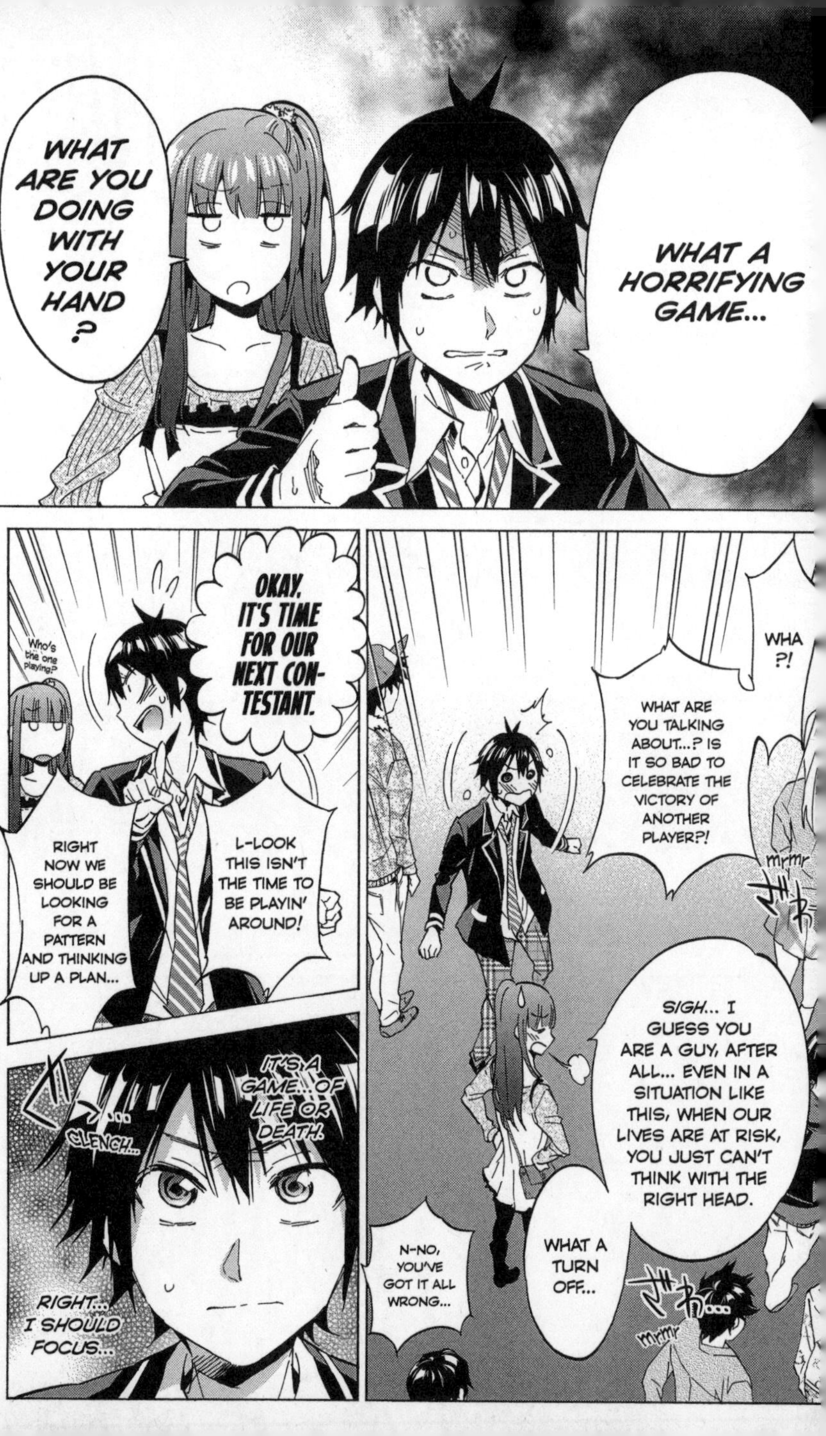
WHAT A HORRIFYING GAME...
WHAT ARE YOU DOING WITH YOUR HAND ?
WHA ?!
WHAT ARE YOU TALKING ABOUT...? IS IT SO BAD TO CELEBRATE THE VICTORY OF ANOTHER PLAYER?!
mrmr
SIGH... I GUESS YOU ARE A GUY, AFTER ALL... EVEN IN A SITUATION LIKE THIS, WHEN OUR LIVES ARE AT RISK, YOU JUST CAN'T THINK WITH THE RIGHT HEAD.
WHAT A TURN OFF...
N-NO, YOU'VE GOT IT ALL WRONG...
mrmr
OKAY. IT'S TIME FOR OUR NEXT CON-TESTANT.
Who's the one playing?
L-LOOK THIS ISN'T THE TIME TO BE PLAYIN' AROUND!
RIGHT NOW WE SHOULD BE LOOKING FOR A PATTERN AND THINKING UP A PLAN...
IT'S A GAME... OF LIFE OR DEATH.
...CLENCH...
RIGHT... I SHOULD FOCUS...

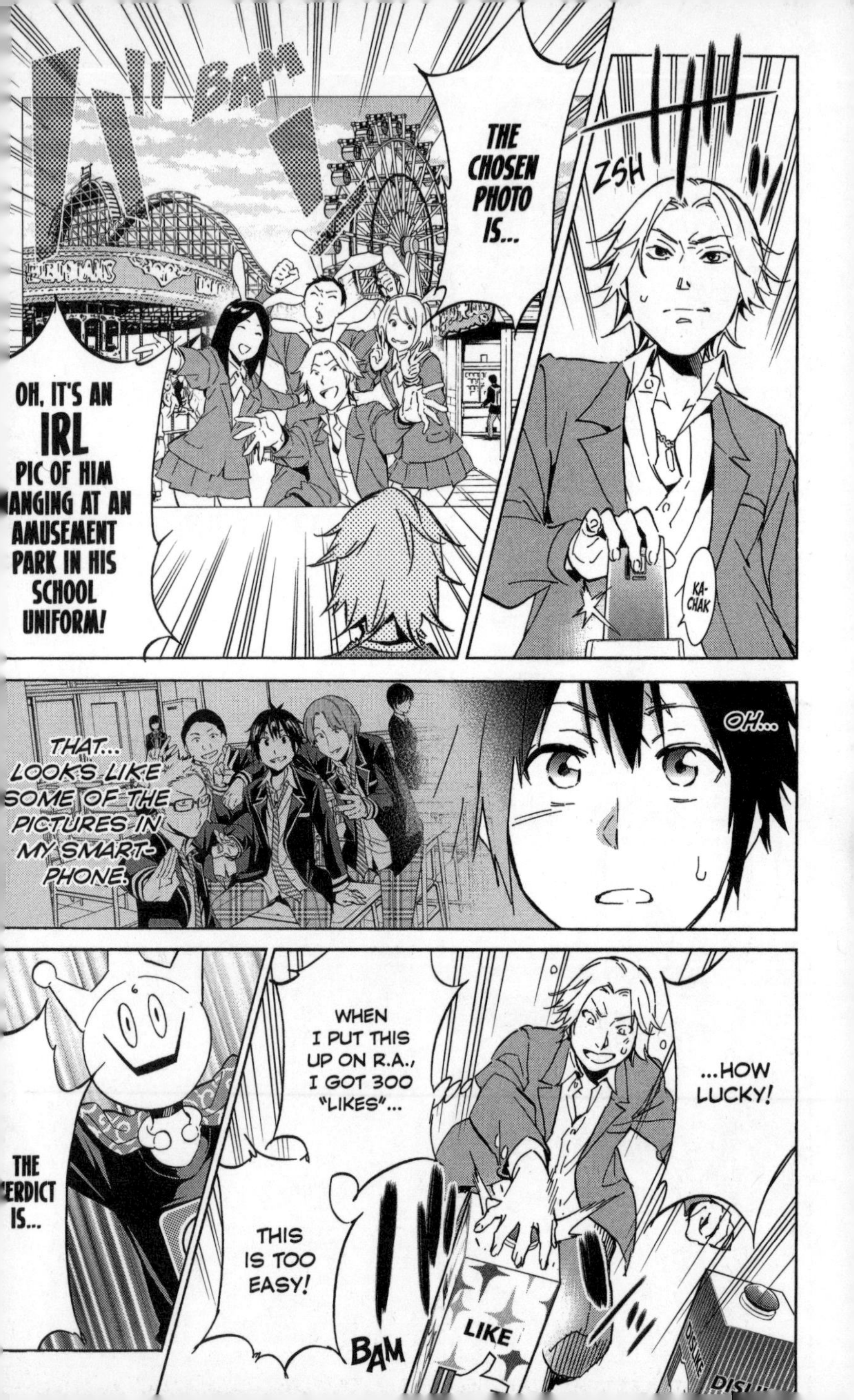

THE CHOSEN PHOTO IS...
ZSH
KA-CHAK
BAM
OH, IT'S AN IRL PIC OF HIM ANGING AT AN AMUSEMENT PARK IN HIS SCHOOL UNIFORM!
OH...
THAT... LOOKS LIKE SOME OF THE PICTURES IN MY SMART-PHONE.
...HOW LUCKY!
WHEN I PUT THIS UP ON R.A., I GOT 300 "LIKES"...
THIS IS TOO EASY!
BAM
LIKE
DISLIKE
THE ERDICT IS...

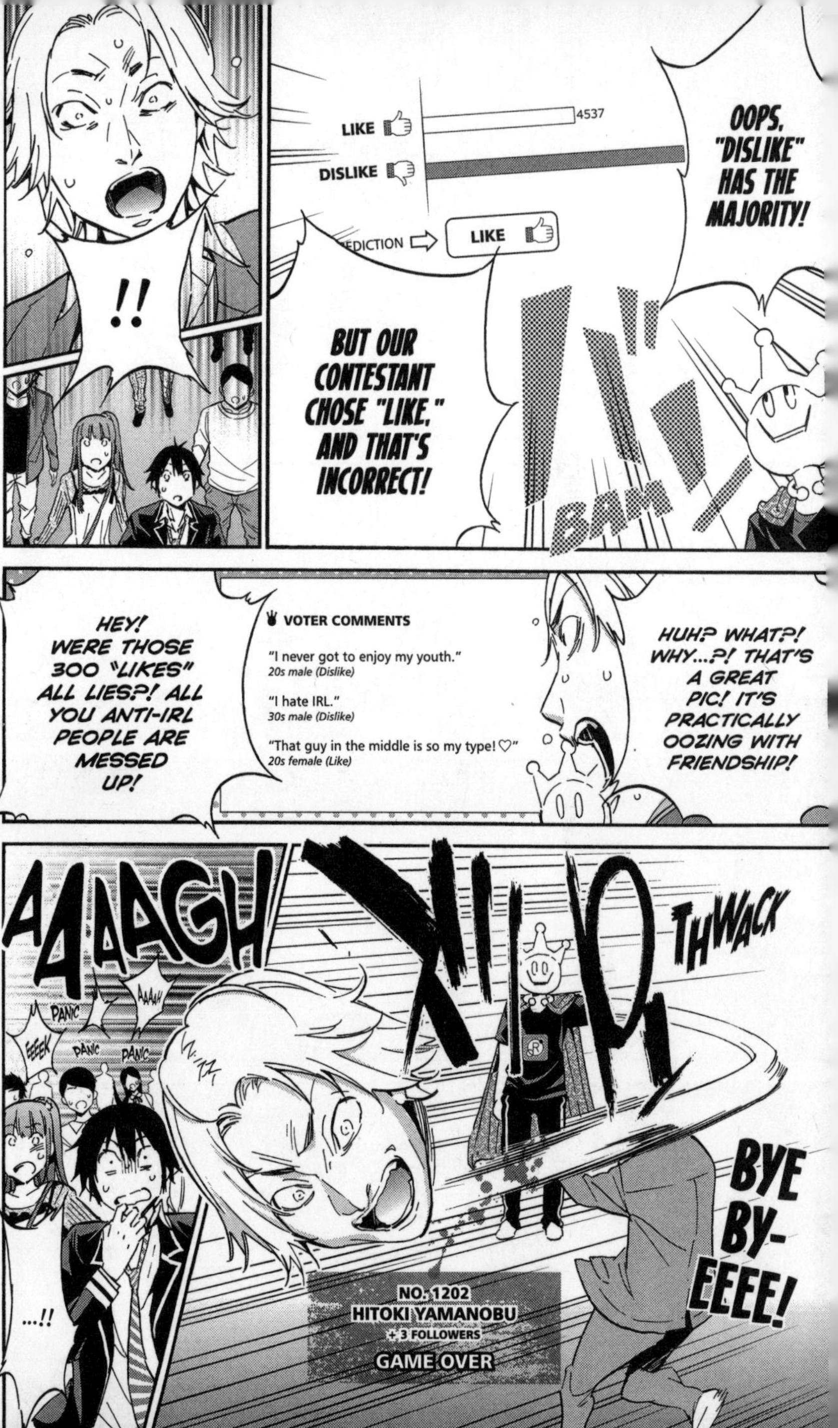
OOPS. "DISLIKE" HAS THE MAJORITY!
LIKE 4537
DISLIKE
EDICTION ⇨ LIKE
BUT OUR CONTESTANT CHOSE "LIKE," AND THAT'S INCORRECT!
BAM
!!
HUH? WHAT?! WHY...?! THAT'S A GREAT PIC! IT'S PRACTICALLY OOZING WITH FRIENDSHIP!
VOTER COMMENTS
"I never got to enjoy my youth." 20s male (Dislike)
"I hate IRL." 30s male (Dislike)
"That guy in the middle is so my type! ♡" 20s female (Like)
HEY! WERE THOSE 300 "LIKES" ALL LIES?! ALL YOU ANTI-IRL PEOPLE ARE MESSED UP!
BYE BY-EEEE!
THWACK
AAAAGH
AAAAH
PANIC
EEEEK
PANIC
PANIC
NO. 1202 HITOKI YAMANOBU + 3 FOLLOWERS
GAME OVER
...!!

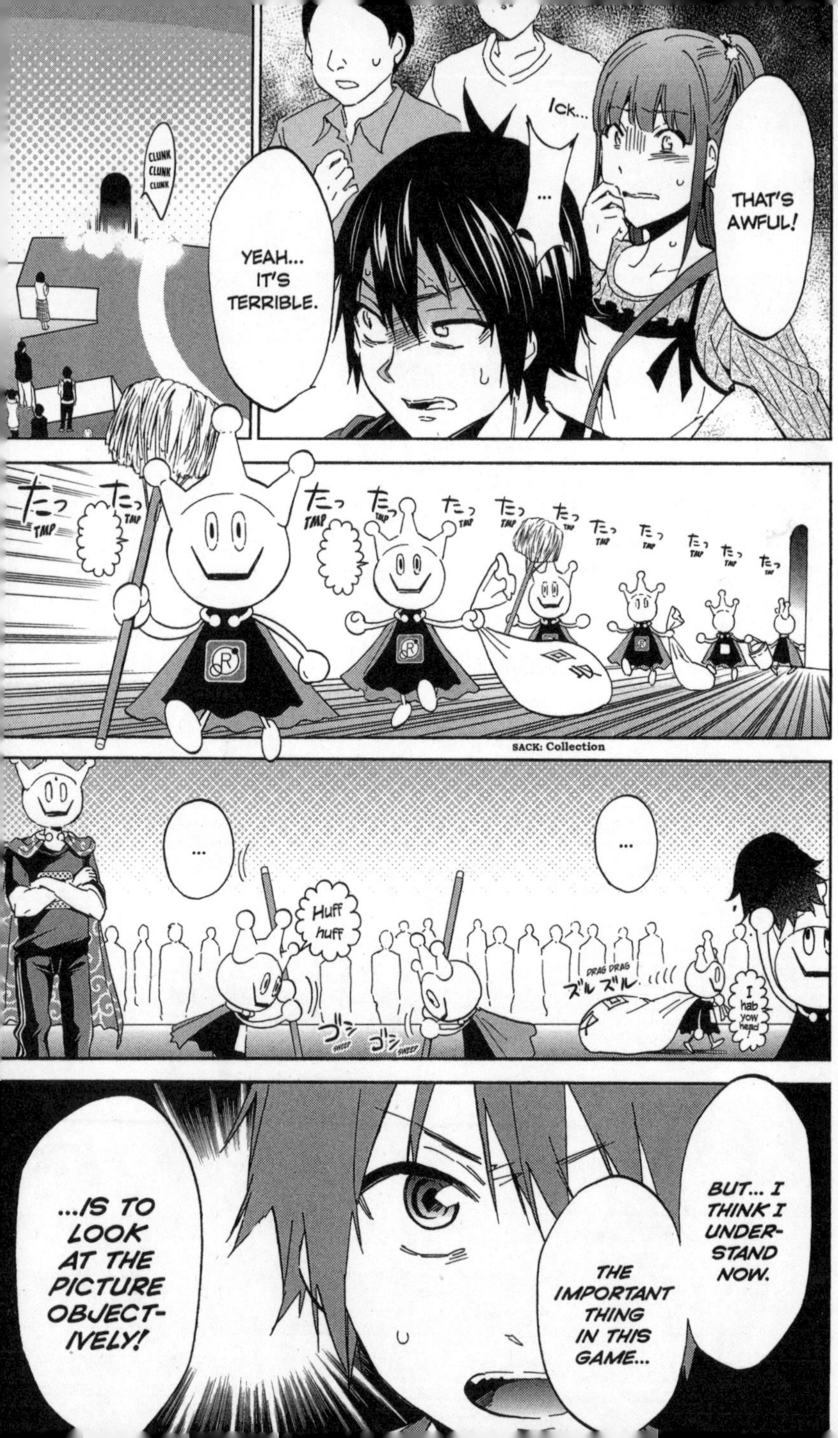
THAT'S AWFUL!
Ick...
...
YEAH... IT'S TERRIBLE.
CLUNK CLUNK CLUNK
たっ TMP
たっ TMP
たっ TMP
たっ TMP
たっ TMP
たっ TMP
たっ TMP
たっ TMP
たっ TMP
たっ TMP
たっ TMP
たっ TMP
SACK: Collection
...
I hab yow head!
ズルズル DRAG DRAG
Huff huff
ゴシ SWEEP
ゴシ SWEEP
...
BUT... I THINK I UNDERSTAND NOW.
THE IMPORTANT THING IN THIS GAME...
...IS TO LOOK AT THE PICTURE OBJECTIVELY!

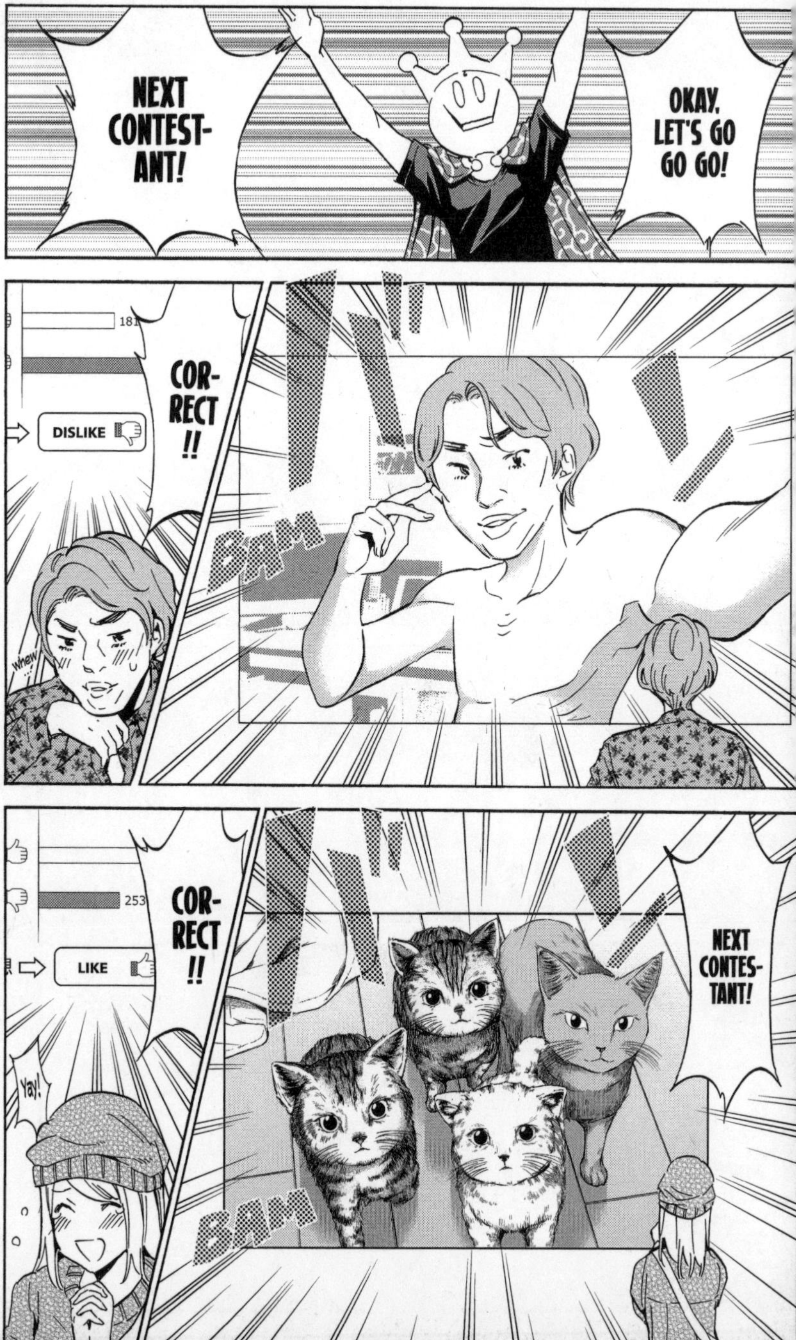
OKAY, LET'S GO GO GO!
NEXT CONTEST-ANT!
BAM
181
DISLIKE
CORRECT!!
whew
NEXT CONTES-TANT!
BAM
253
LIKE
CORRECT!!
Yay!

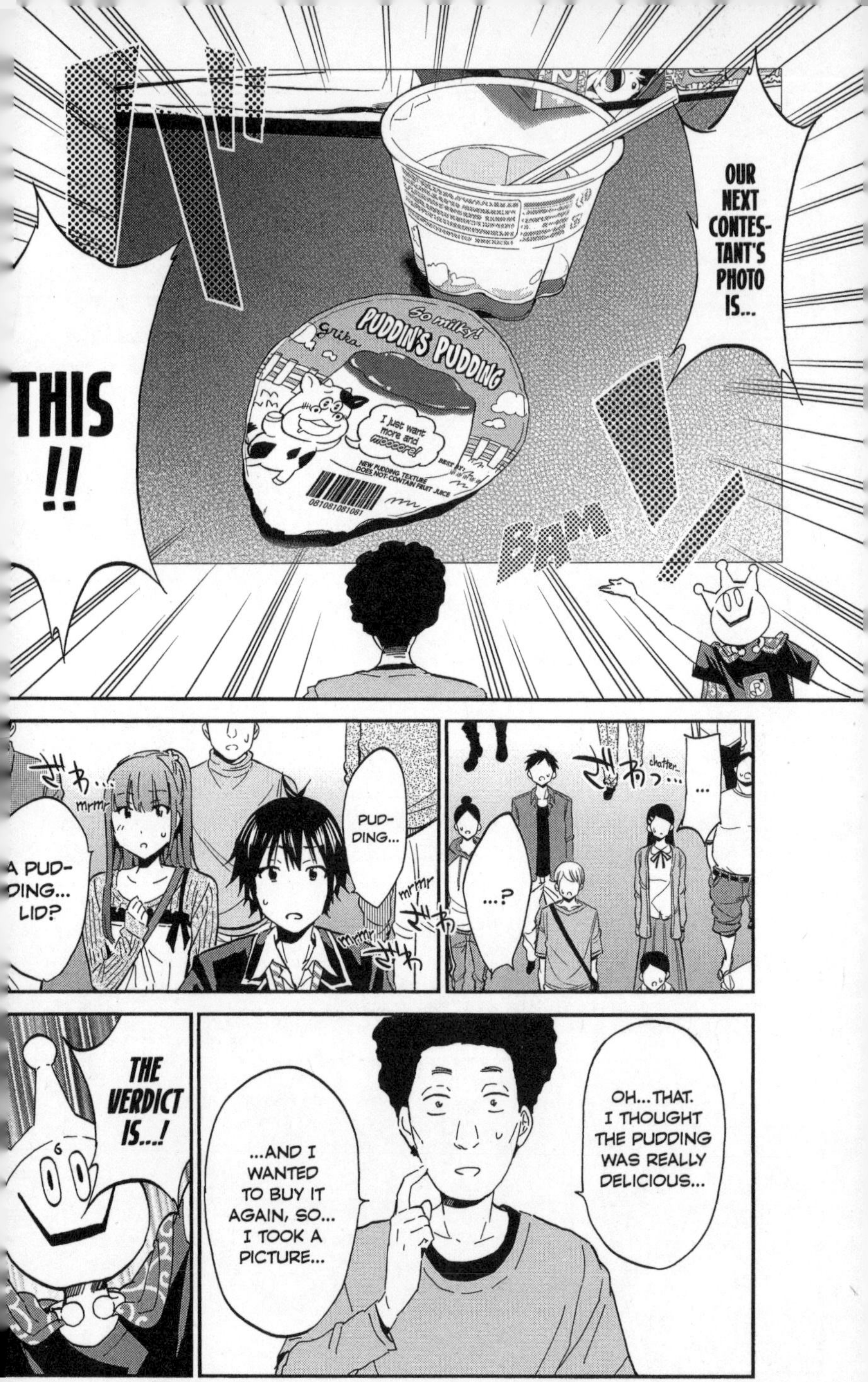

OUR NEXT CONTES-TANT'S PHOTO IS...
THIS!!
So milky!
PUDDIN'S PUDDING
I just want more and mooore!
NEW PUDDING TEXTURE DOES NOT CONTAIN FRUIT JUICE
BAM
chatter...
...
...?
PUD-DING...
mrmr
A PUD-DING... LID?
OH...THAT. I THOUGHT THE PUDDING WAS REALLY DELICIOUS...
...AND I WANTED TO BUY IT AGAIN, SO... I TOOK A PICTURE...
THE VERDICT IS...!

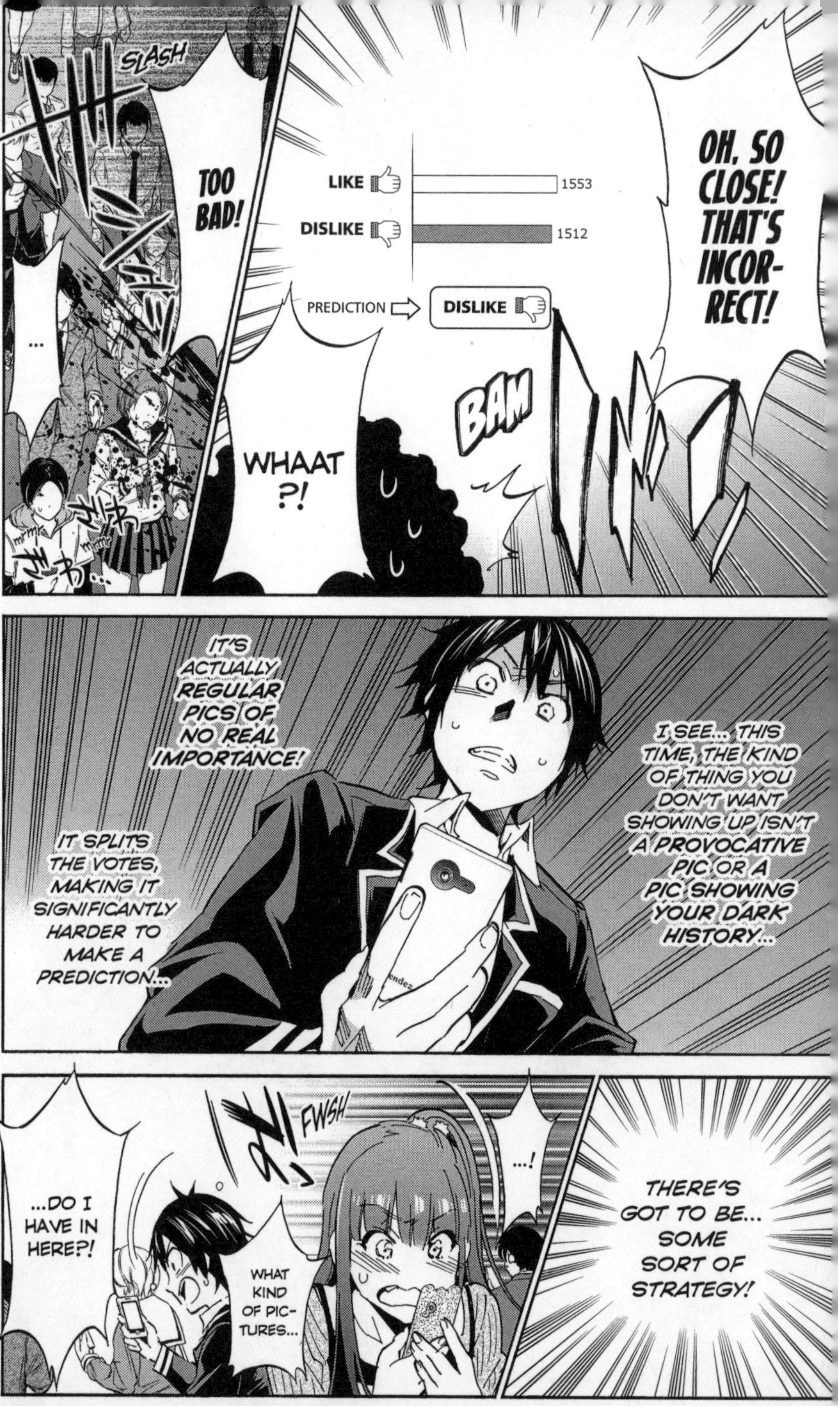
OH, SO CLOSE! THAT'S INCORRECT!
LIKE 1553
DISLIKE 1512
PREDICTION DISLIKE
BAM
WHAAT?!
SLASH
TOO BAD!
...
mrmr
mrmr
I SEE... THIS TIME, THE KIND OF THING YOU DON'T WANT SHOWING UP ISN'T A PROVOCATIVE PIC OR A PIC SHOWING YOUR DARK HISTORY...
IT'S ACTUALLY REGULAR PICS OF NO REAL IMPORTANCE!
IT SPLITS THE VOTES, MAKING IT SIGNIFICANTLY HARDER TO MAKE A PREDICTION...
THERE'S GOT TO BE... SOME SORT OF STRATEGY!
...!
FWSH
WHAT KIND OF PICTURES...
...DO I HAVE IN HERE?!

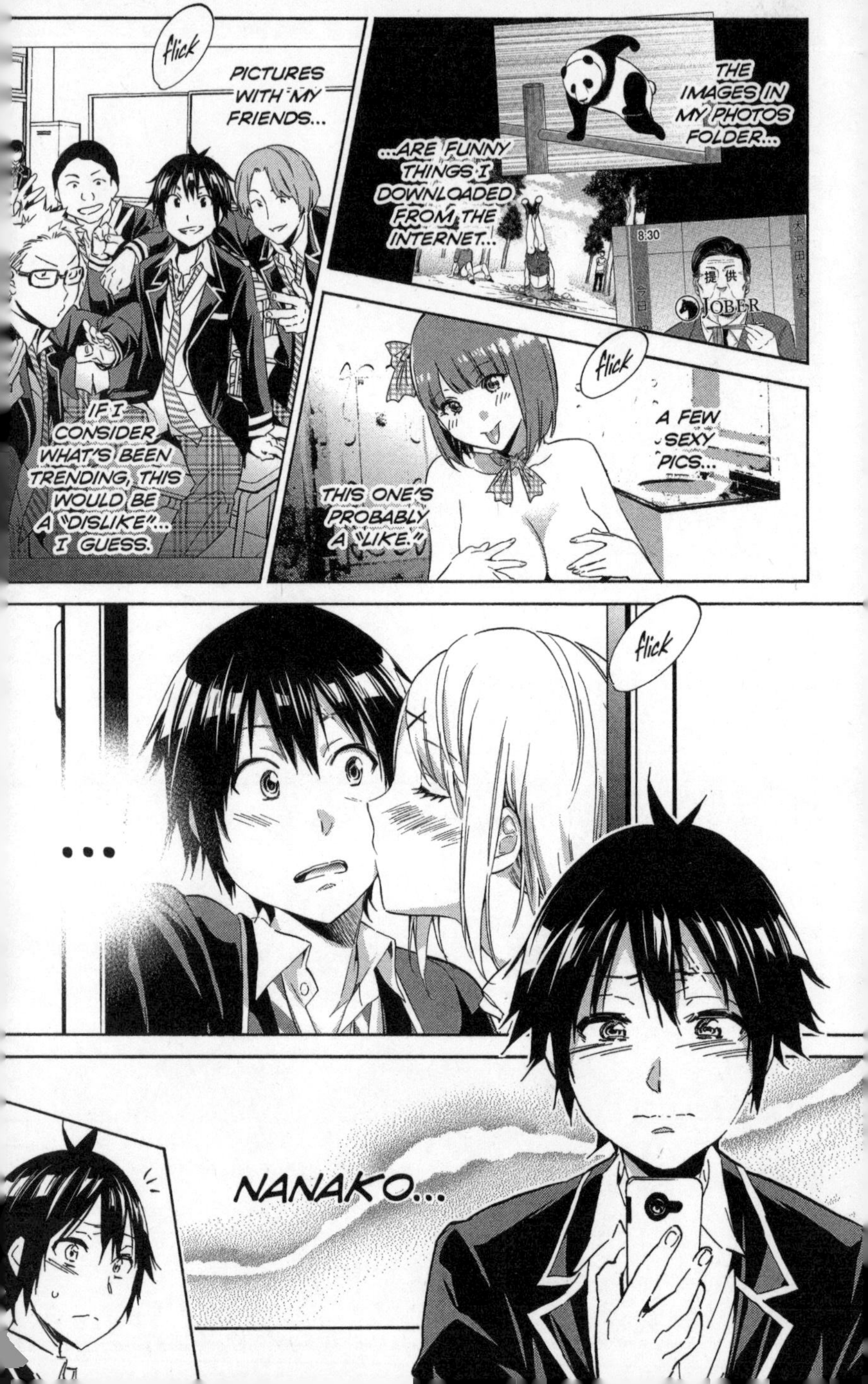
THE IMAGES IN MY PHOTOS FOLDER...
...ARE FUNNY THINGS I DOWNLOADED FROM THE INTERNET...
8:30
提供
JOBER
flick
A FEW SEXY PICS...
THIS ONE'S PROBABLY A "LIKE."
flick
PICTURES WITH MY FRIENDS...
IF I CONSIDER WHAT'S BEEN TRENDING, THIS WOULD BE A "DISLIKE"... I GUESS.
flick
...
NANAKO...

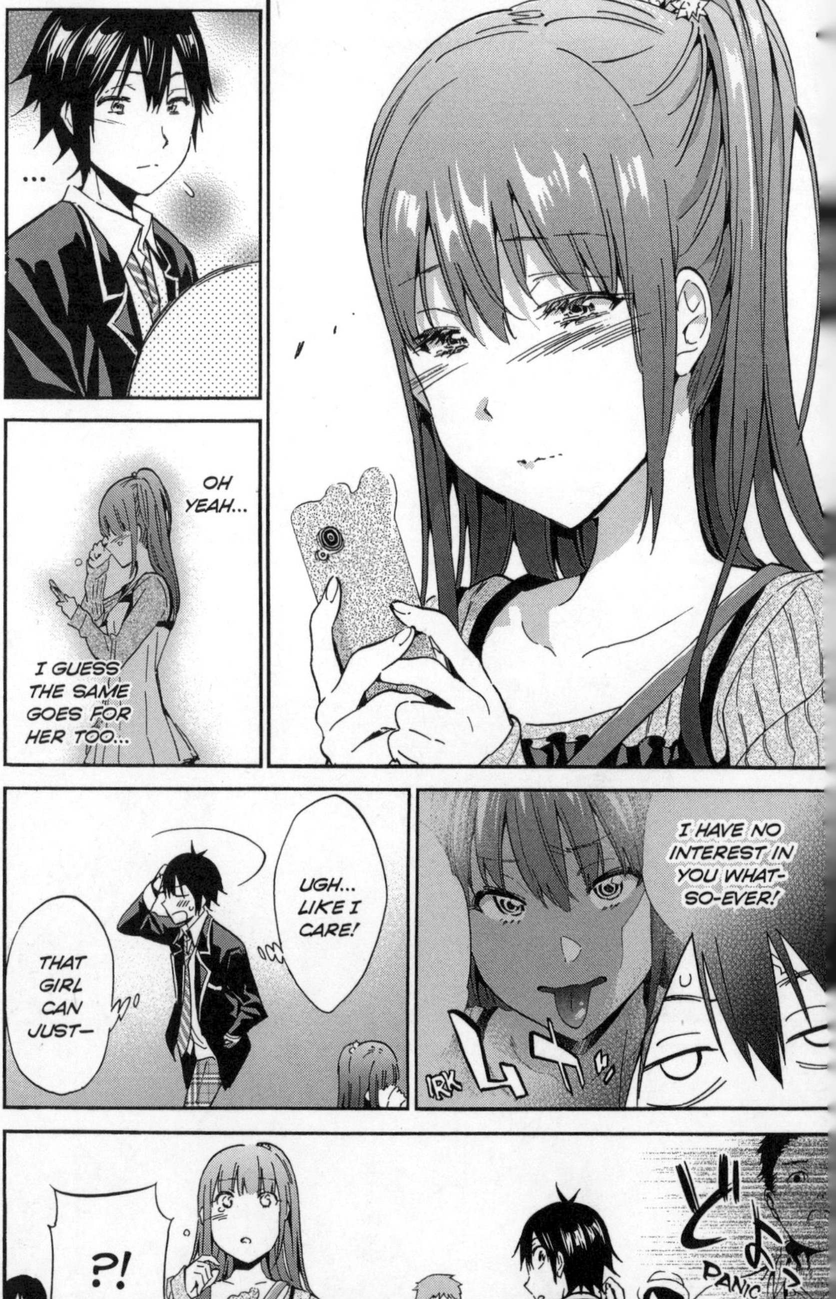
...
OH YEAH...
I GUESS THE SAME GOES FOR HER TOO...
I HAVE NO INTEREST IN YOU WHAT-SO-EVER!
IRK
UGH... LIKE I CARE!
THAT GIRL CAN JUST—
PANIC
?!

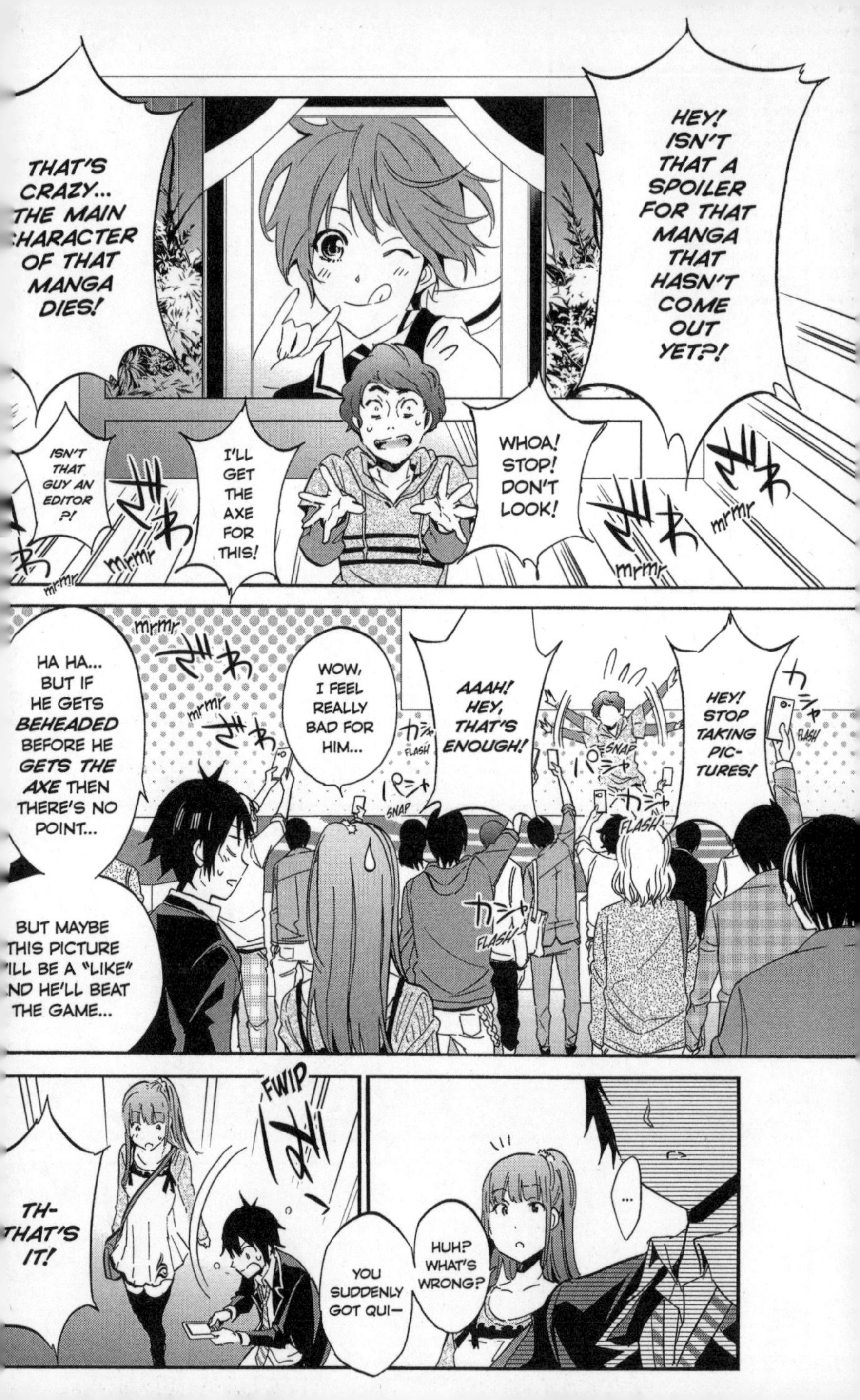
HEY! ISN'T THAT A SPOILER FOR THAT MANGA THAT HASN'T COME OUT YET?!
THAT'S CRAZY... THE MAIN HARACTER OF THAT MANGA DIES!
ざわ mrmr
ざわ mrmr
WHOA! STOP! DON'T LOOK!
I'LL GET THE AXE FOR THIS!
ざわ mrmr
ISN'T THAT GUY AN EDITOR ?!
mrmr
HEY! STOP TAKING PIC- TURES!
カシャ FLASH
AAAH! HEY, THAT'S ENOUGH!
パシャ SNAP
カシャ FLASH
カシャ FLASH
パシャ SNAP
カシャ FLASH
WOW, I FEEL REALLY BAD FOR HIM...
mrmr ざわ
mrmr ざわ
HA HA... BUT IF HE GETS BEHEADED BEFORE HE GETS THE AXE THEN THERE'S NO POINT...
BUT MAYBE THIS PICTURE 'ILL BE A "LIKE" ND HE'LL BEAT THE GAME...
...
HUH? WHAT'S WRONG?
YOU SUDDENLY GOT QUI—
FWIP
TH- THAT'S IT!

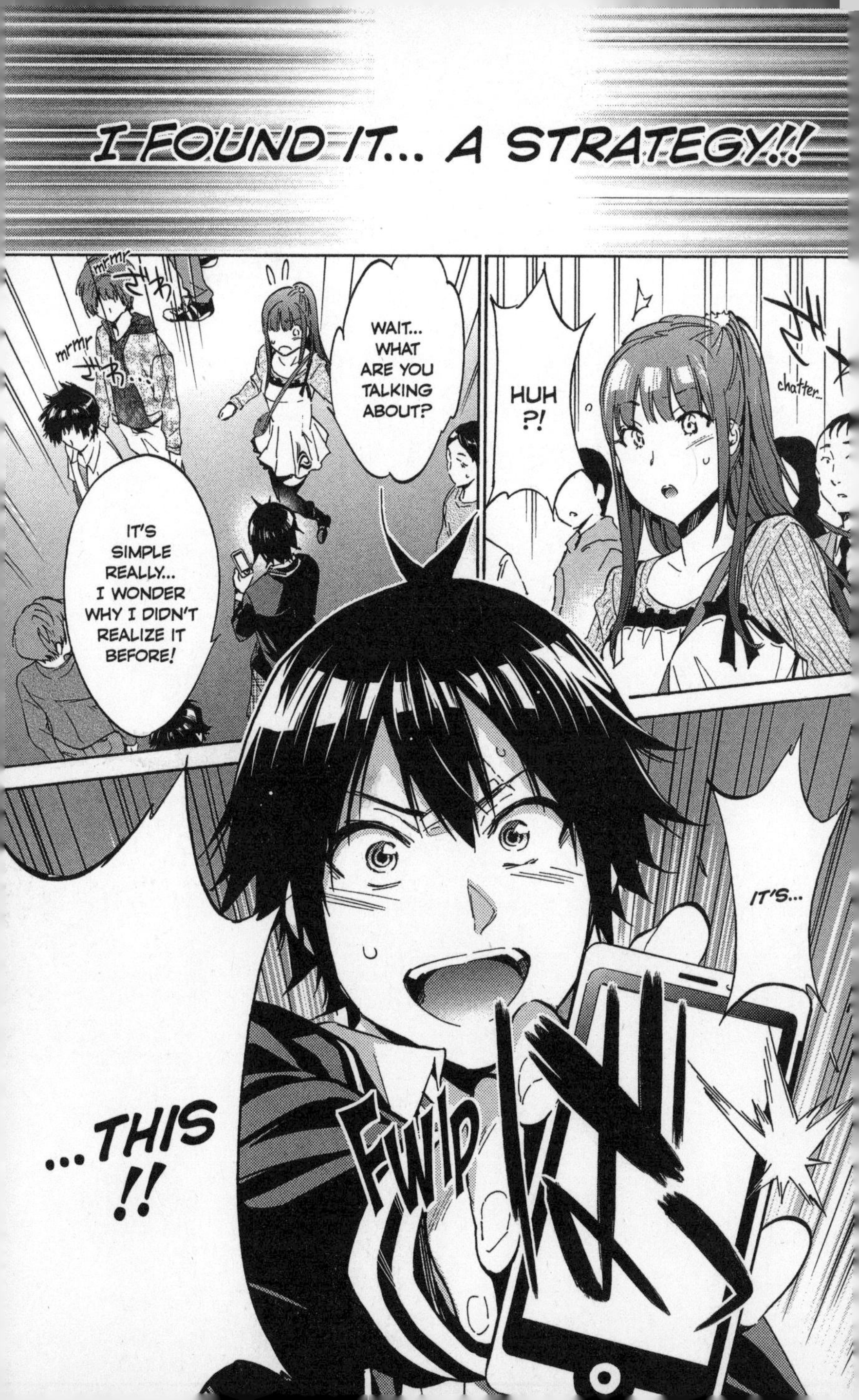
I FOUND IT... A STRATEGY!!
HUH ?!
chatter...
mrmr
WAIT... WHAT ARE YOU TALKING ABOUT?
mrmr
IT'S SIMPLE REALLY... I WONDER WHY I DIDN'T REALIZE IT BEFORE!
IT'S...
FWIP
...THIS !!

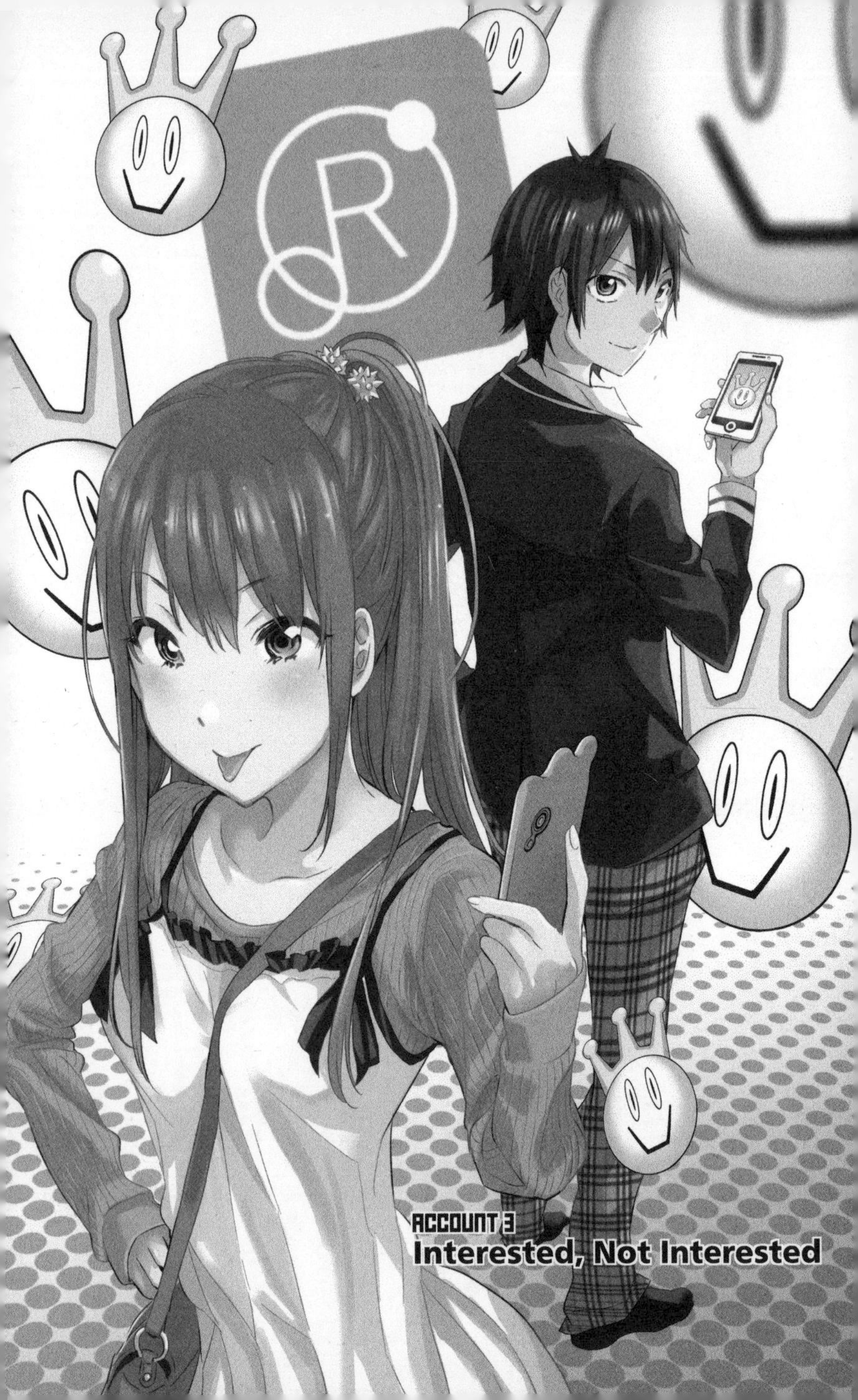

ACCOUNT 3
Interested, Not Interested

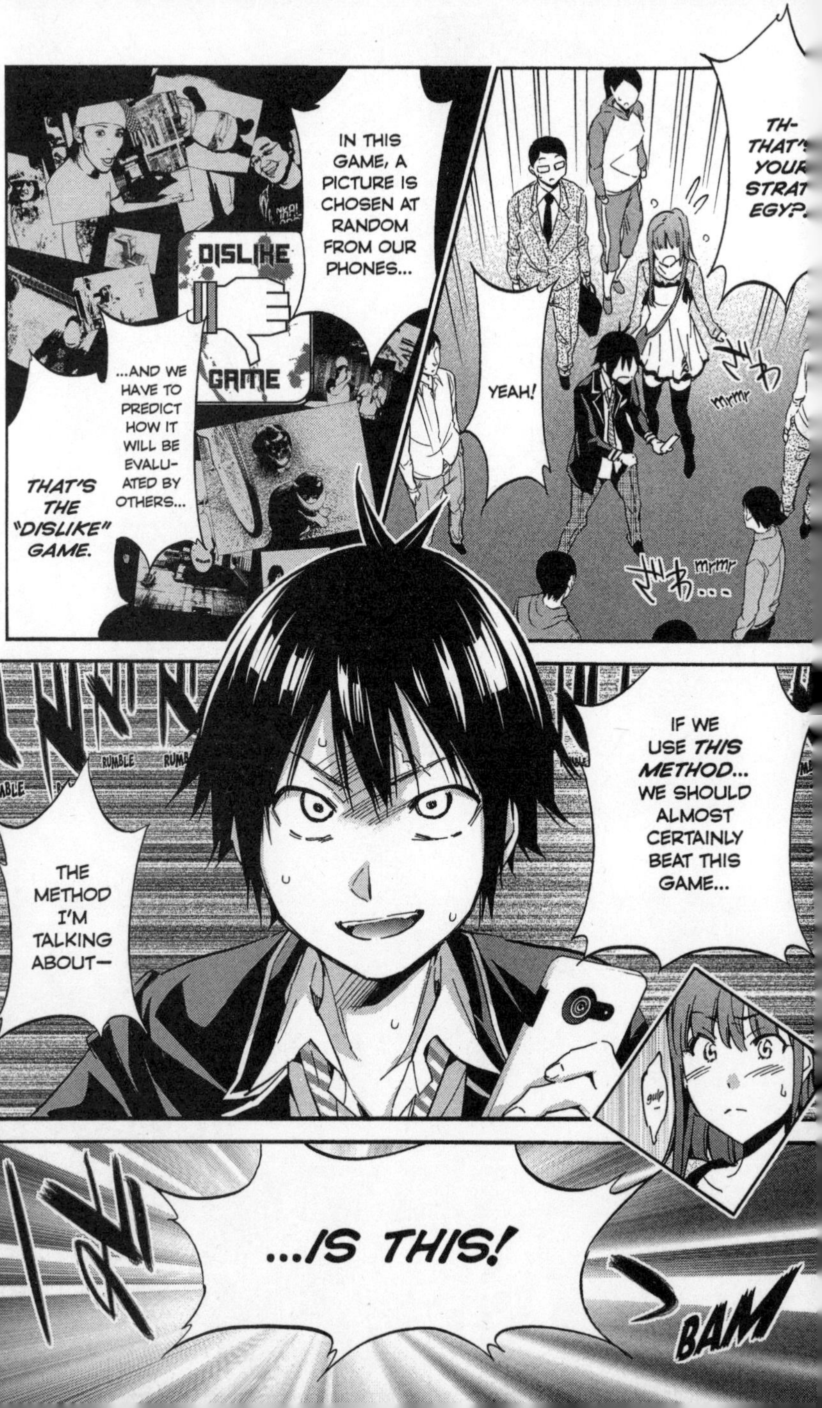
TH-THAT'S YOUR STRATEGY?!
YEAH!
mrmr
mrmr...
IN THIS GAME, A PICTURE IS CHOSEN AT RANDOM FROM OUR PHONES...
DISLIKE GAME
...AND WE HAVE TO PREDICT HOW IT WILL BE EVALUATED BY OTHERS...
THAT'S THE "DISLIKE" GAME.
RUMBLE RUMBLE RUMBLE
IF WE USE THIS METHOD... WE SHOULD ALMOST CERTAINLY BEAT THIS GAME...
THE METHOD I'M TALKING ABOUT—
gulp
...IS THIS!
BAM

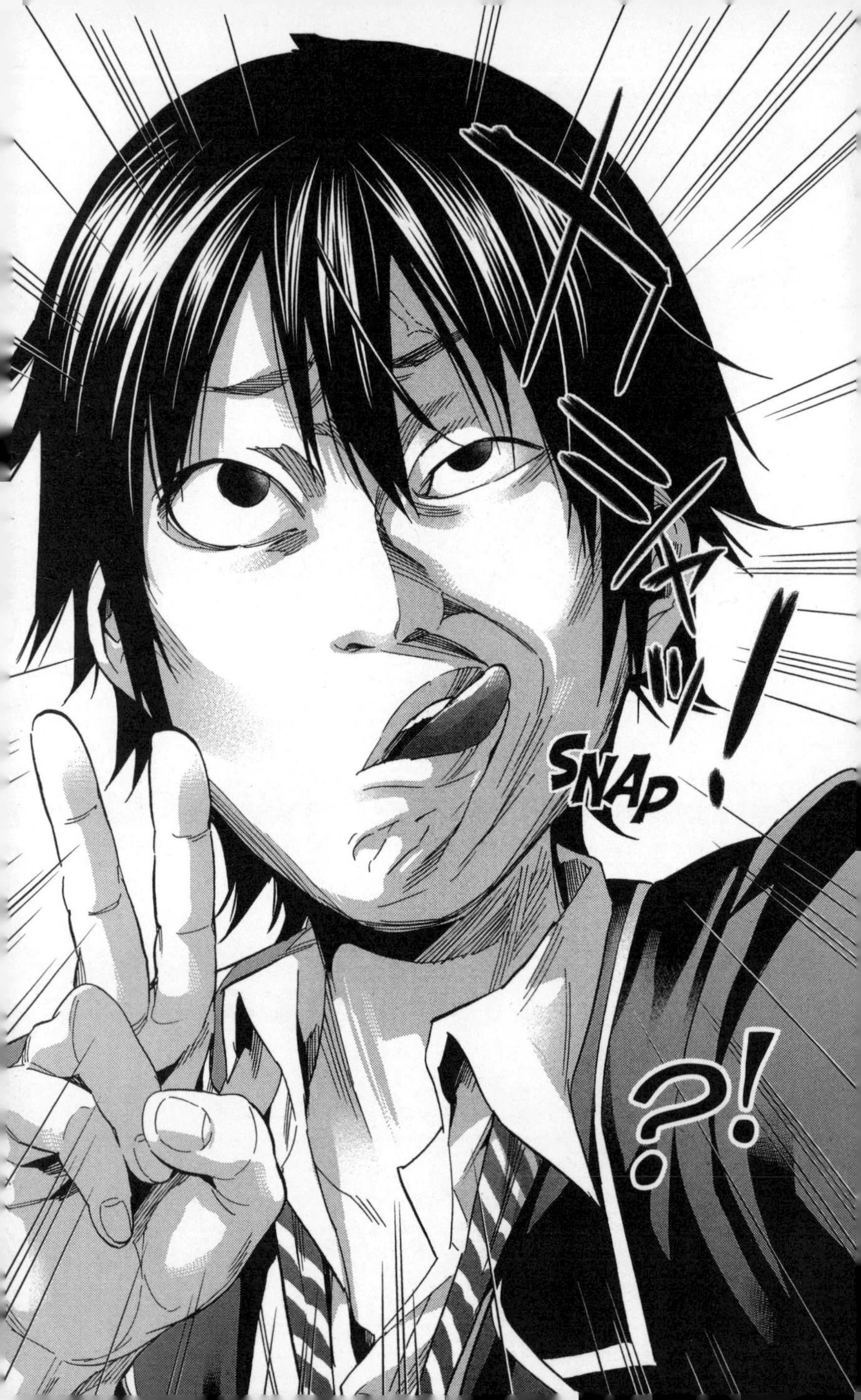
SNAP
!
?!

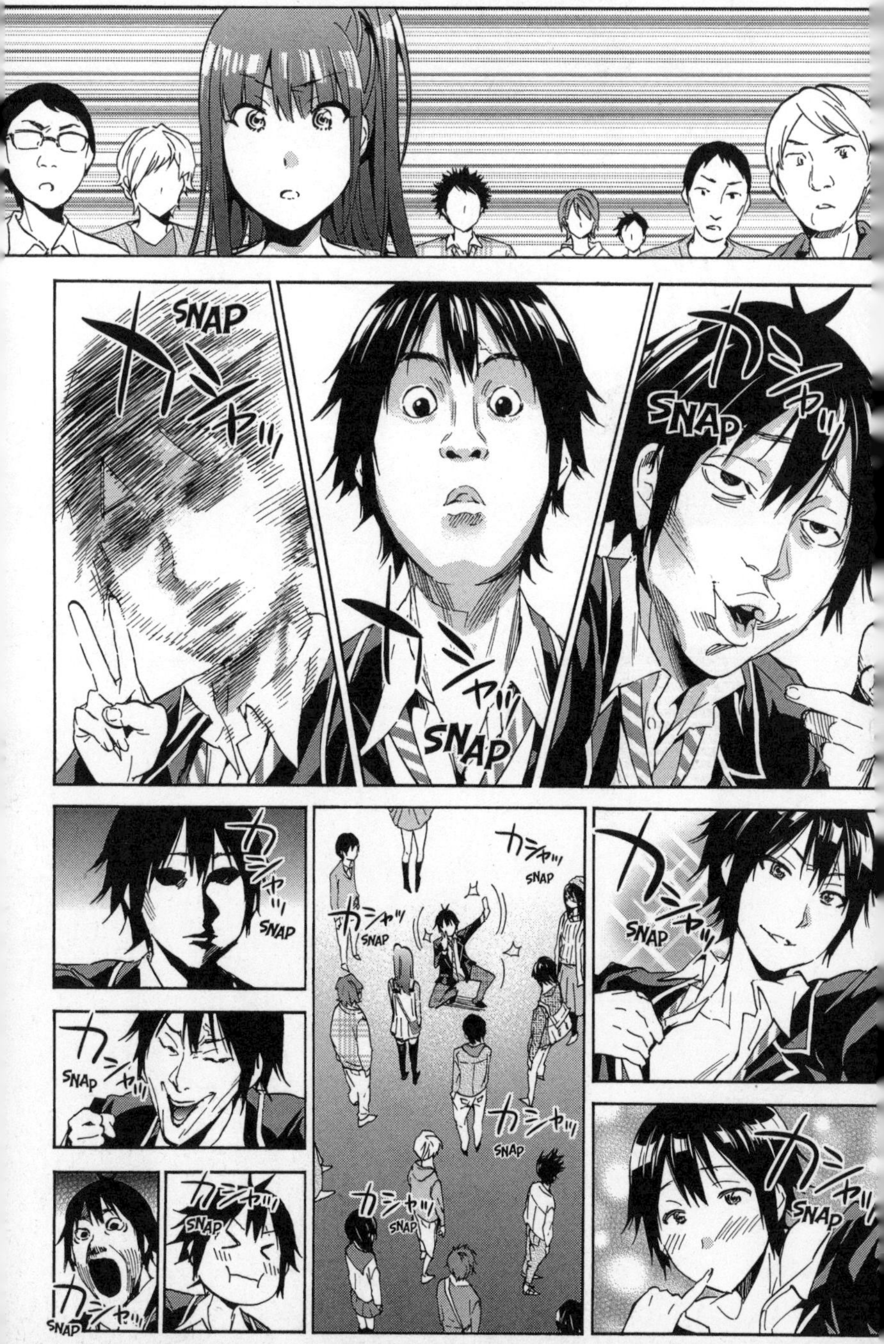
カシャッ
SNAP
カシャッ
SNAP
カシャッ
SNAP
カシャッ
SNAP
カシャッ
SNAP
カシャッ
SNAP
カシャッ
SNAP
カシャッ
SNAP
カシャッ
SNAP
カシャッ
SNAP
カシャッ
SNAP
カシャッ
SNAP
カシャッ
SNAP
カシャッ
SNAP

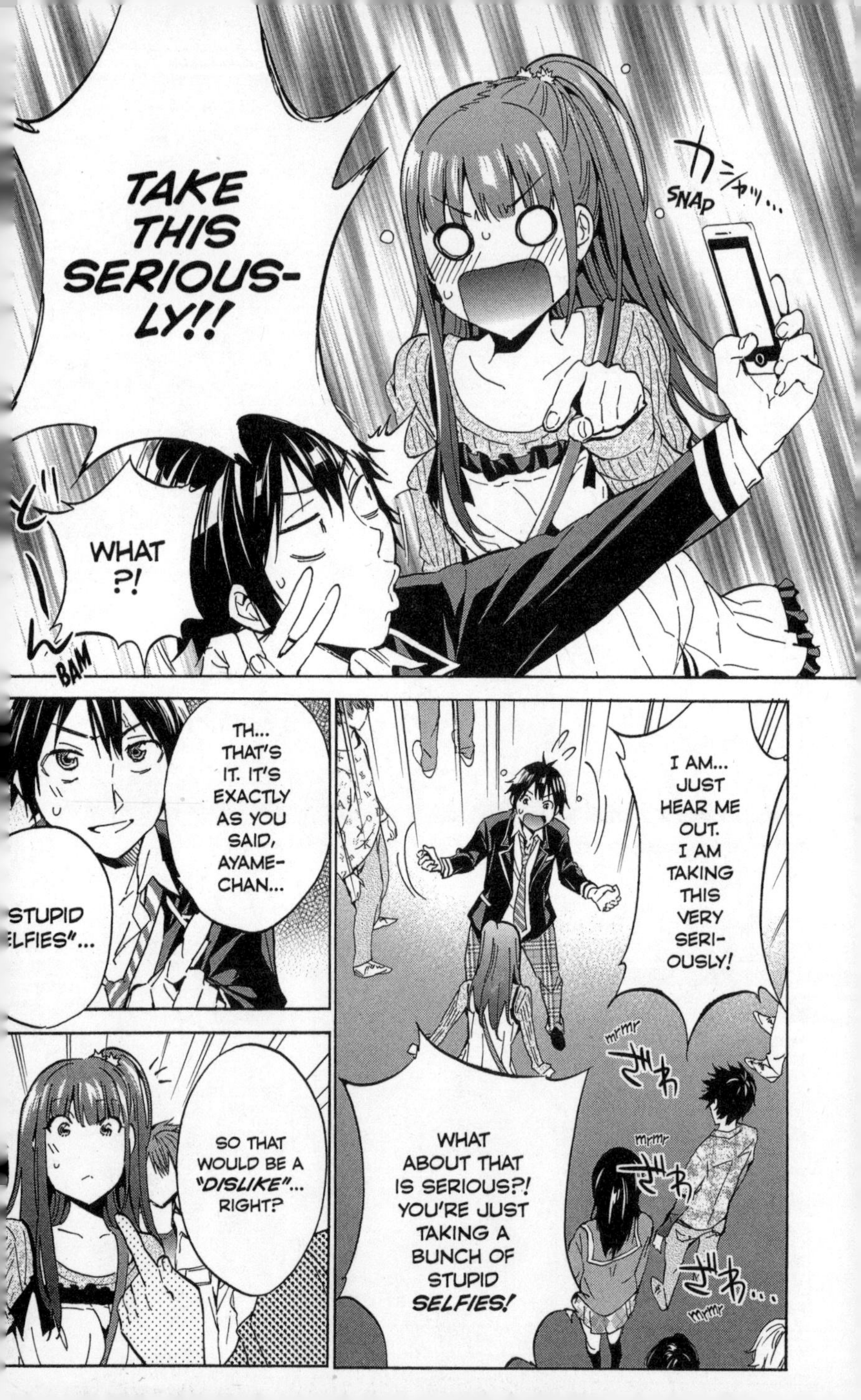
カシャッ...
SNAP
TAKE THIS SERIOUS-LY!!
WHAT?!
BAM
I AM... JUST HEAR ME OUT. I AM TAKING THIS VERY SERI-OUSLY!
WHAT ABOUT THAT IS SERIOUS?! YOU'RE JUST TAKING A BUNCH OF STUPID *SELFIES!*
mrmr
mrmr
mrmr
TH... THAT'S IT. IT'S EXACTLY AS YOU SAID, AYAME-CHAN...
STUPID ELFIES"...
SO THAT WOULD BE A *"DISLIKE"*... RIGHT?

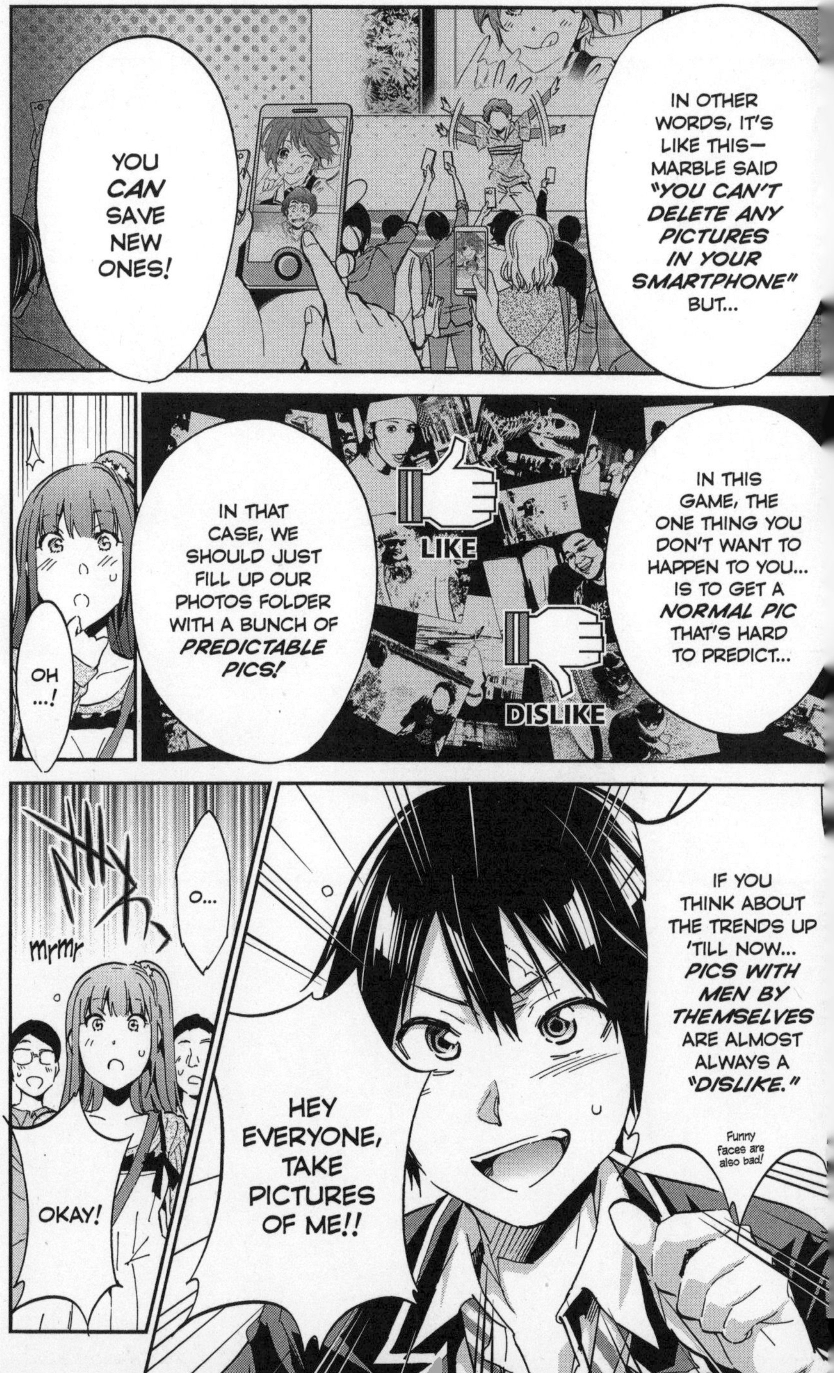
IN OTHER WORDS, IT'S LIKE THIS— MARBLE SAID "YOU CAN'T DELETE ANY PICTURES IN YOUR SMARTPHONE" BUT...
YOU CAN SAVE NEW ONES!
IN THIS GAME, THE ONE THING YOU DON'T WANT TO HAPPEN TO YOU... IS TO GET A NORMAL PIC THAT'S HARD TO PREDICT...
LIKE
DISLIKE
IN THAT CASE, WE SHOULD JUST FILL UP OUR PHOTOS FOLDER WITH A BUNCH OF PREDICTABLE PICS!
OH ...!
IF YOU THINK ABOUT THE TRENDS UP 'TILL NOW... PICS WITH MEN BY THEMSELVES ARE ALMOST ALWAYS A "DISLIKE."
Funny faces are also bad!
HEY EVERYONE, TAKE PICTURES OF ME!!
O...
mrmr
OKAY!

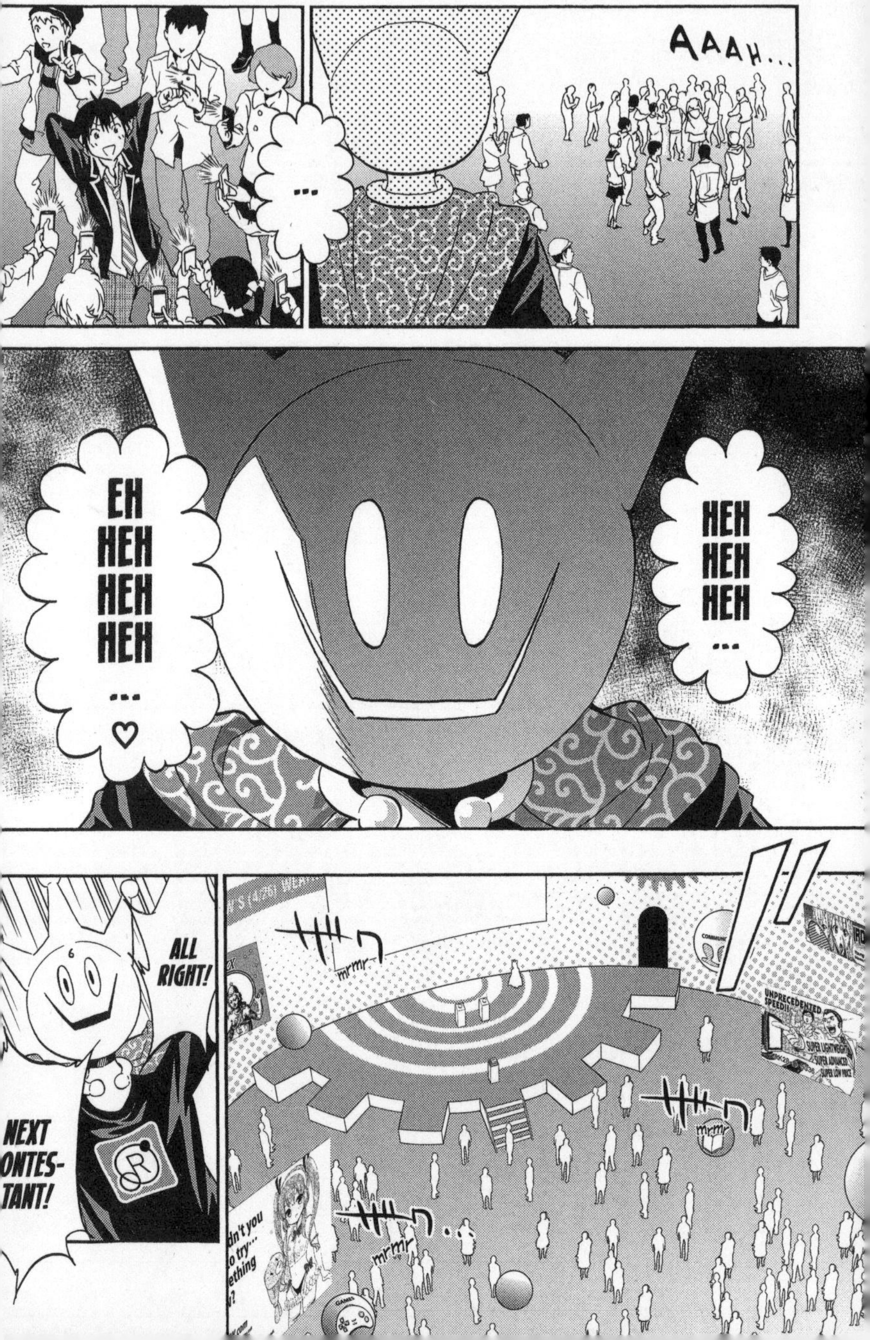
AAAH...
...
HEH HEH HEH ...
EH HEH HEH HEH ... ♡
mrmr
UNPRECEDENTED SPEED!!
SUPER LIGHTWEIGHT
SUPER ADVANCED
SUPER LOW PRICE
mrmr
mrmr
ALL RIGHT!
NEXT ONTES- TANT!

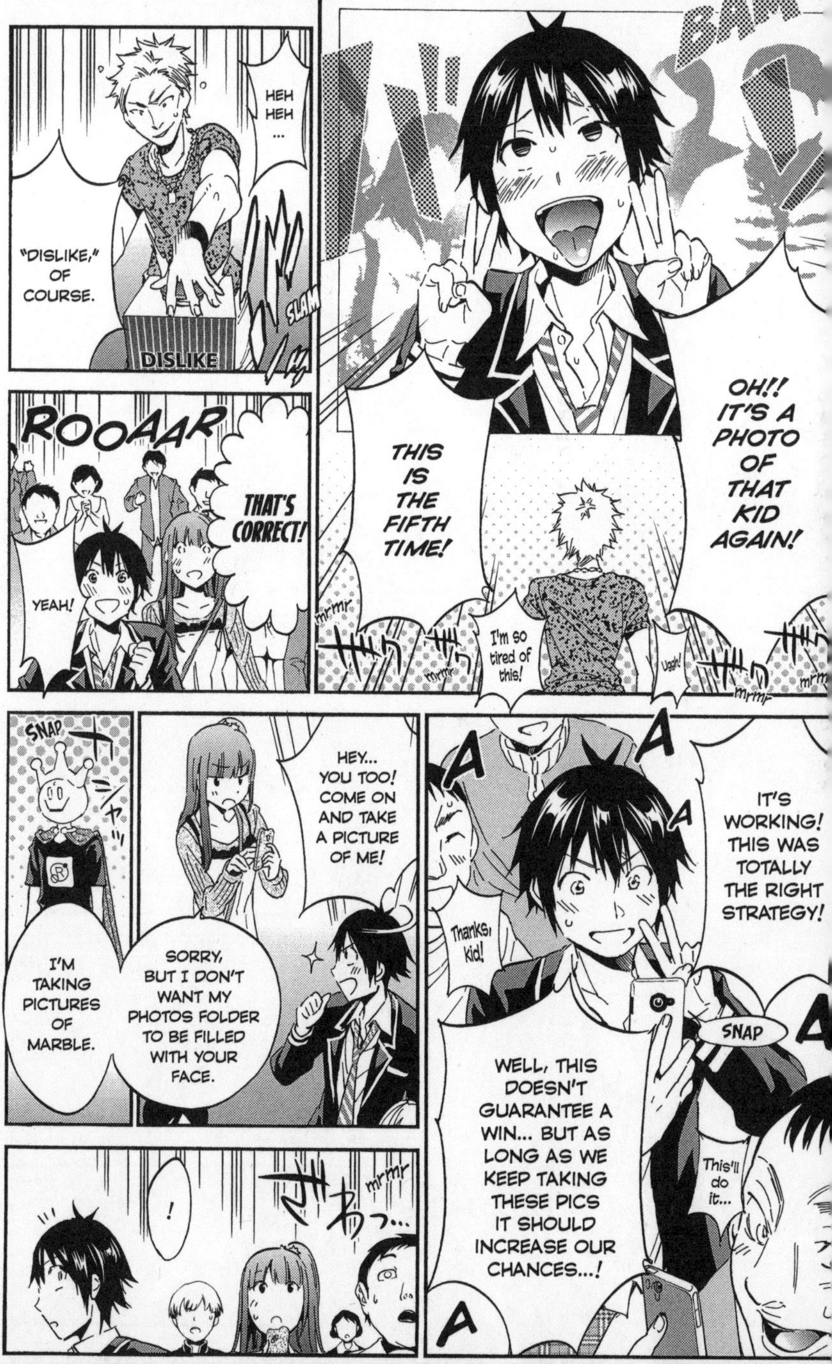
BAM
OH!! IT'S A PHOTO OF THAT KID AGAIN!
THIS IS THE FIFTH TIME!
Ugh!
I'm so tired of this!
mrmr
HEH HEH ...
"DISLIKE," OF COURSE.
SLAM
DISLIKE
ROOAAR
THAT'S CORRECT!
YEAH!
IT'S WORKING! THIS WAS TOTALLY THE RIGHT STRATEGY!
Thanks, kid!
SNAP
WELL, THIS DOESN'T GUARANTEE A WIN... BUT AS LONG AS WE KEEP TAKING THESE PICS IT SHOULD INCREASE OUR CHANCES...!
This'll do it...
HEY... YOU TOO! COME ON AND TAKE A PICTURE OF ME!
SORRY, BUT I DON'T WANT MY PHOTOS FOLDER TO BE FILLED WITH YOUR FACE.
SNAP
I'M TAKING PICTURES OF MARBLE.
!
mrmr

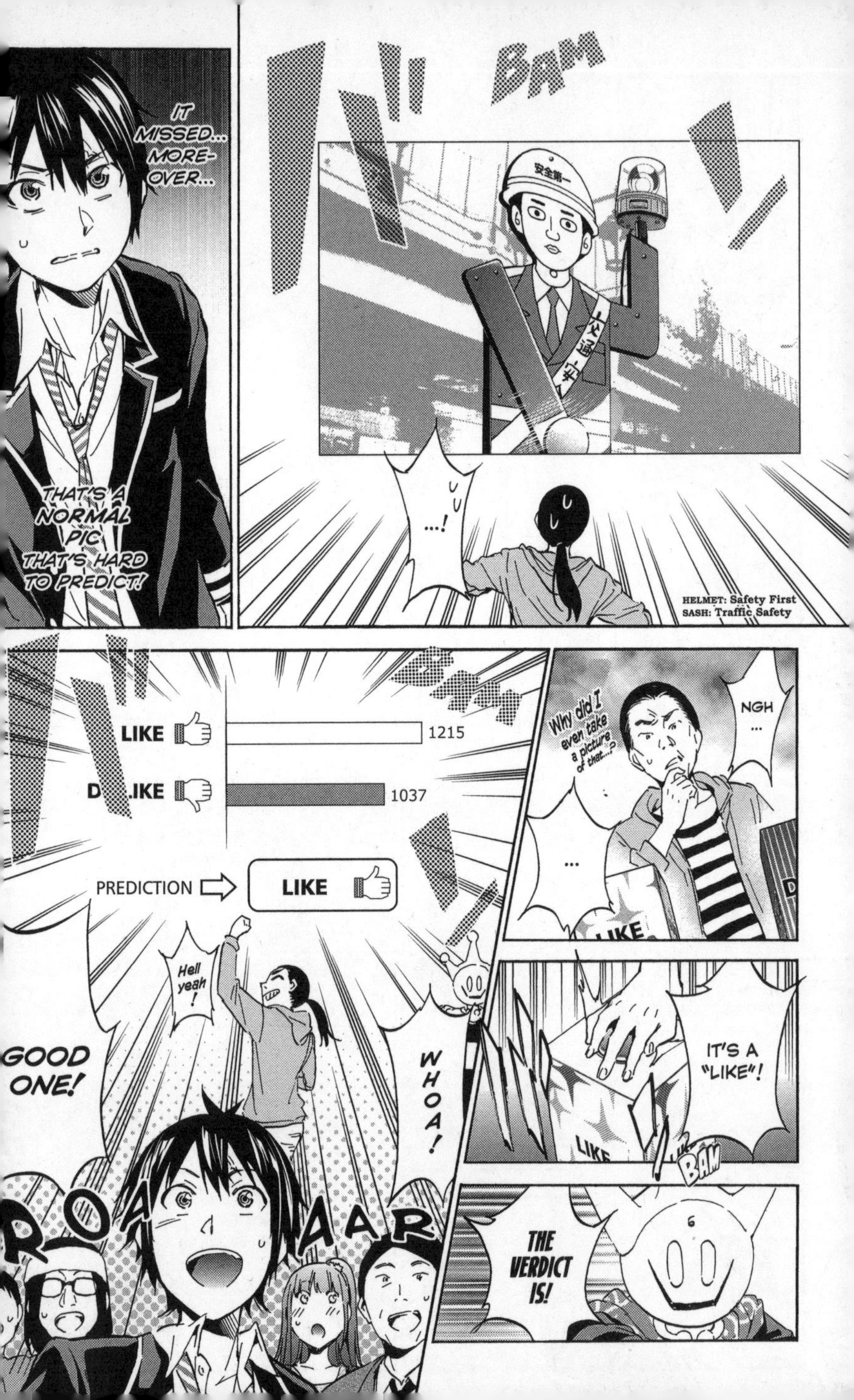
BAM
...!
HELMET: Safety First
SASH: Traffic Safety
IT MISSED... MORE-OVER...
THAT'S A NORMAL PIC THAT'S HARD TO PREDICT!
NGH ...
Why did I even take a picture of that...?
...
IT'S A "LIKE"!
BAM
THE VERDICT IS!
LIKE 1215
1037
PREDICTION LIKE
Hell yeah!
WHOA!
GOOD ONE!
ROAAAR

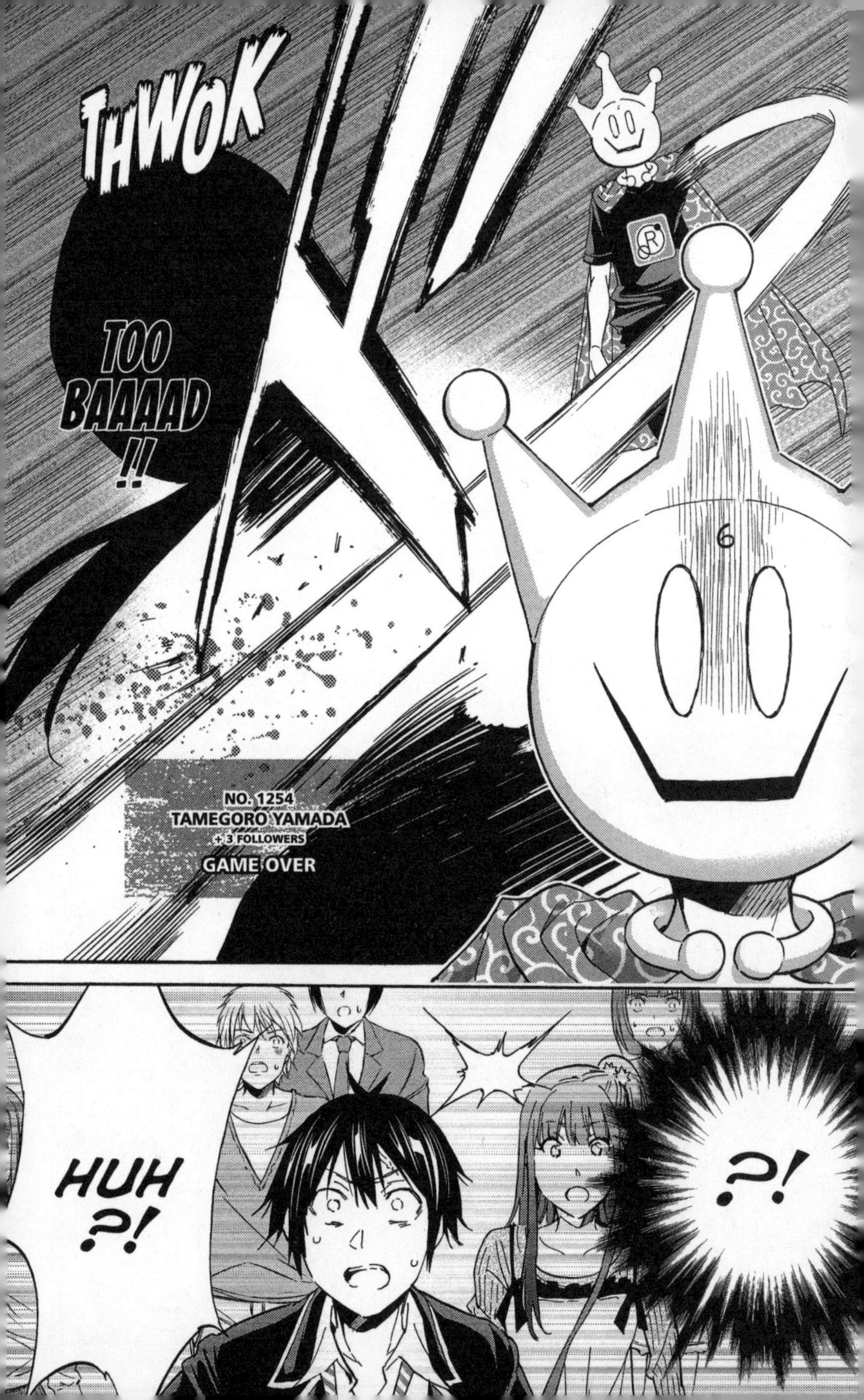
THWOK
TOO BAAAAD!!
NO. 1254
TAMEGORO YAMADA
+ 3 FOLLOWERS
GAME OVER
?!
HUH?!

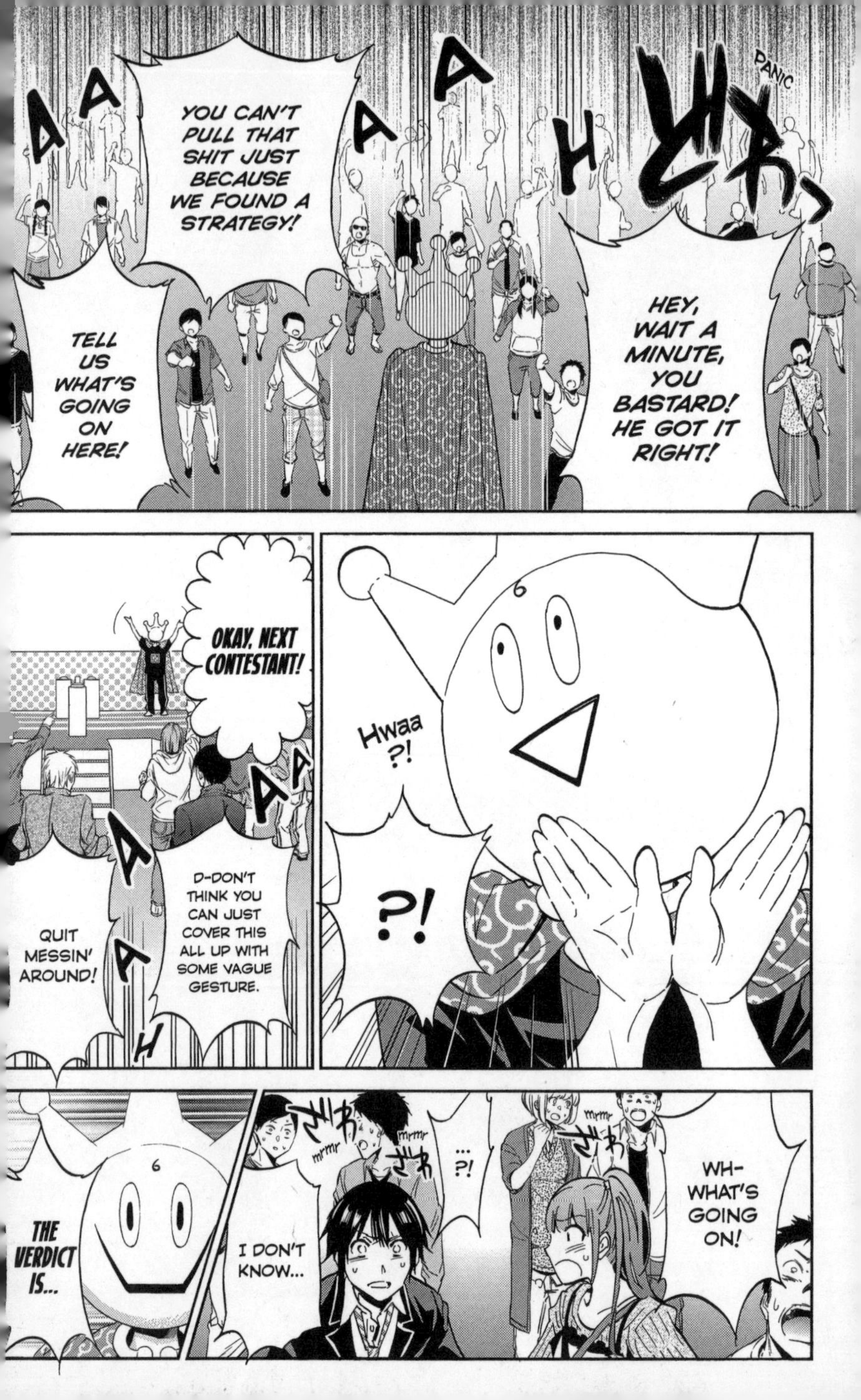
PANIC
HEY, WAIT A MINUTE, YOU BASTARD! HE GOT IT RIGHT!
AAAAH
YOU CAN'T PULL THAT SHIT JUST BECAUSE WE FOUND A STRATEGY!
TELL US WHAT'S GOING ON HERE!
Hwaa ?!
?!
OKAY, NEXT CONTESTANT!
D-DON'T THINK YOU CAN JUST COVER THIS ALL UP WITH SOME VAGUE GESTURE.
AAAH
QUIT MESSIN' AROUND!
mrmr
WH- WHAT'S GOING ON!
mrmr
...?!
I DON'T KNOW...
THE VERDICT IS...

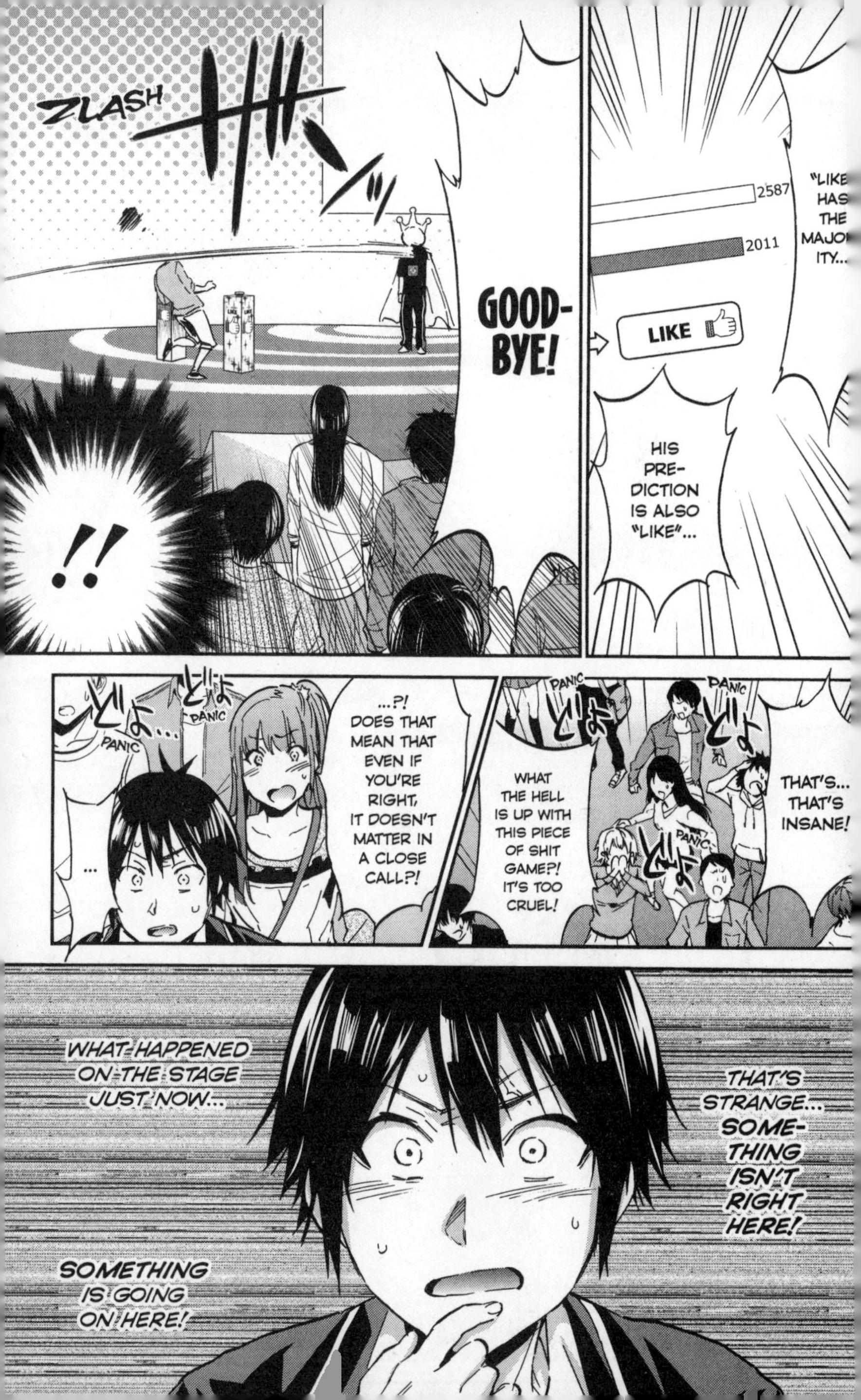
2587
2011
“LIKE HAS THE MAJO ITY...
LIKE
HIS PRE-DICTION IS ALSO “LIKE”...
ZLASH
GOOD-BYE!
!!
PANIC
どよ
PANIC
どよ
THAT'S... THAT'S INSANE!
WHAT THE HELL IS UP WITH THIS PIECE OF SHIT GAME?! IT'S TOO CRUEL!
PANIC
どよ
...?! DOES THAT MEAN THAT EVEN IF YOU'RE RIGHT, IT DOESN'T MATTER IN A CLOSE CALL?!
どよ
PANIC
どよ...
PANIC
...
WHAT HAPPENED ON THE STAGE JUST NOW...
THAT'S STRANGE... SOMETHING ISN'T RIGHT HERE!
SOMETHING IS GOING ON HERE!

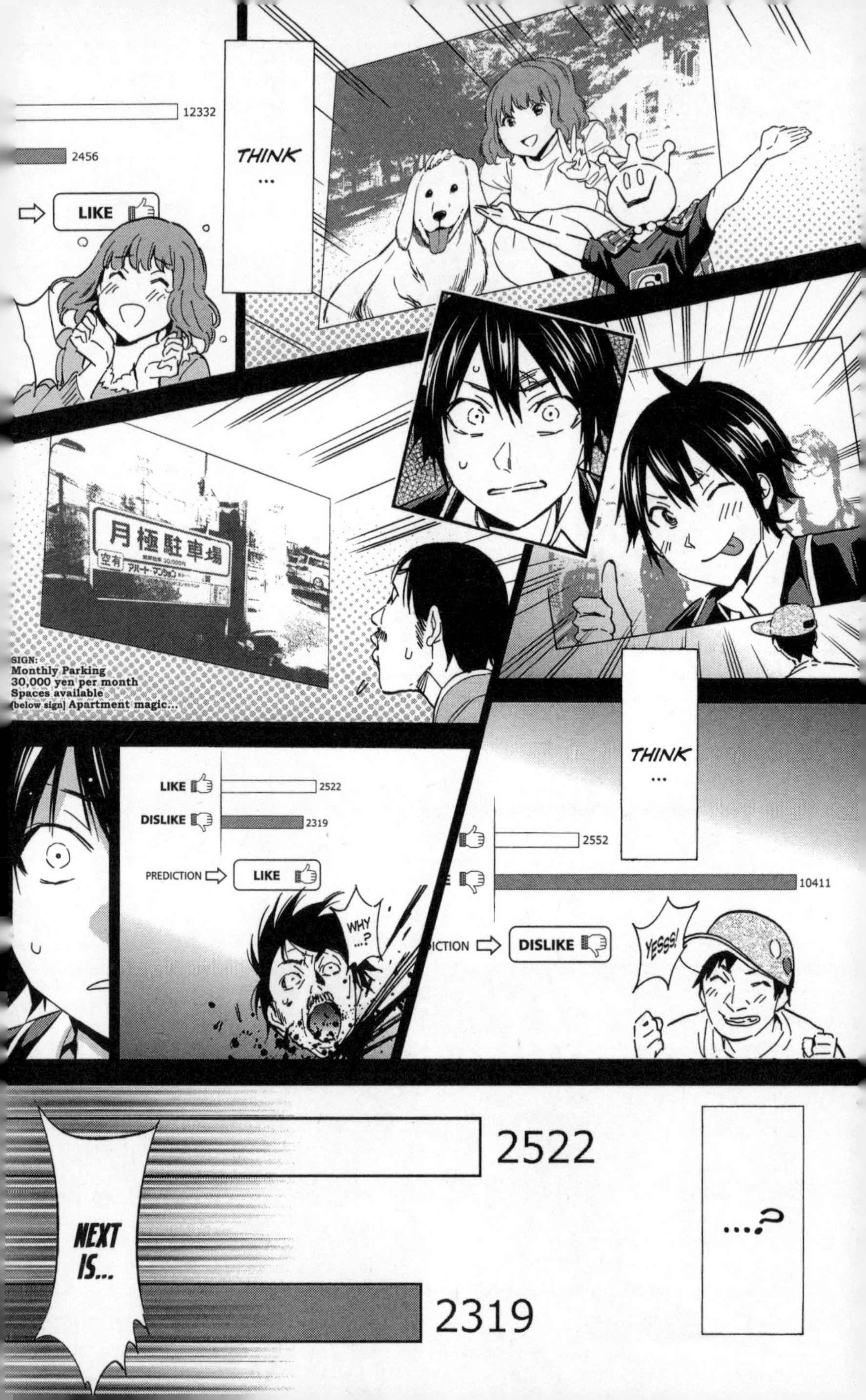
THINK ...
12332
2456
LIKE
月極駐車場
空有
アパート・マンション
SIGN:
Monthly Parking
30,000 yen per month
Spaces available
[below sign] Apartment magic...
THINK ...
2552
10411
DICTION
DISLIKE
YESSS!
LIKE
2522
DISLIKE
2319
PREDICTION
LIKE
WHY ...?
...?
NEXT IS...
2522
2319

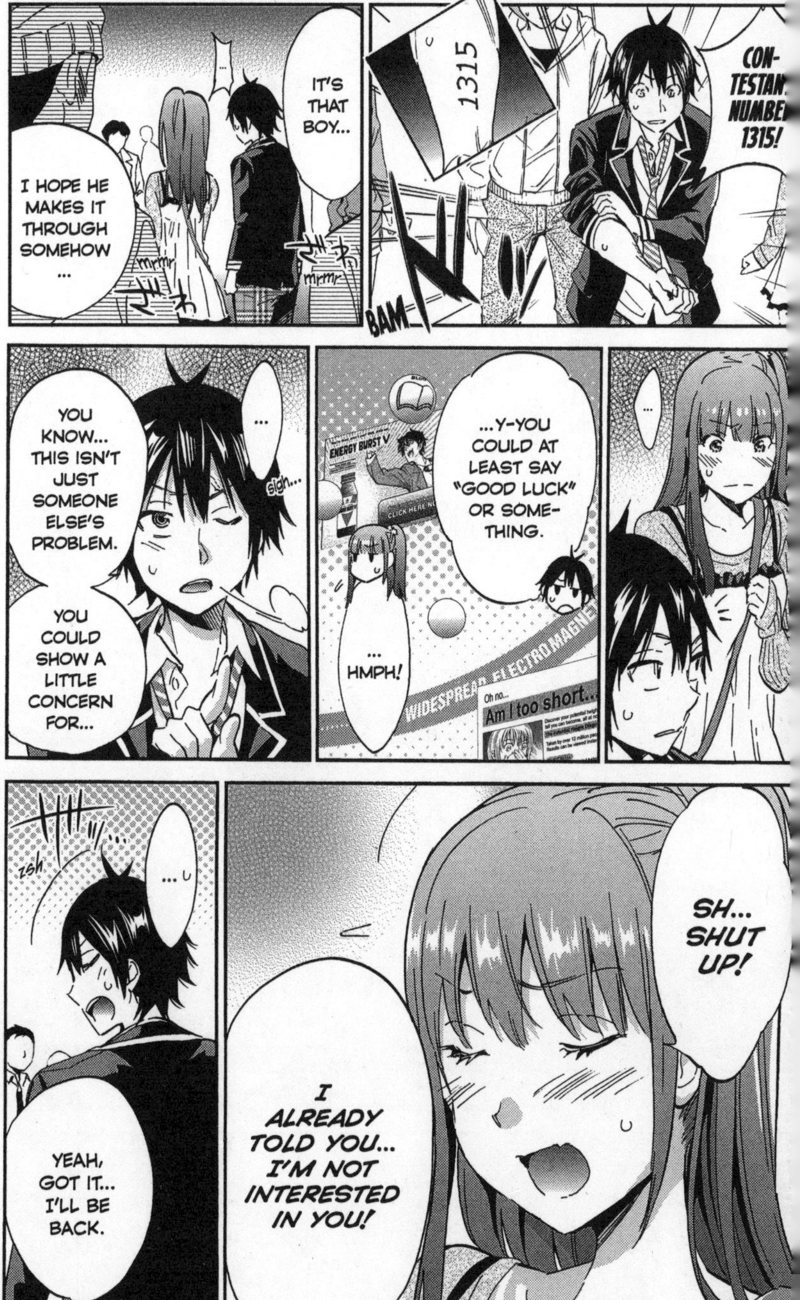
CON-
TESTAN
NUMBE
1315!
1315
BAM
IT'S THAT BOY...
...
I HOPE HE MAKES IT THROUGH SOMEHOW ...
mrmr
mrmr
...
...Y-YOU COULD AT LEAST SAY "GOOD LUCK" OR SOME-THING.
ENERGY BURST V
CLICK HERE N
... HMPH!
WIDESPREAD ELECTROMAGNE
Oh no...
Am I too short...
...
YOU KNOW... THIS ISN'T JUST SOMEONE ELSE'S PROBLEM.
sigh...
YOU COULD SHOW A LITTLE CONCERN FOR...
SH... SHUT UP!
I ALREADY TOLD YOU... I'M NOT INTERESTED IN YOU!
zsh
...
YEAH, GOT IT... I'LL BE BACK.

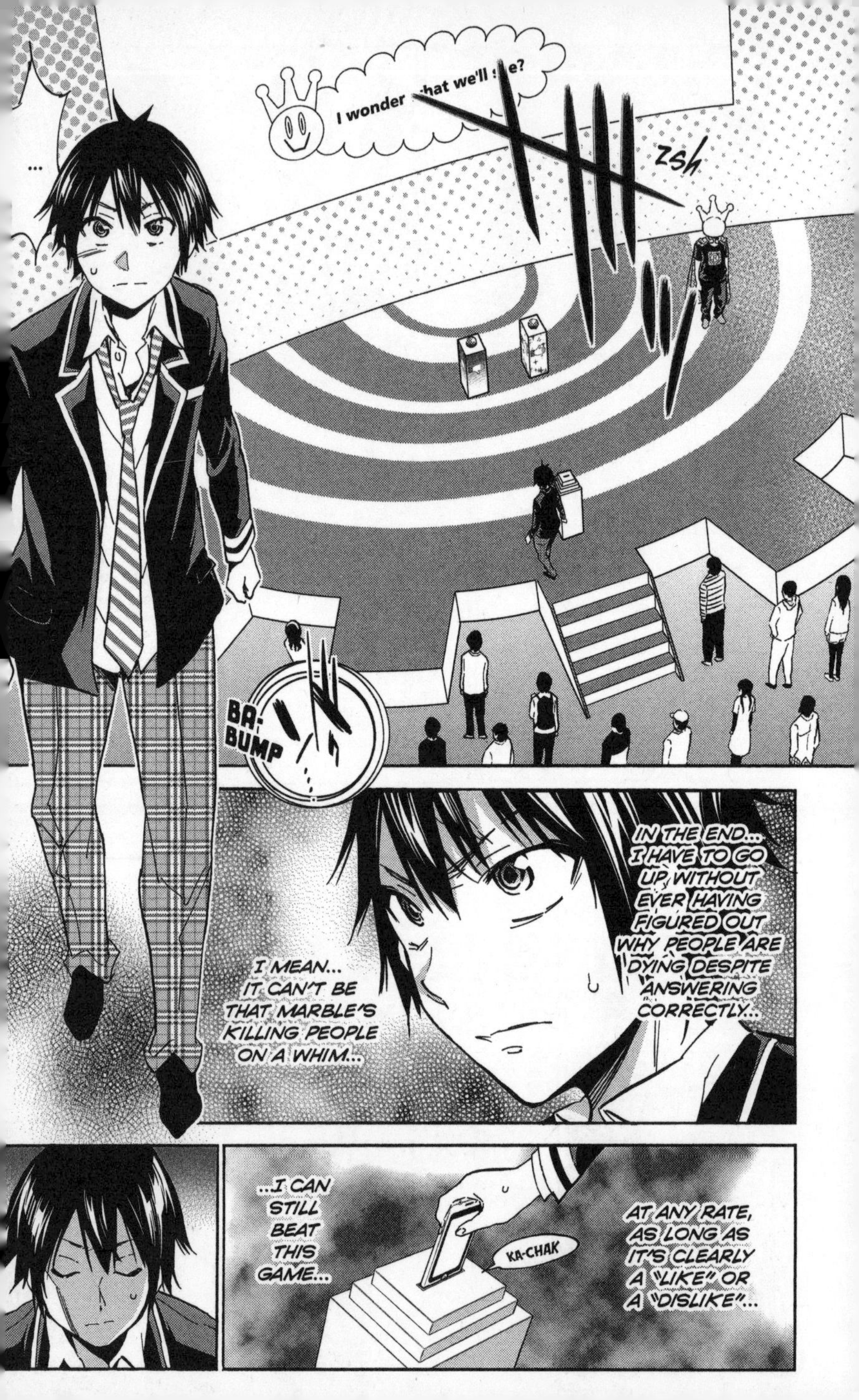

I wonder what we'll see?
ZSH
...
BA-BUMP
IN THE END... I HAVE TO GO UP WITHOUT EVER HAVING FIGURED OUT WHY PEOPLE ARE DYING DESPITE ANSWERING CORRECTLY...
I MEAN... IT CAN'T BE THAT MARBLE'S KILLING PEOPLE ON A WHIM...
AT ANY RATE, AS LONG AS IT'S CLEARLY A "LIKE" OR A "DISLIKE"...
KA-CHAK
...I CAN STILL BEAT THIS GAME...

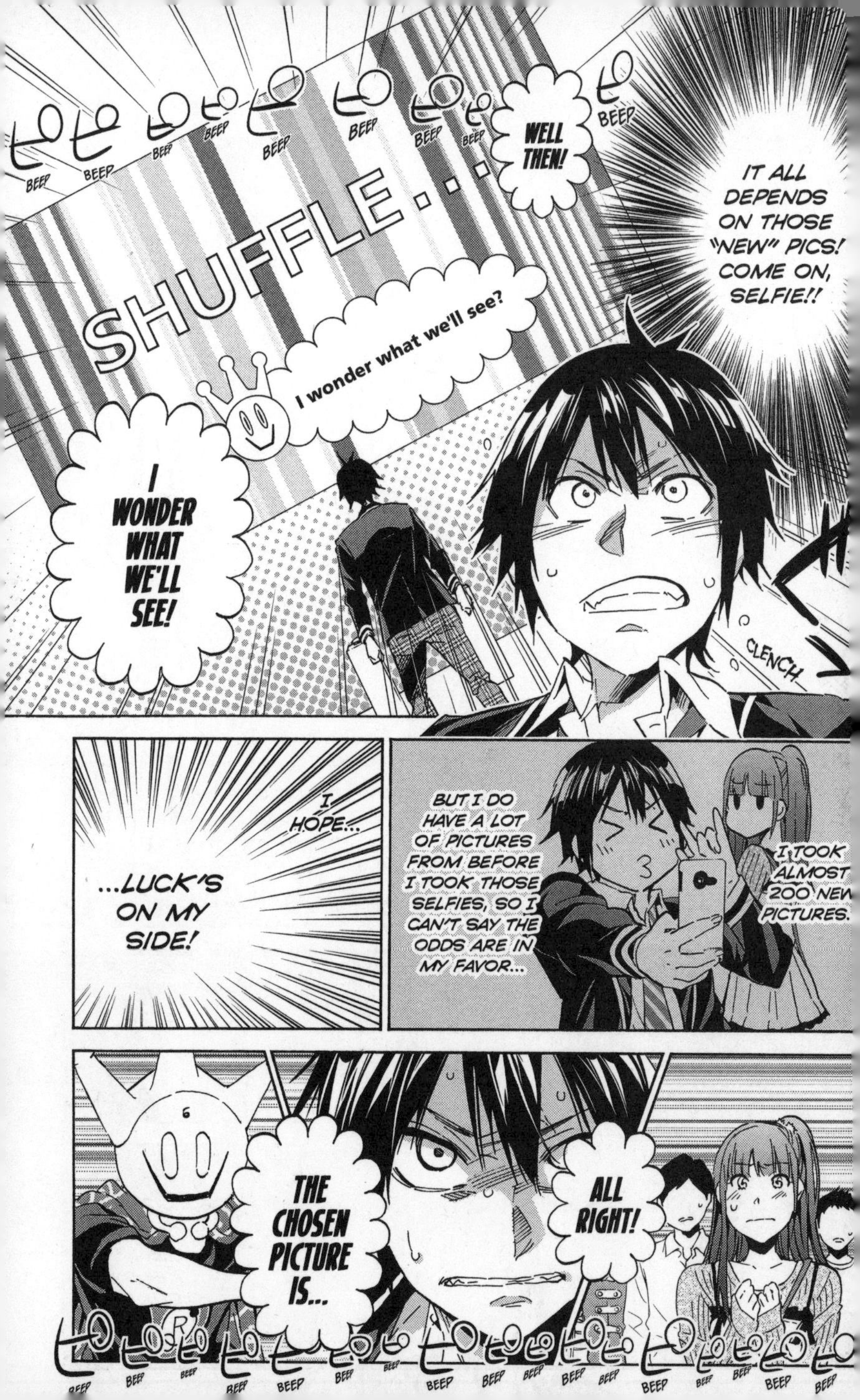
IT ALL DEPENDS ON THOSE "NEW" PICS! COME ON, SELFIE!!
BEEP
WELL THEN!
BEEP BEEP BEEP BEEP BEEP BEEP BEEP BEEP
SHUFFLE...
I wonder what we'll see?
I WONDER WHAT WE'LL SEE!
CLENCH
I TOOK ALMOST 200 NEW PICTURES.
BUT I DO HAVE A LOT OF PICTURES FROM BEFORE I TOOK THOSE SELFIES, SO I CAN'T SAY THE ODDS ARE IN MY FAVOR...
I HOPE...
...LUCK'S ON MY SIDE!
ALL RIGHT!
THE CHOSEN PICTURE IS...
BEEP BEEP BEEP BEEP BEEP BEEP BEEP BEEP BEEP BEEP BEEP BEEP BEEP BEEP BEEP BEEP

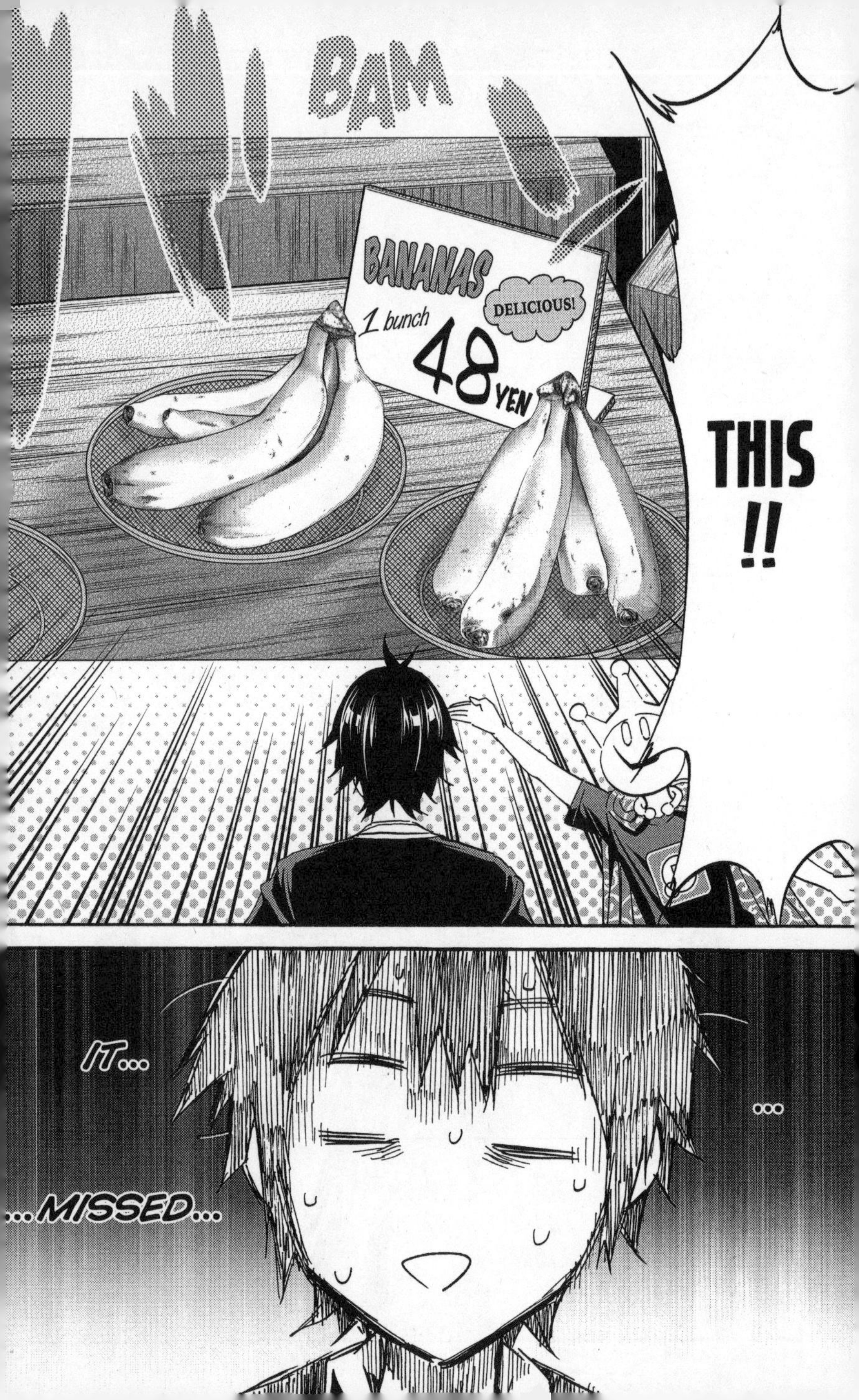

THIS!!
BAM
BANANAS
DELICIOUS!
1 bunch 48 YEN
...
IT...
...MISSED...

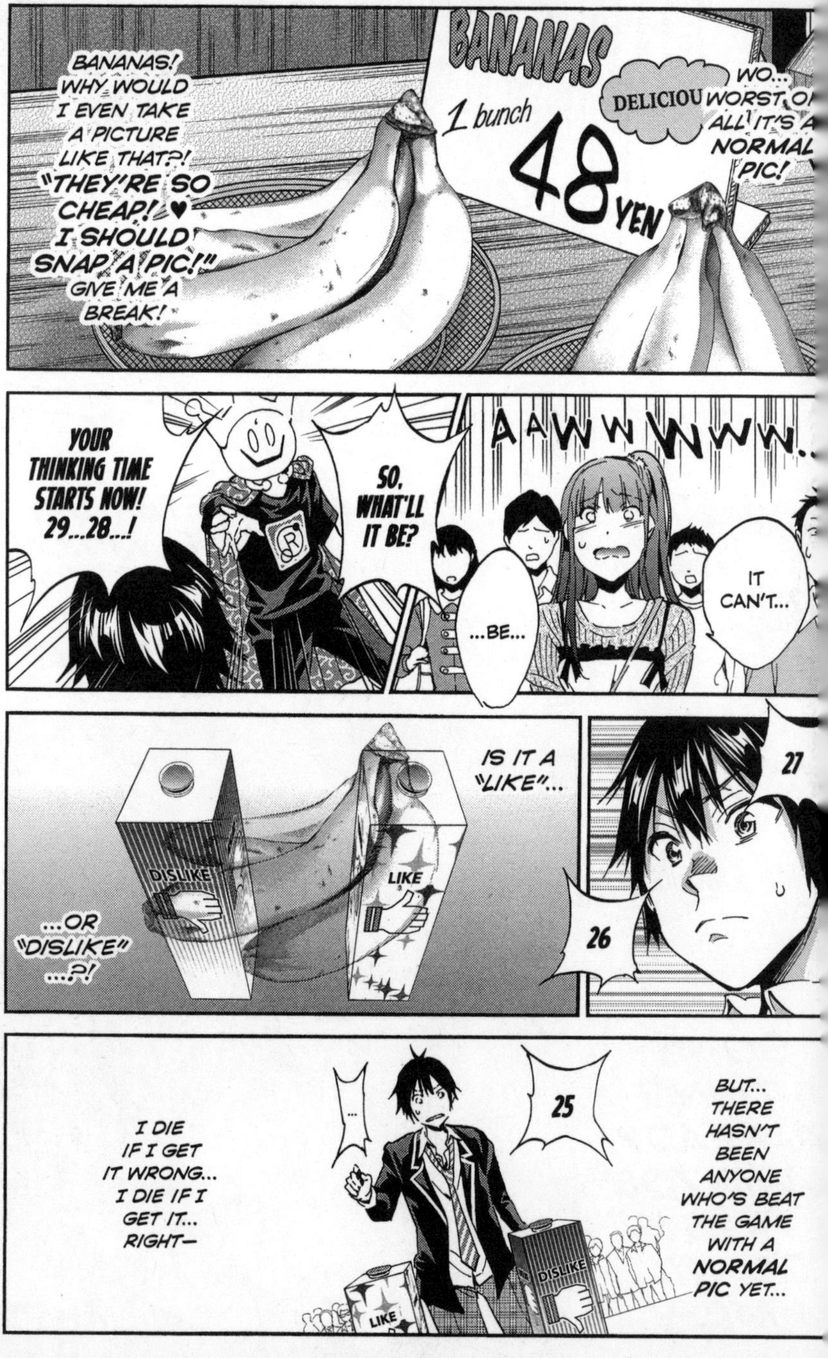
BANANAS
1 bunch
48 YEN
DELICIOU
WO... WORST O ALL IT'S A NORMAL PIC!
BANANAS! WHY WOULD I EVEN TAKE A PICTURE LIKE THAT?! "THEY'RE SO CHEAP! ♥ I SHOULD SNAP A PIC!" GIVE ME A BREAK!
AAWWWWWW...
IT CAN'T...
...BE...
SO, WHAT'LL IT BE?
YOUR THINKING TIME STARTS NOW! 29...28...!
27
26
IS IT A "LIKE"...
DISLIKE
LIKE
...OR "DISLIKE" ...?!
BUT... THERE HASN'T BEEN ANYONE WHO'S BEAT THE GAME WITH A NORMAL PIC YET...
25
...
I DIE IF I GET IT WRONG... I DIE IF I GET IT... RIGHT—
DISLIKE
LIKE

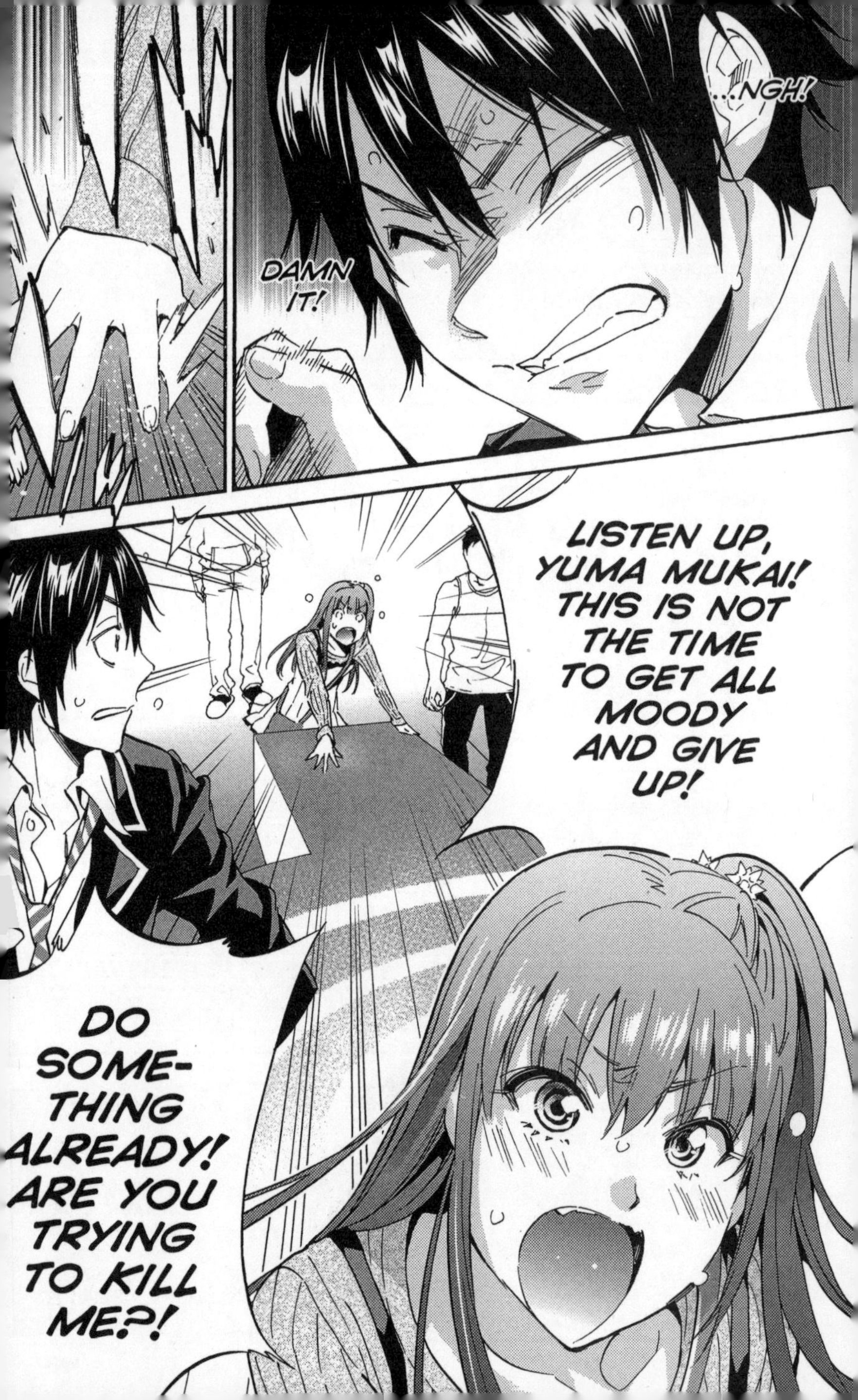
...NGH!
DAMN IT!
LISTEN UP, YUMA MUKAI! THIS IS NOT THE TIME TO GET ALL MOODY AND GIVE UP!
DO SOME-THING ALREADY! ARE YOU TRYING TO KILL ME?!

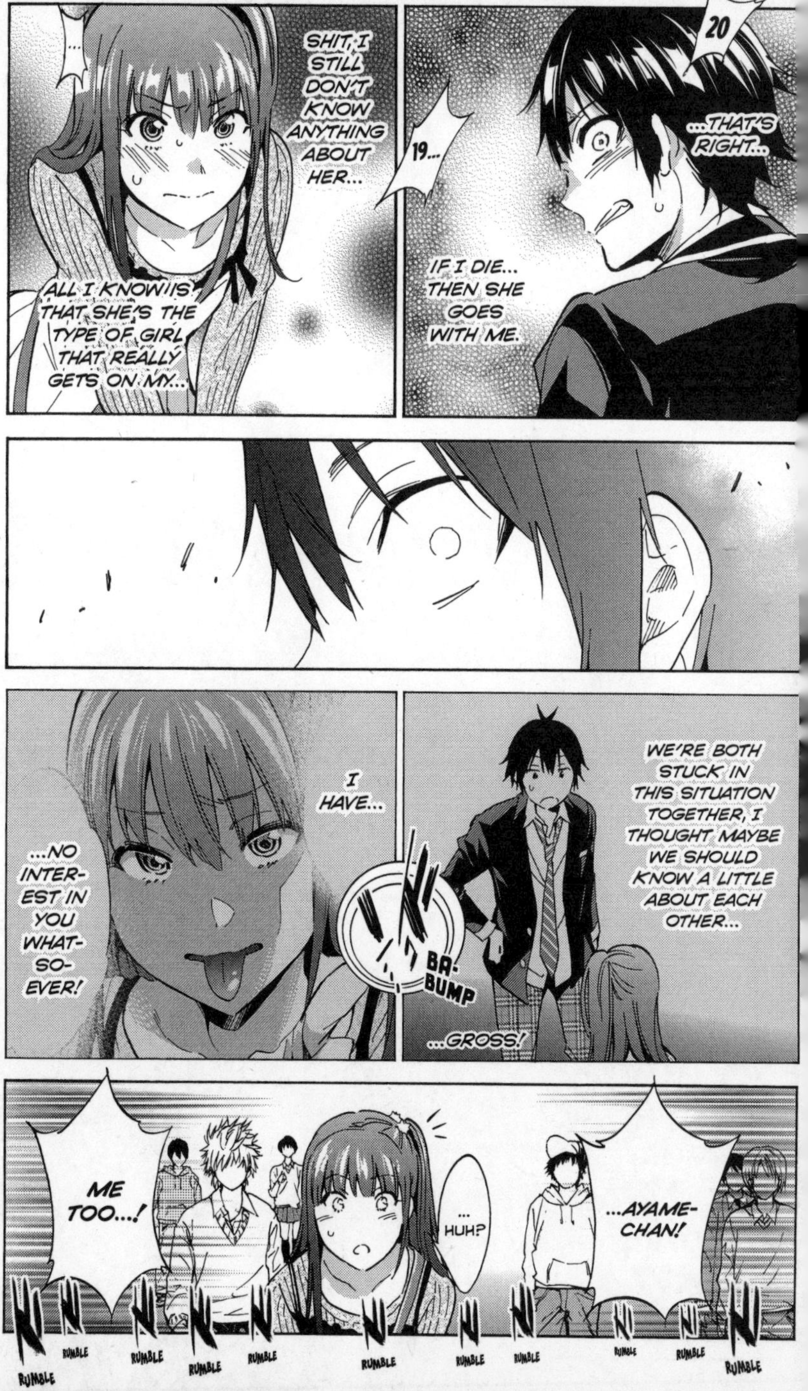
20
...THAT'S RIGHT...
19...
IF I DIE... THEN SHE GOES WITH ME.
...
SHIT, I STILL DON'T KNOW ANYTHING ABOUT HER...
ALL I KNOW IS THAT SHE'S THE TYPE OF GIRL THAT REALLY GETS ON MY...
WE'RE BOTH STUCK IN THIS SITUATION TOGETHER, I THOUGHT MAYBE WE SHOULD KNOW A LITTLE ABOUT EACH OTHER...
BA-BUMP
...GROSS!
I HAVE...
...NO INTER-EST IN YOU WHAT-SO-EVER!
...AYAME-CHAN!
... HUH?
ME TOO...!
RUMBLE RUMBLE RUMBLE RUMBLE RUMBLE RUMBLE RUMBLE RUMBLE RUMBLE RUMBLE RUMBLE RUMBLE

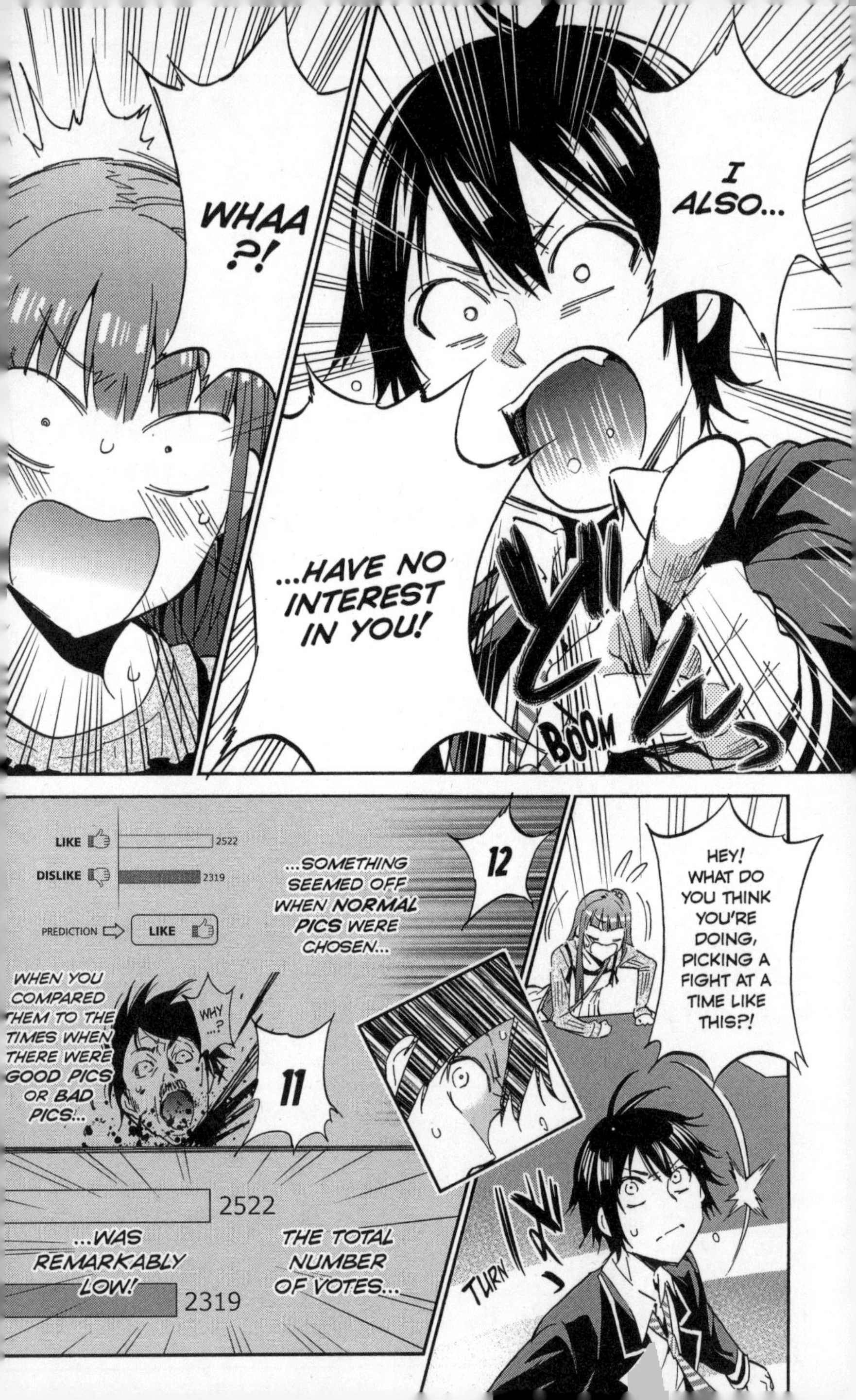
I ALSO...
...HAVE NO INTEREST IN YOU!
BOOM
WHAA ?!
HEY! WHAT DO YOU THINK YOU'RE DOING, PICKING A FIGHT AT A TIME LIKE THIS?!
TURN
12
LIKE 2522
DISLIKE 2319
PREDICTION LIKE
...SOMETHING SEEMED OFF WHEN NORMAL PICS WERE CHOSEN...
WHEN YOU COMPARED THEM TO THE TIMES WHEN THERE WERE GOOD PICS OR BAD PICS...
WHY ...?
11
THE TOTAL NUMBER OF VOTES...
...WAS REMARKABLY LOW!
2522
2319

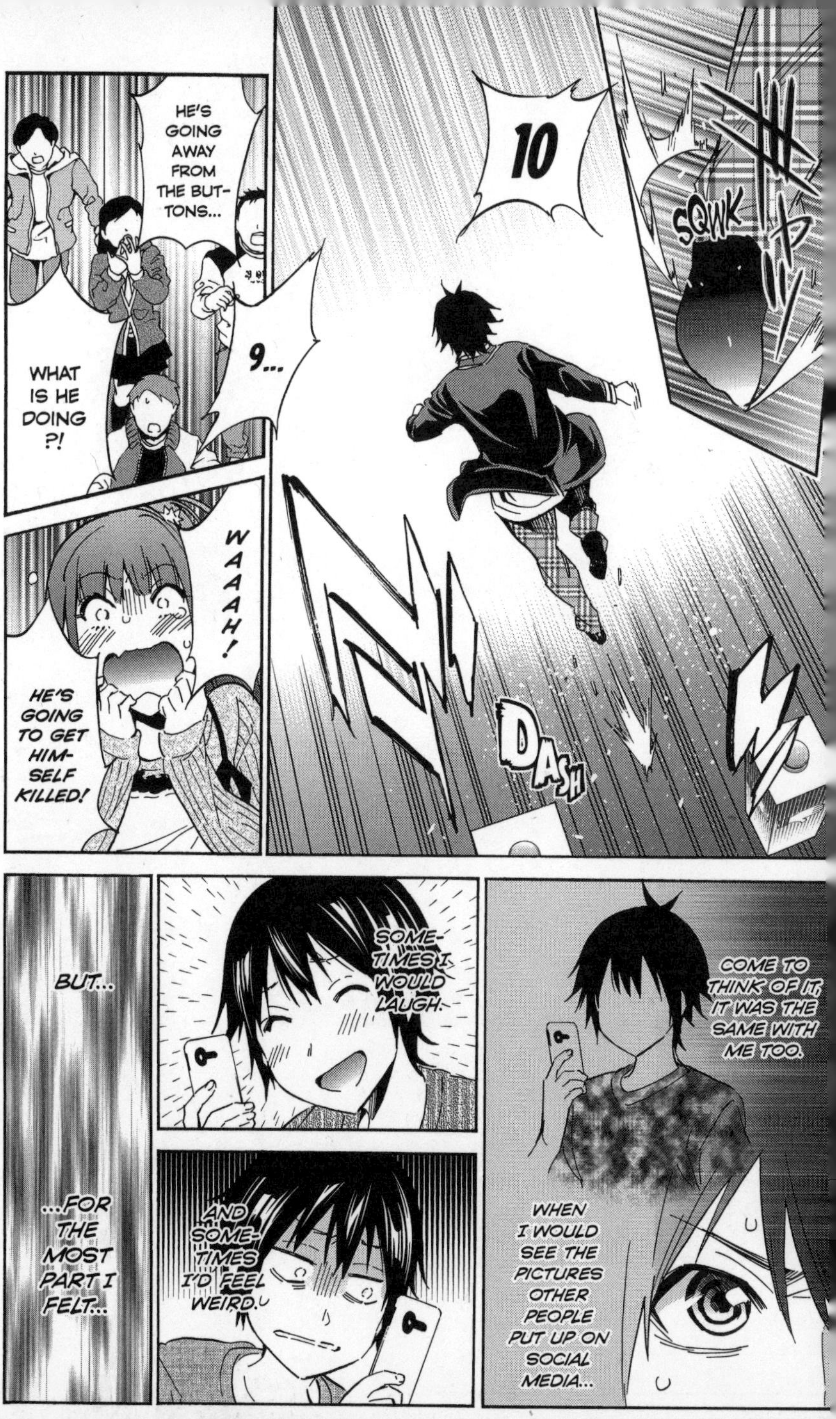
SQWK
10
DASH
9...
HE'S GOING AWAY FROM THE BUT-TONS...
WHAT IS HE DOING ?!
WAAAAH!
HE'S GOING TO GET HIM-SELF KILLED!
COME TO THINK OF IT, IT WAS THE SAME WITH ME TOO.
WHEN I WOULD SEE THE PICTURES OTHER PEOPLE PUT UP ON SOCIAL MEDIA...
SOME-TIMES I WOULD LAUGH.
AND SOME-TIMES I'D FEEL WEIRD.
BUT...
...FOR THE MOST PART I FELT...

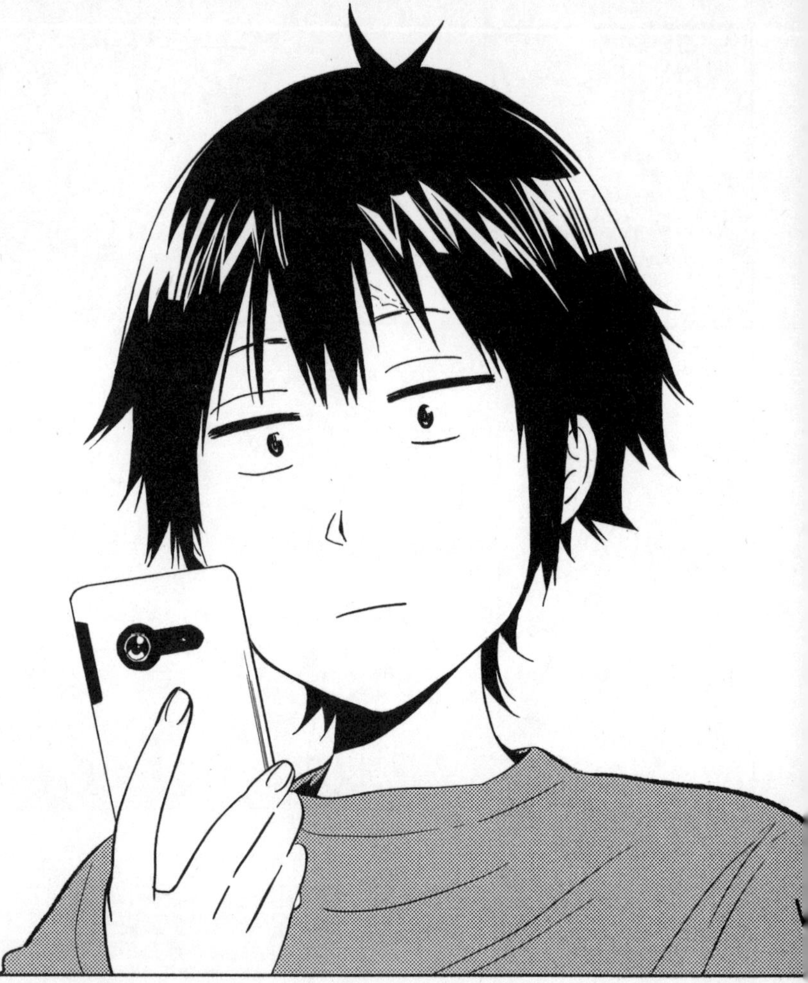

NOTHING.

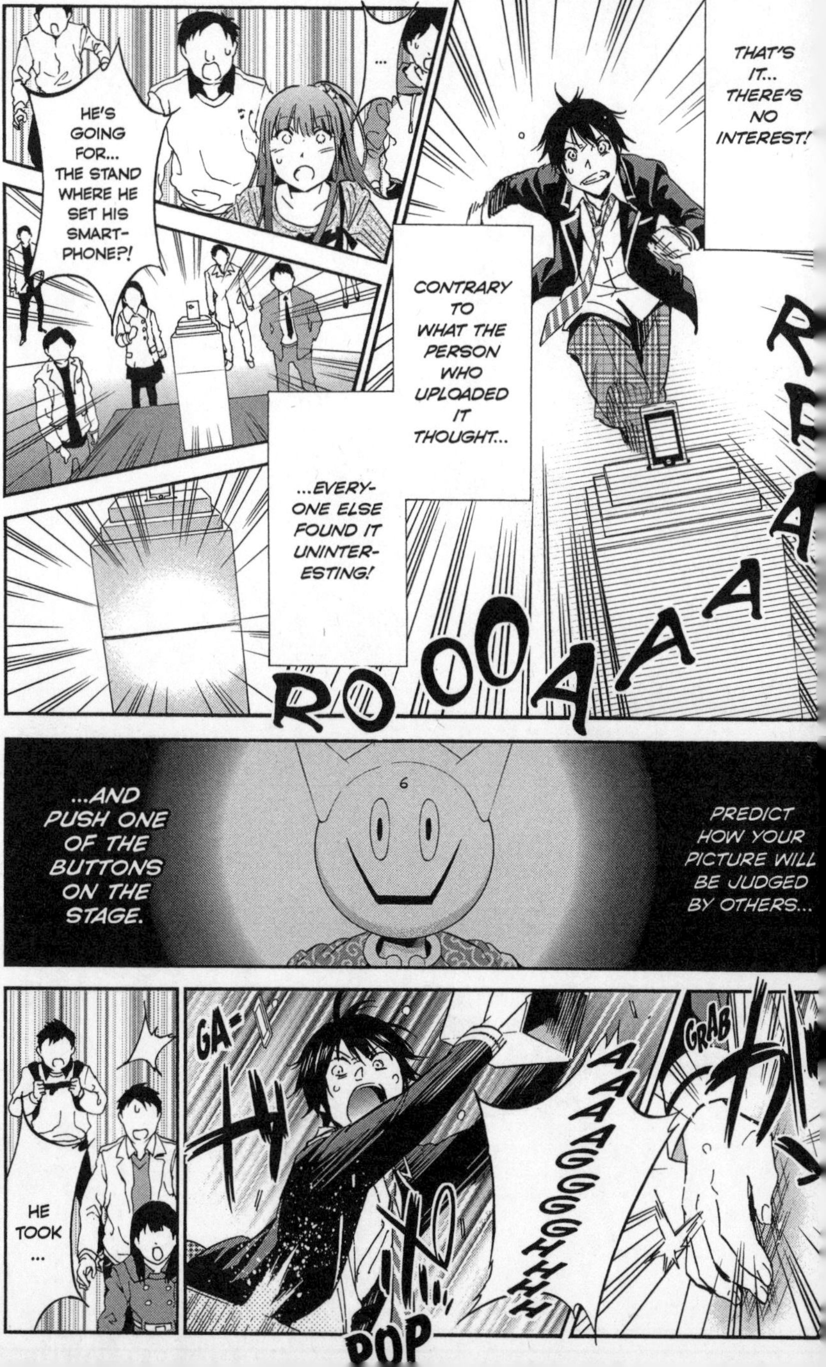

THAT'S IT... THERE'S NO INTEREST!
CONTRARY TO WHAT THE PERSON WHO UPLOADED IT THOUGHT...
...EVERYONE ELSE FOUND IT UNINTERESTING!
ROOOOAAAAARR
...
HE'S GOING FOR... THE STAND WHERE HE SET HIS SMARTPHONE?!
PREDICT HOW YOUR PICTURE WILL BE JUDGED BY OTHERS...
6
...AND PUSH ONE OF THE BUTTONS ON THE STAGE.
GRAB
AAAAAGGGGHHHH
GA-
POP
HE TOOK ...

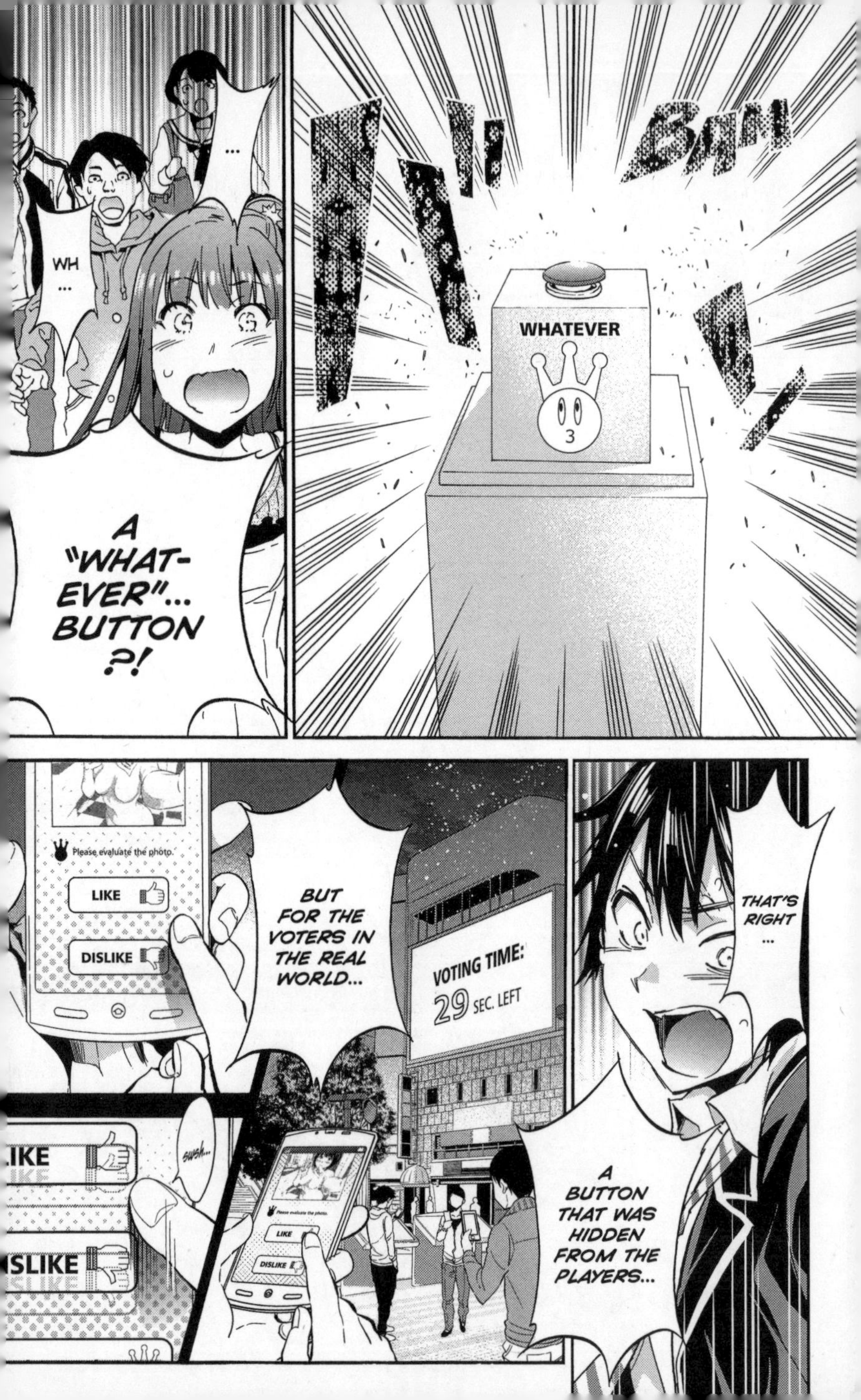
BAM
WHATEVER
3
...
WH ...
A "WHAT-EVER"... BUTTON ?!
THAT'S RIGHT ...
A BUTTON THAT WAS HIDDEN FROM THE PLAYERS...
BUT FOR THE VOTERS IN THE REAL WORLD...
Please evaluate the photo.
LIKE
DISLIKE
VOTING TIME:
29 SEC. LEFT
LIKE
DISLIKE
Please evaluate the photo.
LIKE
DISLIKE

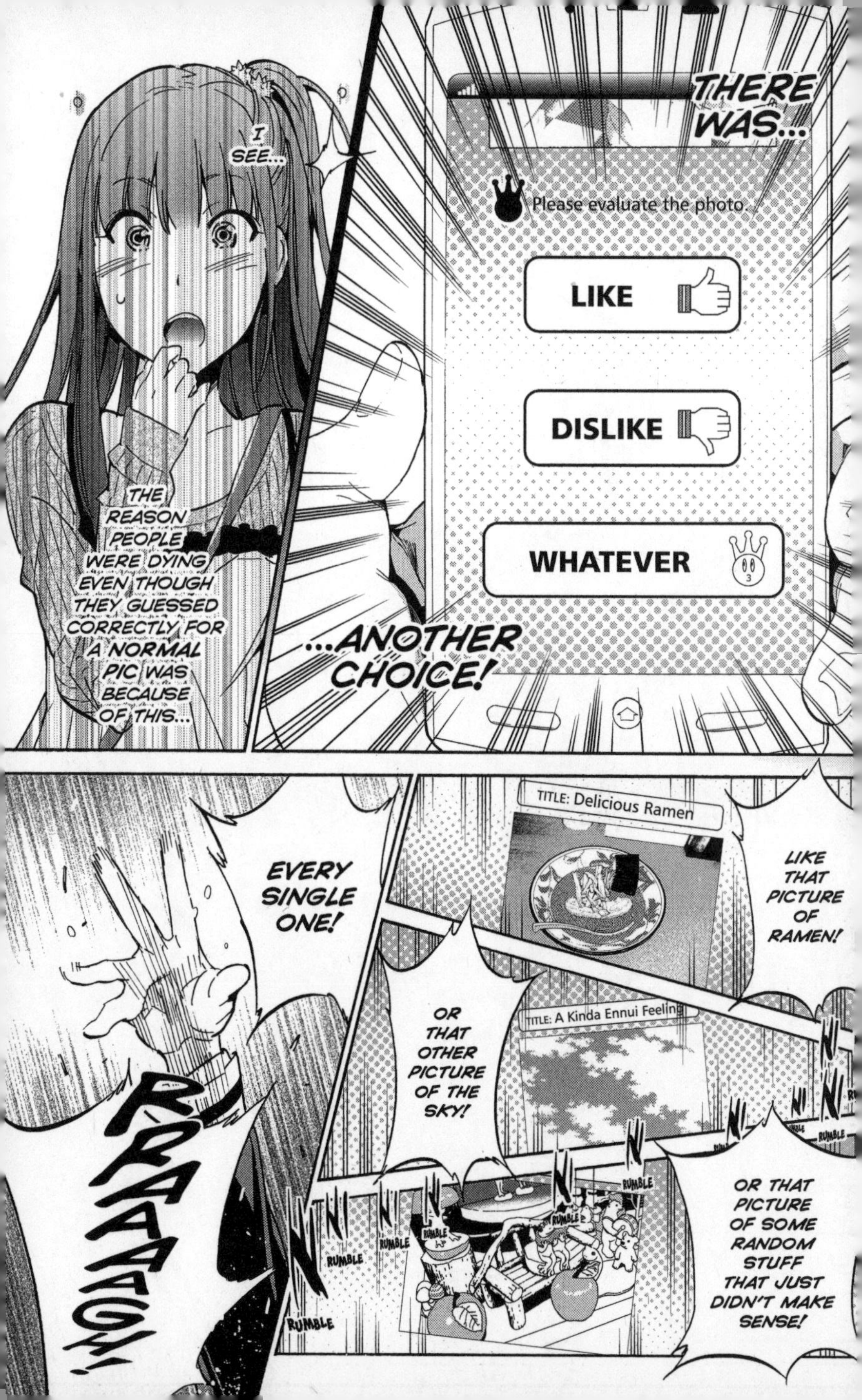
THERE WAS...
Please evaluate the photo.
LIKE
DISLIKE
WHATEVER
...ANOTHER CHOICE!
I SEE...
THE REASON PEOPLE WERE DYING EVEN THOUGH THEY GUESSED CORRECTLY FOR A NORMAL PIC WAS BECAUSE OF THIS...
TITLE: Delicious Ramen
LIKE THAT PICTURE OF RAMEN!
TITLE: A Kinda Ennui Feeling
OR THAT OTHER PICTURE OF THE SKY!
RUMBLE
OR THAT PICTURE OF SOME RANDOM STUFF THAT JUST DIDN'T MAKE SENSE!
EVERY SINGLE ONE!
RRAAAAGH!

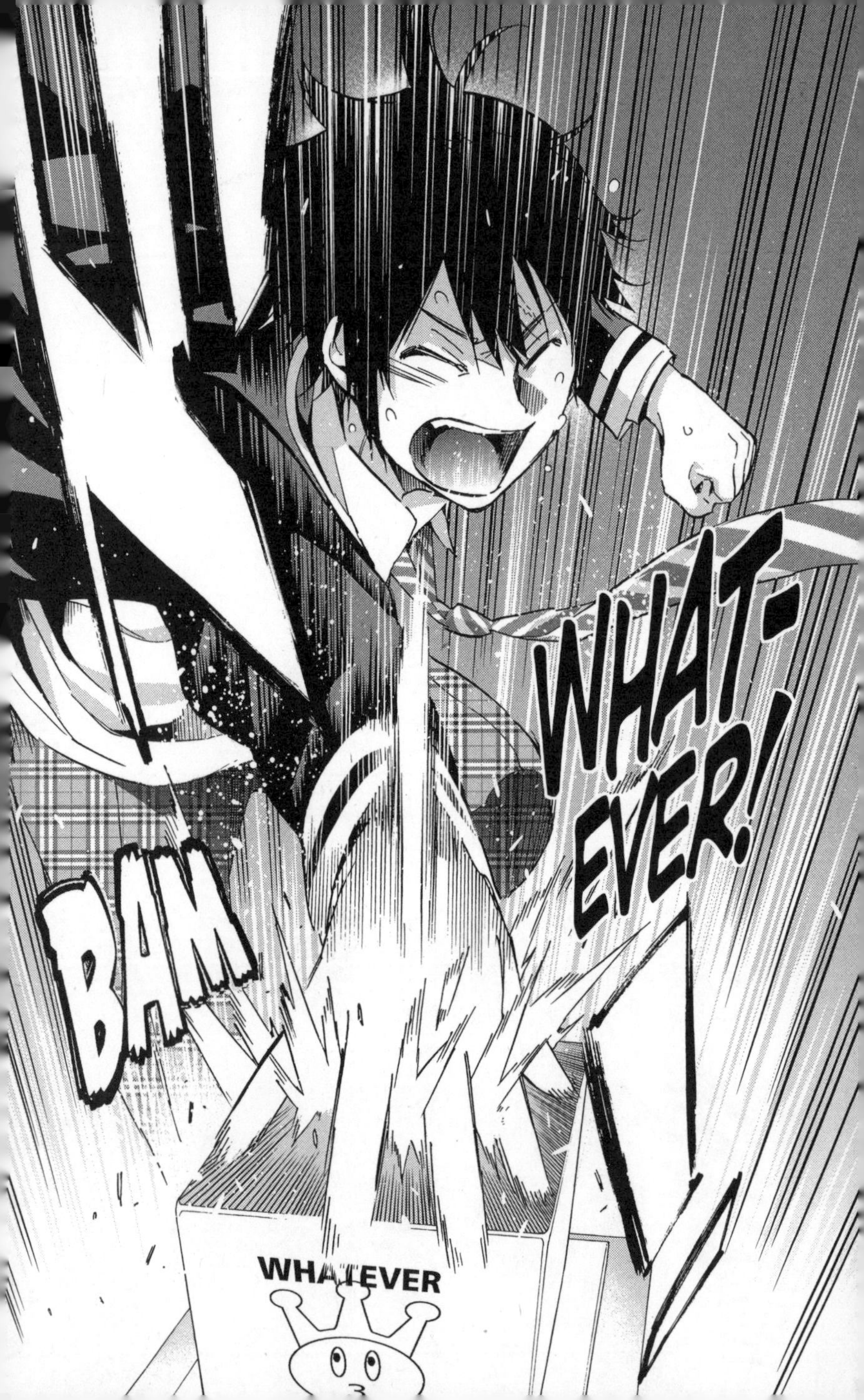
WHAT-EVER!
BAM
WHATEVER

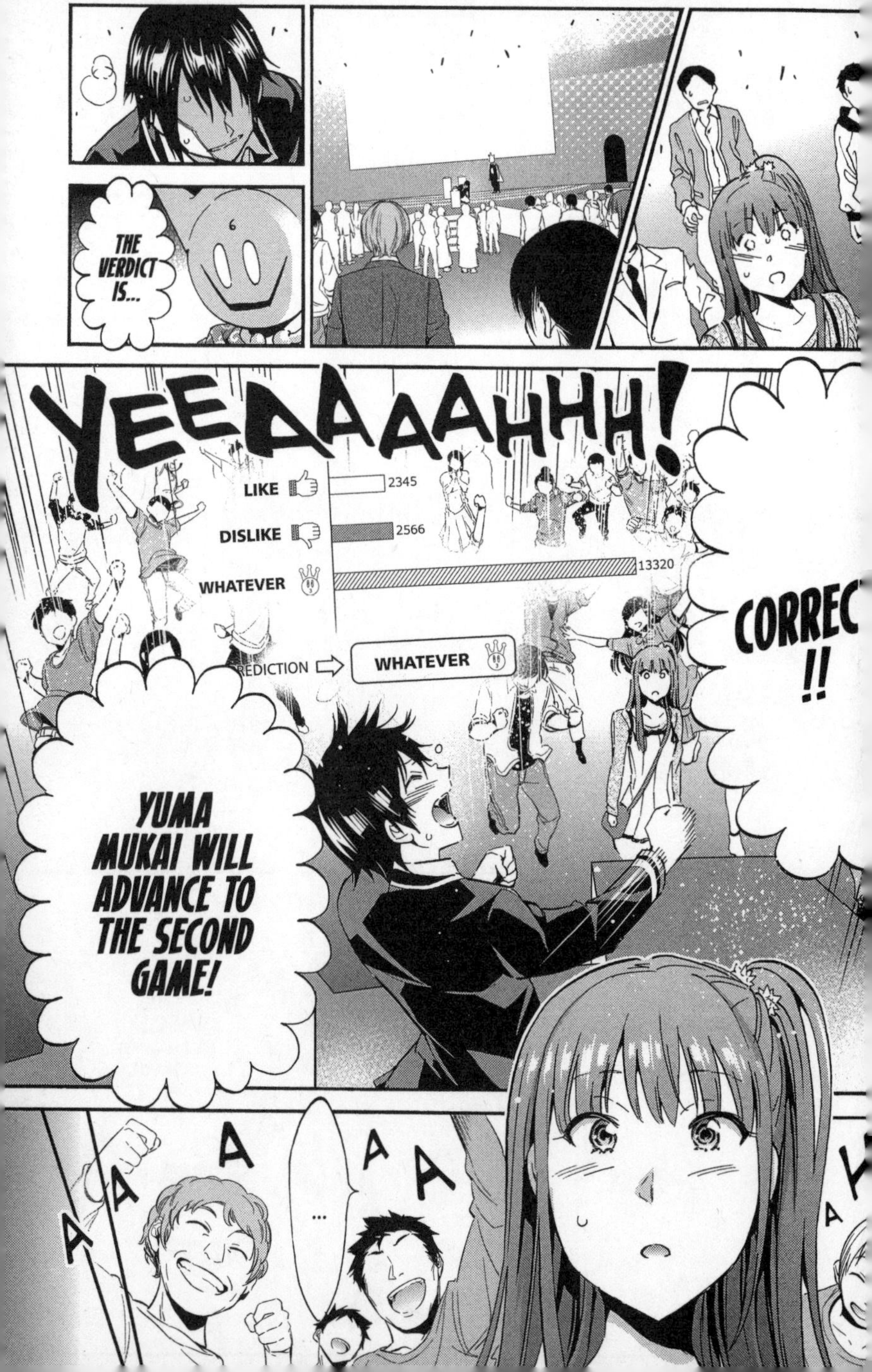
THE VERDICT IS...
YEEAAAAHHH!
CORREC !!
LIKE 2345
DISLIKE 2566
WHATEVER 13320
REDICTION ⇨ WHATEVER
YUMA MUKAI WILL ADVANCE TO THE SECOND GAME!
A A A A A A A
...

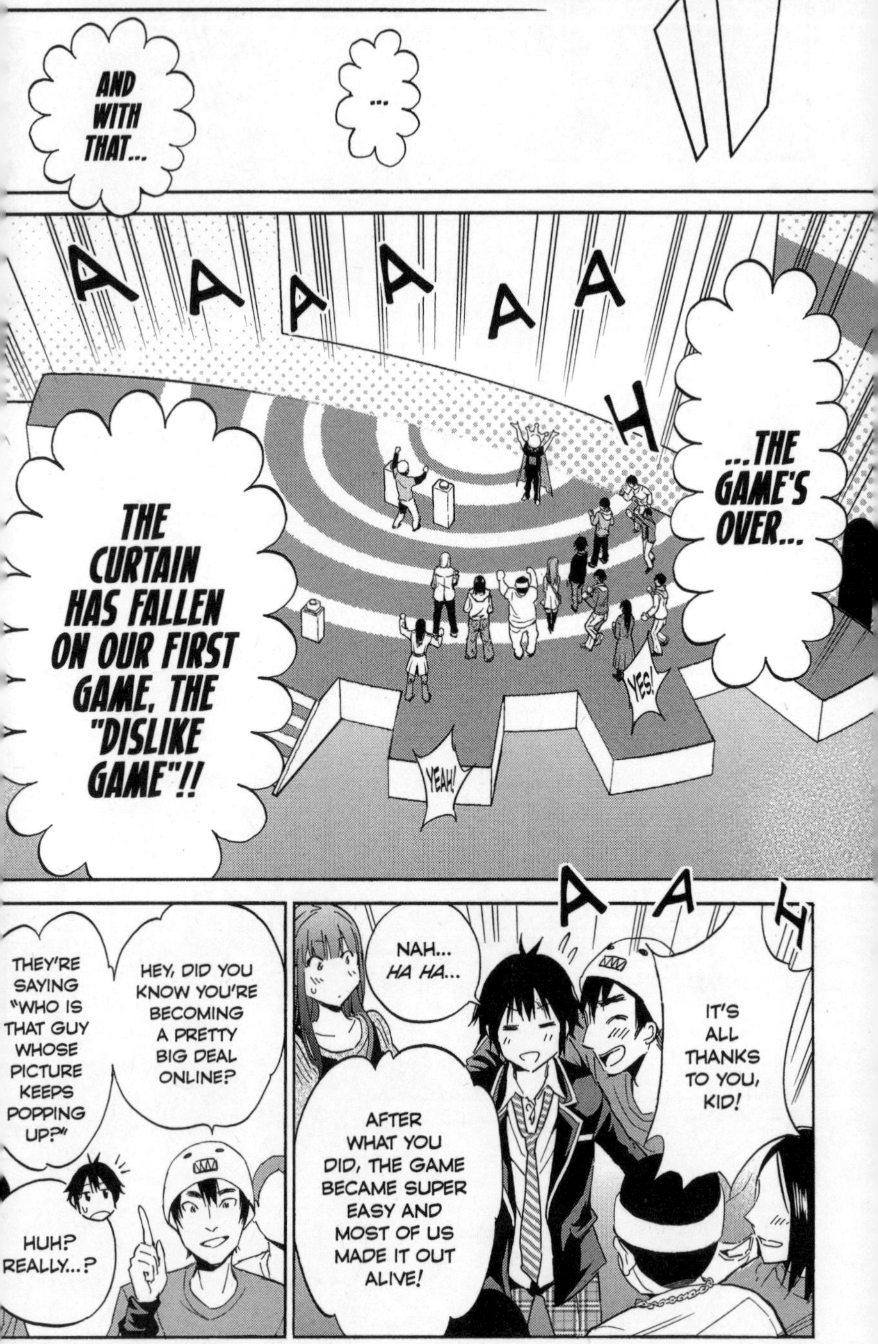
...
AND WITH THAT...
AAAAAAAH
...THE GAME'S OVER...
THE CURTAIN HAS FALLEN ON OUR FIRST GAME, THE "DISLIKE GAME"!!
YES!
YEAH!
AAAH
IT'S ALL THANKS TO YOU, KID!
AFTER WHAT YOU DID, THE GAME BECAME SUPER EASY AND MOST OF US MADE IT OUT ALIVE!
NAH... HA HA...
HEY, DID YOU KNOW YOU'RE BECOMING A PRETTY BIG DEAL ONLINE?
THEY'RE SAYING "WHO IS THAT GUY WHOSE PICTURE KEEPS POPPING UP?"
HUH? REALLY...?

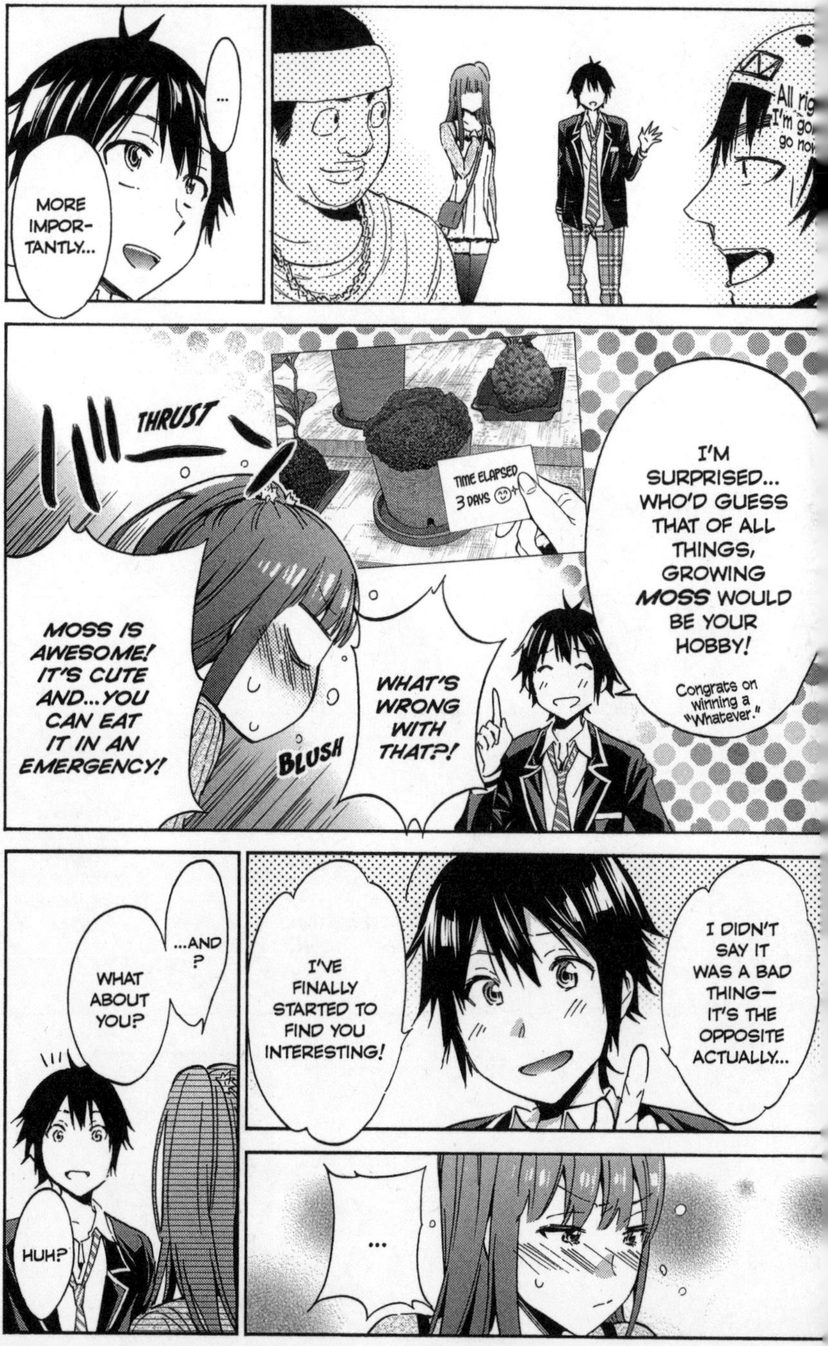
All rig
I'm go
go now
...
MORE IMPORTANTLY...
I'M SURPRISED... WHO'D GUESS THAT OF ALL THINGS, GROWING MOSS WOULD BE YOUR HOBBY!
Congrats on winning a "Whatever."
TIME ELAPSED 3 DAYS
THRUST
WHAT'S WRONG WITH THAT?!
MOSS IS AWESOME! IT'S CUTE AND...YOU CAN EAT IT IN AN EMERGENCY!
BLUSH
I DIDN'T SAY IT WAS A BAD THING— IT'S THE OPPOSITE ACTUALLY...
I'VE FINALLY STARTED TO FIND YOU INTERESTING!
...
...AND ?
WHAT ABOUT YOU?
HUH?

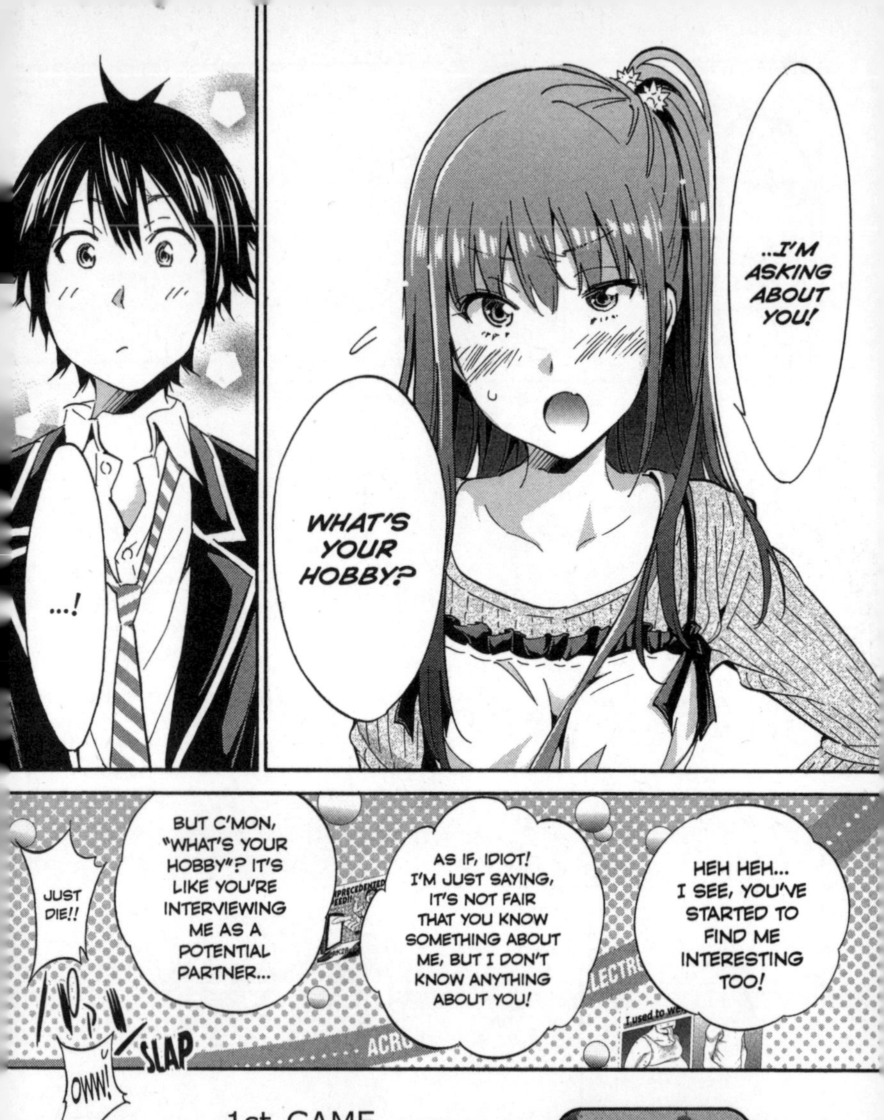
...I'M ASKING ABOUT YOU!
WHAT'S YOUR HOBBY?
...!
HEH HEH... I SEE, YOU'VE STARTED TO FIND ME INTERESTING TOO!
AS IF, IDIOT! I'M JUST SAYING, IT'S NOT FAIR THAT YOU KNOW SOMETHING ABOUT ME, BUT I DON'T KNOW ANYTHING ABOUT YOU!
BUT C'MON, "WHAT'S YOUR HOBBY"? IT'S LIKE YOU'RE INTERVIEWING ME AS A POTENTIAL PARTNER...
JUST DIE!!
SLAP
OWW!

1st GAME ————

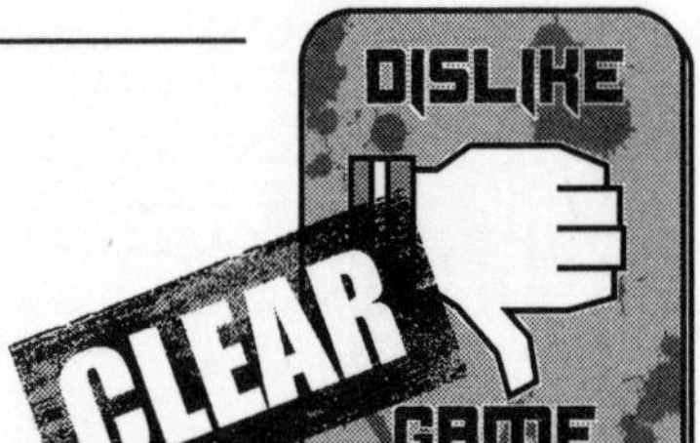
DISLIKE
CLEAR
GAME

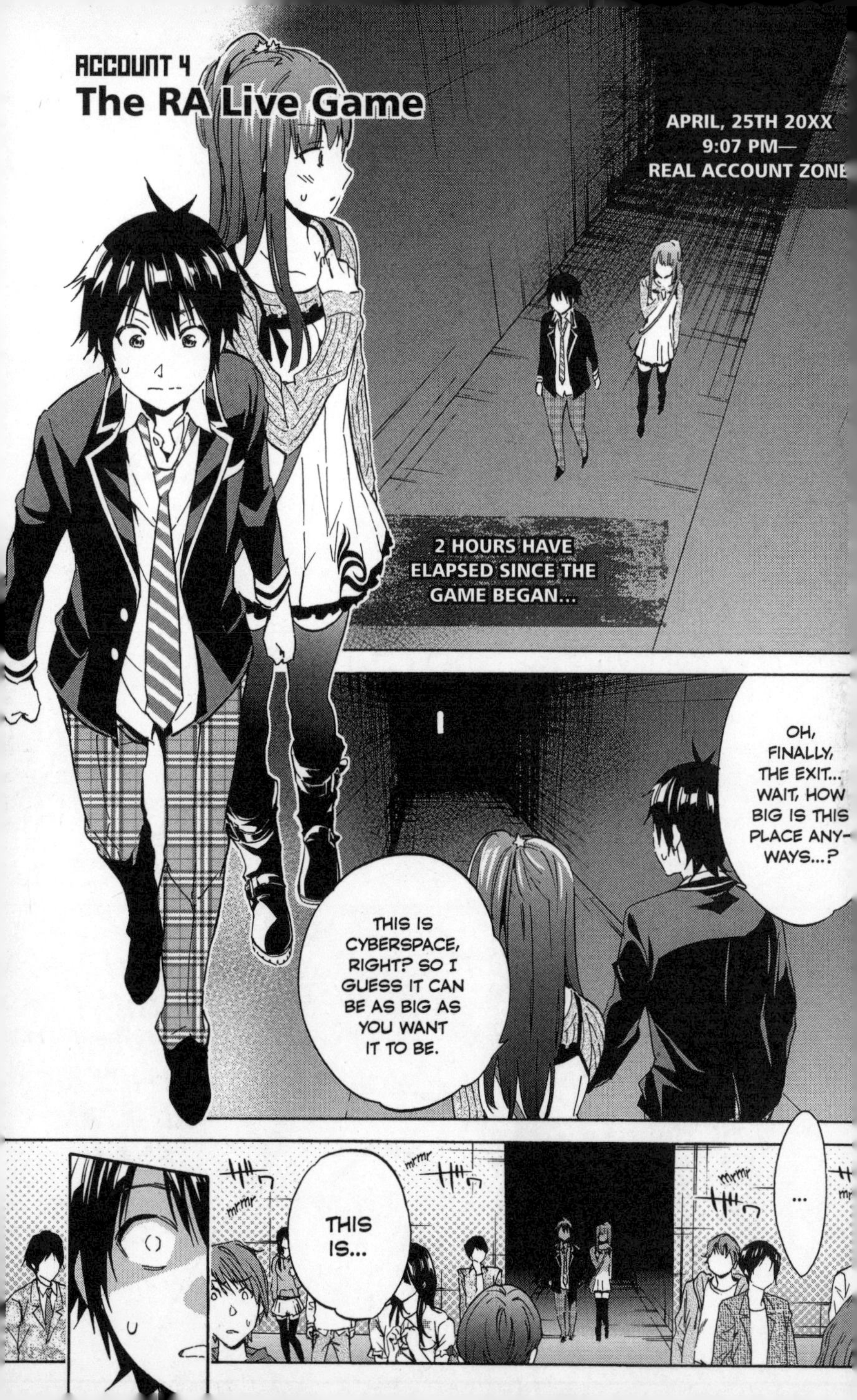
ACCOUNT 4
The RA Live Game
APRIL, 25TH 20XX 9:07 PM— REAL ACCOUNT ZONE
2 HOURS HAVE ELAPSED SINCE THE GAME BEGAN...
OH, FINALLY, THE EXIT... WAIT, HOW BIG IS THIS PLACE ANY-WAYS...?
THIS IS CYBERSPACE, RIGHT? SO I GUESS IT CAN BE AS BIG AS YOU WANT IT TO BE.
...
mrmr
THIS IS...

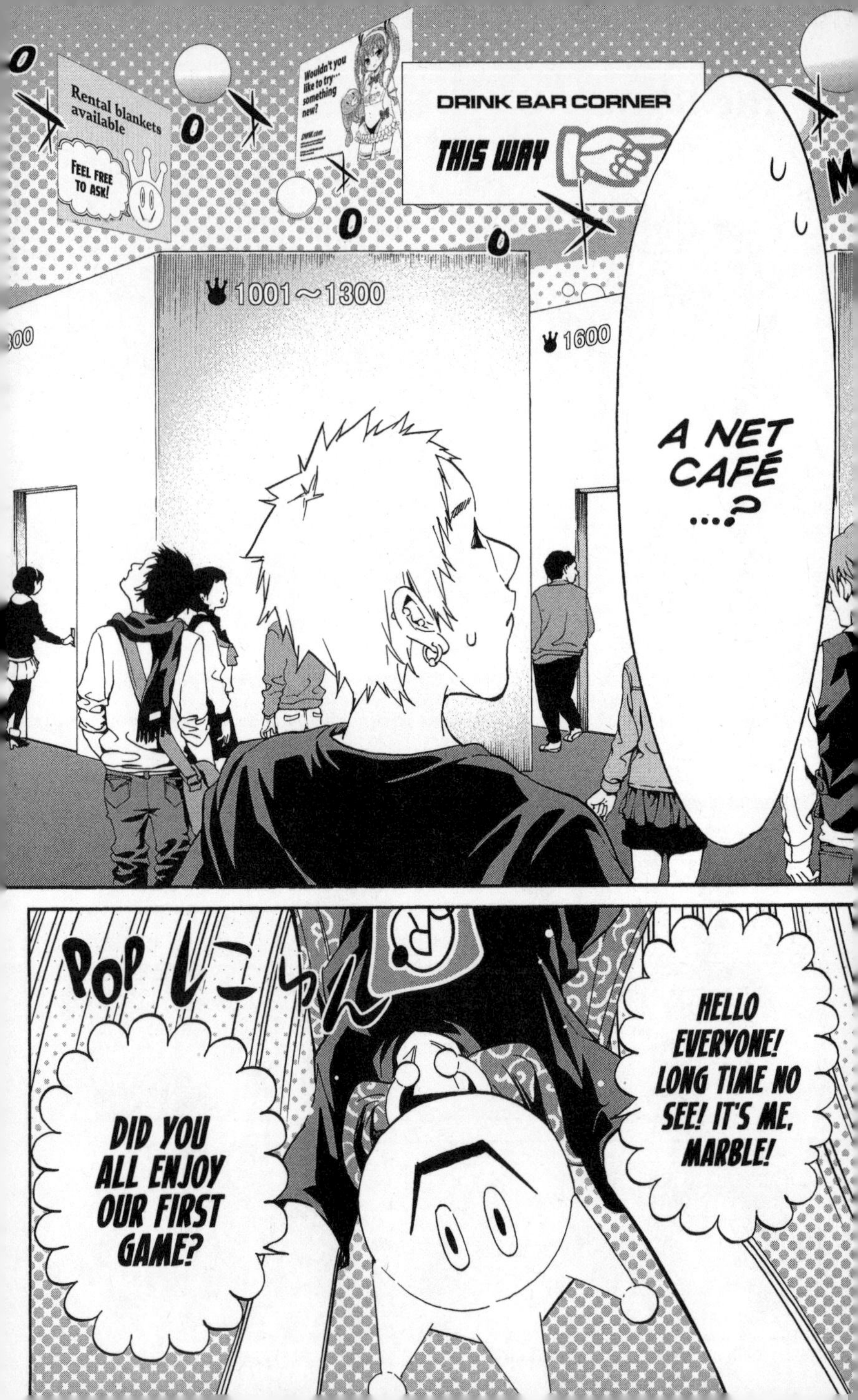
DRINK BAR CORNER
THIS WAY
Wouldn't you like to try… something new?
Rental blankets available
FEEL FREE TO ASK!
A NET CAFÉ …?
1600
1001～1300
HELLO EVERYONE! LONG TIME NO SEE! IT'S ME, MARBLE!
POP
DID YOU ALL ENJOY OUR FIRST GAME?

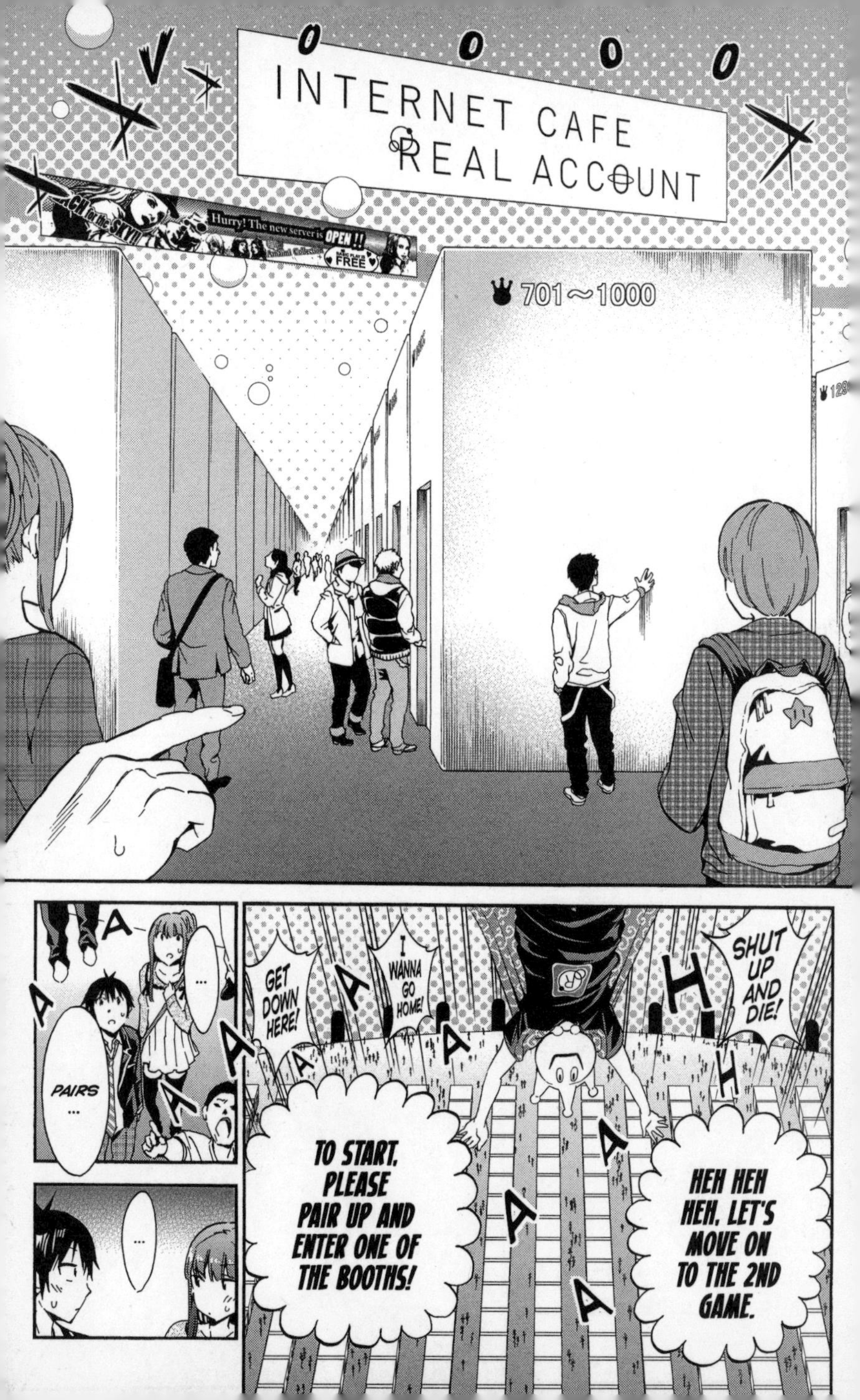

INTERNET CAFE REAL ACCOUNT
Hurry! The new server is OPEN!!
FREE
701～1000
SHUT UP AND DIE!
I WANNA GO HOME!
GET DOWN HERE!
AAAAAAAAHH
HEH HEH HEH. LET'S MOVE ON TO THE 2ND GAME.
TO START. PLEASE PAIR UP AND ENTER ONE OF THE BOOTHS!
...
PAIRS ...
...

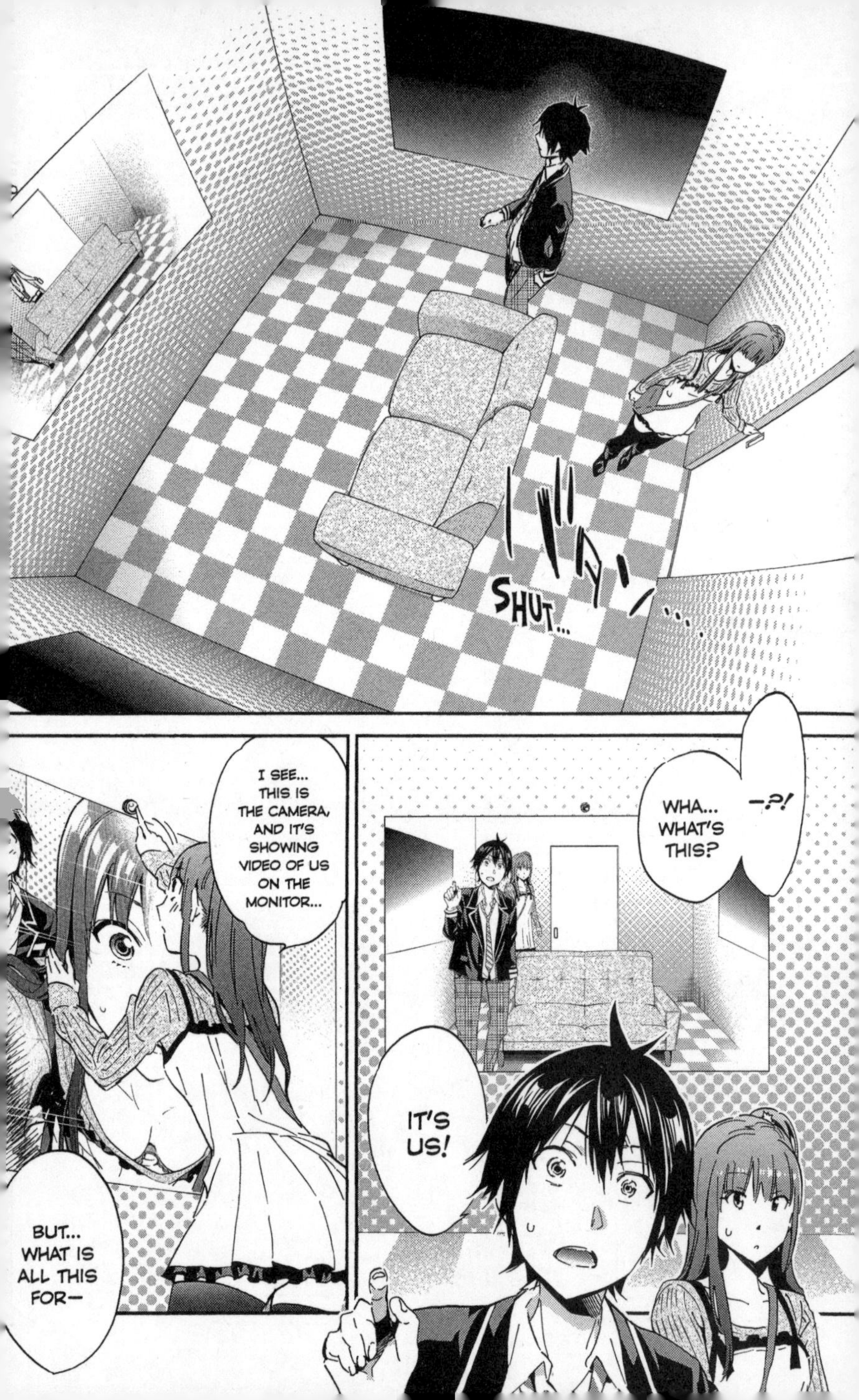
SHUT...
...
—?!
WHA... WHAT'S THIS?
IT'S US!
I SEE... THIS IS THE CAMERA, AND IT'S SHOWING VIDEO OF US ON THE MONITOR...
BUT... WHAT IS ALL THIS FOR—

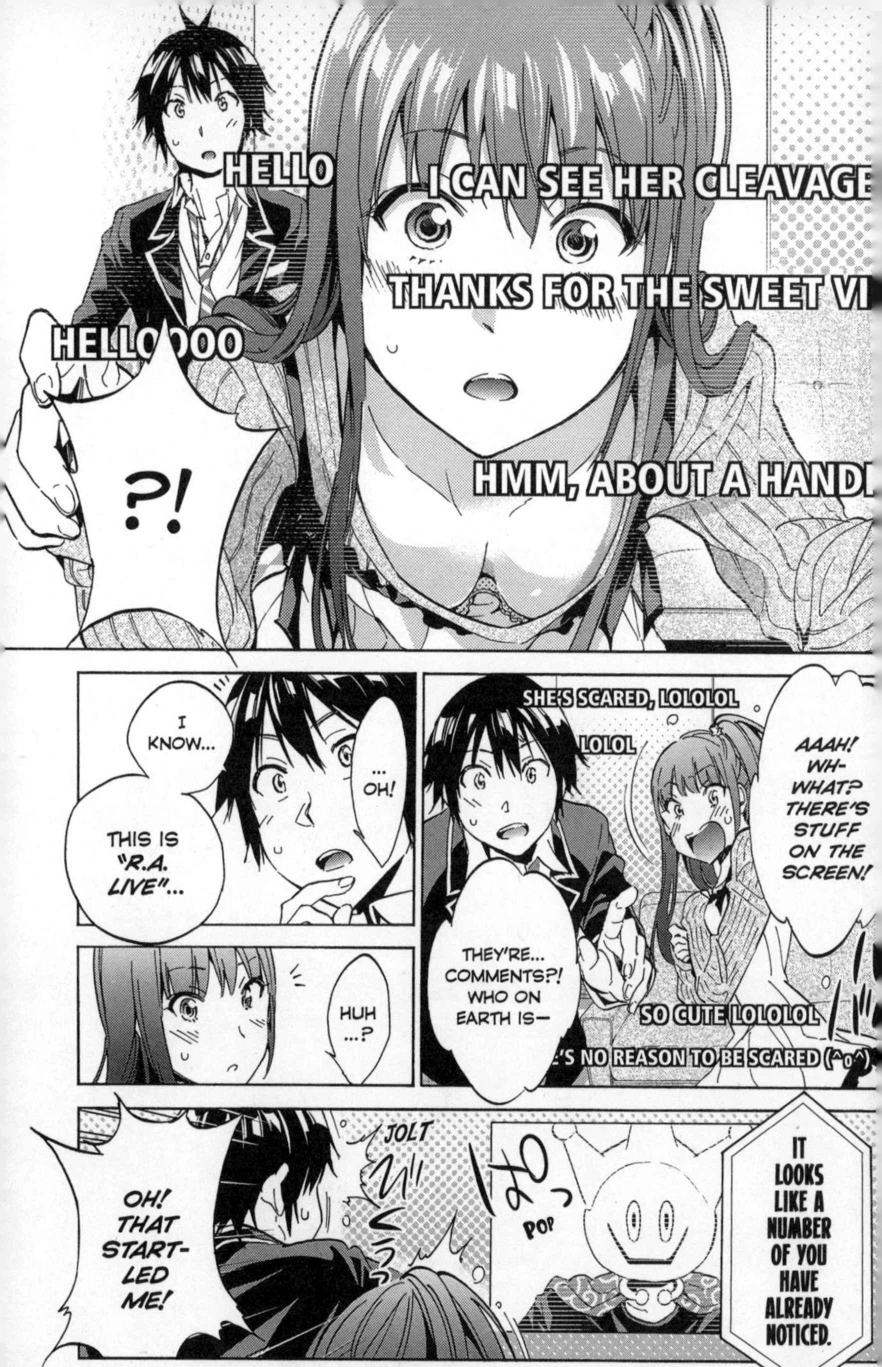
I CAN SEE HER CLEAVAGE
HELLO
THANKS FOR THE SWEET VI
HELLOOOO
HMM, ABOUT A HAND
?!
AAAH! WH-WHAT? THERE'S STUFF ON THE SCREEN!
SHE'S SCARED, LOLOLOL
LOLOL
THEY'RE... COMMENTS?! WHO ON EARTH IS—
SO CUTE LOLOLOL
'S NO REASON TO BE SCARED (^o^)
... OH!
I KNOW...
THIS IS "R.A. LIVE"...
HUH ...?
IT LOOKS LIKE A NUMBER OF YOU HAVE ALREADY NOTICED.
POP
JOLT
OH! THAT START-LED ME!

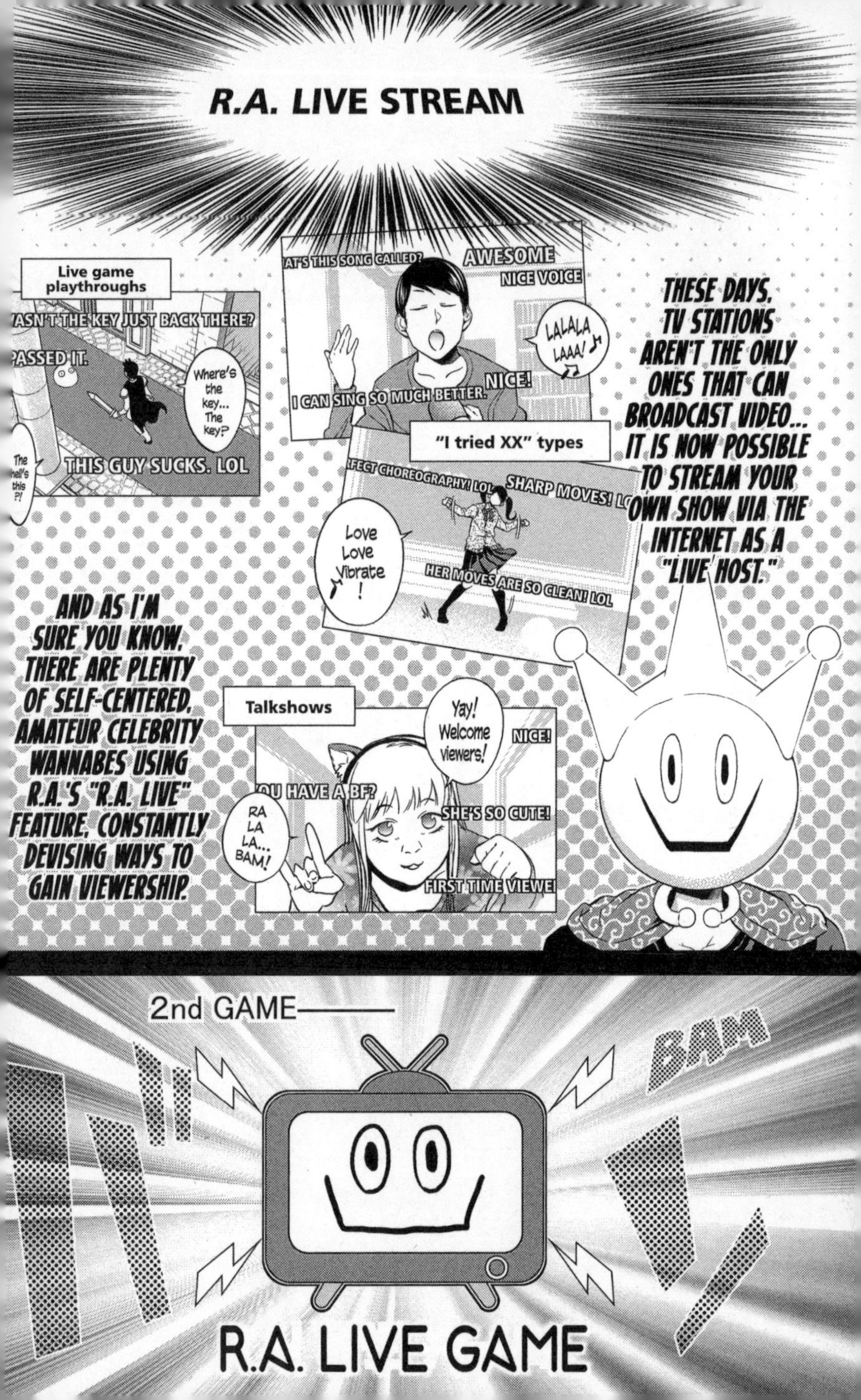
R.A. LIVE STREAM
THESE DAYS, TV STATIONS AREN'T THE ONLY ONES THAT CAN BROADCAST VIDEO... IT IS NOW POSSIBLE TO STREAM YOUR OWN SHOW VIA THE INTERNET AS A "LIVE HOST."
AT'S THIS SONG CALLED?
AWESOME
NICE VOICE
LALALA LAAA!
NICE!
I CAN SING SO MUCH BETTER.
Live game playthroughs
ASN'T THE KEY JUST BACK THERE?
PASSED IT.
Where's the key... The key?
THIS GUY SUCKS. LOL
The hell's this?!
"I tried XX" types
RFECT CHOREOGRAPHY! LOL
SHARP MOVES! LO
Love Love Vibrate!
HER MOVES ARE SO CLEAN! LOL
Talkshows
Yay! Welcome viewers!
NICE!
OU HAVE A BF?
SHE'S SO CUTE!
RA LA LA... BAM!
FIRST TIME VIEWE
AND AS I'M SURE YOU KNOW, THERE ARE PLENTY OF SELF-CENTERED, AMATEUR CELEBRITY WANNABES USING R.A.'S "R.A. LIVE" FEATURE, CONSTANTLY DEVISING WAYS TO GAIN VIEWERSHIP.
2nd GAME——
BAM
R.A. LIVE GAME

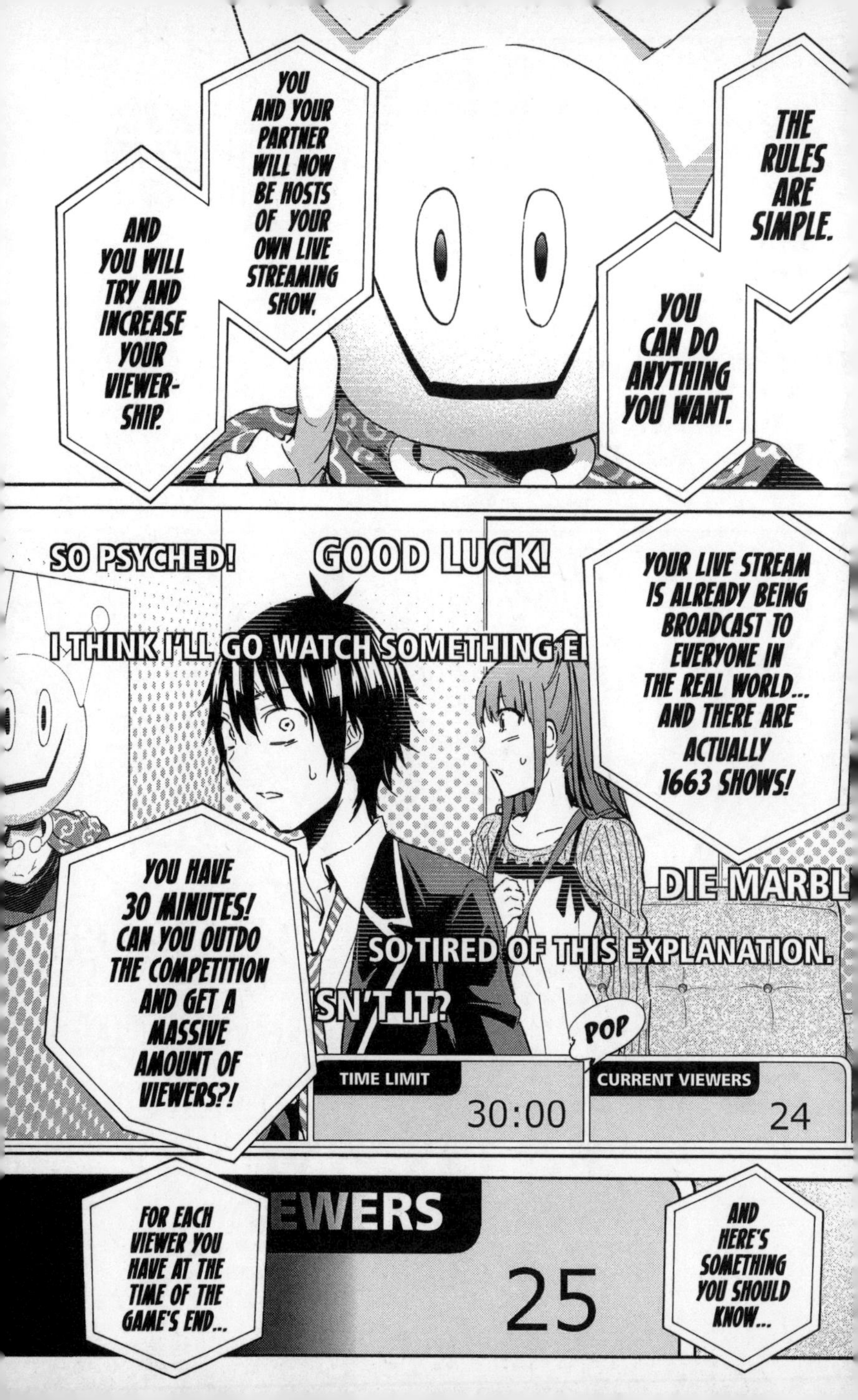
THE RULES ARE SIMPLE.
YOU CAN DO ANYTHING YOU WANT.
YOU AND YOUR PARTNER WILL NOW BE HOSTS OF YOUR OWN LIVE STREAMING SHOW.
AND YOU WILL TRY AND INCREASE YOUR VIEWER-SHIP.
YOUR LIVE STREAM IS ALREADY BEING BROADCAST TO EVERYONE IN THE REAL WORLD... AND THERE ARE ACTUALLY 1663 SHOWS!
GOOD LUCK!
SO PSYCHED!
I THINK I'LL GO WATCH SOMETHING E
DIE MARBL
SO TIRED OF THIS EXPLANATION.
SN'T IT?
POP
CURRENT VIEWERS
24
TIME LIMIT
30:00
YOU HAVE 30 MINUTES! CAN YOU OUTDO THE COMPETITION AND GET A MASSIVE AMOUNT OF VIEWERS?!
AND HERE'S SOMETHING YOU SHOULD KNOW...
EWERS
25
FOR EACH VIEWER YOU HAVE AT THE TIME OF THE GAME'S END...

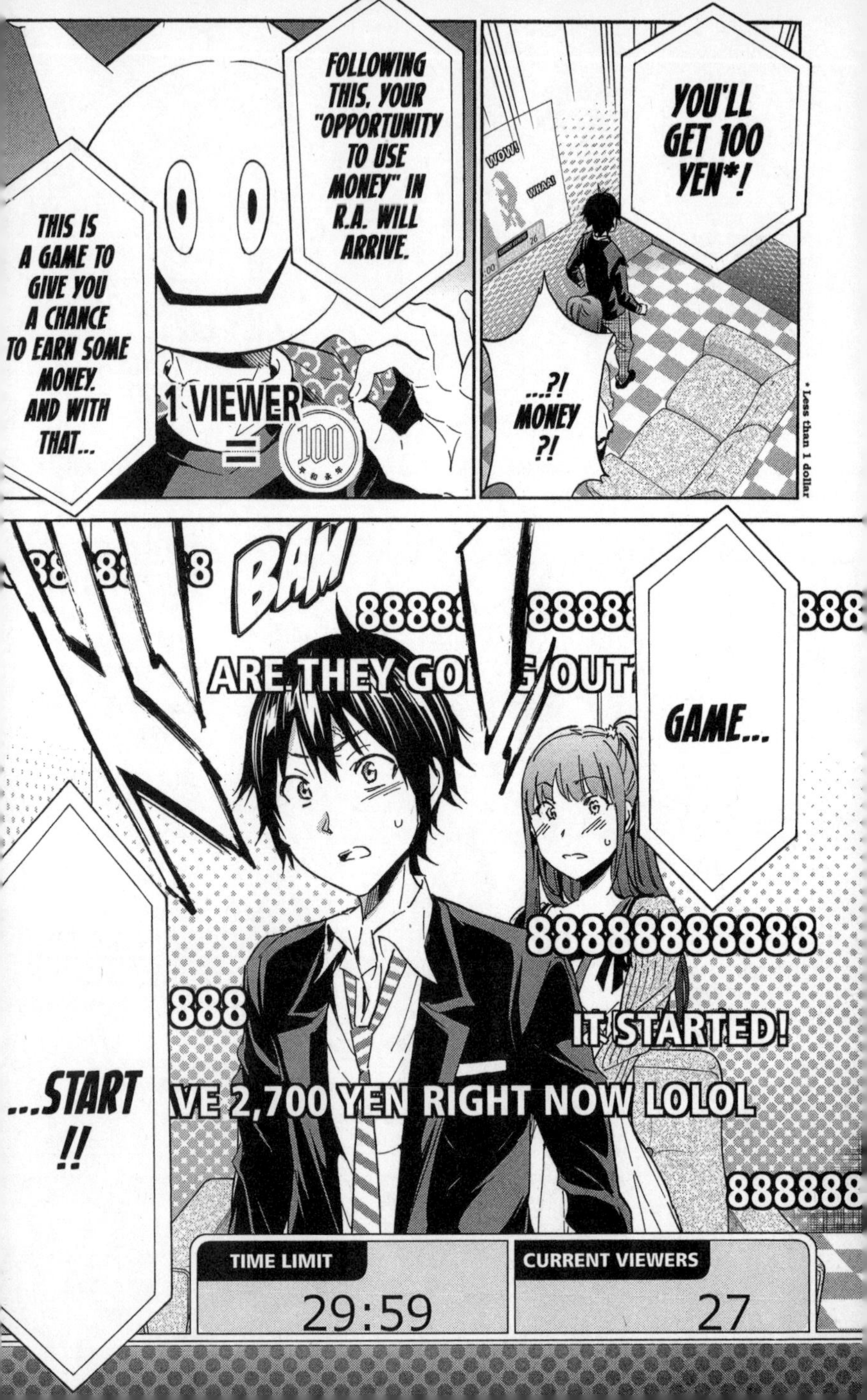
YOU'LL GET 100 YEN*!
WOW!
WHAA!
...?! MONEY ?!
*Less than 1 dollar
FOLLOWING THIS, YOUR "OPPORTUNITY TO USE MONEY" IN R.A. WILL ARRIVE.
THIS IS A GAME TO GIVE YOU A CHANCE TO EARN SOME MONEY. AND WITH THAT...
1 VIEWER = 100
GAME...
BAM
...START !!
ARE THEY GOI G OUT
88888888888
888
IT STARTED!
VE 2,700 YEN RIGHT NOW LOLOL
888888
TIME LIMIT
29:59
CURRENT VIEWERS
27

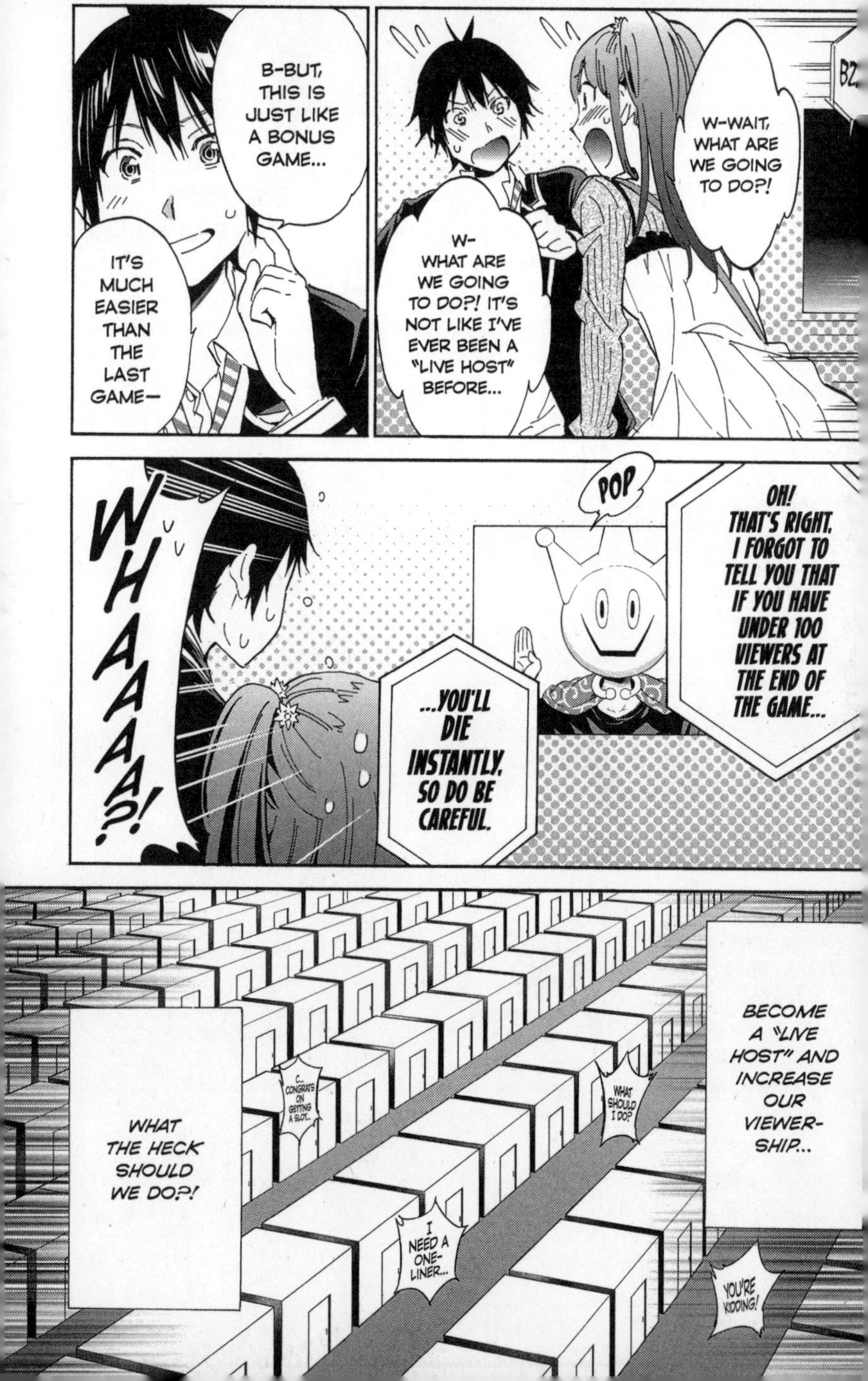
BZ
W-WAIT, WHAT ARE WE GOING TO DO?!
W- WHAT ARE WE GOING TO DO?! IT'S NOT LIKE I'VE EVER BEEN A "LIVE HOST" BEFORE...
B-BUT, THIS IS JUST LIKE A BONUS GAME...
IT'S MUCH EASIER THAN THE LAST GAME—
OH! THAT'S RIGHT. I FORGOT TO TELL YOU THAT IF YOU HAVE UNDER 100 VIEWERS AT THE END OF THE GAME...
POP
...YOU'LL DIE INSTANTLY, SO DO BE CAREFUL.
WHAAAAA?!
BECOME A "LIVE HOST" AND INCREASE OUR VIEWERSHIP...
WHAT SHOULD I DO?
YOU'RE KIDDING!
I NEED A ONE-LINER...
C... CONGRATS ON GETTING A SLOT...
WHAT THE HECK SHOULD WE DO?!

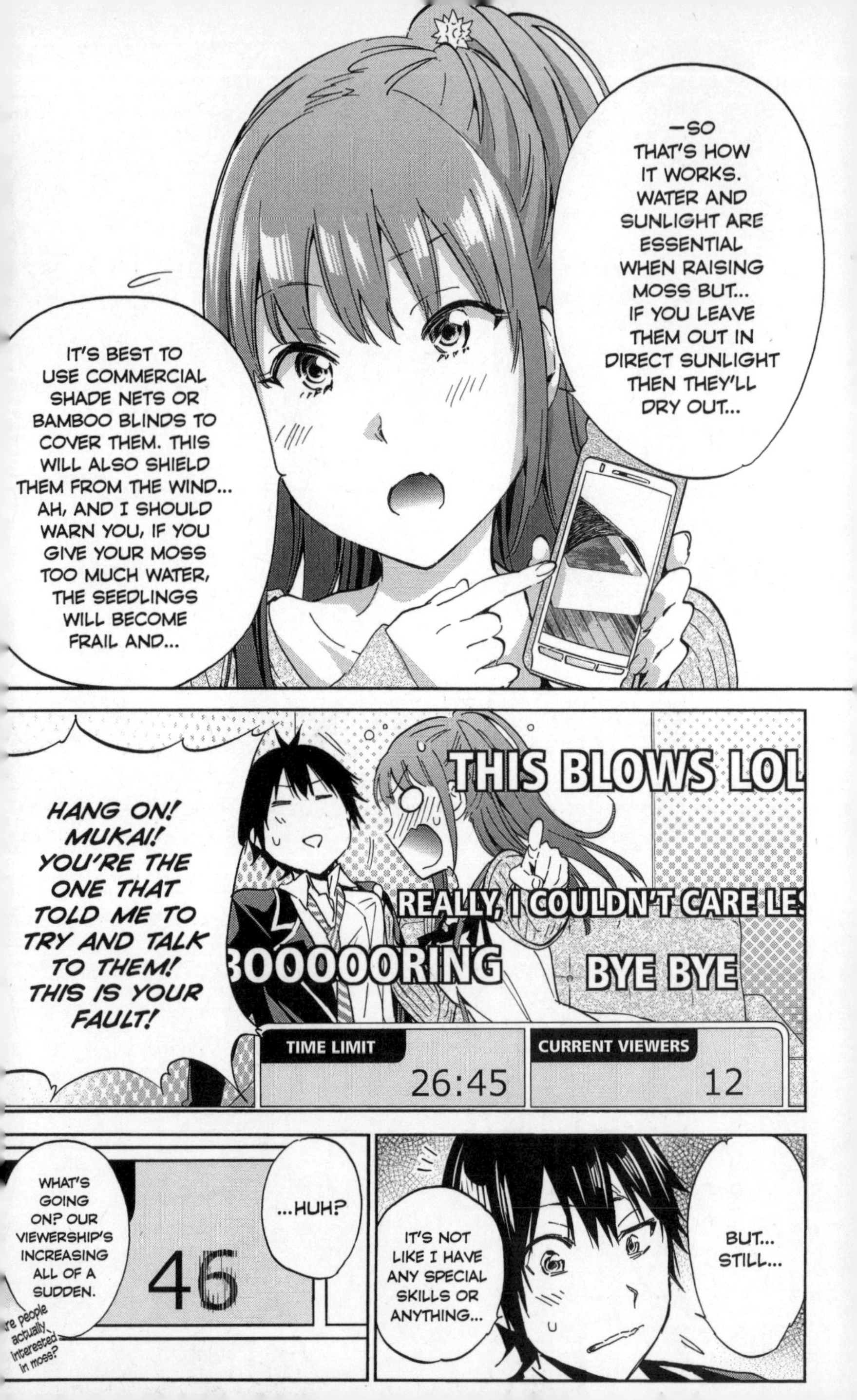
—SO THAT'S HOW IT WORKS. WATER AND SUNLIGHT ARE ESSENTIAL WHEN RAISING MOSS BUT... IF YOU LEAVE THEM OUT IN DIRECT SUNLIGHT THEN THEY'LL DRY OUT...
IT'S BEST TO USE COMMERCIAL SHADE NETS OR BAMBOO BLINDS TO COVER THEM. THIS WILL ALSO SHIELD THEM FROM THE WIND... AH, AND I SHOULD WARN YOU, IF YOU GIVE YOUR MOSS TOO MUCH WATER, THE SEEDLINGS WILL BECOME FRAIL AND...
THIS BLOWS LOL
REALLY, I COULDN'T CARE LES
BYE BYE
OOOOORING
HANG ON! MUKAI! YOU'RE THE ONE THAT TOLD ME TO TRY AND TALK TO THEM! THIS IS YOUR FAULT!
TIME LIMIT
26:45
CURRENT VIEWERS
12
BUT... STILL...
IT'S NOT LIKE I HAVE ANY SPECIAL SKILLS OR ANYTHING...
...HUH?
WHAT'S GOING ON? OUR VIEWERSHIP'S INCREASING ALL OF A SUDDEN.
46
re people actually interested in moss?

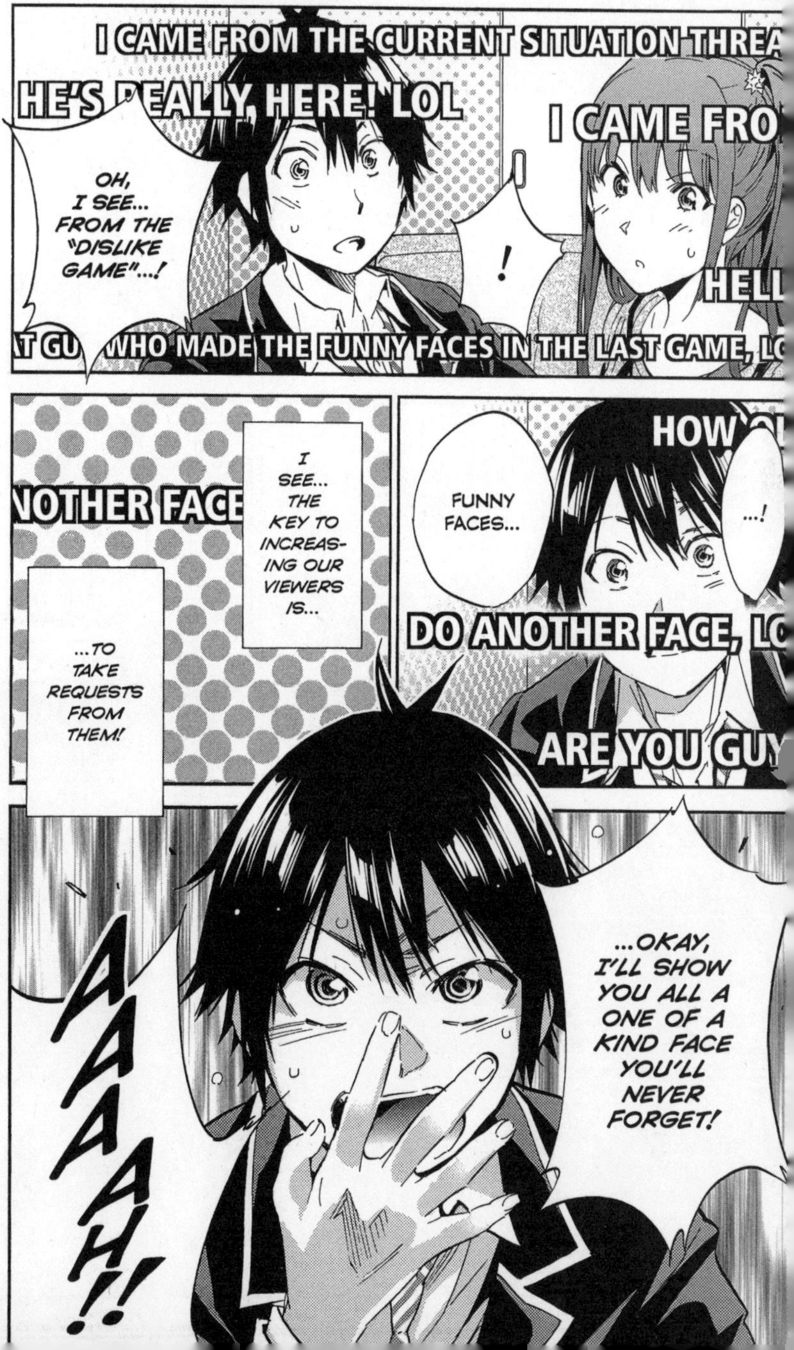
I CAME FROM THE CURRENT SITUATION THREA
I CAME FRO
HE'S REALLY HERE! LOL
!
HELL
OH, I SEE... FROM THE "DISLIKE GAME"...!
T GU WHO MADE THE FUNNY FACES IN THE LAST GAME, LO
HOW O
...!
FUNNY FACES...
DO ANOTHER FACE, LO
ARE YOU GUY
I SEE... THE KEY TO INCREAS-ING OUR VIEWERS IS...
NOTHER FACE
...TO TAKE REQUESTS FROM THEM!
...OKAY, I'LL SHOW YOU ALL A ONE OF A KIND FACE YOU'LL NEVER FORGET!
AAAAAH!!

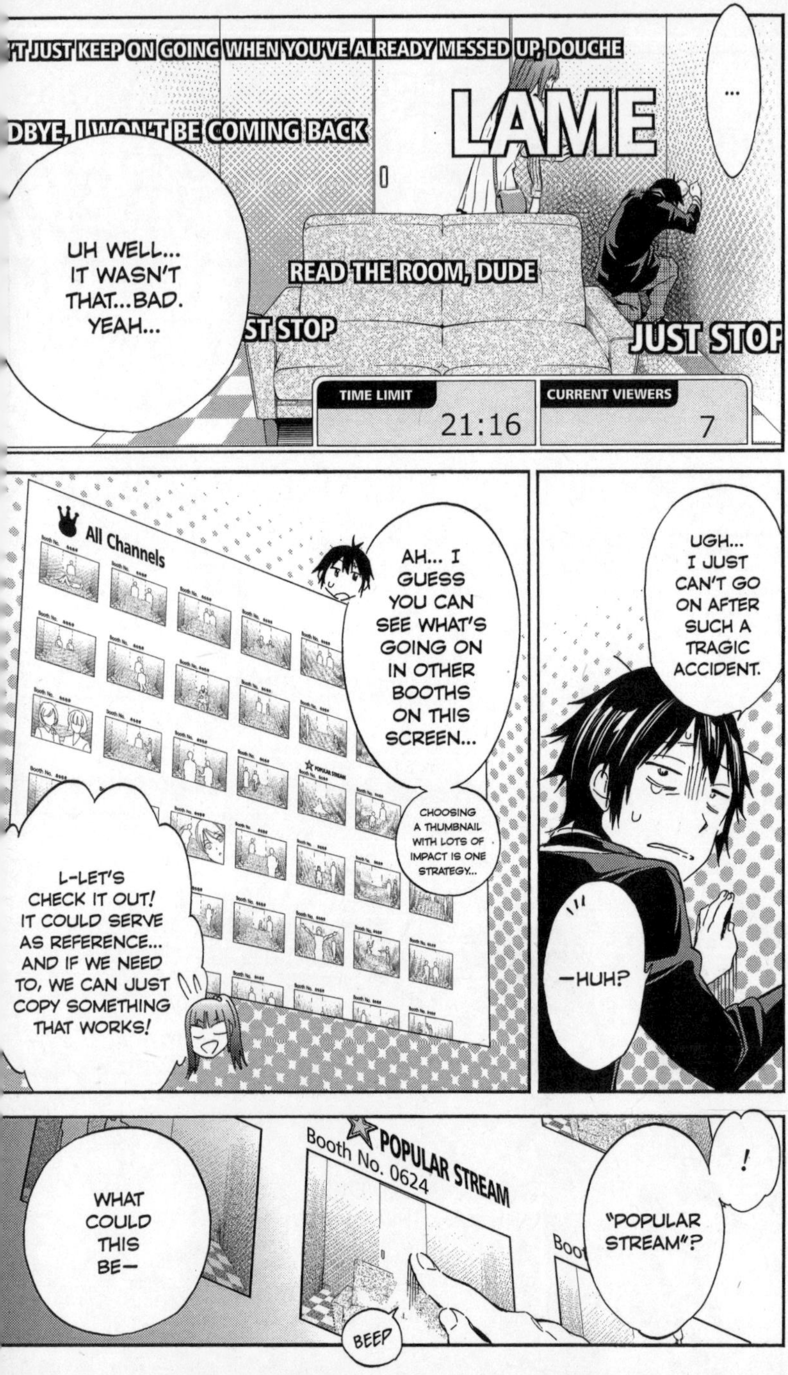
...
'T JUST KEEP ON GOING WHEN YOU'VE ALREADY MESSED UP, DOUCHE
LAME
DBYE, I WON'T BE COMING BACK
READ THE ROOM, DUDE
JUST STOP
UH WELL... IT WASN'T THAT...BAD. YEAH...
ST STOP
TIME LIMIT
21:16
CURRENT VIEWERS
7
UGH... I JUST CAN'T GO ON AFTER SUCH A TRAGIC ACCIDENT.
—HUH?
AH... I GUESS YOU CAN SEE WHAT'S GOING ON IN OTHER BOOTHS ON THIS SCREEN...
CHOOSING A THUMBNAIL WITH LOTS OF IMPACT IS ONE STRATEGY...
All Channels
L-LET'S CHECK IT OUT! IT COULD SERVE AS REFERENCE... AND IF WE NEED TO, WE CAN JUST COPY SOMETHING THAT WORKS!
!
"POPULAR STREAM"?
POPULAR STREAM
Booth No. 0624
WHAT COULD THIS BE—
BEEP

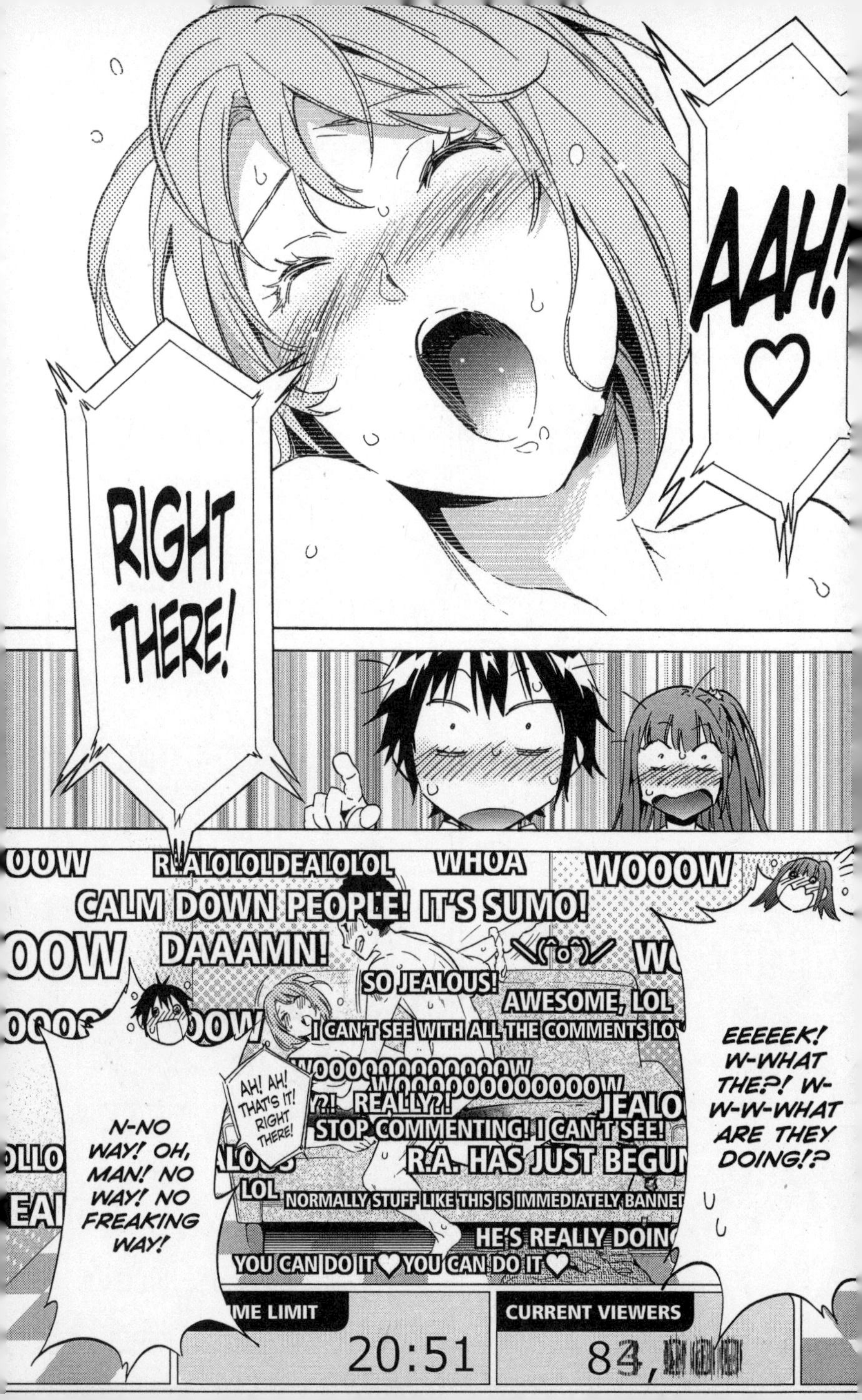
AAH! ♥
RIGHT THERE!
EEEEEK! W-WHAT THE?! W-W-W-WHAT ARE THEY DOING!?
WOOOW
WHOA
CALM DOWN PEOPLE! IT'S SUMO!
DAAAMN!
SO JEALOUS!
AWESOME, LOL
WOOOOOOOOOOOOOW
WOOOOOOOOOOOOW
REALLY?!
STOP COMMENTING! I CAN'T SEE!
R.A. HAS JUST BEGUN
LOL
YOU CAN DO IT♥ YOU CAN DO IT♥
AH! AH! THAT'S IT! RIGHT THERE!
N-NO WAY! OH, MAN! NO WAY! NO FREAKING WAY!
CURRENT VIEWERS
20:51

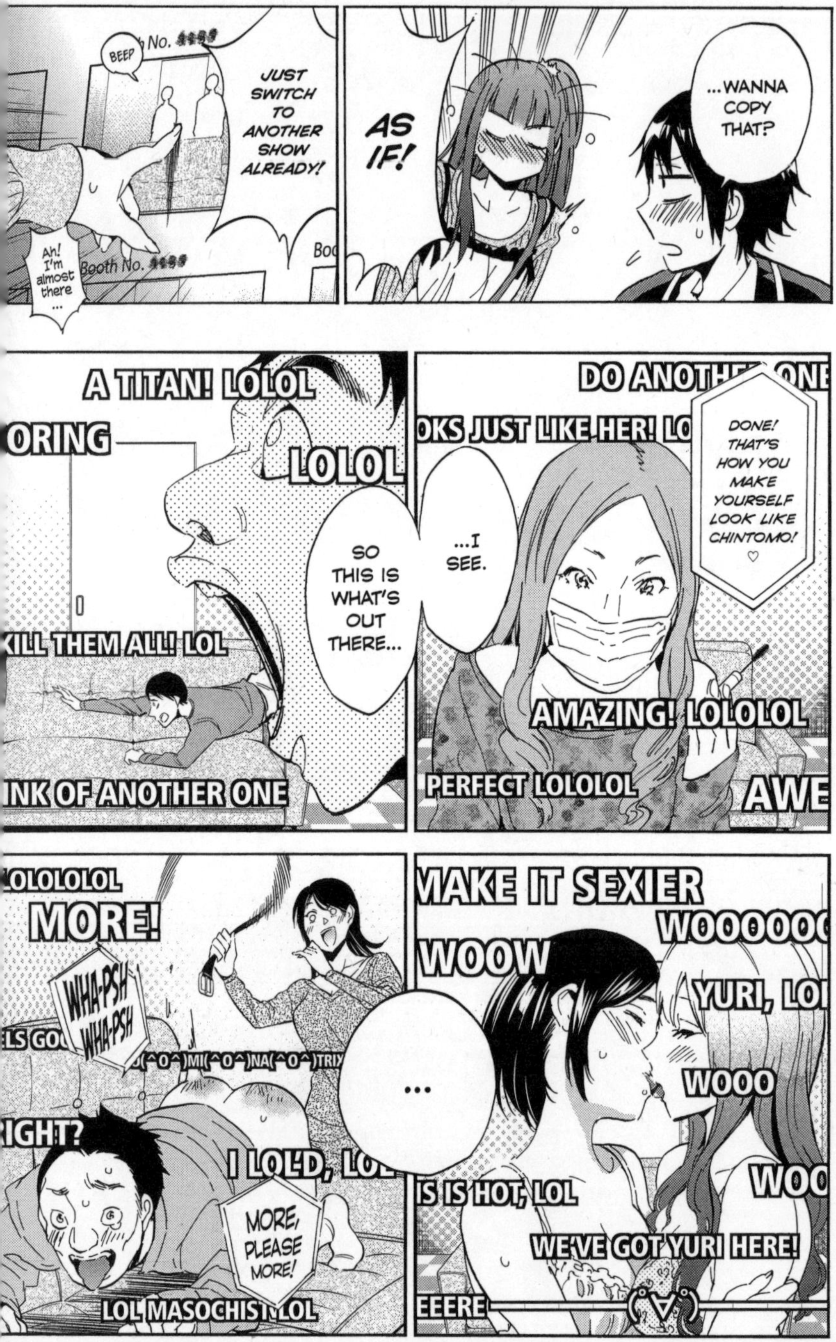
...WANNA COPY THAT?
AS IF!
JUST SWITCH TO ANOTHER SHOW ALREADY!
BEEP
Booth No.
Booth No.
Ah! I'm almost there ...
DONE! THAT'S HOW YOU MAKE YOURSELF LOOK LIKE CHINTOMO! ♡
DO ANOTHE ONE
OKS JUST LIKE HER! LO
...I SEE.
AMAZING! LOLOLOL
PERFECT LOLOLOL
AWE
SO THIS IS WHAT'S OUT THERE...
A TITAN! LOLOL
ORING
LOLOL
KILL THEM ALL! LOL
INK OF ANOTHER ONE
MAKE IT SEXIER
WOOOOOO
WOOW
YURI, LOI
WOOO
WOO
IS IS HOT, LOL
WE'VE GOT YURI HERE!
EEERE
(°∀°)
...
LOLOLOLOL
MORE!
WHA-PSH WHA-PSH
ELS GOO
(^O^)MI(^O^)NA(^O^)TRIX
IGHT?
I LOL'D, LOL
MORE, PLEASE MORE!
LOL MASOCHIST LOL

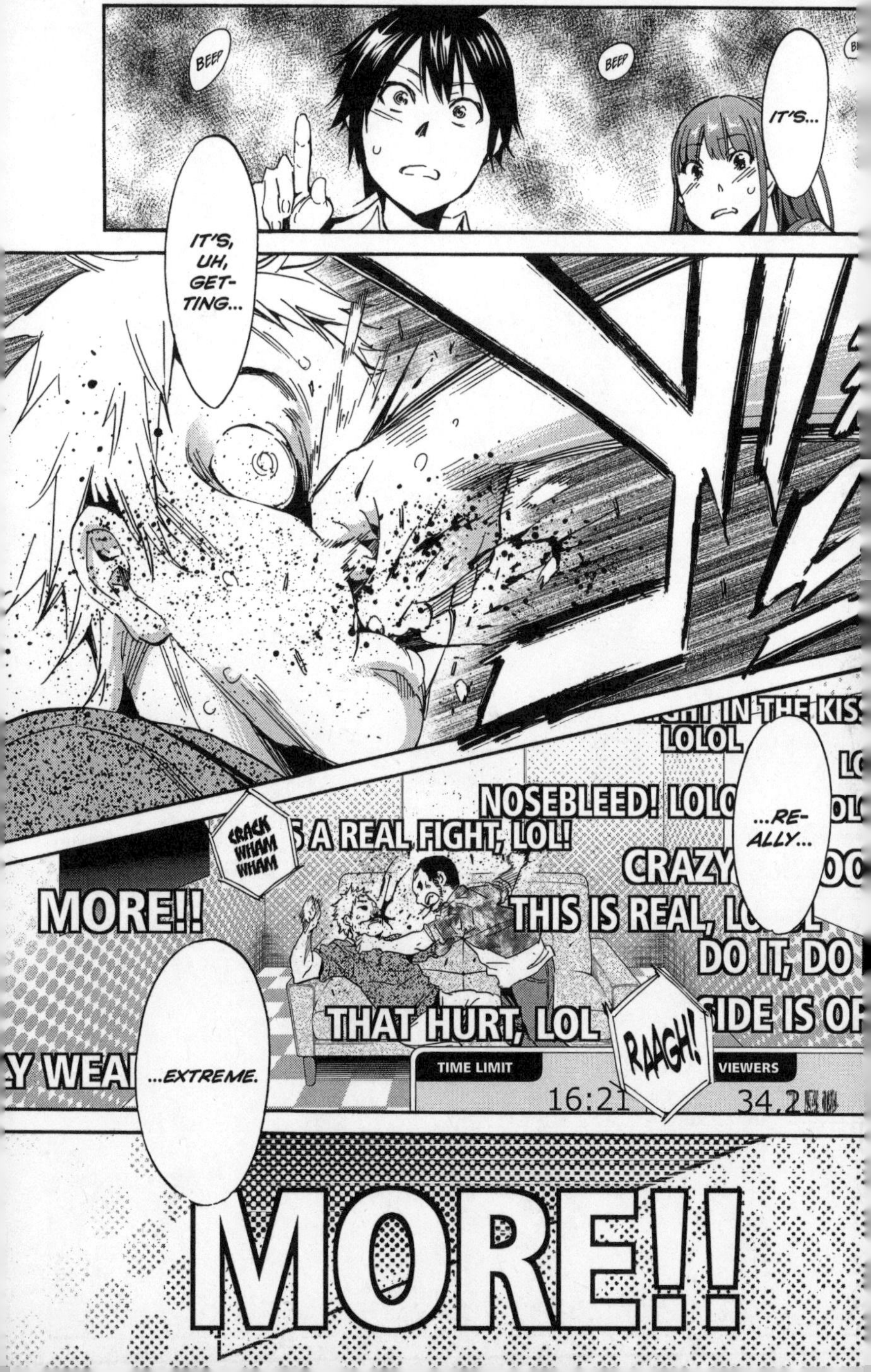
IT'S...
BEEP
BEEP
IT'S, UH, GETTING...
IGHT IN THE KISS
LOLOL
NOSEBLEED! LOLO
...REALLY...
S A REAL FIGHT, LOL!
CRAZY
THIS IS REAL, LO
DO IT, DO
SIDE IS OF
CRACK WHAM WHAM
MORE!!
THAT HURT, LOL
RAAGH!
Y WEAR
...EXTREME.
TIME LIMIT
16:21
VIEWERS
34.2
MORE!!

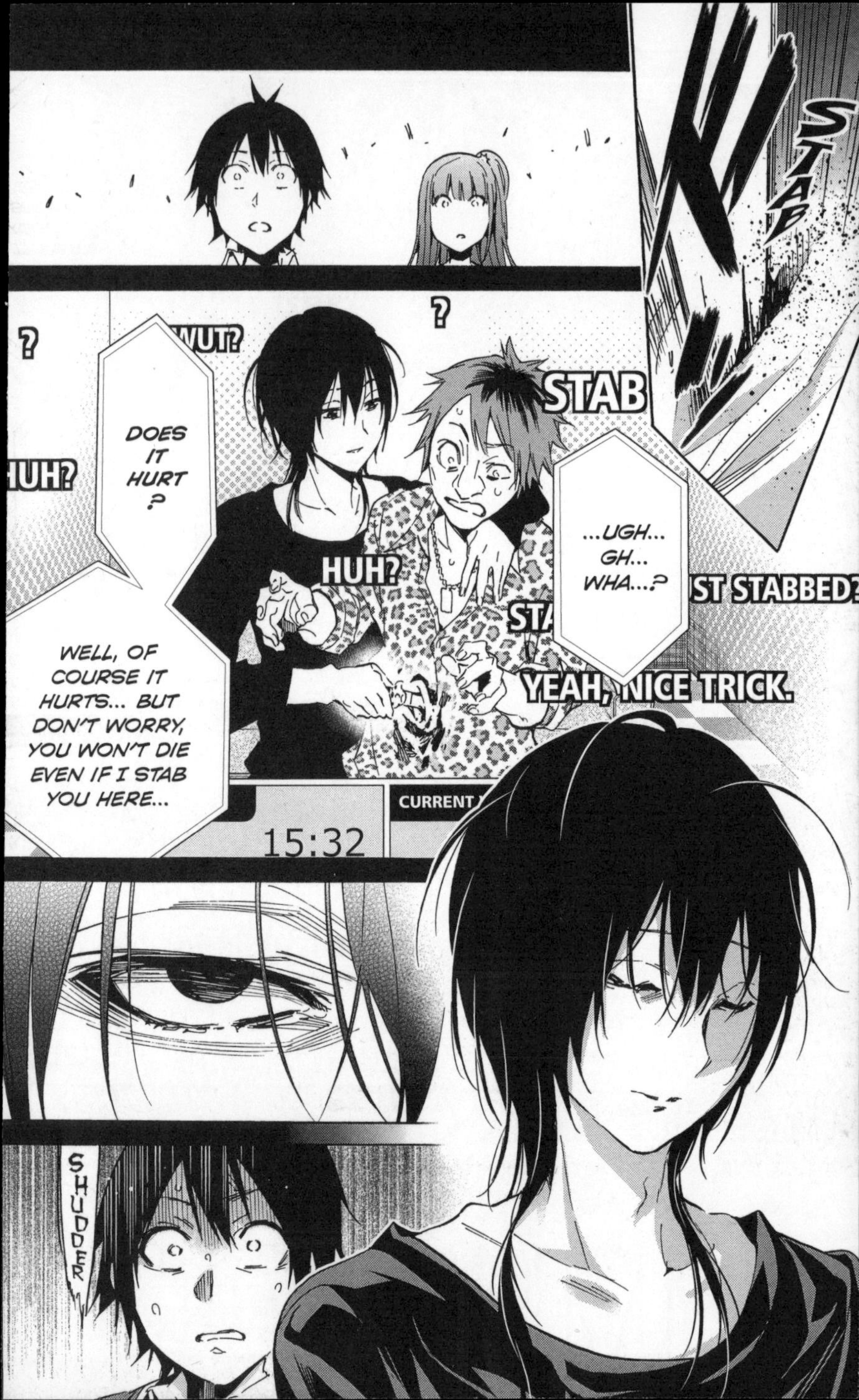
STAB!
STAB
...UGH... GH... WHA...?
ST STABBED?
STA
YEAH, NICE TRICK.
?
HUH?
DOES IT HURT?
WUT?
?
HUH?
WELL, OF COURSE IT HURTS... BUT DON'T WORRY, YOU WON'T DIE EVEN IF I STAB YOU HERE...
CURRENT
15:32
SHUDDER

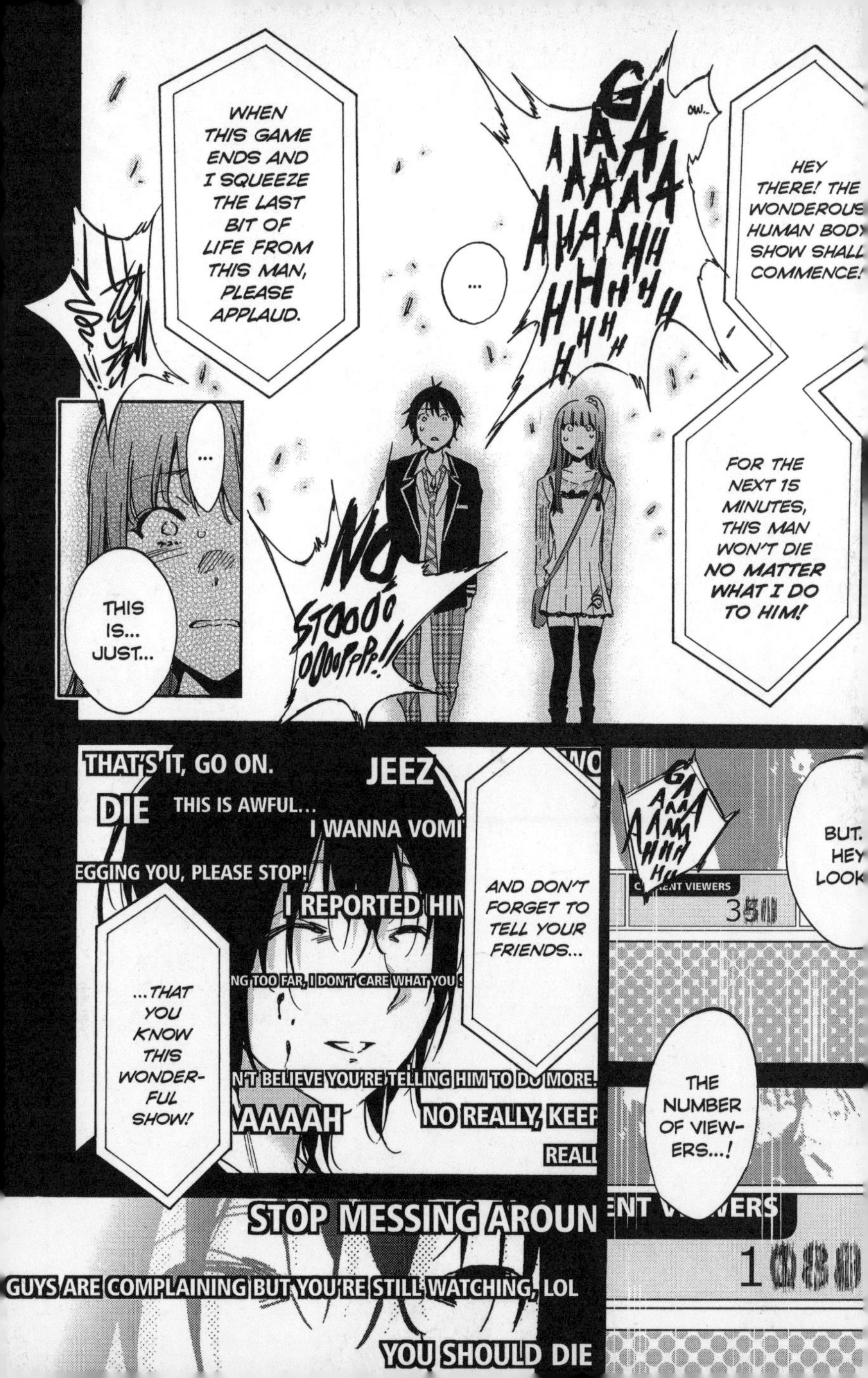
HEY THERE! THE WONDEROUS HUMAN BODY SHOW SHALL COMMENCE!
ow..
GAAAAAAAAAHHHHHHHHHHHH
...
WHEN THIS GAME ENDS AND I SQUEEZE THE LAST BIT OF LIFE FROM THIS MAN, PLEASE APPLAUD.
FOR THE NEXT 15 MINUTES, THIS MAN WON'T DIE NO MATTER WHAT I DO TO HIM!
NO STOOOOOOOPPP!!
...
THIS IS... JUST...
GAAAAAAHHHH
BUT. HEY LOOK
THE NUMBER OF VIEWERS...!
AND DON'T FORGET TO TELL YOUR FRIENDS...
...THAT YOU KNOW THIS WONDERFUL SHOW!
THAT'S IT, GO ON.
JEEZ
DIE
THIS IS AWFUL...
I WANNA VOMI
EGGING YOU, PLEASE STOP!
I REPORTED HIM
NG TOO FAR, I DON'T CARE WHAT YOU S
N'T BELIEVE YOU'RE TELLING HIM TO DO MORE.
AAAAAH
NO REALLY, KEEP
REALL
STOP MESSING AROUN
GUYS ARE COMPLAINING BUT YOU'RE STILL WATCHING, LOL
YOU SHOULD DIE

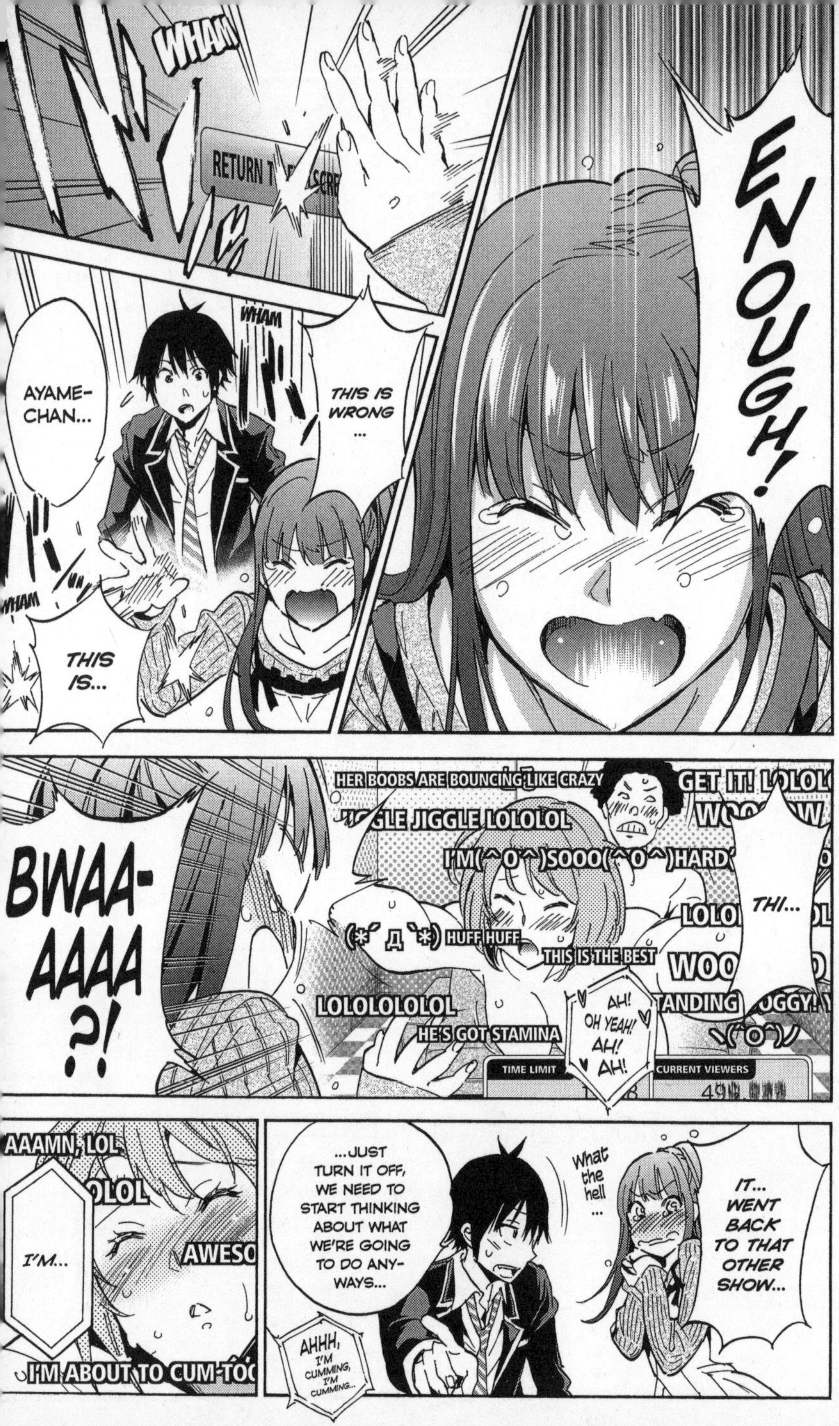
ENOUGH!
WHAM
RETURN T
SCRE
WHAM
THIS IS WRONG ...
AYAME-CHAN...
WHAM
THIS IS...
THI...
HER BOOBS ARE BOUNCING LIKE CRAZY
GET IT! LOLOL
JIGGLE JIGGLE LOLOLOL
I'M(^O^)SOOO(^O^)HARD
(*´Д`*) HUFF HUFF
THIS IS THE BEST
LOLOLOLOLOL
HE'S GOT STAMINA
\(^O^)/
AH! OH YEAH! AH! AH!
TIME LIMIT
CURRENT VIEWERS
BWAA-AAAA?!
IT... WENT BACK TO THAT OTHER SHOW...
What the hell ...
...JUST TURN IT OFF, WE NEED TO START THINKING ABOUT WHAT WE'RE GOING TO DO ANY-WAYS...
AHHH, I'M CUMMING, I'M CUMMING...
AAAMN, LOL
OLOL
I'M...
AWESO
I'M ABOUT TO CUM TOO

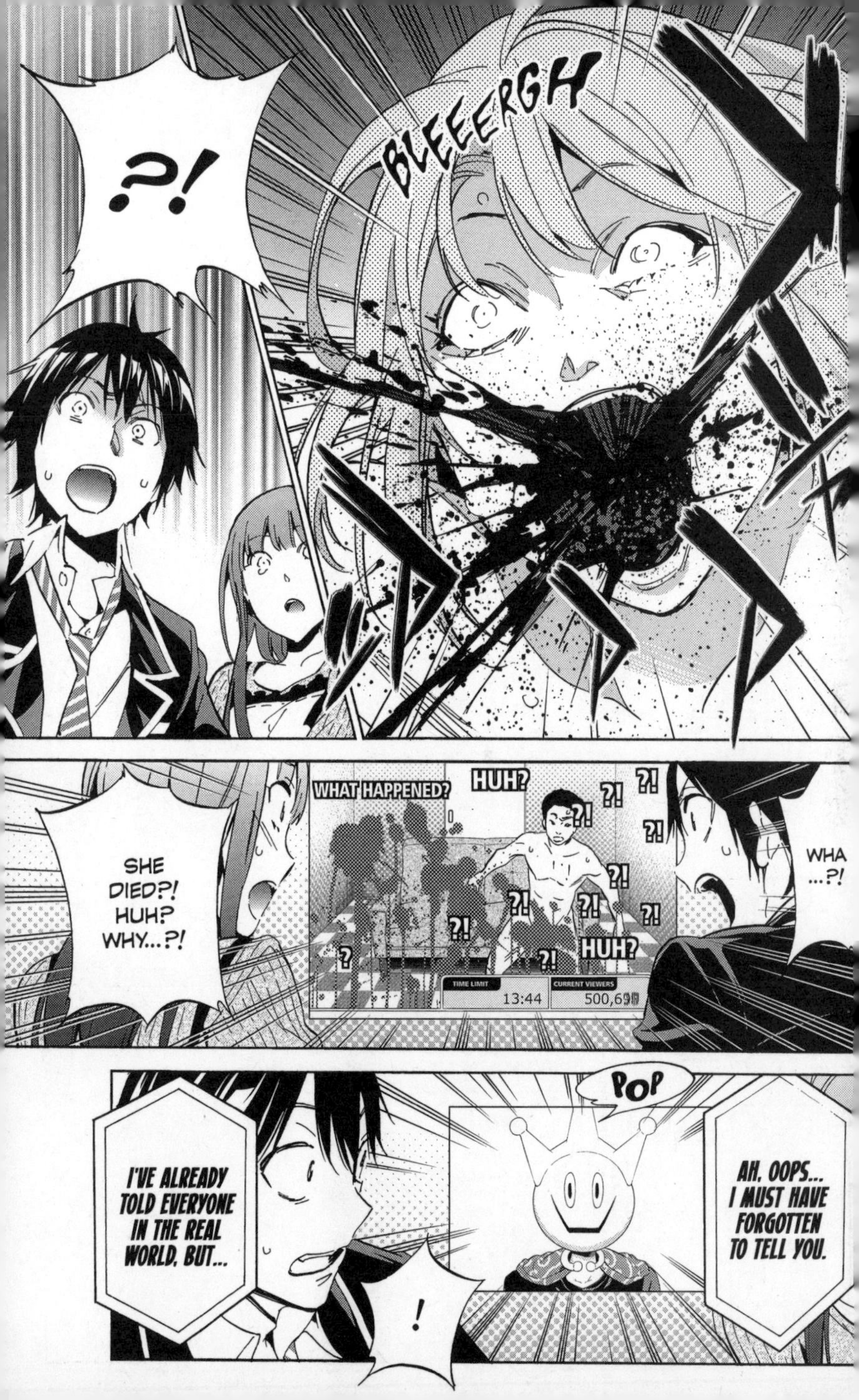
BLEEERGH
?!
WHA ...?!
HUH?
WHAT HAPPENED?
HUH?
TIME LIMIT
13:44
CURRENT VIEWERS
SHE DIED?! HUH? WHY...?!
AH, OOPS... I MUST HAVE FORGOTTEN TO TELL YOU.
POP
I'VE ALREADY TOLD EVERYONE IN THE REAL WORLD, BUT...
!

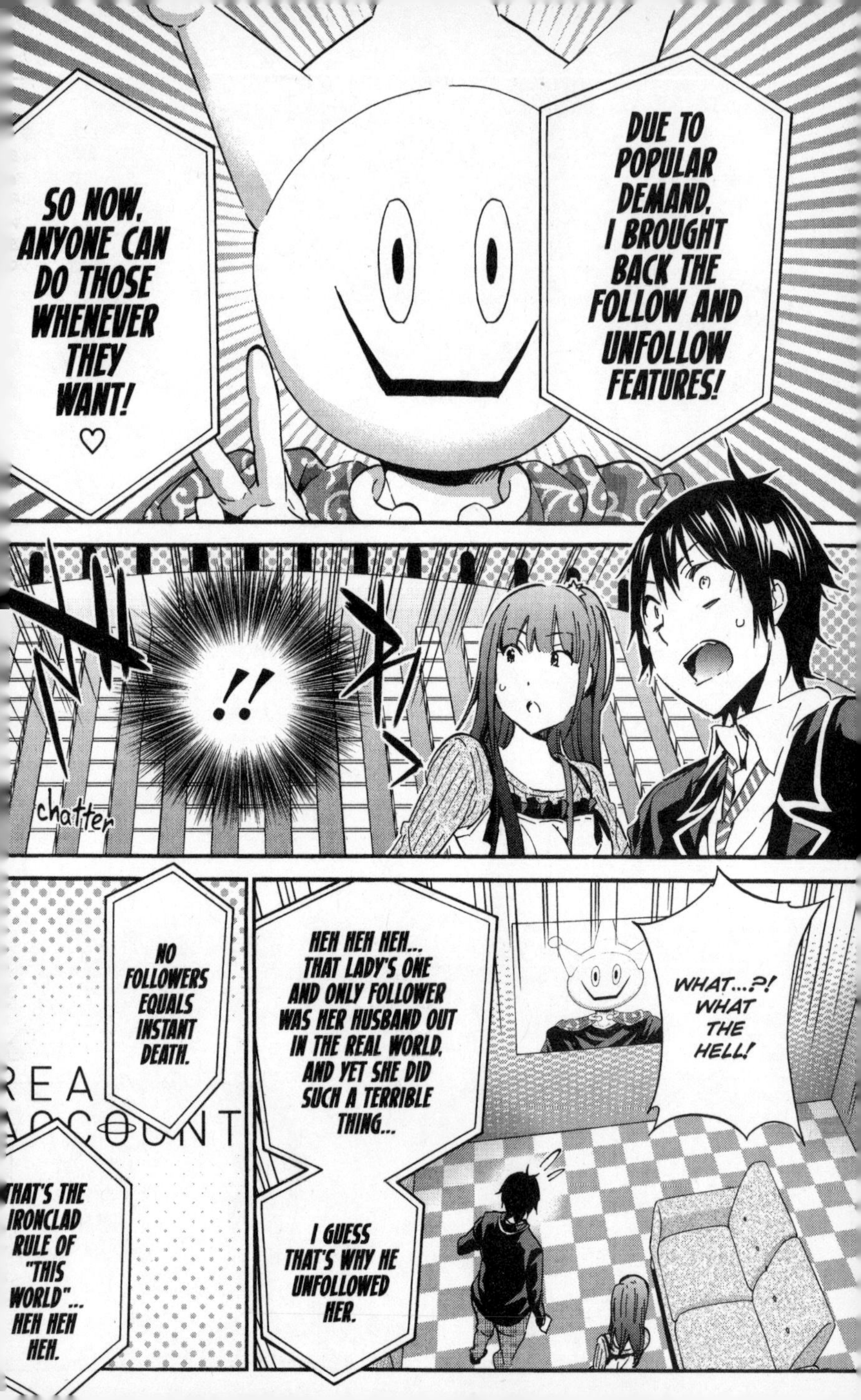
DUE TO POPULAR DEMAND, I BROUGHT BACK THE FOLLOW AND UNFOLLOW FEATURES!
SO NOW, ANYONE CAN DO THOSE WHENEVER THEY WANT! ♡
!!
chatter
WHAT...?! WHAT THE HELL!
HEH HEH HEH... THAT LADY'S ONE AND ONLY FOLLOWER WAS HER HUSBAND OUT IN THE REAL WORLD, AND YET SHE DID SUCH A TERRIBLE THING...
I GUESS THAT'S WHY HE UNFOLLOWED HER.
NO FOLLOWERS EQUALS INSTANT DEATH.
THAT'S THE IRONCLAD RULE OF "THIS WORLD"... HEH HEH HEH.

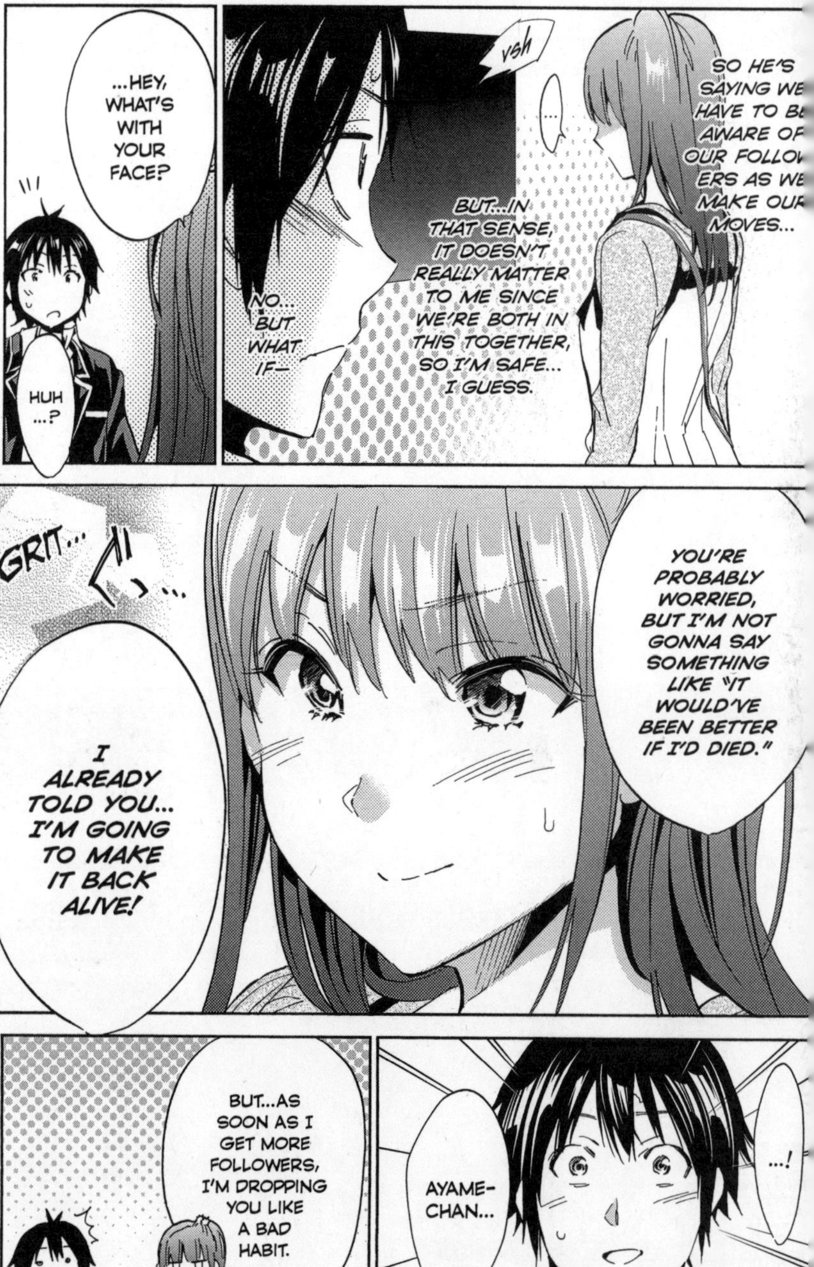
SO HE'S SAYING WE HAVE TO BE AWARE OF OUR FOLLOWERS AS WE MAKE OUR MOVES...
...
vsh
BUT...IN THAT SENSE, IT DOESN'T REALLY MATTER TO ME SINCE WE'RE BOTH IN THIS TOGETHER, SO I'M SAFE... I GUESS.
NO... BUT WHAT IF—
...HEY, WHAT'S WITH YOUR FACE?
HUH ...?
YOU'RE PROBABLY WORRIED, BUT I'M NOT GONNA SAY SOMETHING LIKE "IT WOULD'VE BEEN BETTER IF I'D DIED."
GRIT...
I ALREADY TOLD YOU... I'M GOING TO MAKE IT BACK ALIVE!
...!
AYAME-CHAN...
BUT...AS SOON AS I GET MORE FOLLOWERS, I'M DROPPING YOU LIKE A BAD HABIT.

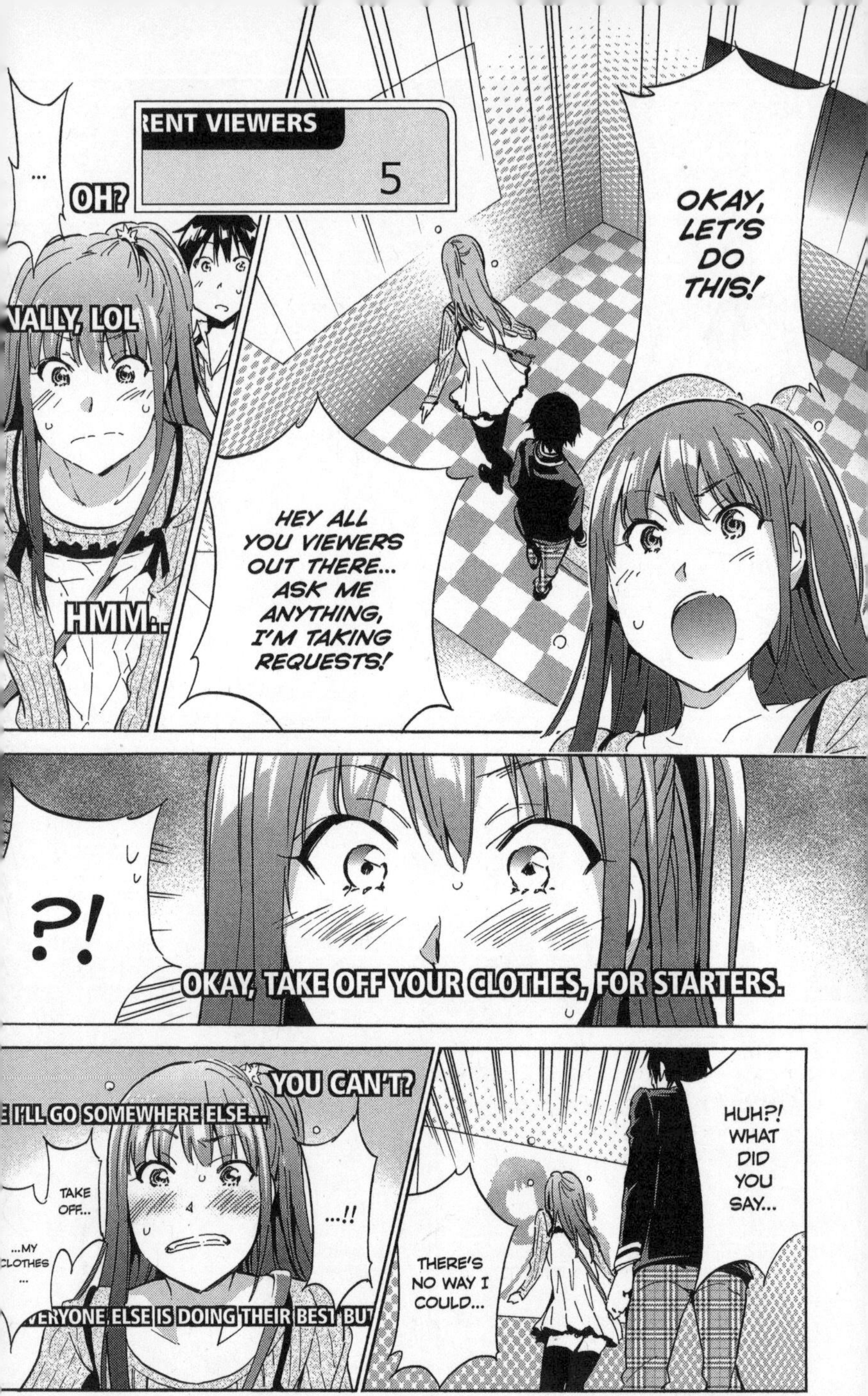
OKAY, LET'S DO THIS!
HEY ALL YOU VIEWERS OUT THERE... ASK ME ANYTHING, I'M TAKING REQUESTS!
RENT VIEWERS
5
OH?
...
NALLY, LOL
HMM..
?!
OKAY, TAKE OFF YOUR CLOTHES, FOR STARTERS.
HUH?! WHAT DID YOU SAY...
THERE'S NO WAY I COULD...
YOU CAN'T?
E I'LL GO SOMEWHERE ELSE...
...!!
TAKE OFF...
...MY CLOTHES ...
VERYONE ELSE IS DOING THEIR BEST BUT

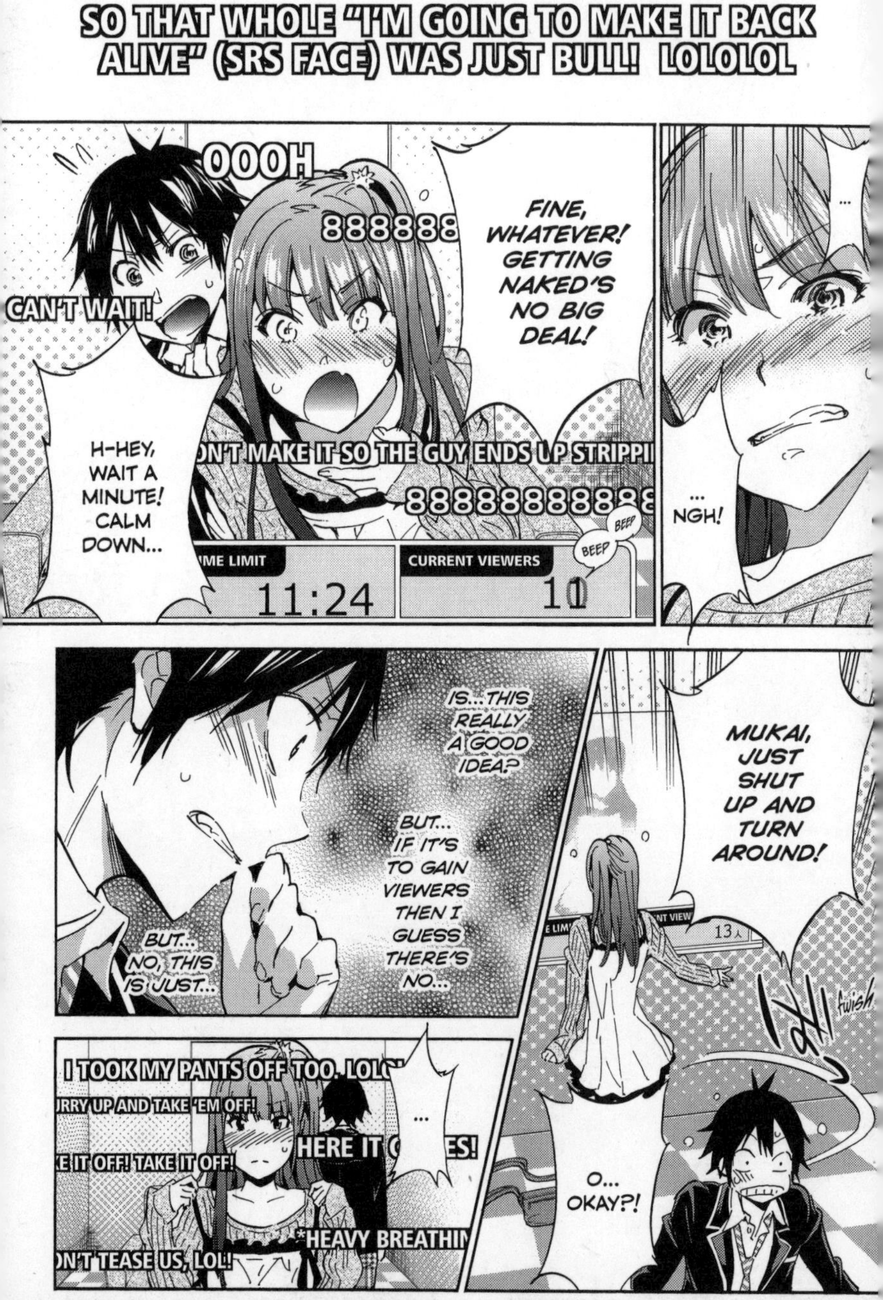
SO THAT WHOLE "I'M GOING TO MAKE IT BACK ALIVE" (SRS FACE) WAS JUST BULL! LOLOLOL
...
... NGH!
OOOH
888888
FINE, WHATEVER! GETTING NAKED'S NO BIG DEAL!
CAN'T WAIT!
H-HEY, WAIT A MINUTE! CALM DOWN...
ON'T MAKE IT SO THE GUY ENDS UP STRIPPI
8888888888
BEEP
BEEP
IME LIMIT
11:24
CURRENT VIEWERS
11
MUKAI, JUST SHUT UP AND TURN AROUND!
13人
fwish
O... OKAY?!
IS... THIS REALLY A GOOD IDEA?
BUT... IF IT'S TO GAIN VIEWERS THEN I GUESS THERE'S NO...
BUT... NO, THIS IS JUST...
I TOOK MY PANTS OFF TOO. LOL
...
URRY UP AND TAKE 'EM OFF!
HERE IT C ES!
KE IT OFF! TAKE IT OFF!
*HEAVY BREATHIN
ON'T TEASE US, LOL!

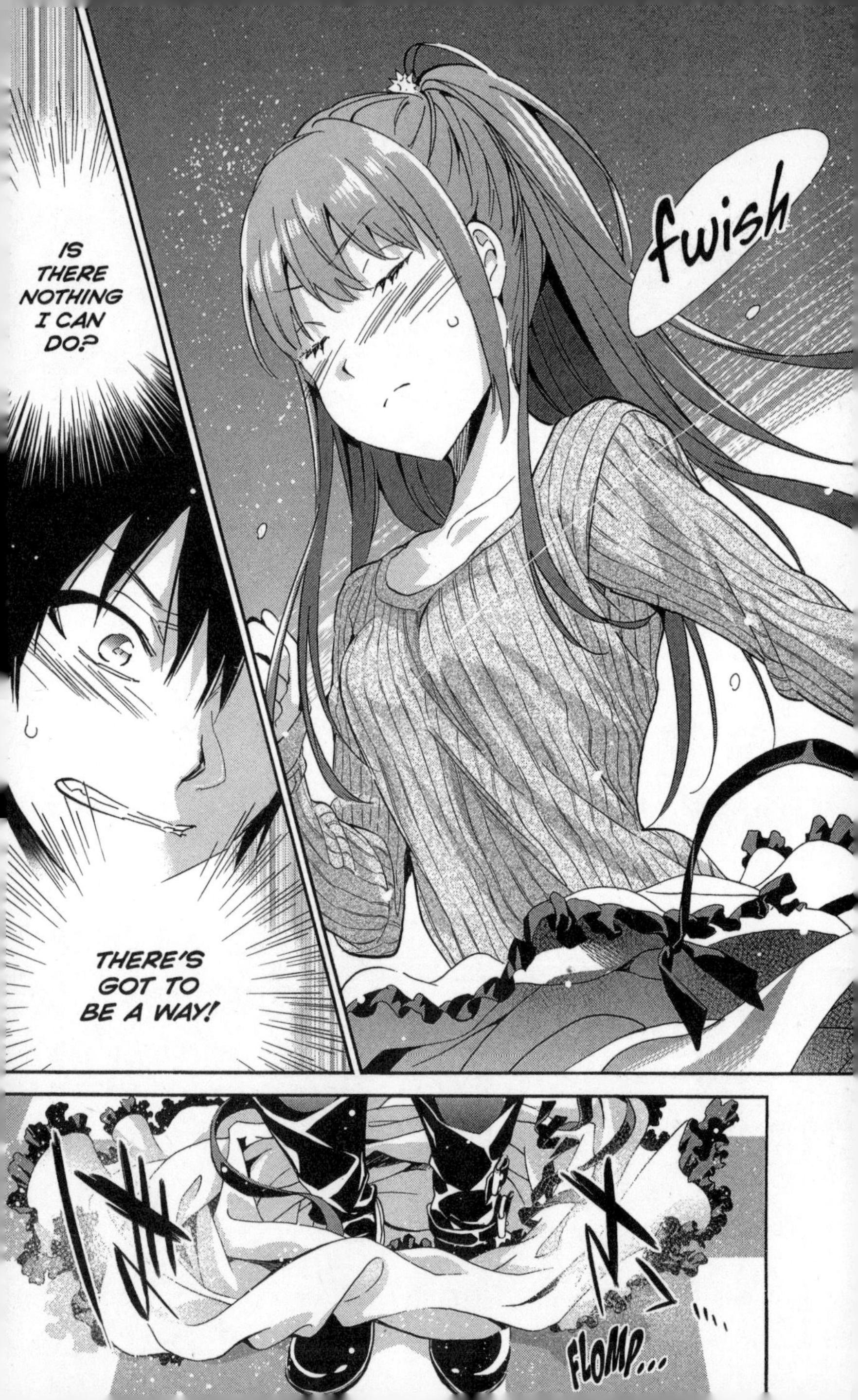
fwish
IS THERE NOTHING I CAN DO?
THERE'S GOT TO BE A WAY!
FLOMP...

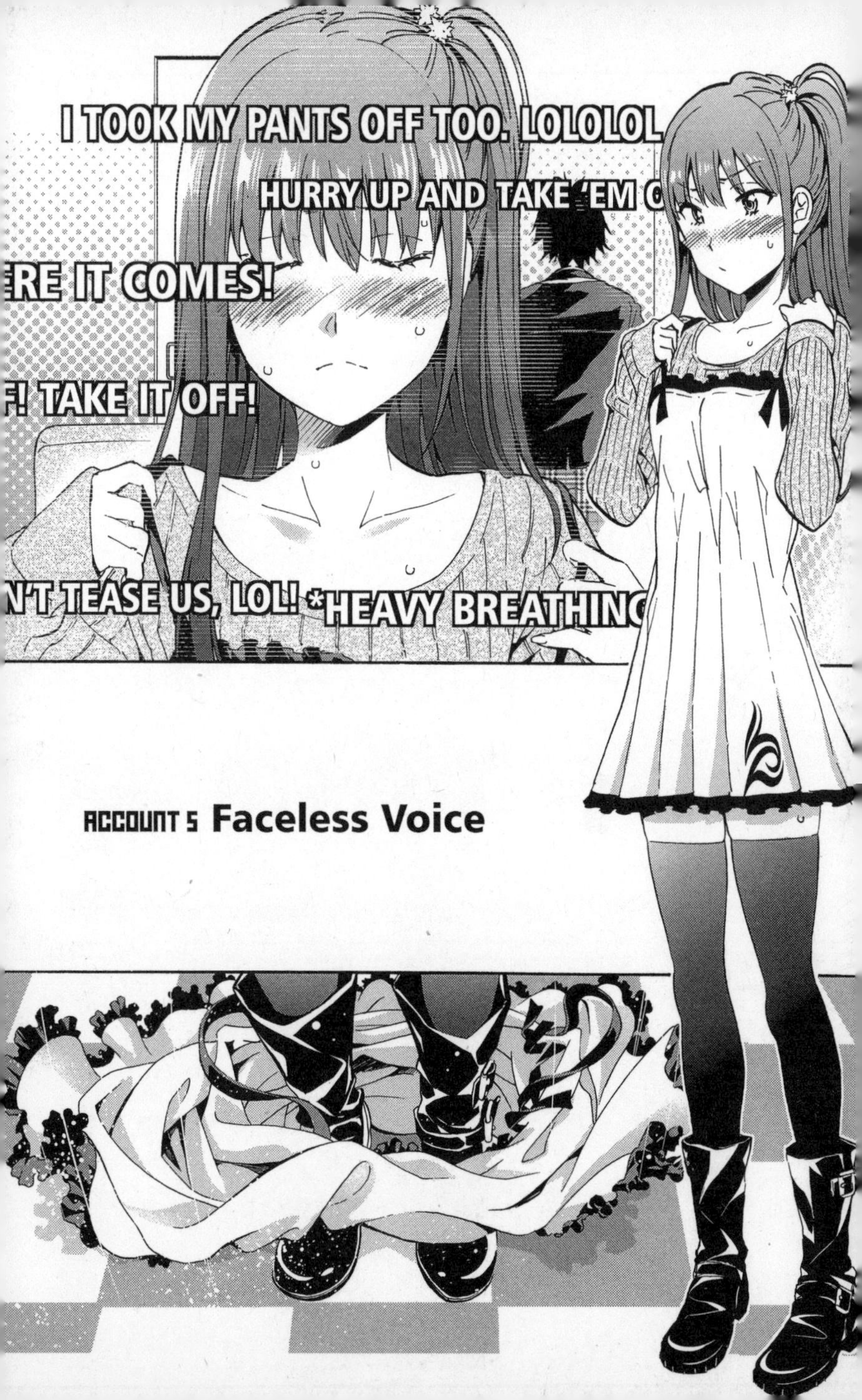

I TOOK MY PANTS OFF TOO. LOLOLOL
HURRY UP AND TAKE 'EM O
ERE IT COMES!
F! TAKE IT OFF!
N'T TEASE US, LOL! *HEAVY BREATHING
ACCOUNT 5 Faceless Voice

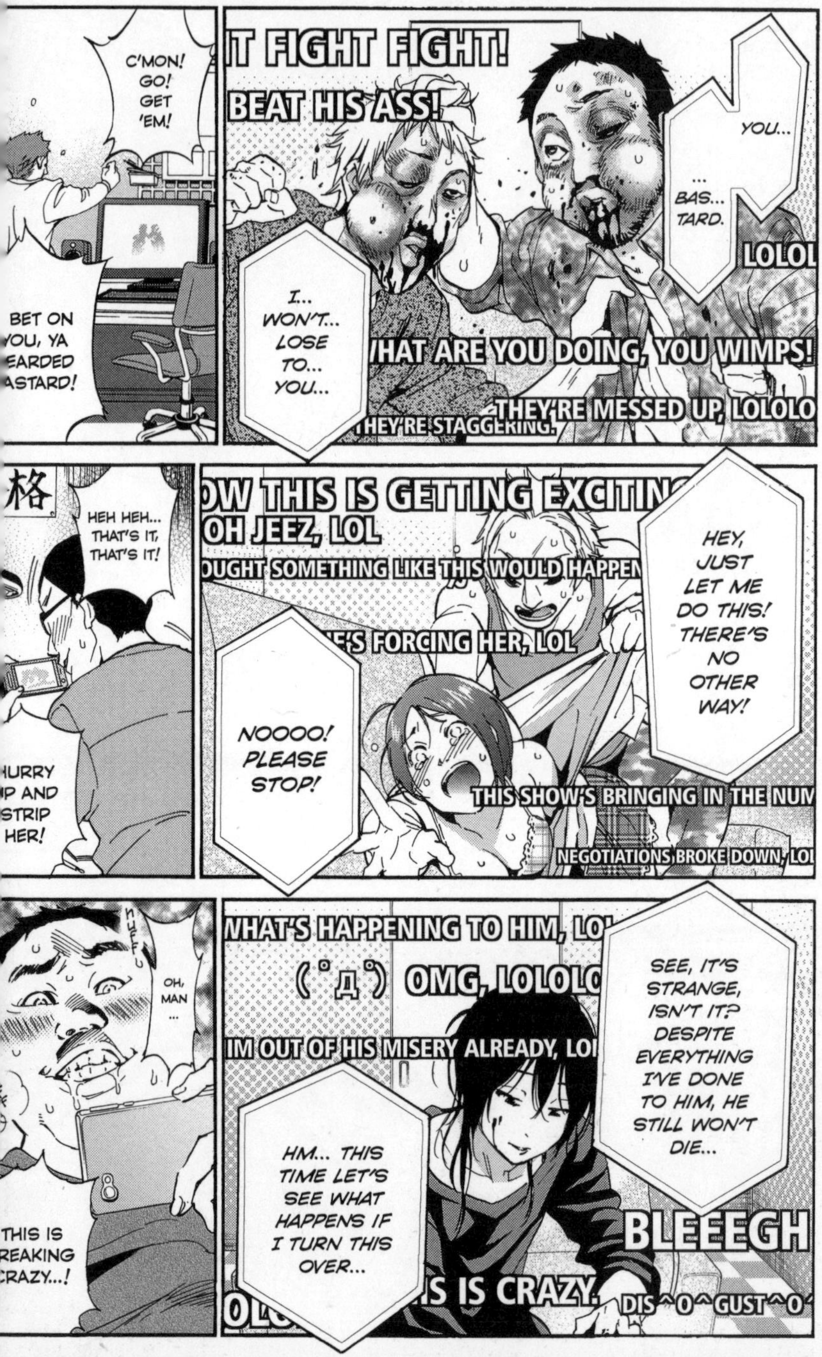
T FIGHT FIGHT!
BEAT HIS ASS!
YOU...
... BAS... TARD.
LOLOL
I... WON'T... LOSE TO... YOU...
HAT ARE YOU DOING, YOU WIMPS!
THEY'RE MESSED UP, LOLOLO
THEY'RE STAGGERING.
C'MON! GO! GET 'EM!
BET ON YOU, YA EARDED ASTARD!
OW THIS IS GETTING EXCITIN
OH JEEZ, LOL
OUGHT SOMETHING LIKE THIS WOULD HAPPEN
HEY, JUST LET ME DO THIS! THERE'S NO OTHER WAY!
E'S FORCING HER, LOL
NOOOO! PLEASE STOP!
THIS SHOW'S BRINGING IN THE NUM
NEGOTIATIONS BROKE DOWN, LOL
格
HEH HEH... THAT'S IT, THAT'S IT!
HURRY P AND STRIP HER!
HAT'S HAPPENING TO HIM, LO
(゜д゜) OMG, LOLOLO
SEE, IT'S STRANGE, ISN'T IT? DESPITE EVERYTHING I'VE DONE TO HIM, HE STILL WON'T DIE...
IM OUT OF HIS MISERY ALREADY, LOL
HM... THIS TIME LET'S SEE WHAT HAPPENS IF I TURN THIS OVER...
BLEEEGH
S IS CRAZY.
OLO
DIS^O^GUST^O^
HUFF
OH, MAN ...
THIS IS REAKING CRAZY...!

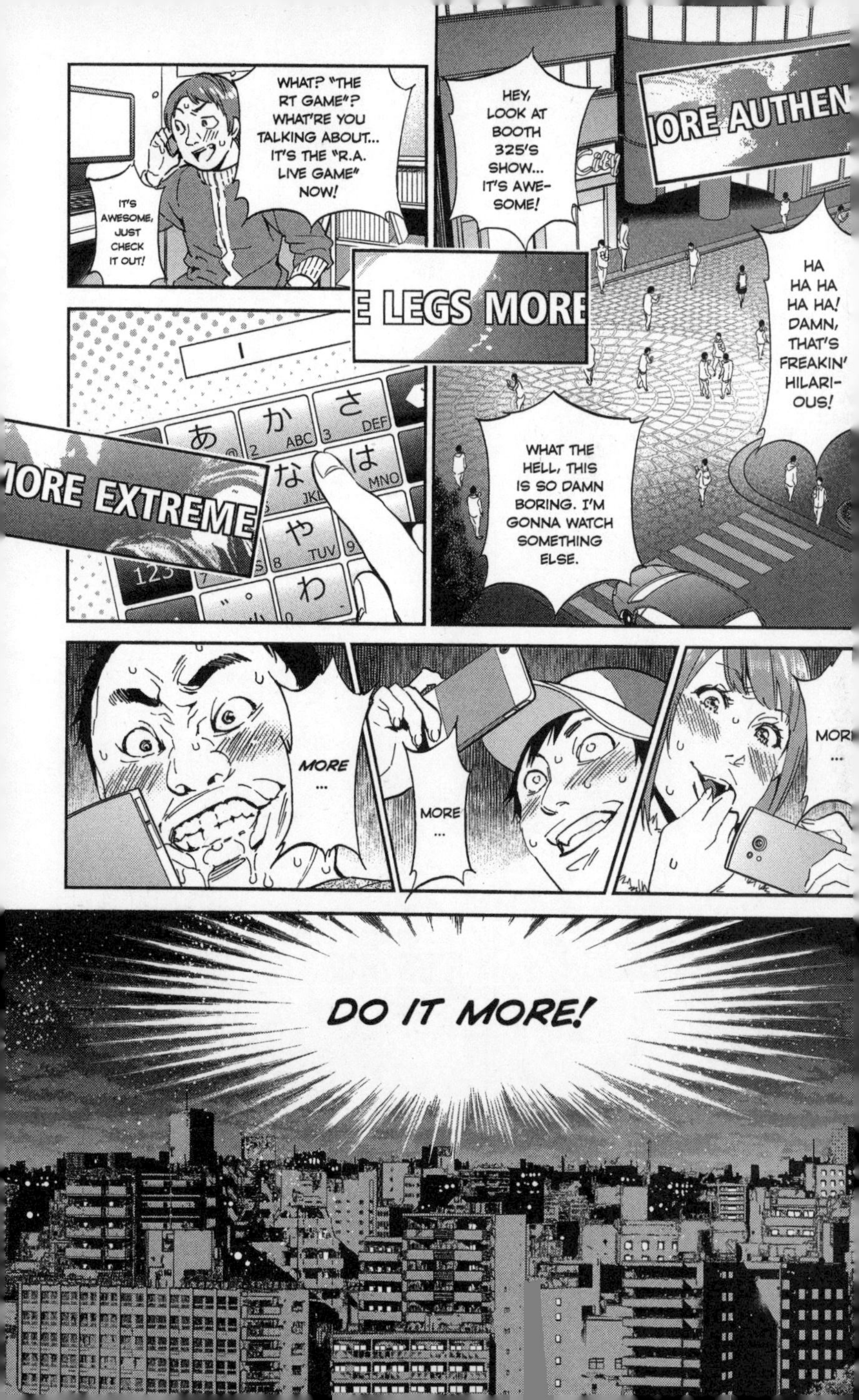
HEY, LOOK AT BOOTH 325'S SHOW... IT'S AWE-SOME!
IORE AUTHEN
HA HA HA HA HA! DAMN, THAT'S FREAKIN' HILARI-OUS!
E LEGS MORE
WHAT THE HELL, THIS IS SO DAMN BORING. I'M GONNA WATCH SOMETHING ELSE.
WHAT? "THE RT GAME"? WHAT'RE YOU TALKING ABOUT... IT'S THE "R.A. LIVE GAME" NOW!
IT'S AWESOME, JUST CHECK IT OUT!
IORE EXTREME
MORE ...
MORE ...
MORE ...
DO IT MORE!

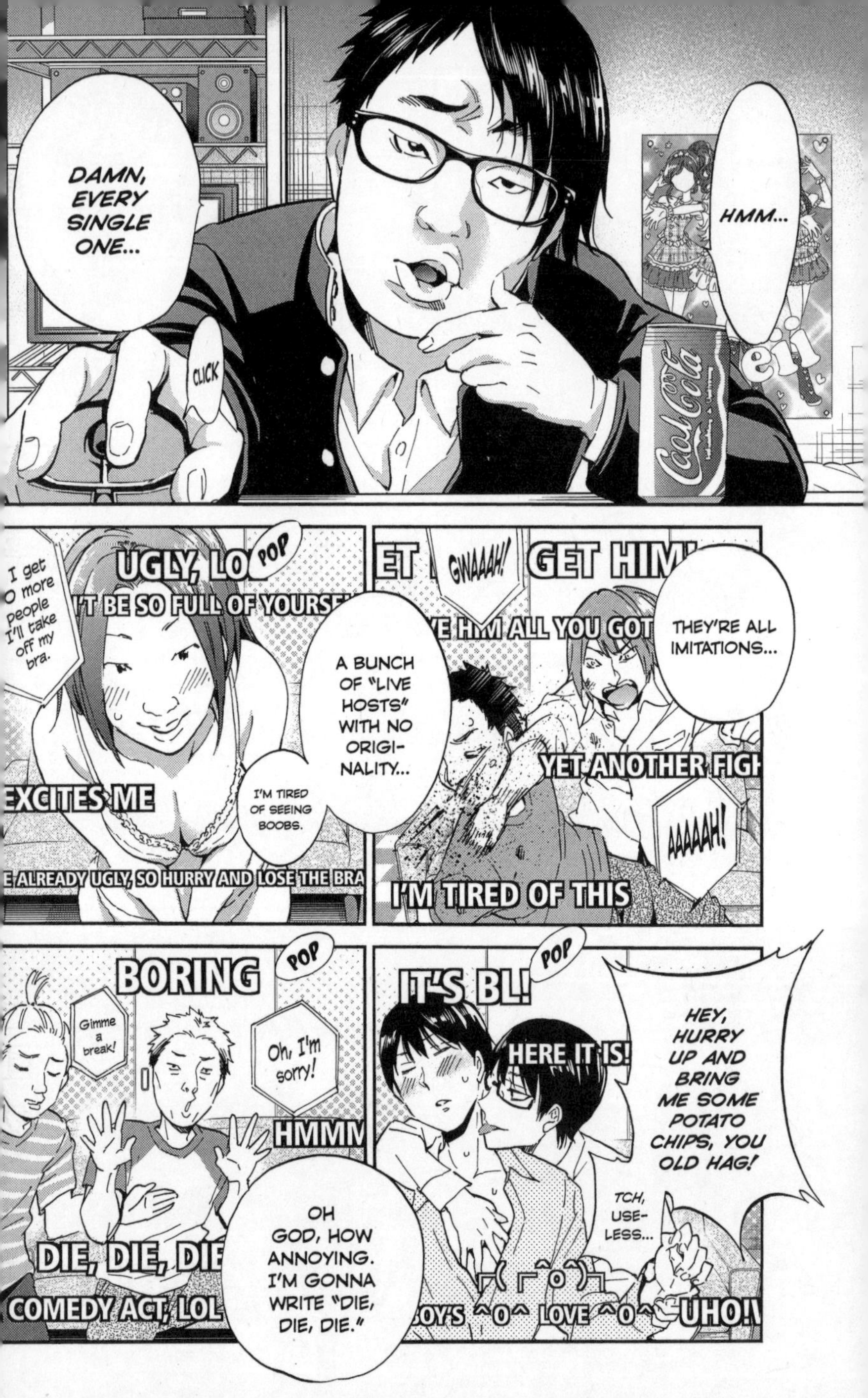
HMM...
DAMN, EVERY SINGLE ONE...
CLICK
Coca-Cola
GET HIM!
GWAAAH!
ET
THEY'RE ALL IMITATIONS...
VE HIM ALL YOU GOT
YET ANOTHER FIGH
AAAAAH!
I'M TIRED OF THIS
A BUNCH OF "LIVE HOSTS" WITH NO ORIGI-NALITY...
POP
UGLY, LO
I get O more people I'll take off my bra.
'T BE SO FULL OF YOURSE
EXCITES ME
I'M TIRED OF SEEING BOOBS.
E ALREADY UGLY, SO HURRY AND LOSE THE BRA
POP
IT'S BL!
HEY, HURRY UP AND BRING ME SOME POTATO CHIPS, YOU OLD HAG!
HERE IT IS!
TCH, USE-LESS...
┌(┌^o^)┐
BOY'S ^o^ LOVE ^o^ UHO!
POP
BORING
Oh, I'm sorry!
Gimme a break!
HMMM
OH GOD, HOW ANNOYING. I'M GONNA WRITE "DIE, DIE, DIE."
DIE, DIE, DIE
COMEDY ACT, LOL

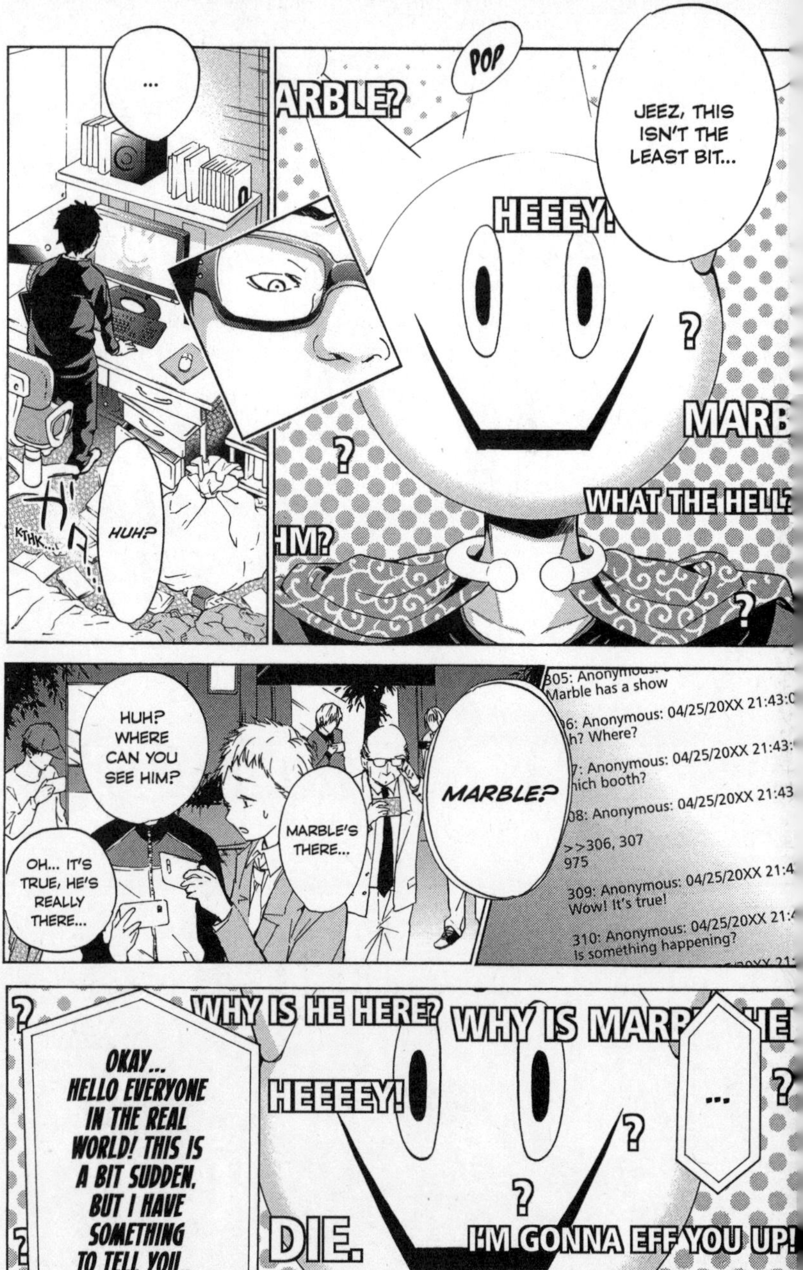
POP
JEEZ, THIS ISN'T THE LEAST BIT...
ARBLE?
HEEEY!
?
MARB
?
WHAT THE HELL?
HM?
?
...
HUH?
KTHK...
305: Anonymous:
Marble has a show
6: Anonymous: 04/25/20XX 21:43:0
h? Where?
7: Anonymous: 04/25/20XX 21:43:
hich booth?
08: Anonymous: 04/25/20XX 21:43
>>306, 307
975
309: Anonymous: 04/25/20XX 21:4
Wow! It's true!
310: Anonymous: 04/25/20XX 21:4
Is something happening?
MARBLE?
MARBLE'S THERE...
HUH? WHERE CAN YOU SEE HIM?
OH... IT'S TRUE, HE'S REALLY THERE...
...
?
WHY IS MARB
HE
?
WHY IS HE HERE?
?
HEEEEY!
?
I'M GONNA EFF YOU UP!
DIE.
?
OKAY... HELLO EVERYONE IN THE REAL WORLD! THIS IS A BIT SUDDEN, BUT I HAVE SOMETHING TO TELL YOU...

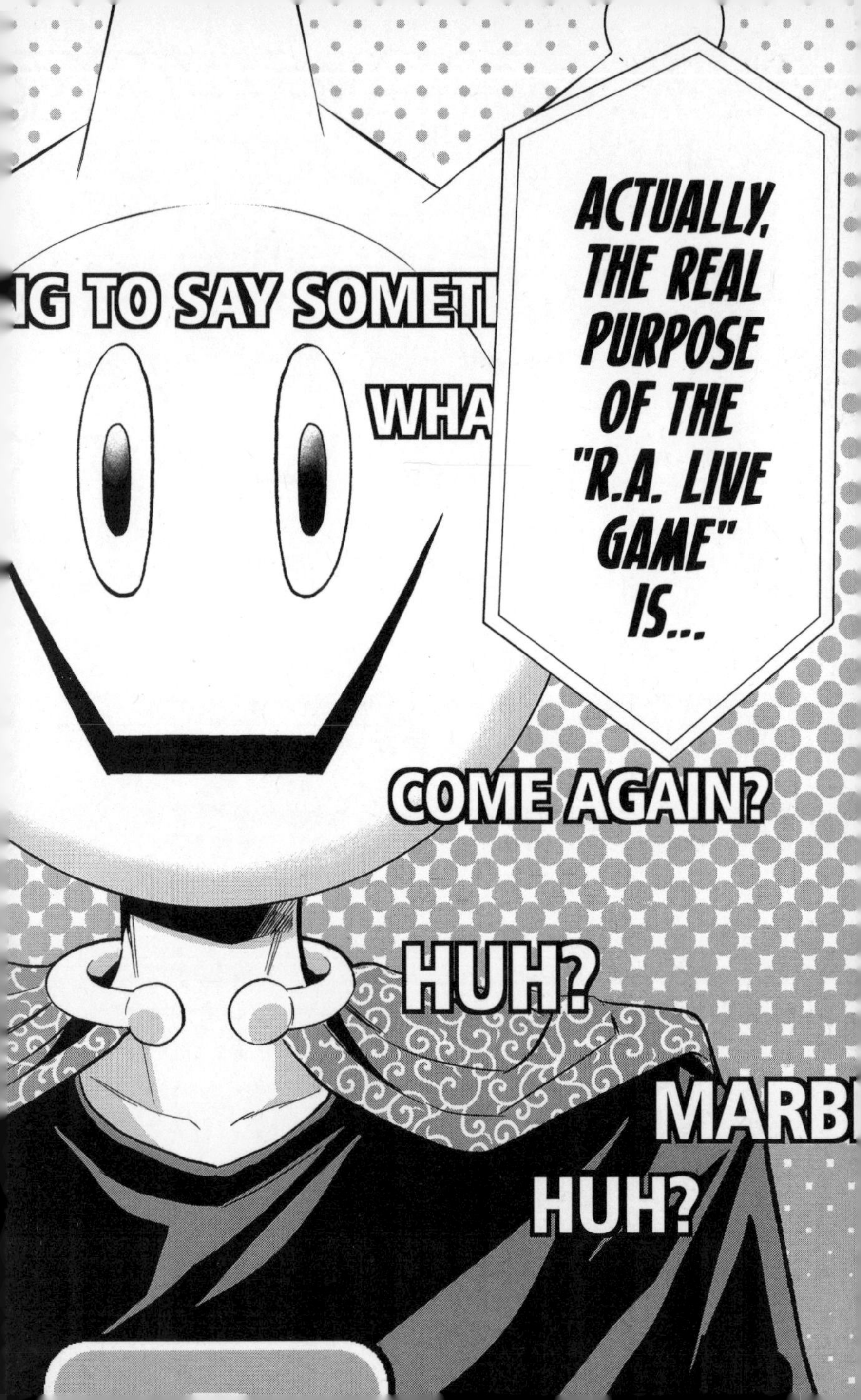
ACTUALLY, THE REAL PURPOSE OF THE "R.A. LIVE GAME" IS...
G TO SAY SOMET
WHA
COME AGAIN?
HUH?
MARB
HUH?

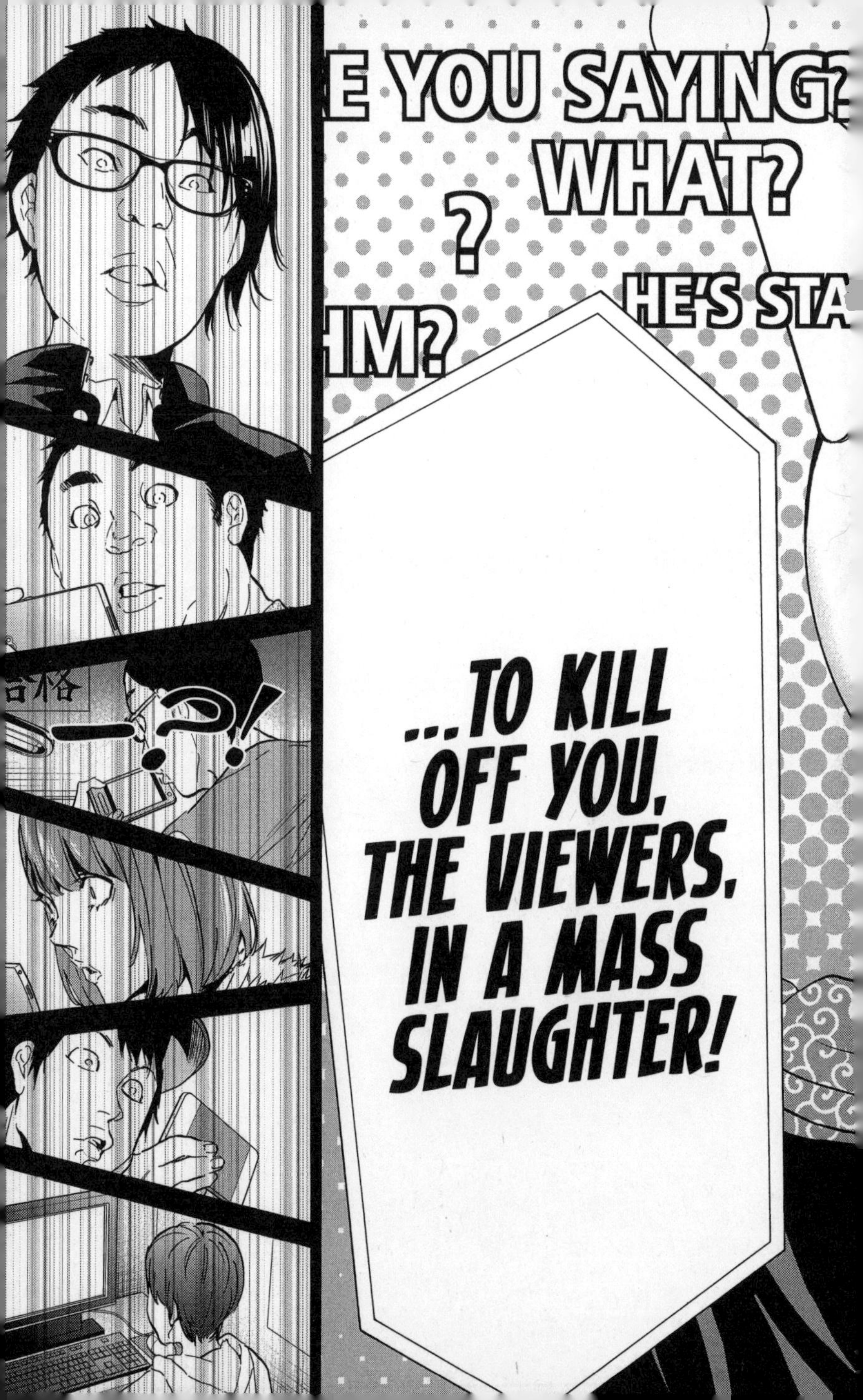
E YOU SAYING?
WHAT?
?
HE'S STA
HM?
...TO KILL OFF YOU, THE VIEWERS, IN A MASS SLAUGHTER!

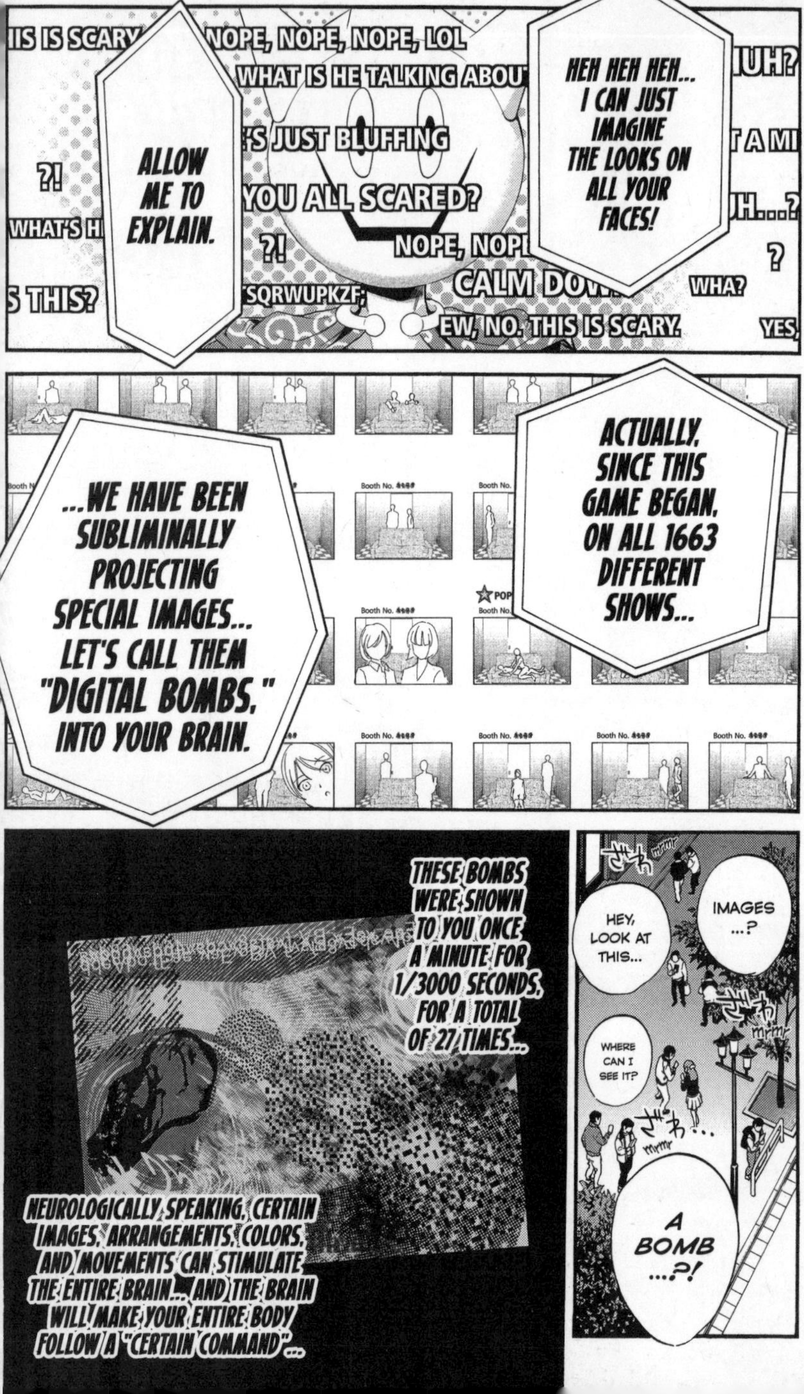
HEH HEH HEH... I CAN JUST IMAGINE THE LOOKS ON ALL YOUR FACES!
ALLOW ME TO EXPLAIN.
NOPE, NOPE, NOPE, LOL
YOU ALL SCARED?
?!
CALM DOW
WHA?
EW, NO. THIS IS SCARY.
?
ACTUALLY, SINCE THIS GAME BEGAN, ON ALL 1663 DIFFERENT SHOWS...
...WE HAVE BEEN SUBLIMINALLY PROJECTING SPECIAL IMAGES... LET'S CALL THEM "DIGITAL BOMBS," INTO YOUR BRAIN.
mrmr
IMAGES ...?
HEY, LOOK AT THIS...
mrmr
WHERE CAN I SEE IT?
mrmr
A BOMB ...?!
THESE BOMBS WERE SHOWN TO YOU ONCE A MINUTE FOR 1/3000 SECONDS, FOR A TOTAL OF 27 TIMES...
NEUROLOGICALLY SPEAKING, CERTAIN IMAGES, ARRANGEMENTS, COLORS, AND MOVEMENTS CAN STIMULATE THE ENTIRE BRAIN... AND THE BRAIN WILL MAKE YOUR ENTIRE BODY FOLLOW A "CERTAIN COMMAND"...

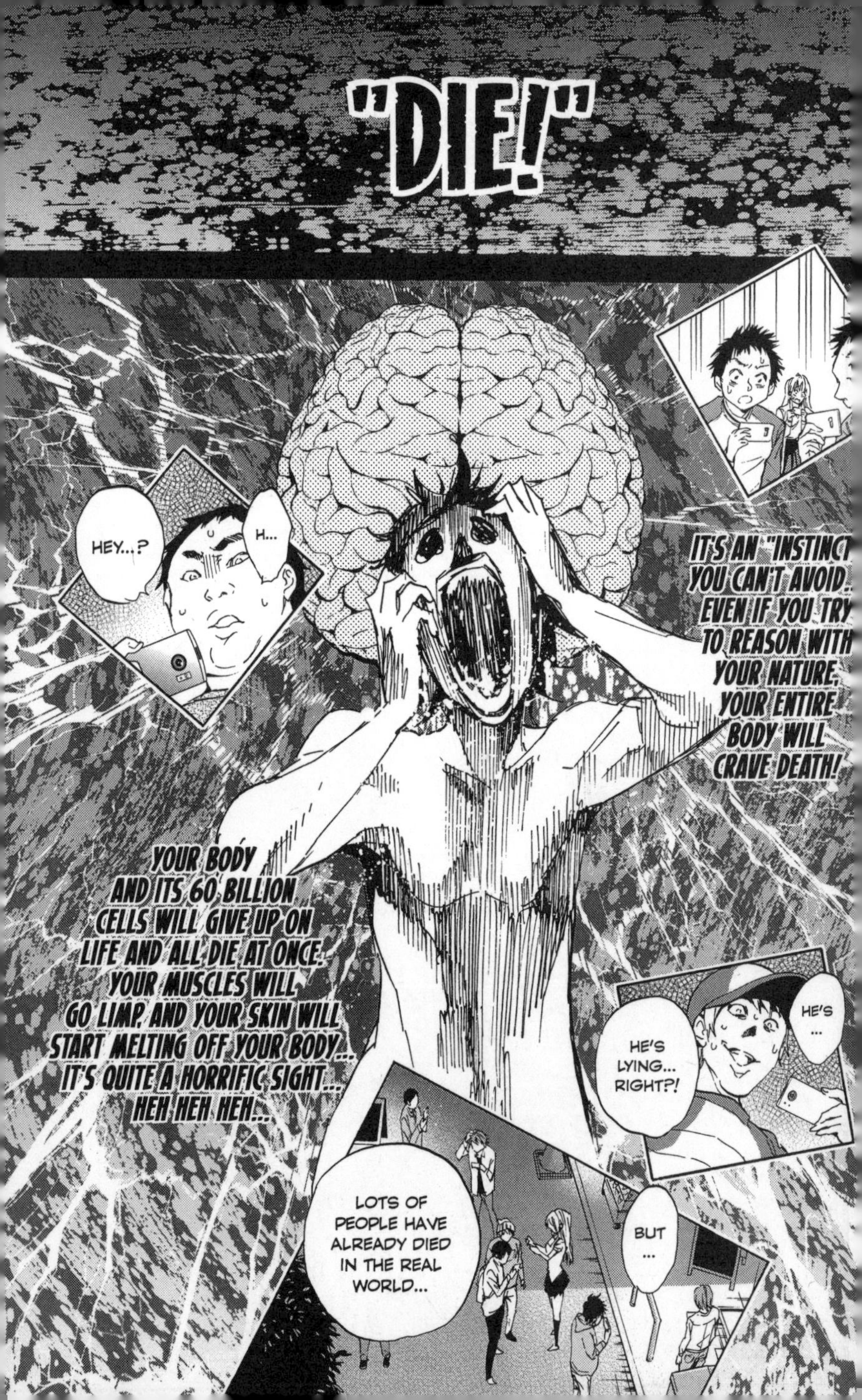
"DIE!"
H...
HEY...?
IT'S AN "INSTINCT" YOU CAN'T AVOID... EVEN IF YOU TRY TO REASON WITH YOUR NATURE, YOUR ENTIRE BODY WILL CRAVE DEATH!
YOUR BODY AND ITS 60 BILLION CELLS WILL GIVE UP ON LIFE AND ALL DIE AT ONCE. YOUR MUSCLES WILL GO LIMP, AND YOUR SKIN WILL START MELTING OFF YOUR BODY... IT'S QUITE A HORRIFIC SIGHT... HEH HEH HEH...
HE'S ...
HE'S LYING... RIGHT?!
BUT ...
LOTS OF PEOPLE HAVE ALREADY DIED IN THE REAL WORLD...

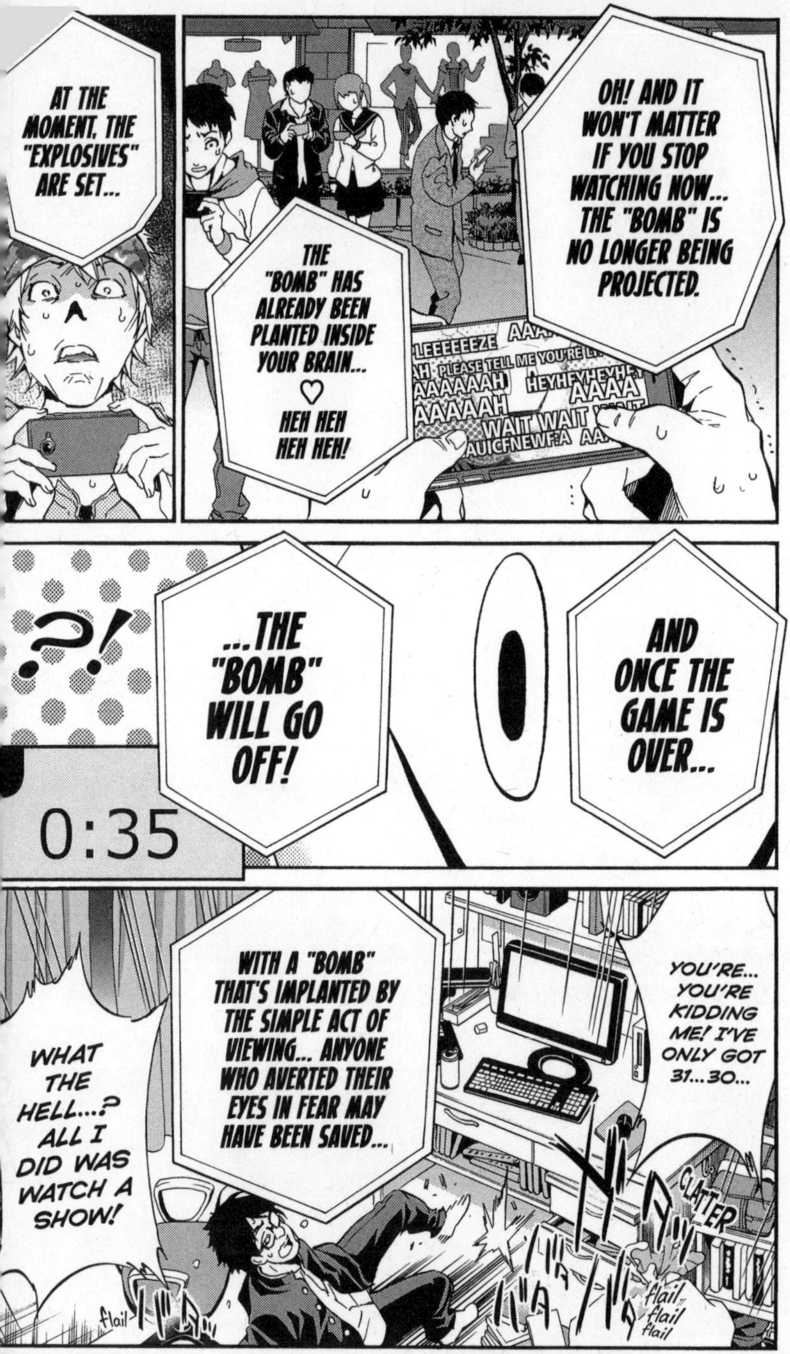
OH! AND IT WON'T MATTER IF YOU STOP WATCHING NOW... THE "BOMB" IS NO LONGER BEING PROJECTED.
THE "BOMB" HAS ALREADY BEEN PLANTED INSIDE YOUR BRAIN... ♡ HEH HEH HEH HEH!
AAAAAAAH
AAAA
AAAAAAH
WAIT WAIT
AUICFNEWFA
AT THE MOMENT, THE "EXPLOSIVES" ARE SET...
AND ONCE THE GAME IS OVER...
...THE "BOMB" WILL GO OFF!
?!
0:35
YOU'RE... YOU'RE KIDDING ME! I'VE ONLY GOT 31...30...
CLATTER
flail flail flail
WITH A "BOMB" THAT'S IMPLANTED BY THE SIMPLE ACT OF VIEWING... ANYONE WHO AVERTED THEIR EYES IN FEAR MAY HAVE BEEN SAVED...
WHAT THE HELL...? ALL I DID WAS WATCH A SHOW!
flail

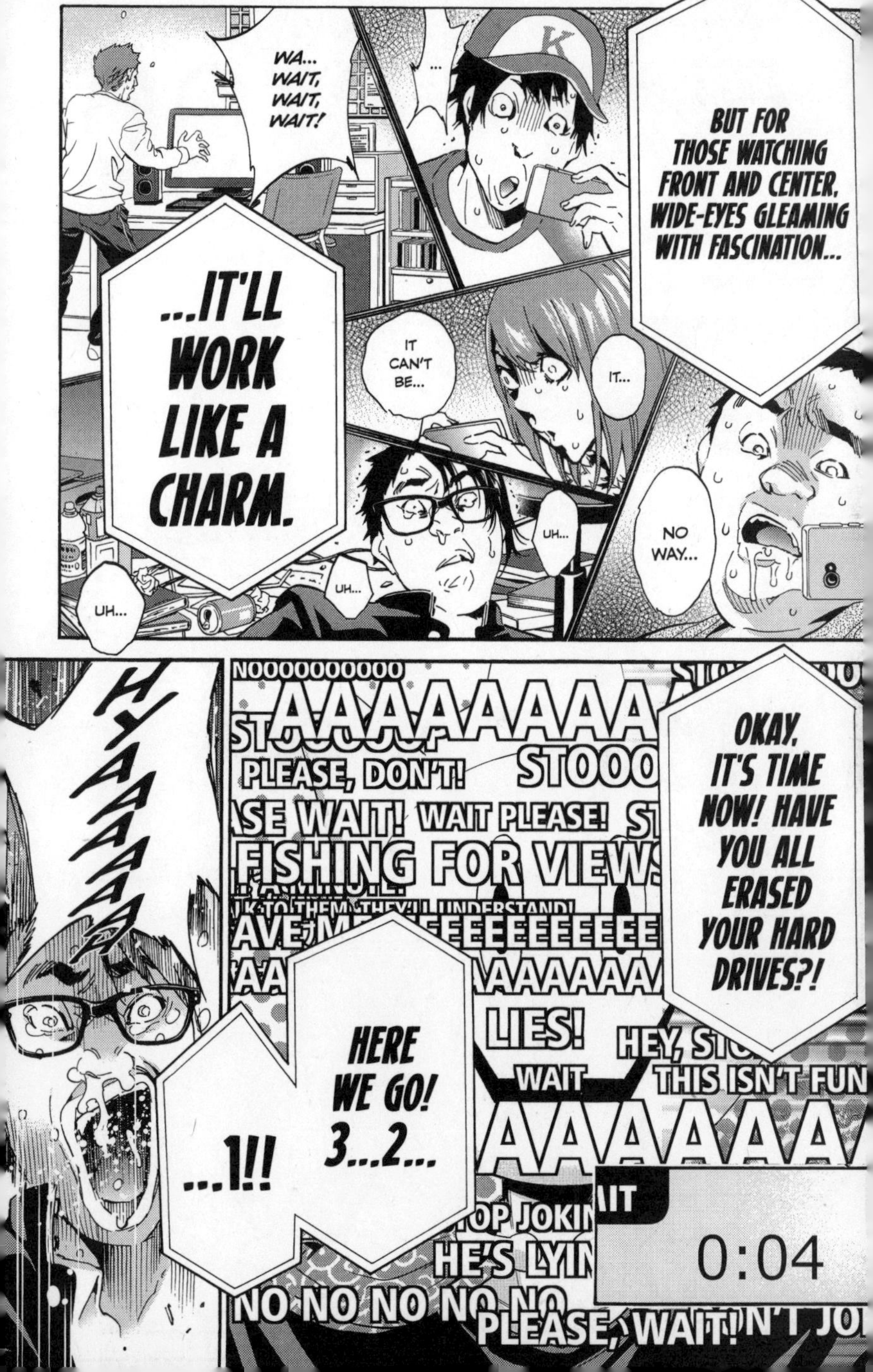
BUT FOR THOSE WATCHING FRONT AND CENTER, WIDE-EYES GLEAMING WITH FASCINATION...
...
WA... WAIT, WAIT, WAIT!
IT...
IT CAN'T BE...
NO WAY...
UH...
UH...
UH...
...IT'LL WORK LIKE A CHARM.
OKAY, IT'S TIME NOW! HAVE YOU ALL ERASED YOUR HARD DRIVES?!
NOOOOOOOOOO
AAAAAAAAA
PLEASE, DON'T!
STOOOO
WAIT PLEASE!
FISHING FOR VIEWS
LIES!
WAIT
THIS ISN'T FUN
AAAAAAA
HE'S LYIN
NO NO NO NO NO
PLEASE, WAIT!
0:04
HERE WE GO! 3...2...
...1!!
HYAAAAAAA

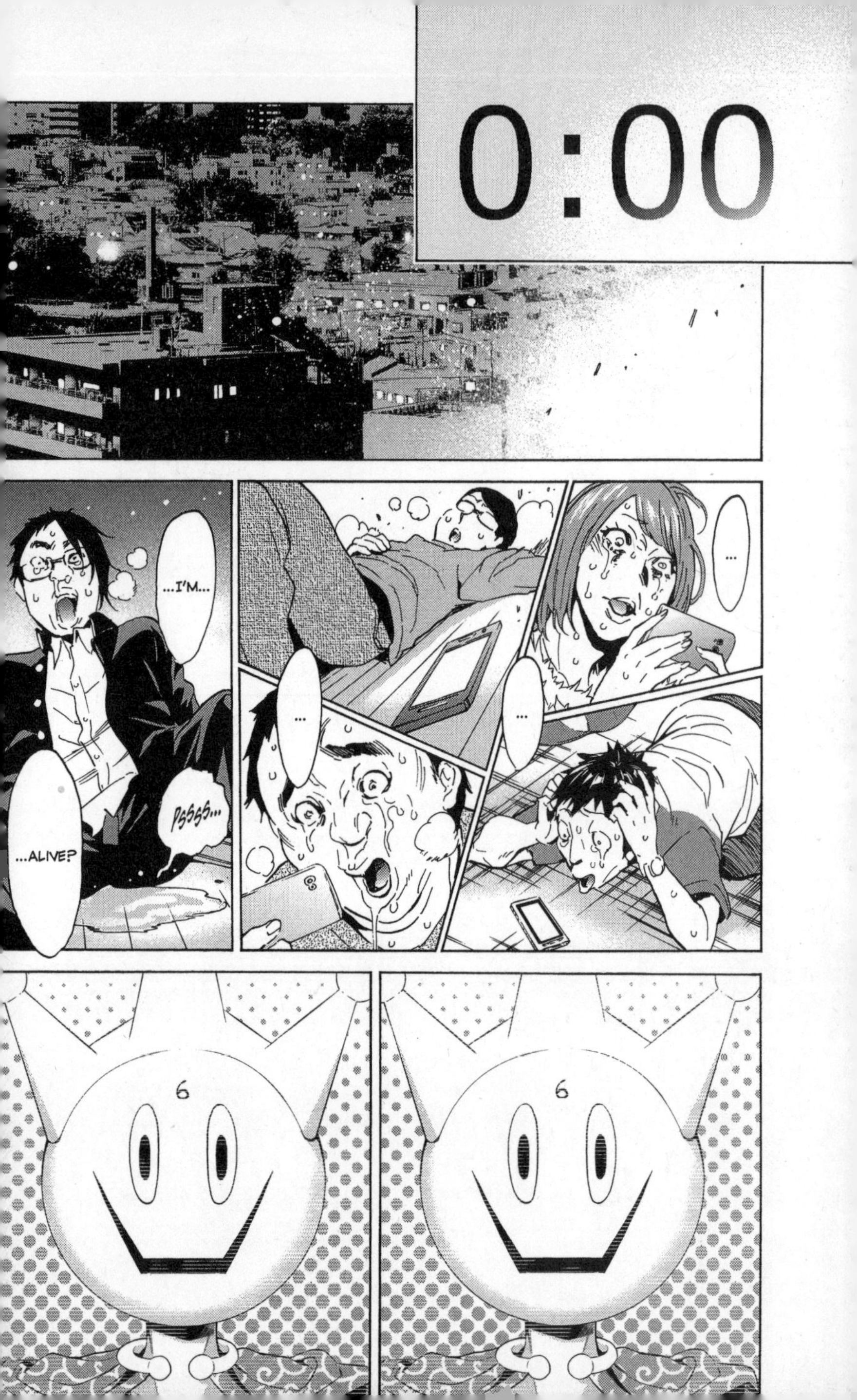
0:00
...
...
...
...I'M...
...ALIVE?
PSSSS...
6
6

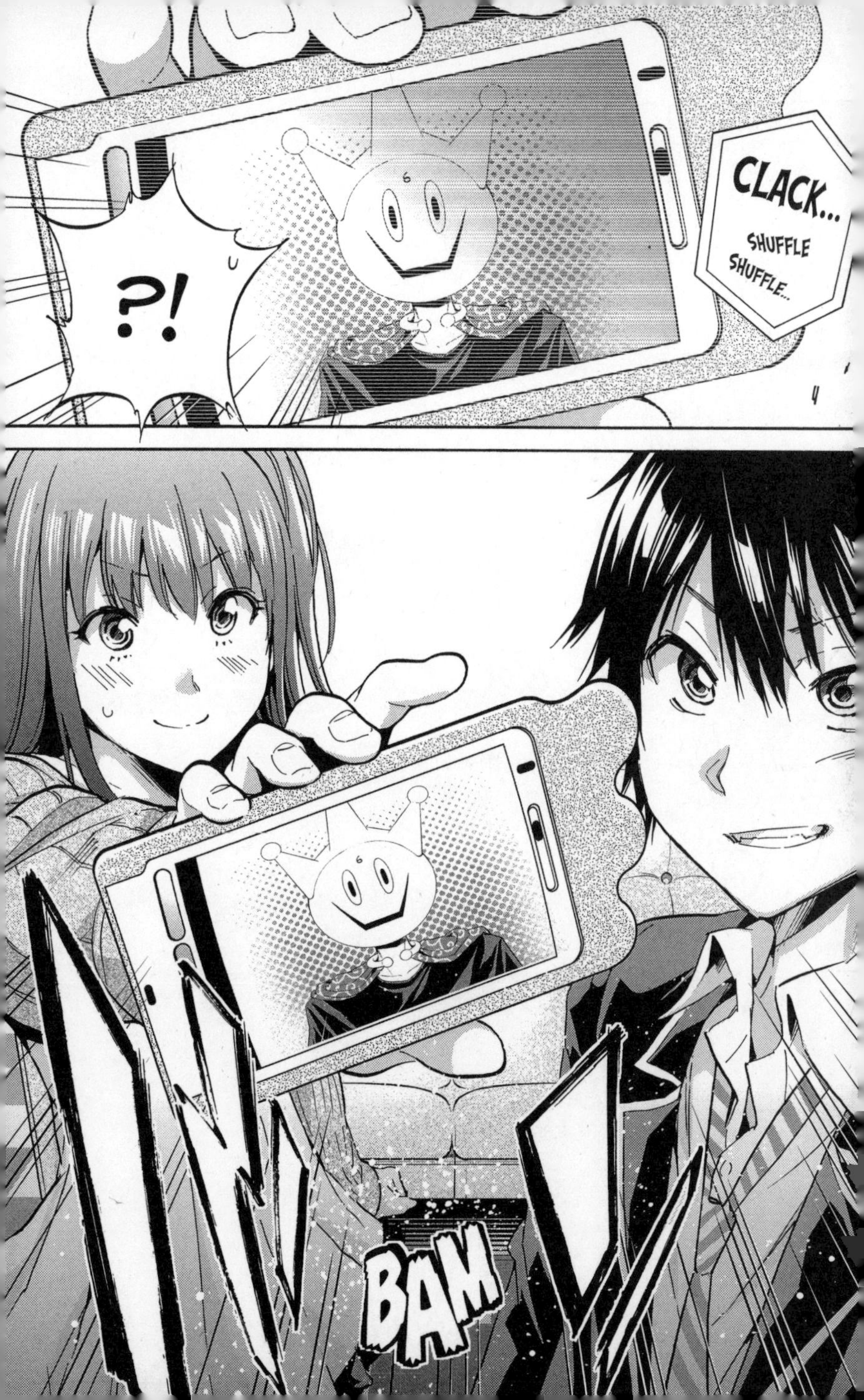
CLACK...
SHUFFLE SHUFFLE...
?!
BAM

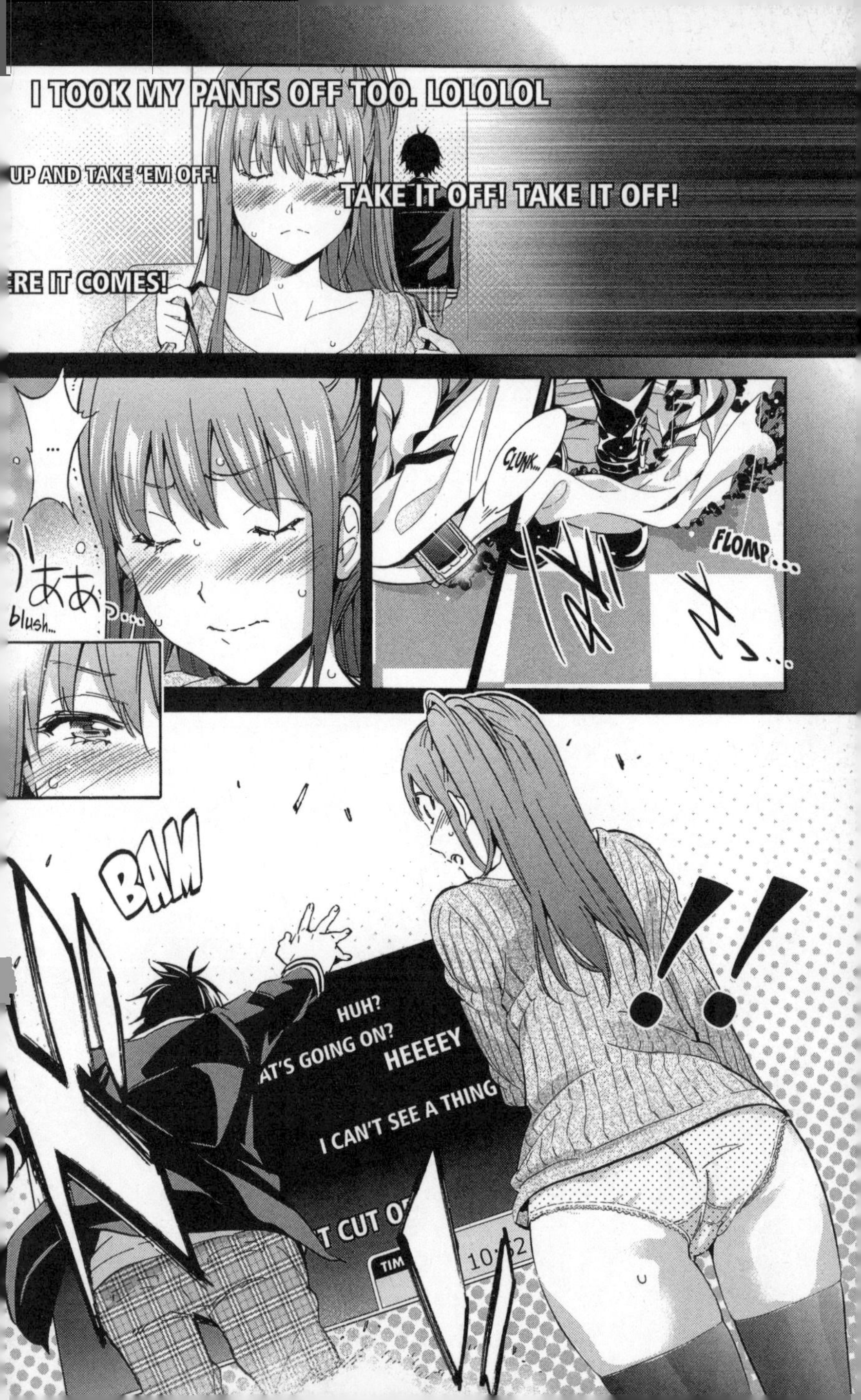
I TOOK MY PANTS OFF TOO. LOLOLOL
TAKE IT OFF! TAKE IT OFF!
UP AND TAKE 'EM OFF!
ERE IT COMES!
CLUNK...
FLOMP...
...
ああ
blush...
BAM
HUH?
AT'S GOING ON?
HEEEEY
I CAN'T SEE A THING
T CUT O

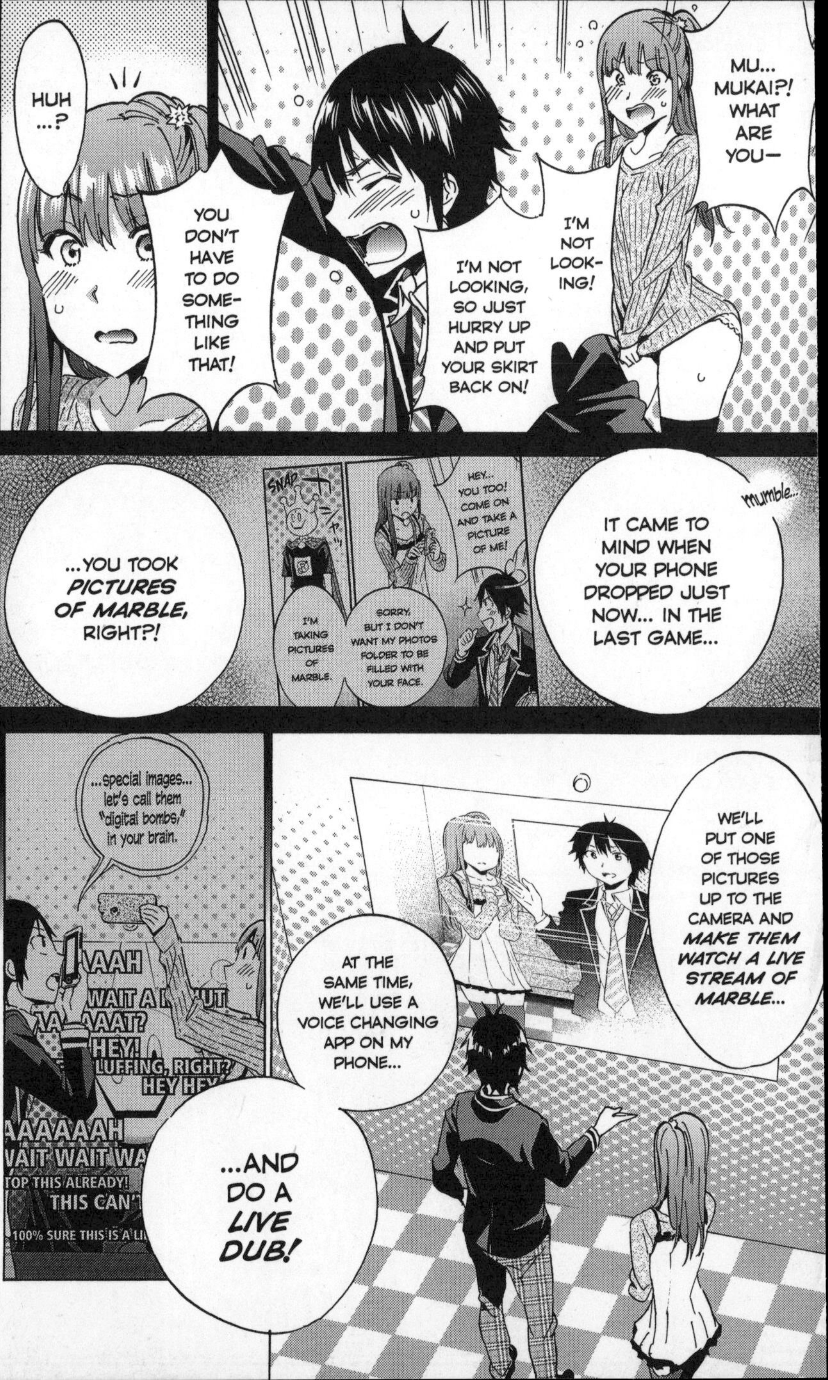
MU... MUKAI?! WHAT ARE YOU—
I'M NOT LOOKING!
I'M NOT LOOKING, SO JUST HURRY UP AND PUT YOUR SKIRT BACK ON!
YOU DON'T HAVE TO DO SOMETHING LIKE THAT!
HUH ...?
mumble...
IT CAME TO MIND WHEN YOUR PHONE DROPPED JUST NOW... IN THE LAST GAME...
HEY... YOU TOO! COME ON AND TAKE A PICTURE OF ME!
SNAP
SORRY, BUT I DON'T WANT MY PHOTOS FOLDER TO BE FILLED WITH YOUR FACE.
I'M TAKING PICTURES OF MARBLE.
...YOU TOOK *PICTURES OF MARBLE,* RIGHT?!
WE'LL PUT ONE OF THOSE PICTURES UP TO THE CAMERA AND *MAKE THEM WATCH A LIVE STREAM OF MARBLE...*
AT THE SAME TIME, WE'LL USE A VOICE CHANGING APP ON MY PHONE...
...AND DO A *LIVE DUB!*
...special images... let's call them "digital bombs," in your brain.
HEY!
HEY HEY
AAAAAAH

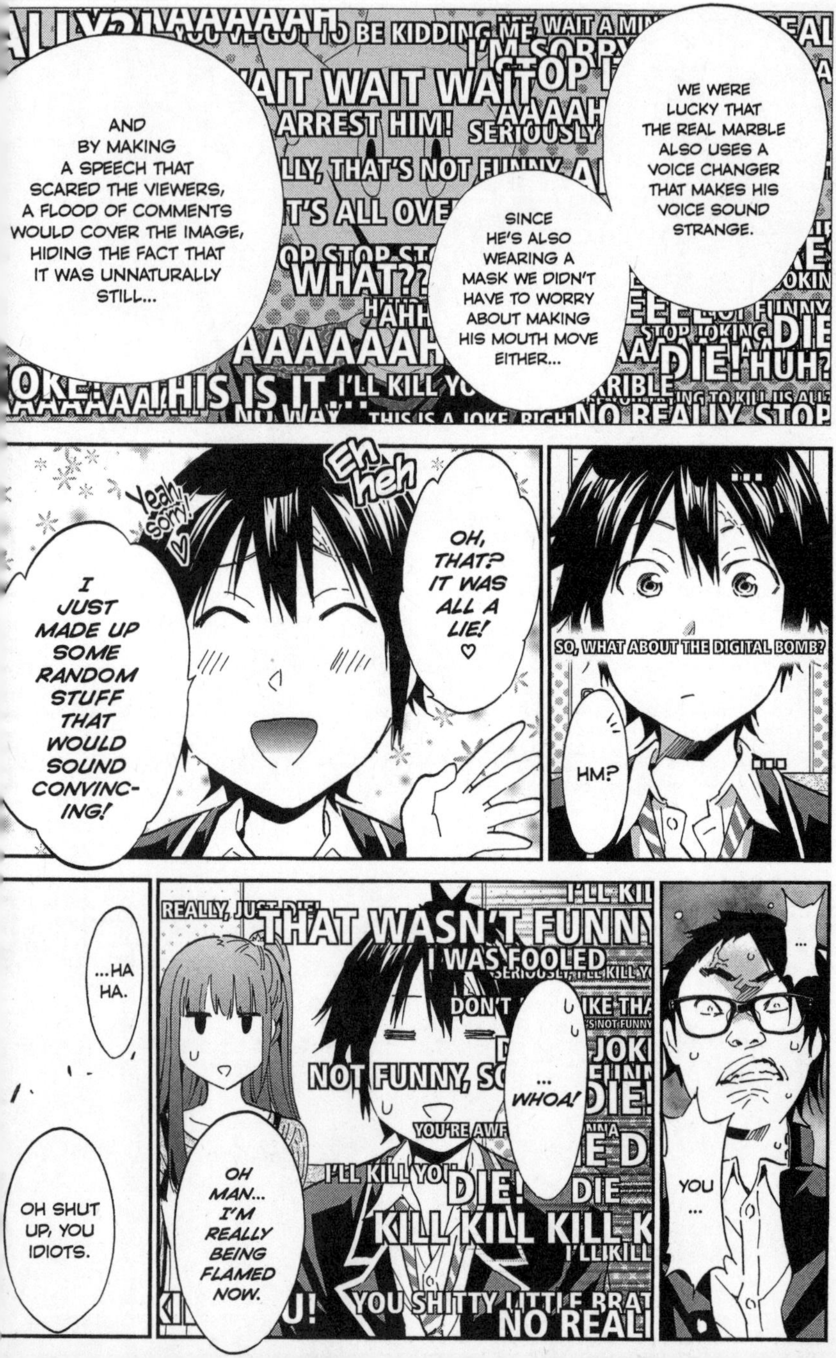
YOU'VE GOT TO BE KIDDING ME
WAIT A MIN
I'M SORRY
STOP IT
WAIT WAIT WAIT
ARREST HIM!
SERIOUSLY
THAT'S NOT FUNNY
IT'S ALL OVE
WHAT??
DIE!
HUH?
THIS IS IT...
I'LL KILL YO
THIS IS A JOKE, RIGHT
NO REALLY STOP
WE WERE LUCKY THAT THE REAL MARBLE ALSO USES A VOICE CHANGER THAT MAKES HIS VOICE SOUND STRANGE.
SINCE HE'S ALSO WEARING A MASK WE DIDN'T HAVE TO WORRY ABOUT MAKING HIS MOUTH MOVE EITHER...
AND BY MAKING A SPEECH THAT SCARED THE VIEWERS, A FLOOD OF COMMENTS WOULD COVER THE IMAGE, HIDING THE FACT THAT IT WAS UNNATURALLY STILL...
...
SO, WHAT ABOUT THE DIGITAL BOMB?
HM?
...
Eh heh
OH, THAT? IT WAS ALL A LIE! ♡
Yeah, sorry! ♡
I JUST MADE UP SOME RANDOM STUFF THAT WOULD SOUND CONVINC-ING!
...
YOU ...
REALLY, JUST DIE!
THAT WASN'T FUNNY
I WAS FOOLED
NOT FUNNY
I'LL KILL YOU
KILL KILL KILL K
YOU SHITTY LITTLE BRAT
NO REALI
... WHOA!
OH MAN... I'M REALLY BEING FLAMED NOW.
...HA HA.
OH SHUT UP, YOU IDIOTS.

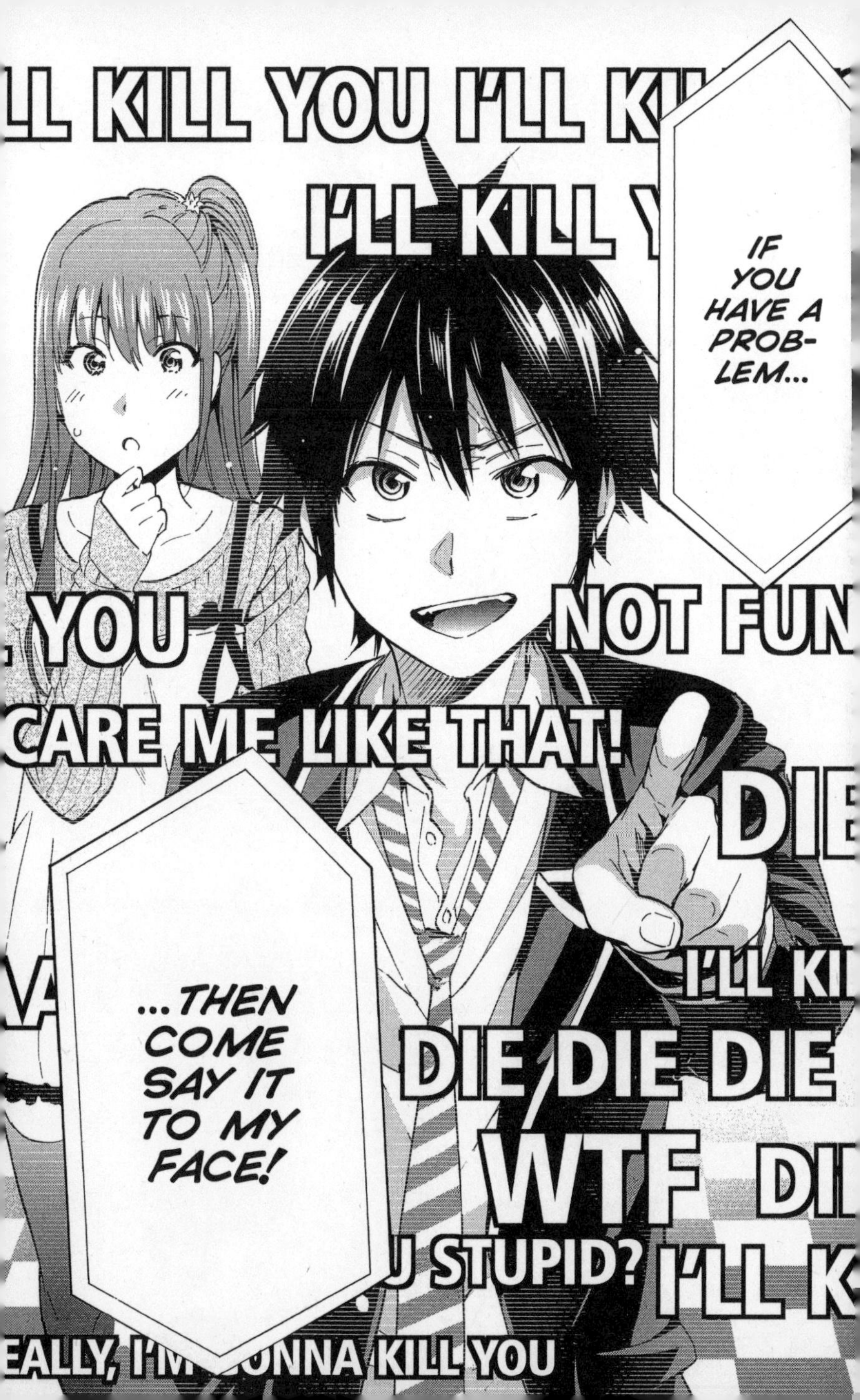
IF YOU HAVE A PROB- LEM...
...THEN COME SAY IT TO MY FACE!
LL KILL YOU I'LL K
I'LL KILL Y
YOU
NOT FUN
CARE ME LIKE THAT!
DIE
I'LL KI
DIE DIE DIE
WTF
DI
U STUPID?
I'LL K
EALLY, I'M GONNA KILL YOU

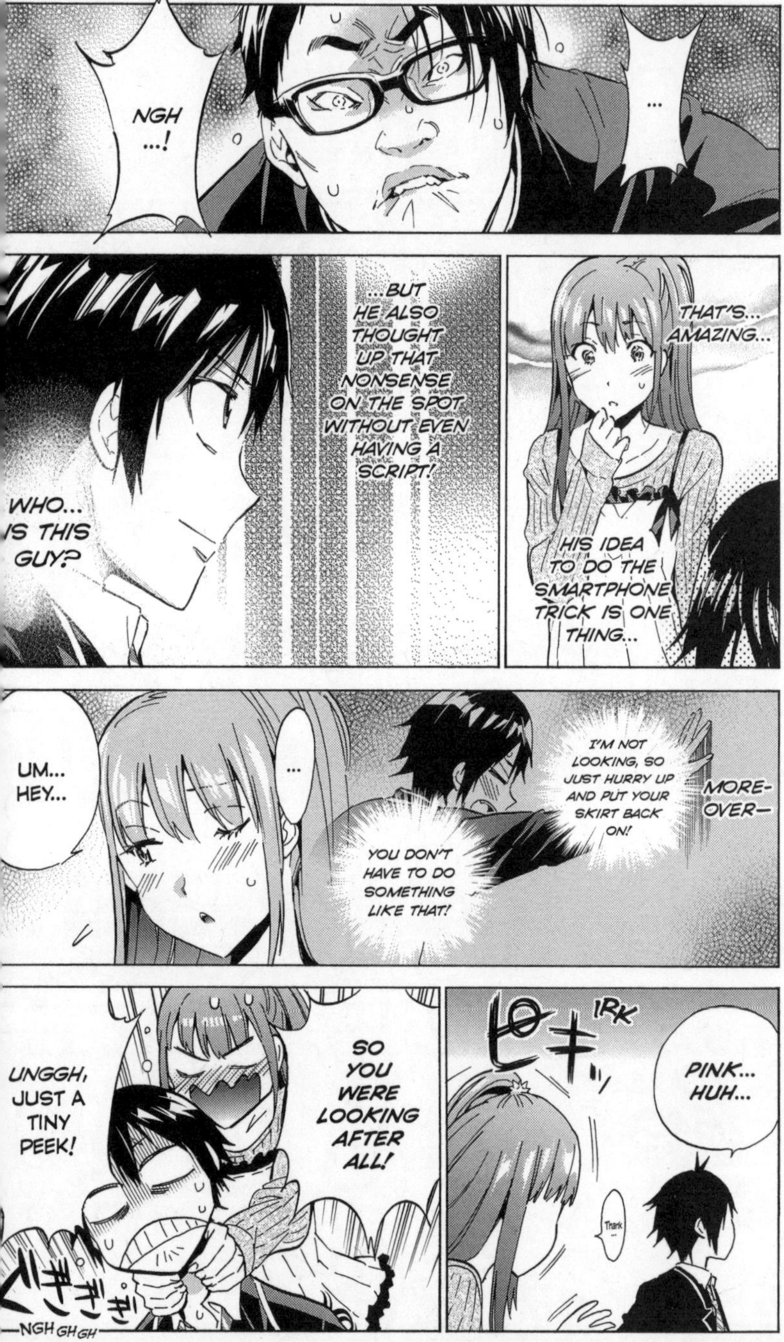
...
NGH ...!
THAT'S... AMAZING...
HIS IDEA TO DO THE SMARTPHONE TRICK IS ONE THING...
...BUT HE ALSO THOUGHT UP THAT NONSENSE ON THE SPOT WITHOUT EVEN HAVING A SCRIPT!
WHO... IS THIS GUY?
MORE-OVER—
I'M NOT LOOKING, SO JUST HURRY UP AND PUT YOUR SKIRT BACK ON!
YOU DON'T HAVE TO DO SOMETHING LIKE THAT!
...
UM... HEY...
IRK
PINK... HUH...
Thank...
SO YOU WERE LOOKING AFTER ALL!
UNGGH, JUST A TINY PEEK!
NGH GH GH

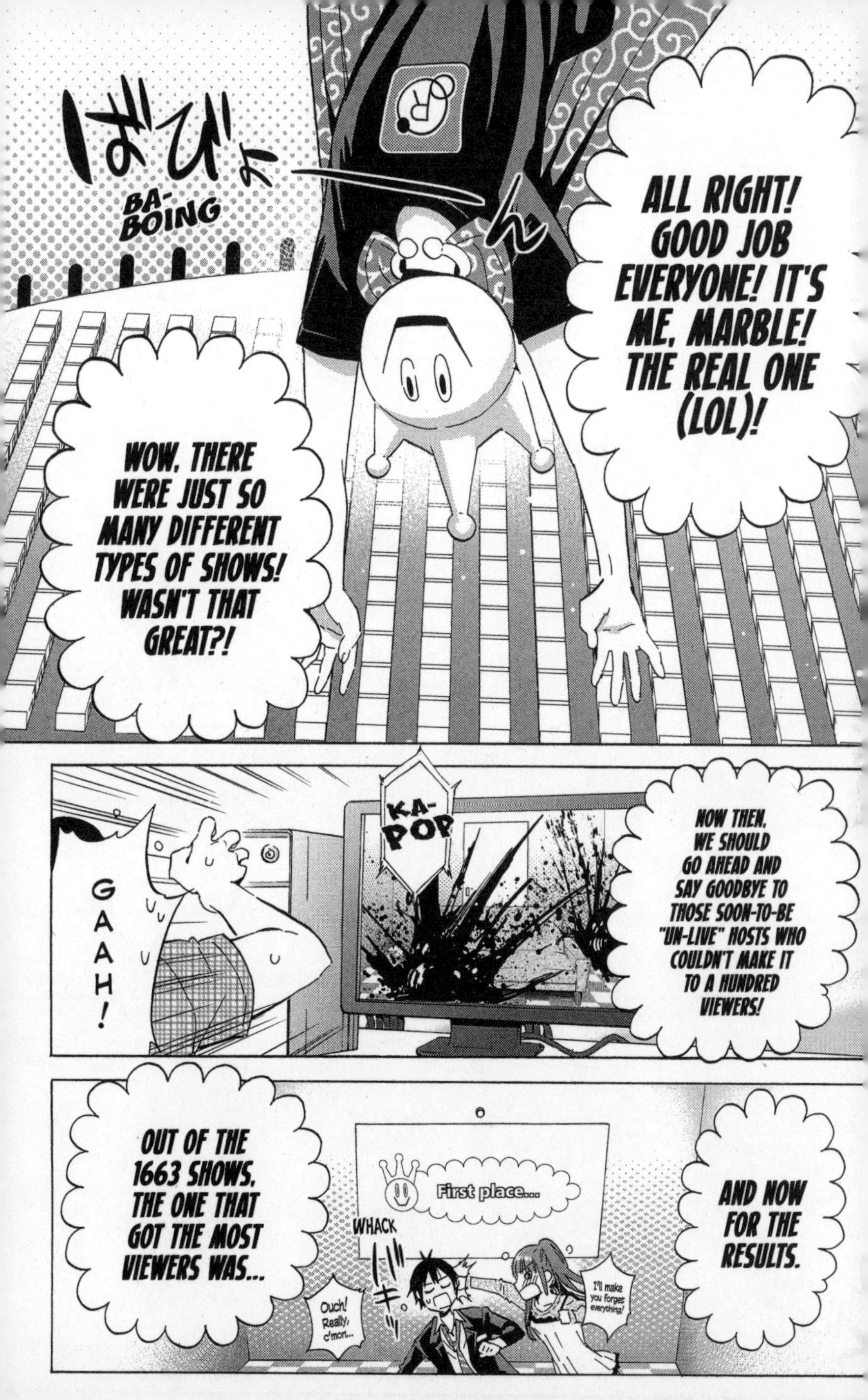
BA-BOING
ALL RIGHT! GOOD JOB EVERYONE! IT'S ME, MARBLE! THE REAL ONE (LOL)!
WOW, THERE WERE JUST SO MANY DIFFERENT TYPES OF SHOWS! WASN'T THAT GREAT?!
NOW THEN, WE SHOULD GO AHEAD AND SAY GOODBYE TO THOSE SOON-TO-BE "UN-LIVE" HOSTS WHO COULDN'T MAKE IT TO A HUNDRED VIEWERS!
KA-POP
GAAH!
AND NOW FOR THE RESULTS.
OUT OF THE 1663 SHOWS, THE ONE THAT GOT THE MOST VIEWERS WAS...
First place...
I'll make you forget everything!
WHACK
Ouch! Really, c'mon...

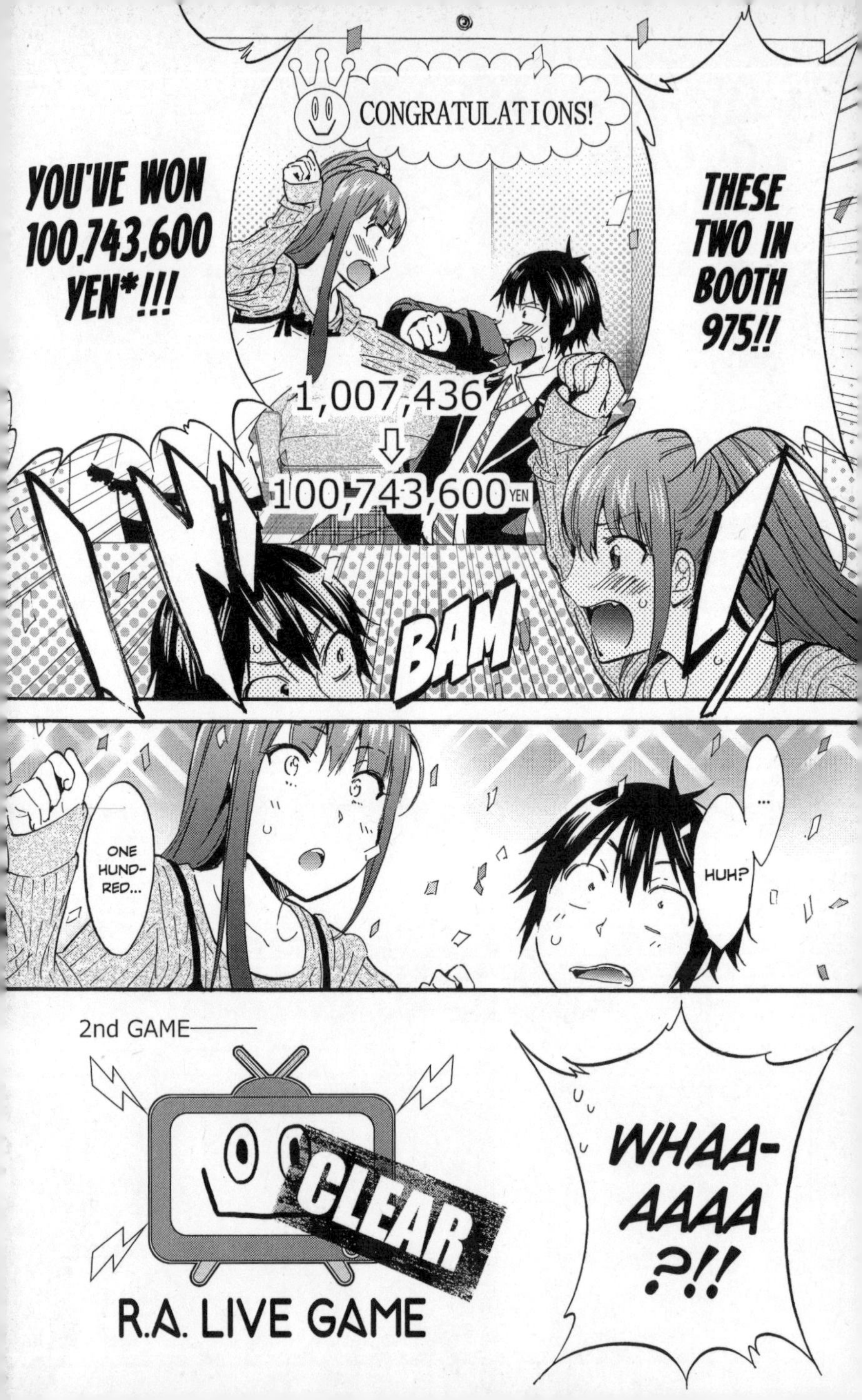
THESE TWO IN BOOTH 975!!
CONGRATULATIONS!
YOU'VE WON 100,743,600 YEN*!!!
1,007,436 ⇩ 100,743,600 YEN
BAM
... HUH?
ONE HUNDRED...
WHAA-AAAA ?!!
2nd GAME——
CLEAR
R.A. LIVE GAME

ACCOUNT 6 Boy Meets Girl

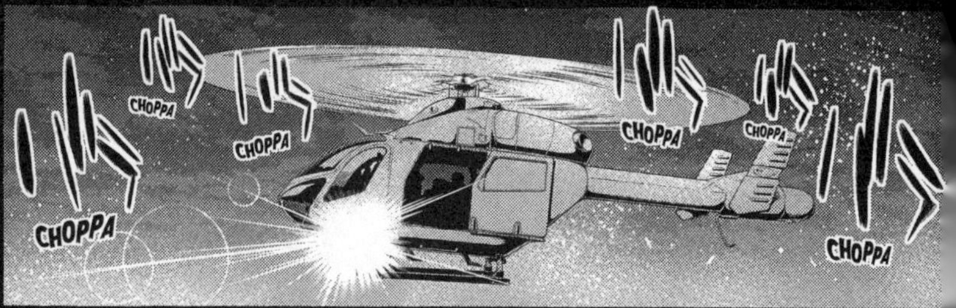
CHOPPA
CHOPPA
CHOPPA
CHOPPA
CHOPPA
CHOPPA

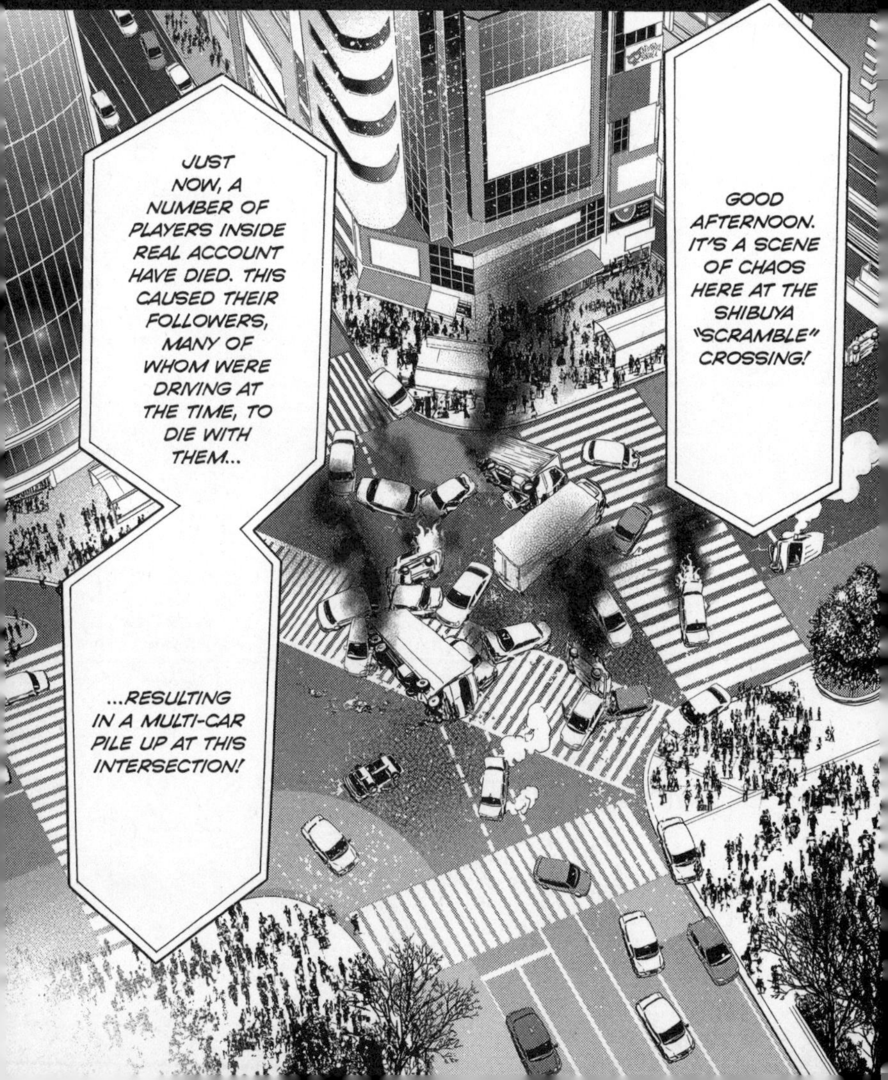
GOOD AFTERNOON. IT'S A SCENE OF CHAOS HERE AT THE SHIBUYA "SCRAMBLE" CROSSING!
JUST NOW, A NUMBER OF PLAYERS INSIDE REAL ACCOUNT HAVE DIED. THIS CAUSED THEIR FOLLOWERS, MANY OF WHOM WERE DRIVING AT THE TIME, TO DIE WITH THEM...
...RESULTING IN A MULTI-CAR PILE UP AT THIS INTERSECTION!

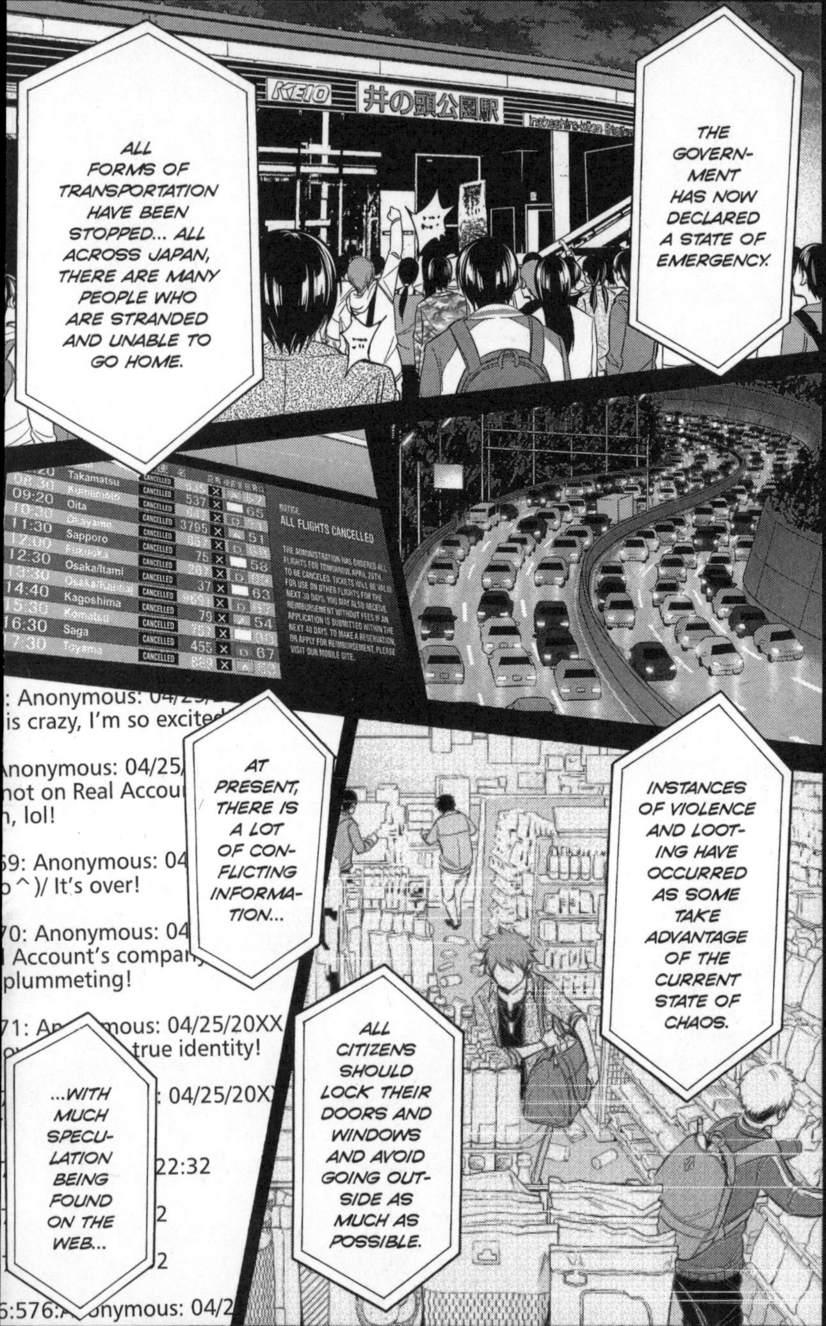
KEIO
井の頭公園駅
THE GOVERNMENT HAS NOW DECLARED A STATE OF EMERGENCY.
ALL FORMS OF TRANSPORTATION HAVE BEEN STOPPED... ALL ACROSS JAPAN, THERE ARE MANY PEOPLE WHO ARE STRANDED AND UNABLE TO GO HOME.
ALL FLIGHTS CANCELLED
INSTANCES OF VIOLENCE AND LOOTING HAVE OCCURRED AS SOME TAKE ADVANTAGE OF THE CURRENT STATE OF CHAOS.
ALL CITIZENS SHOULD LOCK THEIR DOORS AND WINDOWS AND AVOID GOING OUTSIDE AS MUCH AS POSSIBLE.
AT PRESENT, THERE IS A LOT OF CONFLICTING INFORMATION...
...WITH MUCH SPECULATION BEING FOUND ON THE WEB...

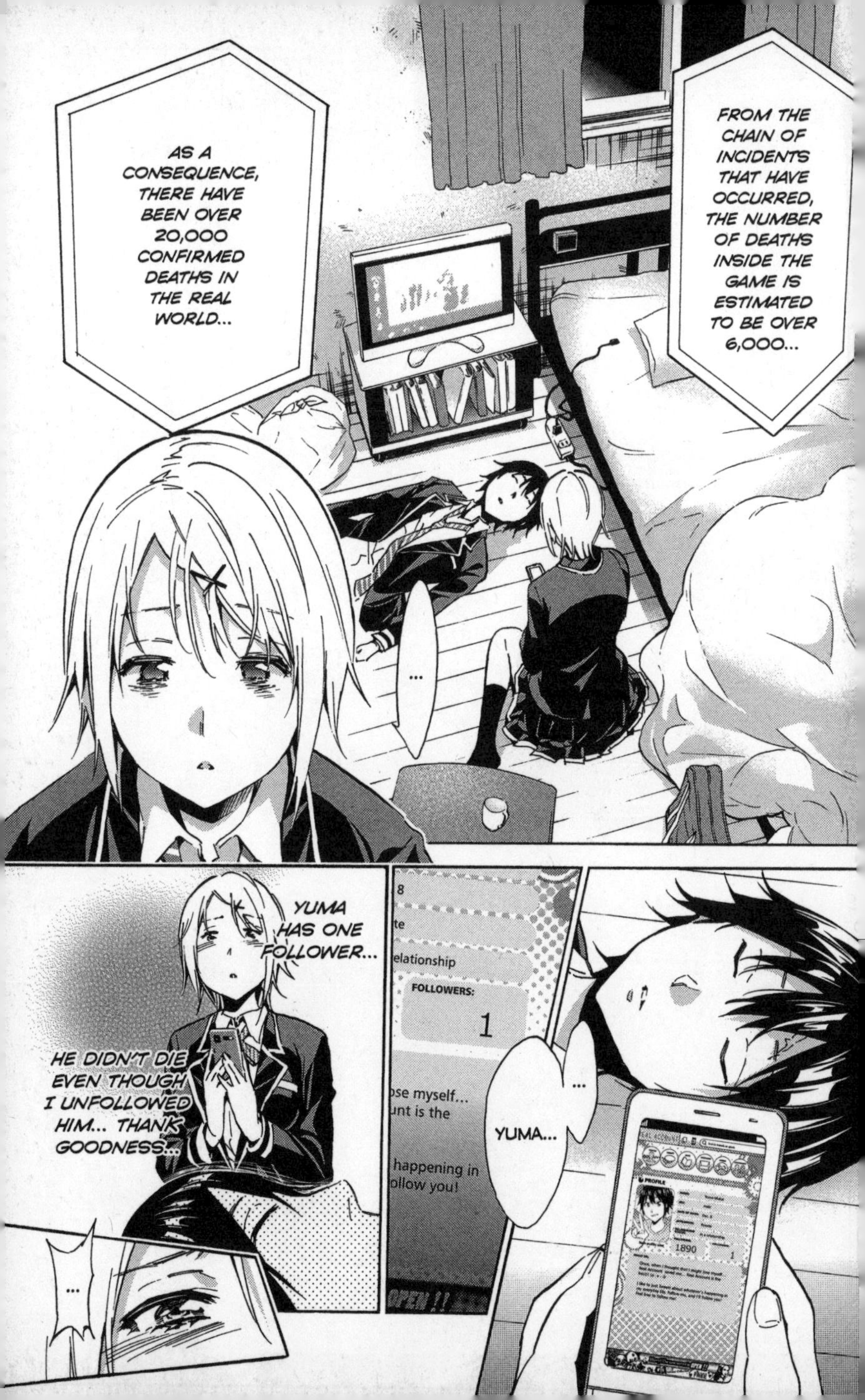
FROM THE CHAIN OF INCIDENTS THAT HAVE OCCURRED, THE NUMBER OF DEATHS INSIDE THE GAME IS ESTIMATED TO BE OVER 6,000...
AS A CONSEQUENCE, THERE HAVE BEEN OVER 20,000 CONFIRMED DEATHS IN THE REAL WORLD...
...
...
YUMA...
FOLLOWERS:
1
YUMA HAS ONE FOLLOWER...
HE DIDN'T DIE EVEN THOUGH I UNFOLLOWED HIM... THANK GOODNESS...
...

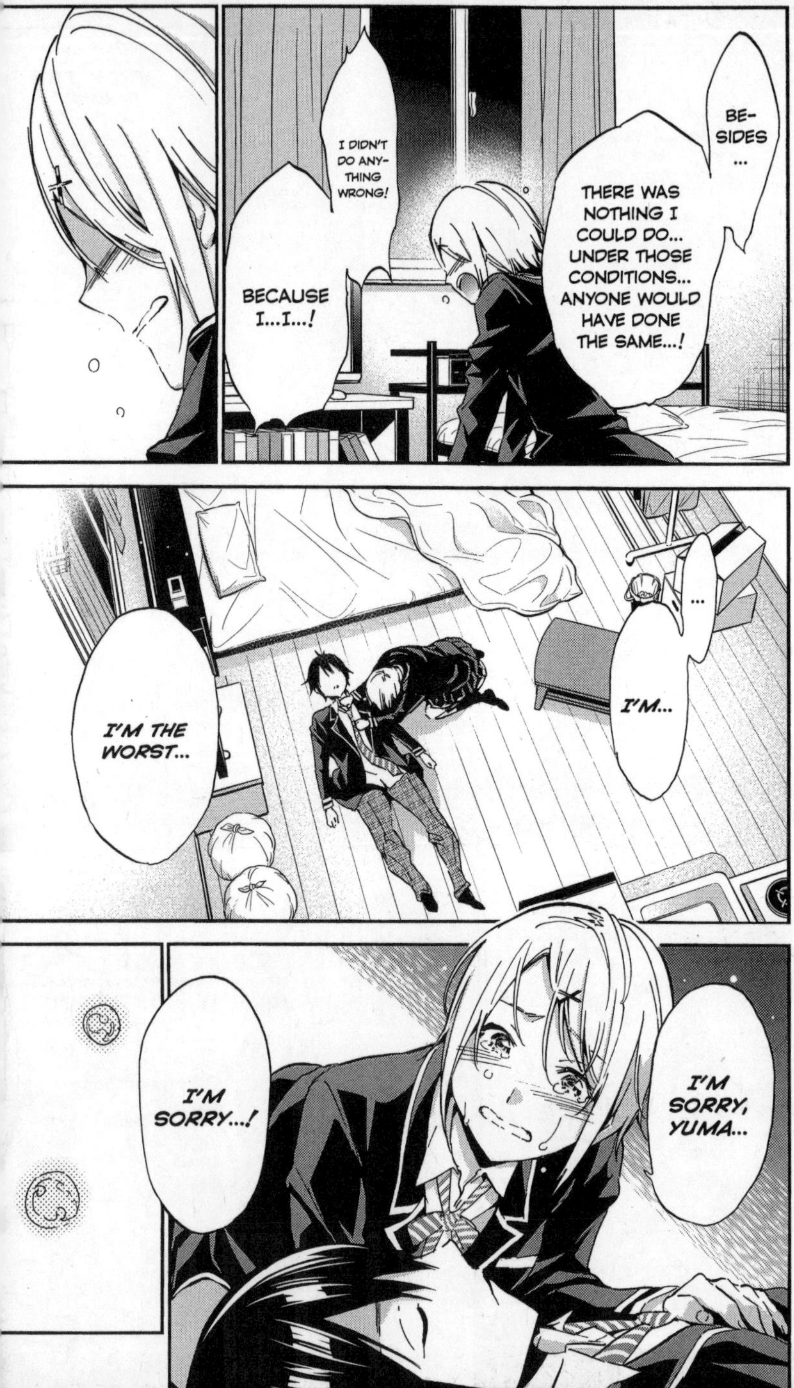
BE-SIDES ...
THERE WAS NOTHING I COULD DO... UNDER THOSE CONDITIONS... ANYONE WOULD HAVE DONE THE SAME...!
I DIDN'T DO ANY-THING WRONG!
BECAUSE I...I...!
...
I'M...
I'M THE WORST...
I'M SORRY, YUMA...
I'M SORRY...!

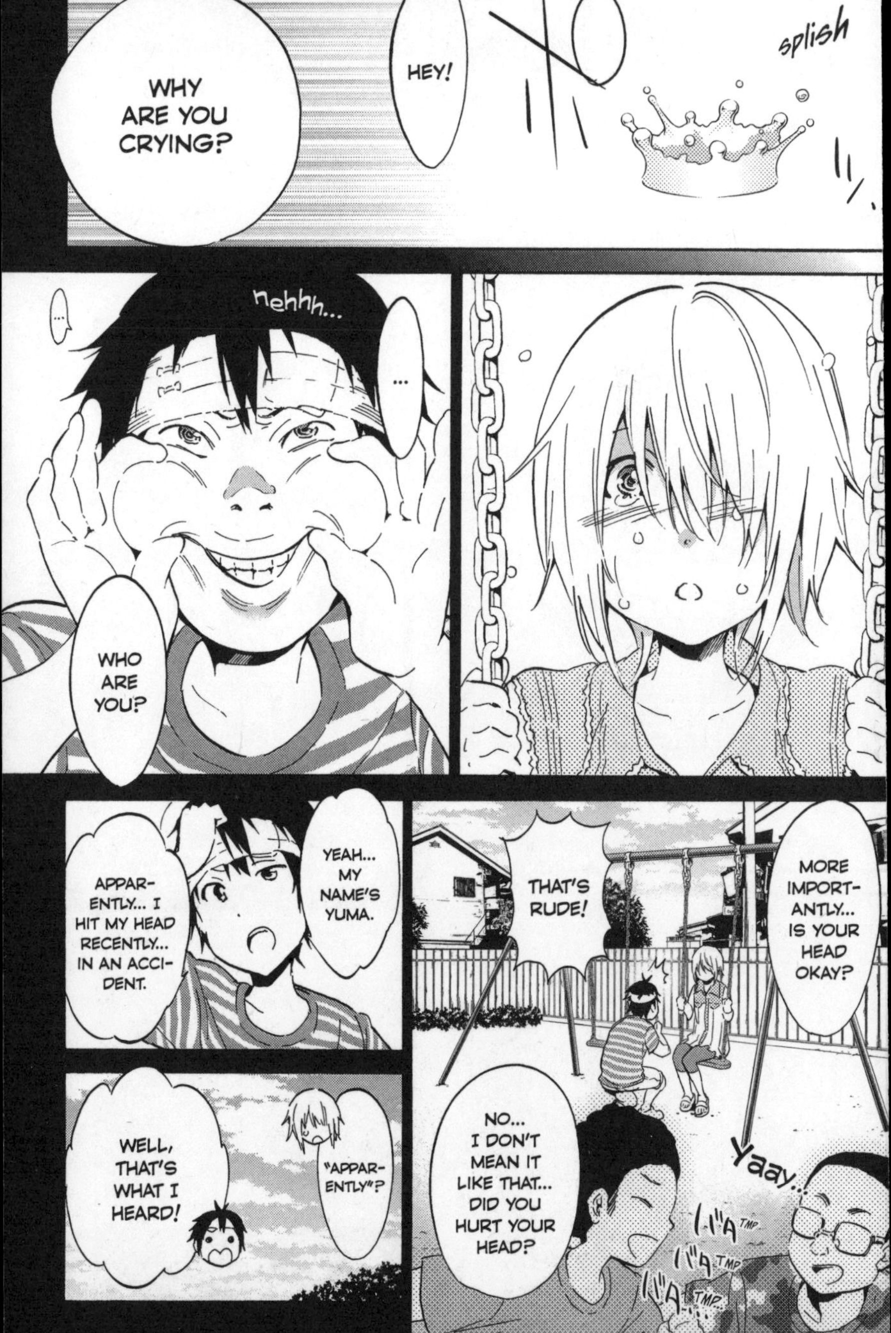
splish
HEY!
WHY ARE YOU CRYING?
nehhh...
...
...
WHO ARE YOU?
MORE IMPORTANTLY... IS YOUR HEAD OKAY?
THAT'S RUDE!
Yaay...
NO... I DON'T MEAN IT LIKE THAT... DID YOU HURT YOUR HEAD?
TMP
TMP
TMP
YEAH... MY NAME'S YUMA.
APPARENTLY... I HIT MY HEAD RECENTLY... IN AN ACCIDENT.
"APPARENTLY"?
WELL, THAT'S WHAT I HEARD!

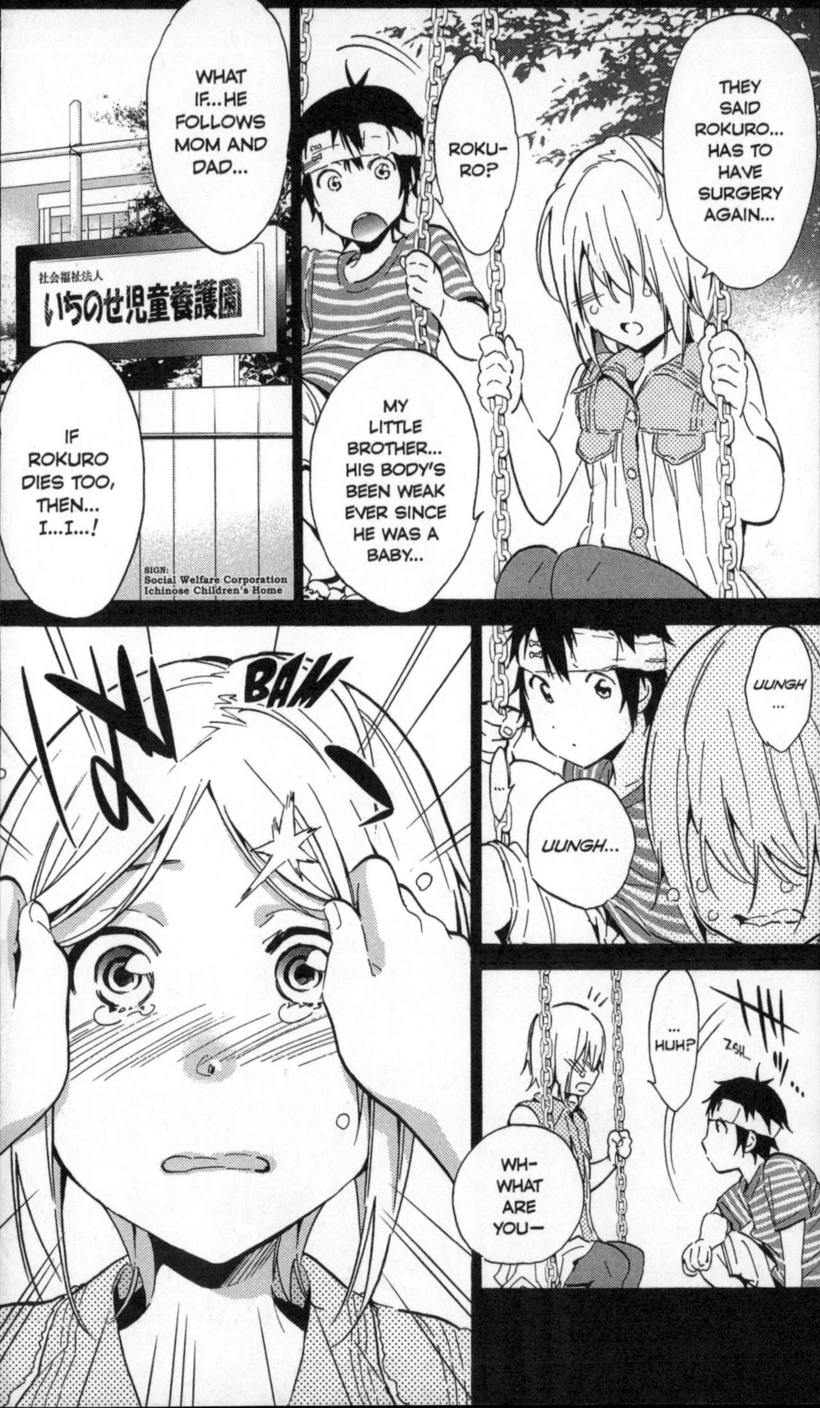
THEY SAID ROKURO... HAS TO HAVE SURGERY AGAIN...
ROKURO?
MY LITTLE BROTHER... HIS BODY'S BEEN WEAK EVER SINCE HE WAS A BABY...
WHAT IF...HE FOLLOWS MOM AND DAD...
社会福祉法人
いちのせ児童養護園
IF ROKURO DIES TOO, THEN... I...I...!
SIGN: Social Welfare Corporation Ichinose Children's Home
UUNGH ...
...
UUNGH...
... HUH?
ZSH...
WH- WHAT ARE YOU—
BAM

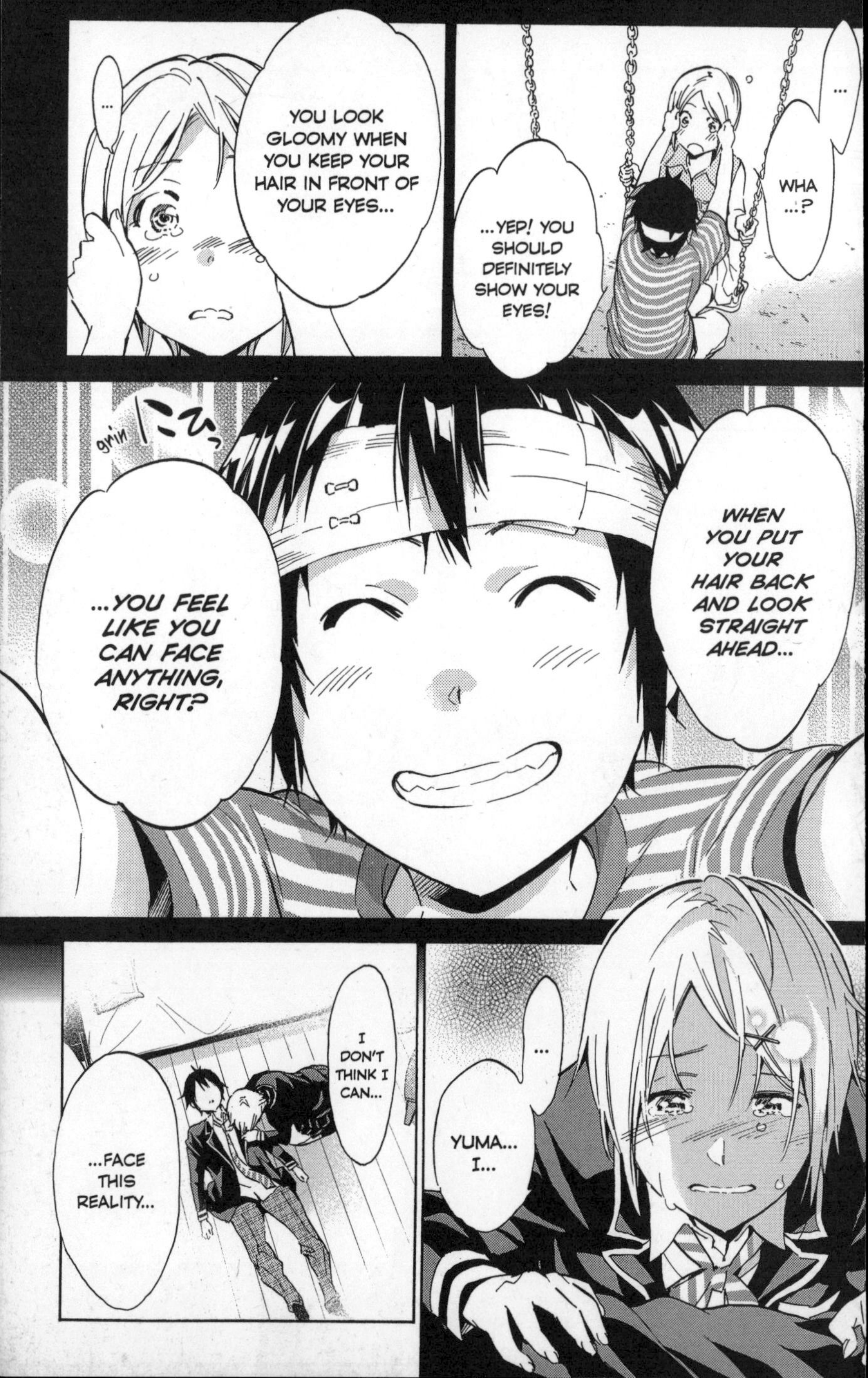
...
WHA ...?
...YEP! YOU SHOULD DEFINITELY SHOW YOUR EYES!
YOU LOOK GLOOMY WHEN YOU KEEP YOUR HAIR IN FRONT OF YOUR EYES...
...
WHEN YOU PUT YOUR HAIR BACK AND LOOK STRAIGHT AHEAD...
grin
...YOU FEEL LIKE YOU CAN FACE ANYTHING, RIGHT?
...
YUMA... I...
I DON'T THINK I CAN...
...FACE THIS REALITY...

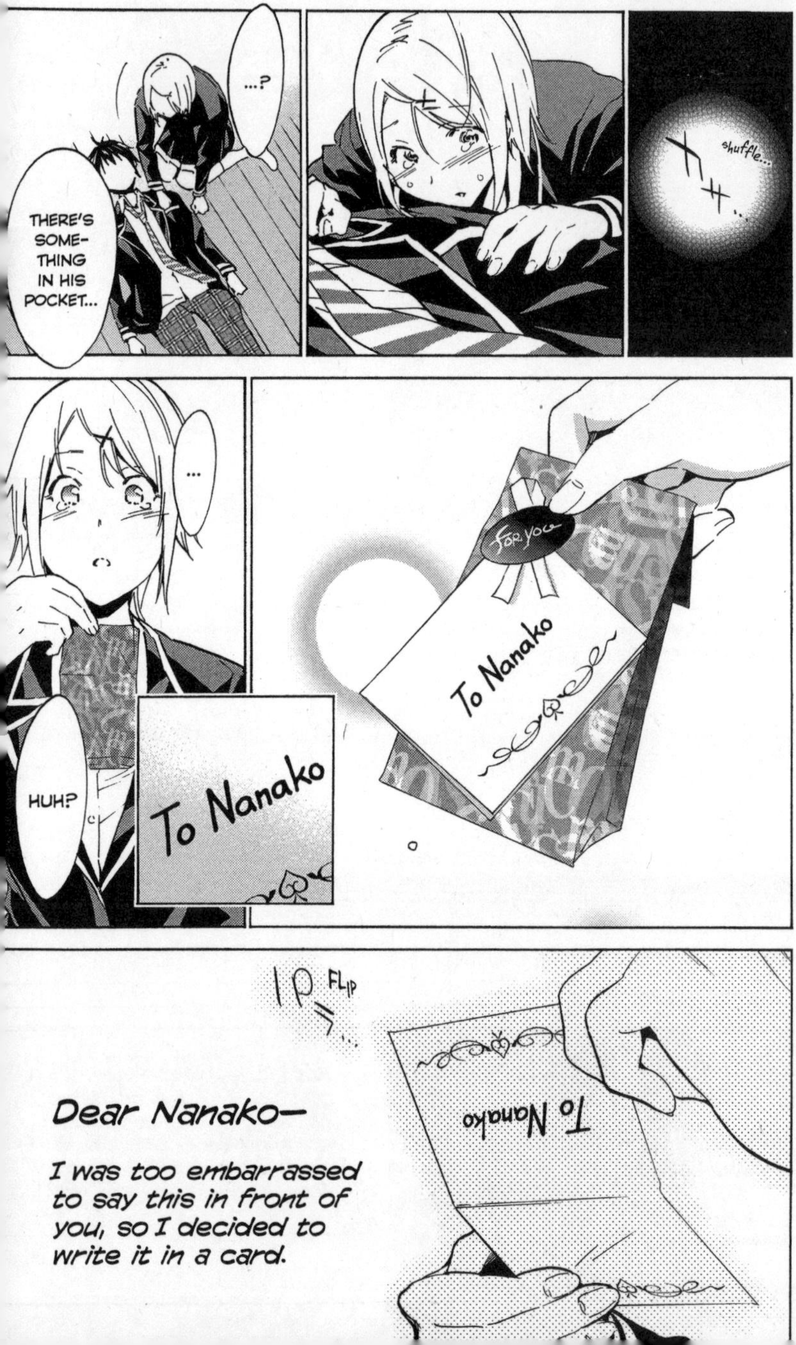
shuffle...
...?
THERE'S SOMETHING IN HIS POCKET...
For you
To Nanako
...
HUH?
To Nanako
FLIP
To Nanako
Dear Nanako—
I was too embarrassed to say this in front of you, so I decided to write it in a card.

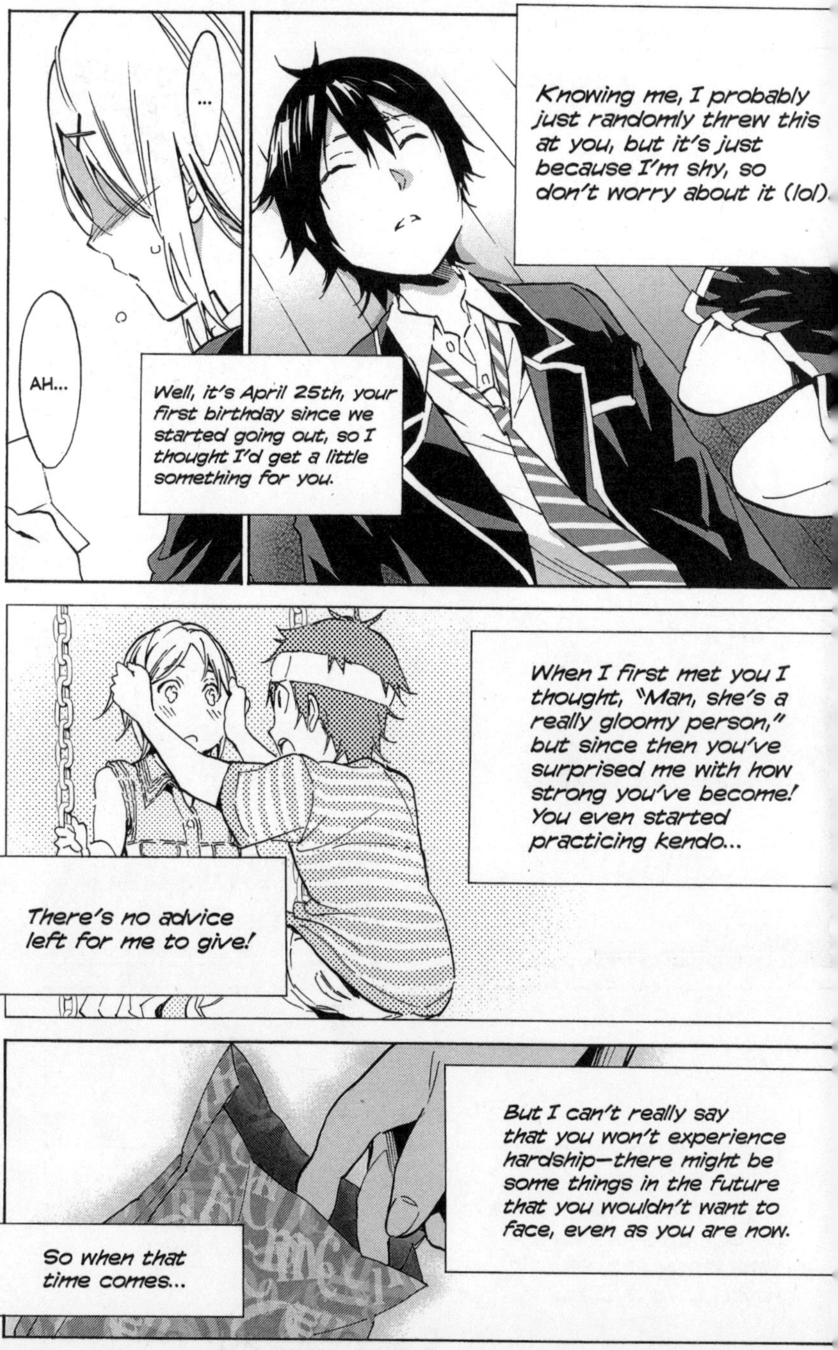
Knowing me, I probably just randomly threw this at you, but it's just because I'm shy, so don't worry about it (lol).
Well, it's April 25th, your first birthday since we started going out, so I thought I'd get a little something for you.
...
AH...
When I first met you I thought, "Man, she's a really gloomy person," but since then you've surprised me with how strong you've become! You even started practicing kendo...
There's no advice left for me to give!
But I can't really say that you won't experience hardship—there might be some things in the future that you wouldn't want to face, even as you are now.
So when that time comes...

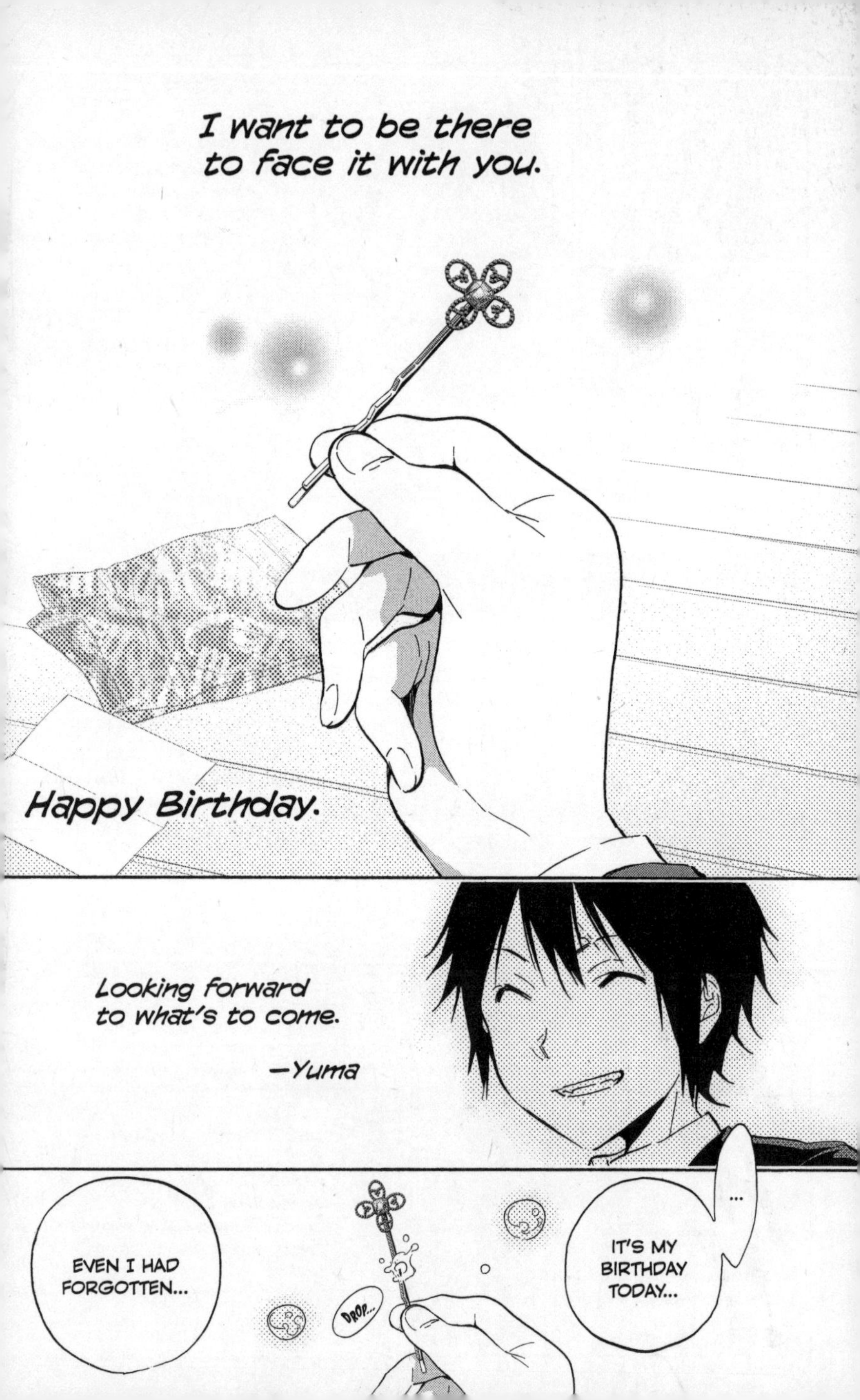
I want to be there to face it with you.
Happy Birthday.
Looking forward to what's to come.
—Yuma
...
IT'S MY BIRTHDAY TODAY...
DROP...
EVEN I HAD FORGOTTEN...

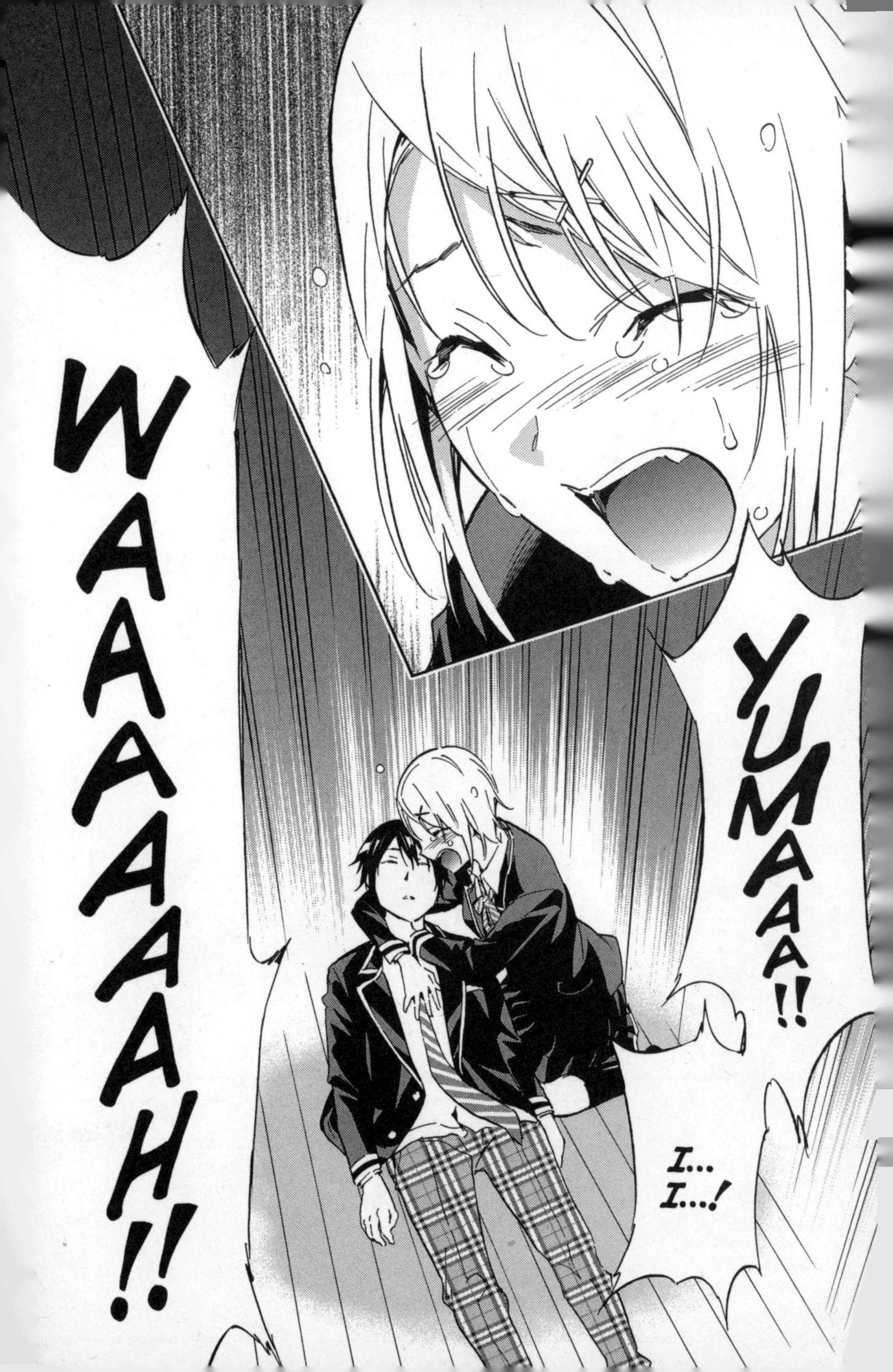
YUMAAA!!
I... I...!
WAAAAAAH!!

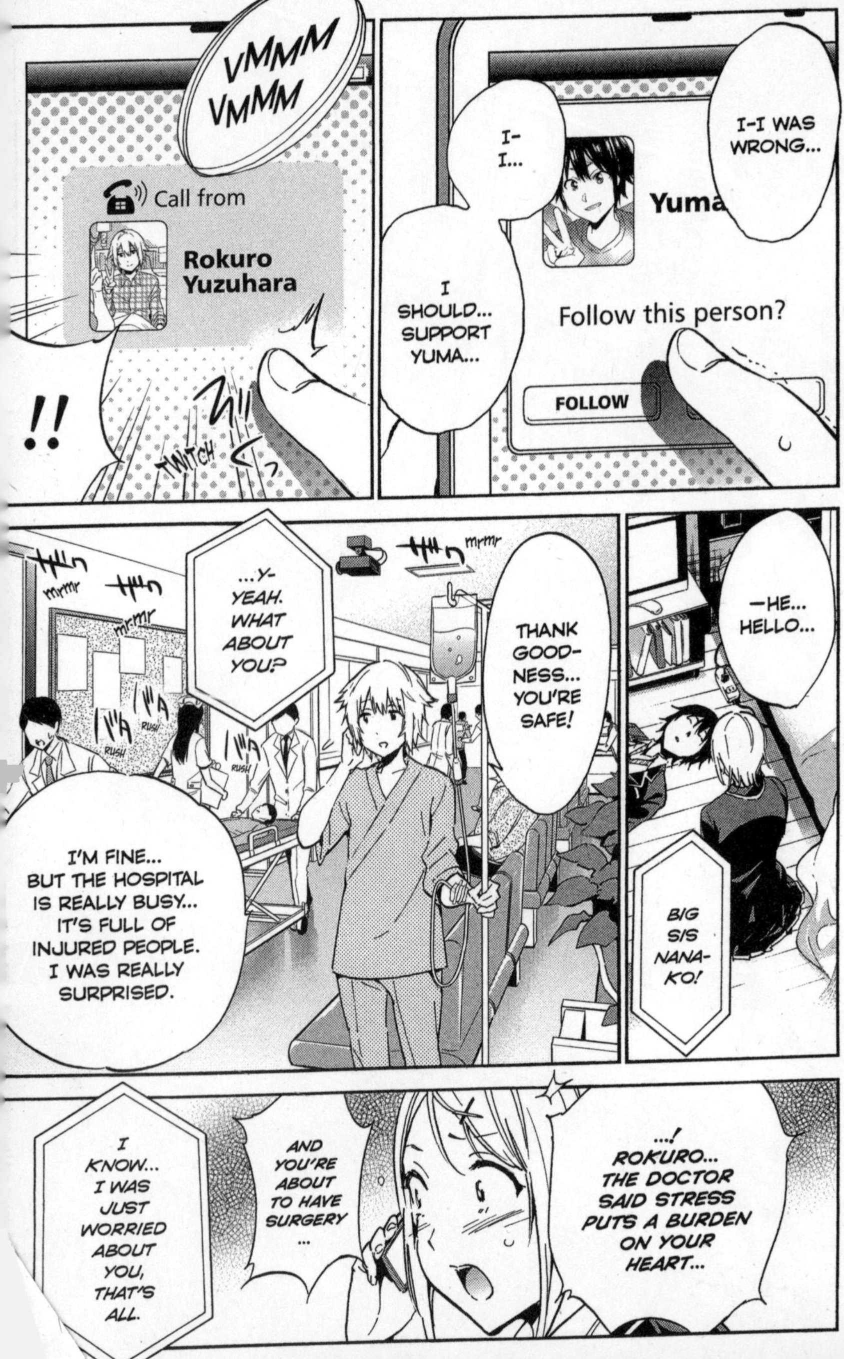
I-I WAS WRONG...
I- I...
Yuma
I SHOULD... SUPPORT YUMA...
Follow this person?
FOLLOW
VMMM VMMM
Call from
Rokuro Yuzuhara
TWITCH
!!
—HE... HELLO...
BIG SIS NANAKO!
THANK GOODNESS... YOU'RE SAFE!
...Y-YEAH. WHAT ABOUT YOU?
mrmr
mrmr
mrmr
mrmr
RUSH
RUSH
RUSH
I'M FINE... BUT THE HOSPITAL IS REALLY BUSY... IT'S FULL OF INJURED PEOPLE. I WAS REALLY SURPRISED.
...! ROKURO... THE DOCTOR SAID STRESS PUTS A BURDEN ON YOUR HEART...
AND YOU'RE ABOUT TO HAVE SURGERY...
I KNOW... I WAS JUST WORRIED ABOUT YOU, THAT'S ALL.

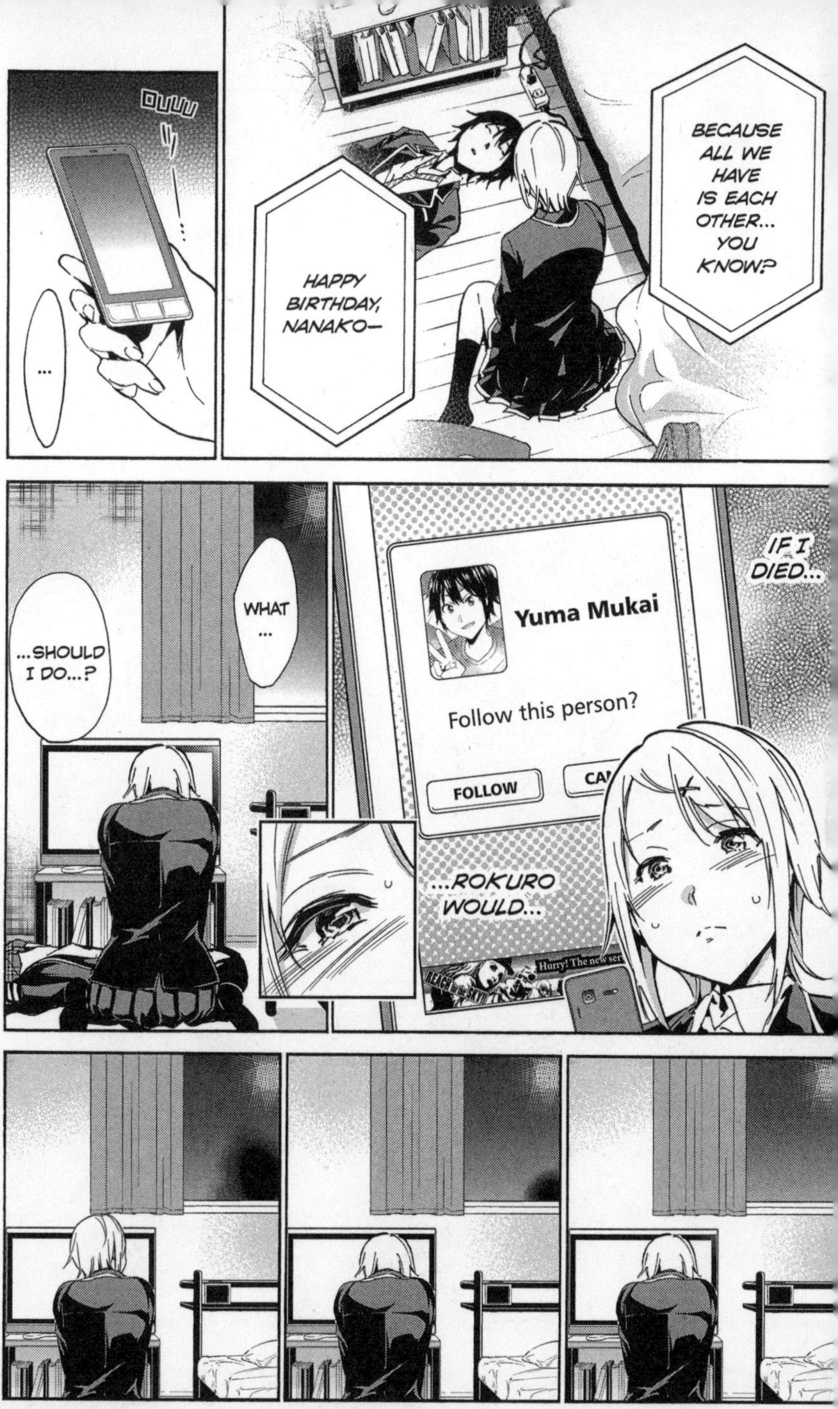
BECAUSE ALL WE HAVE IS EACH OTHER... YOU KNOW?
HAPPY BIRTHDAY, NANAKO—
...
IF I DIED...
Yuma Mukai
Follow this person?
FOLLOW
...ROKURO WOULD...
WHAT ...
...SHOULD I DO...?

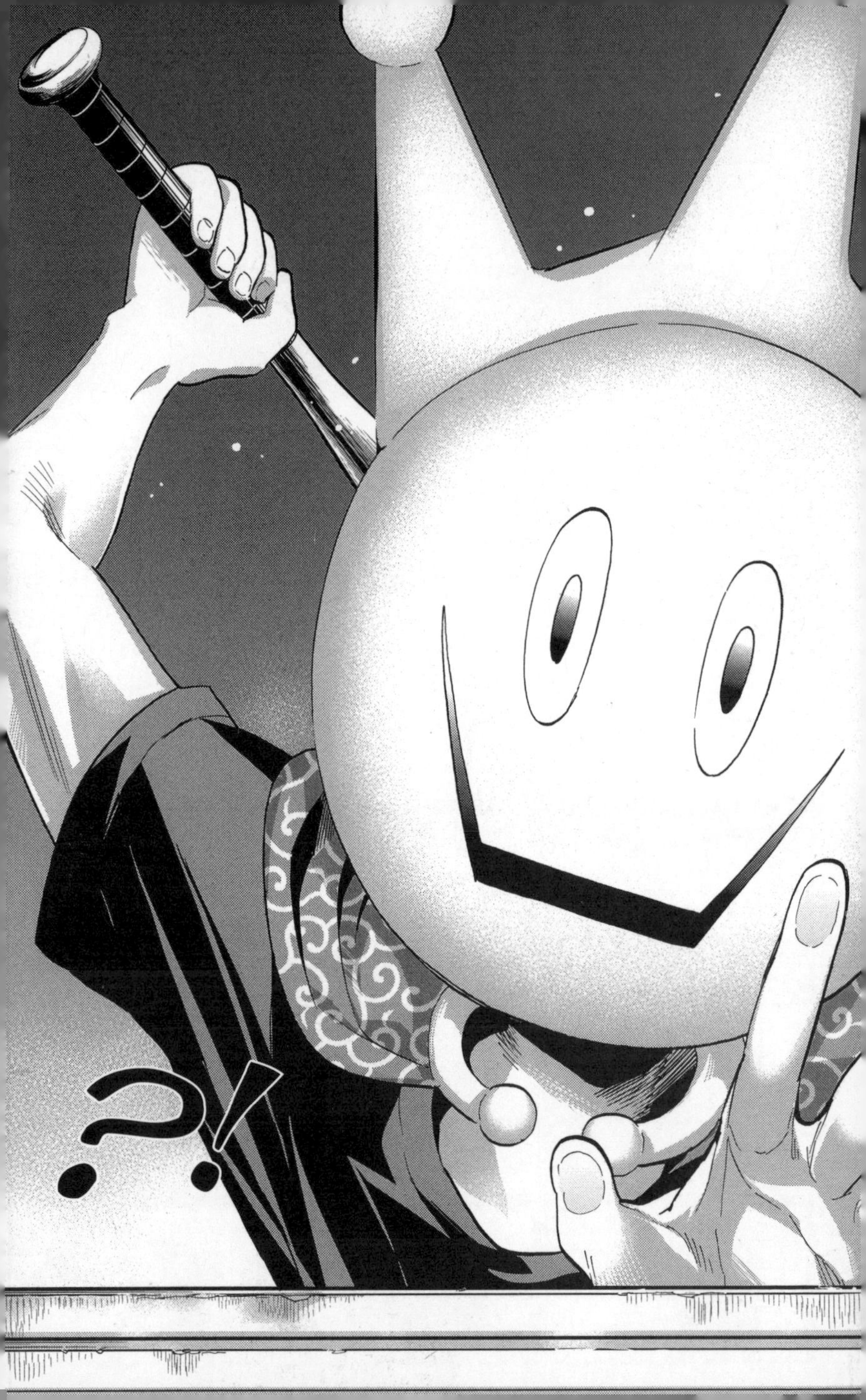
?!

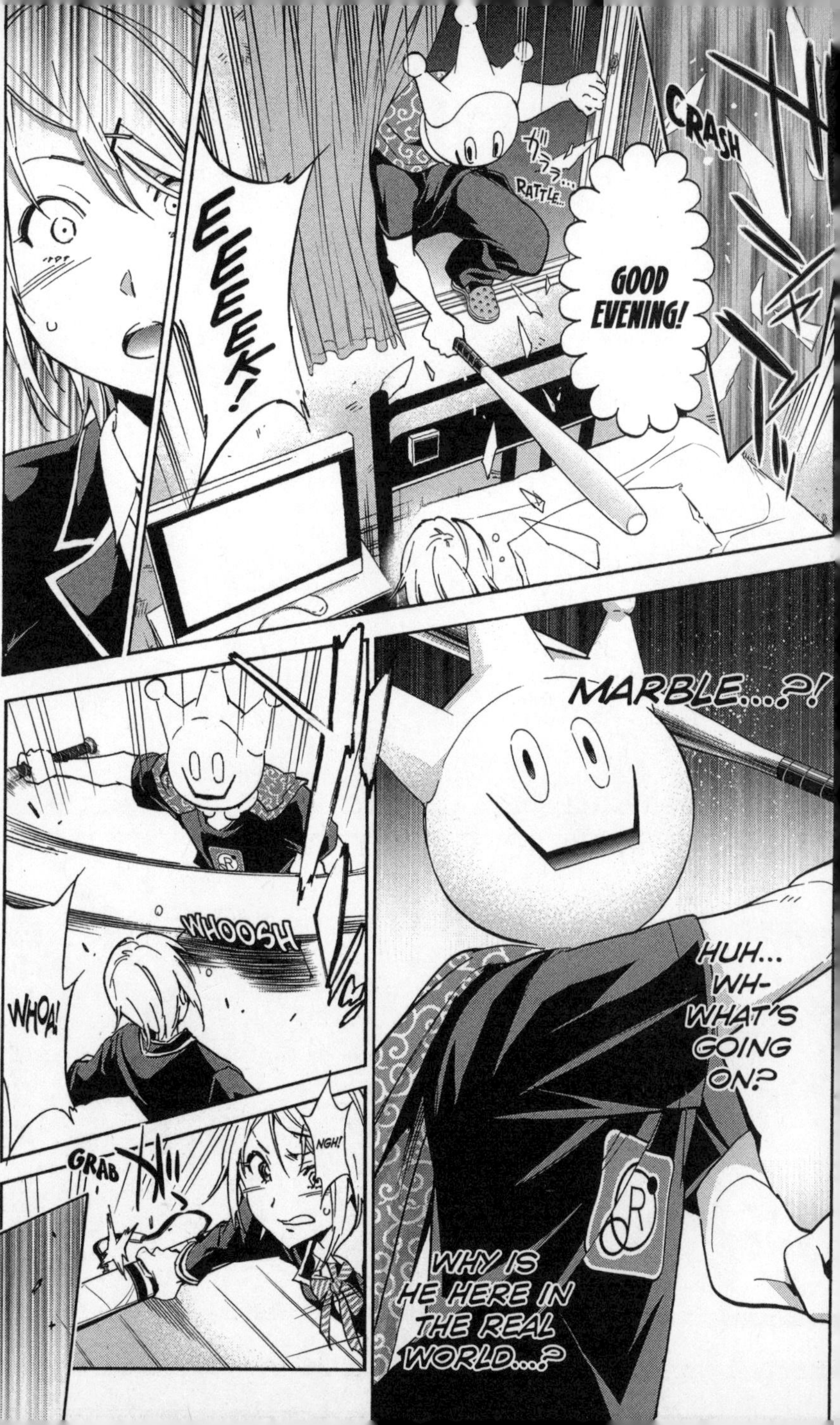
CRASH
ガラ…
RATTLE...
GOOD EVENING!
EEEEEK!
MARBLE...?!
HUH... WH-WHAT'S GOING ON?
WHY IS HE HERE IN THE REAL WORLD...?
WHOOSH
WHOA!
NGH!
GRAB

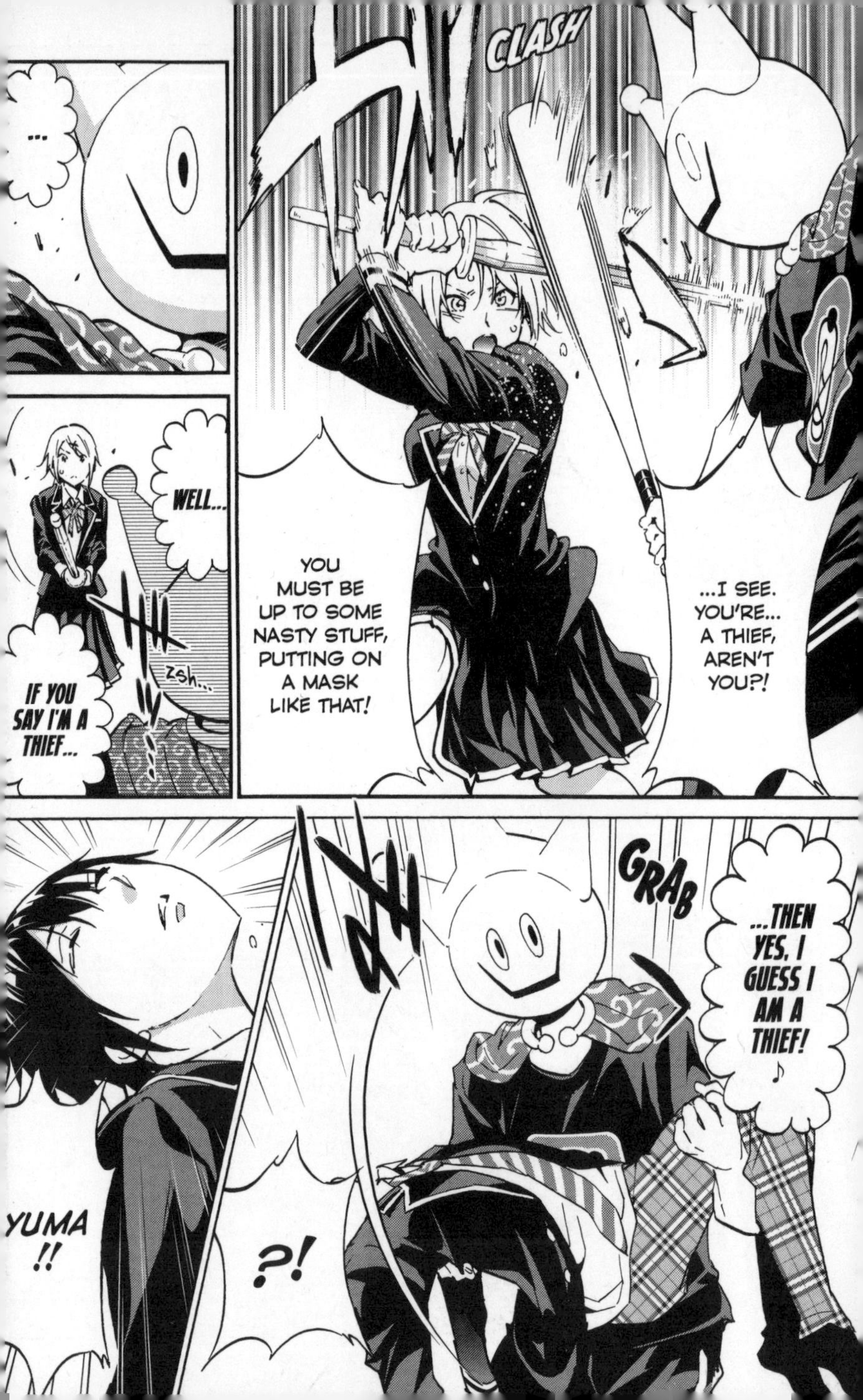
CLASH
...I SEE. YOU'RE... A THIEF, AREN'T YOU?!
YOU MUST BE UP TO SOME NASTY STUFF, PUTTING ON A MASK LIKE THAT!
...
WELL...
zsh...
IF YOU SAY I'M A THIEF...
GRAB
...THEN YES, I GUESS I AM A THIEF! ♪
?!
YUMA!!

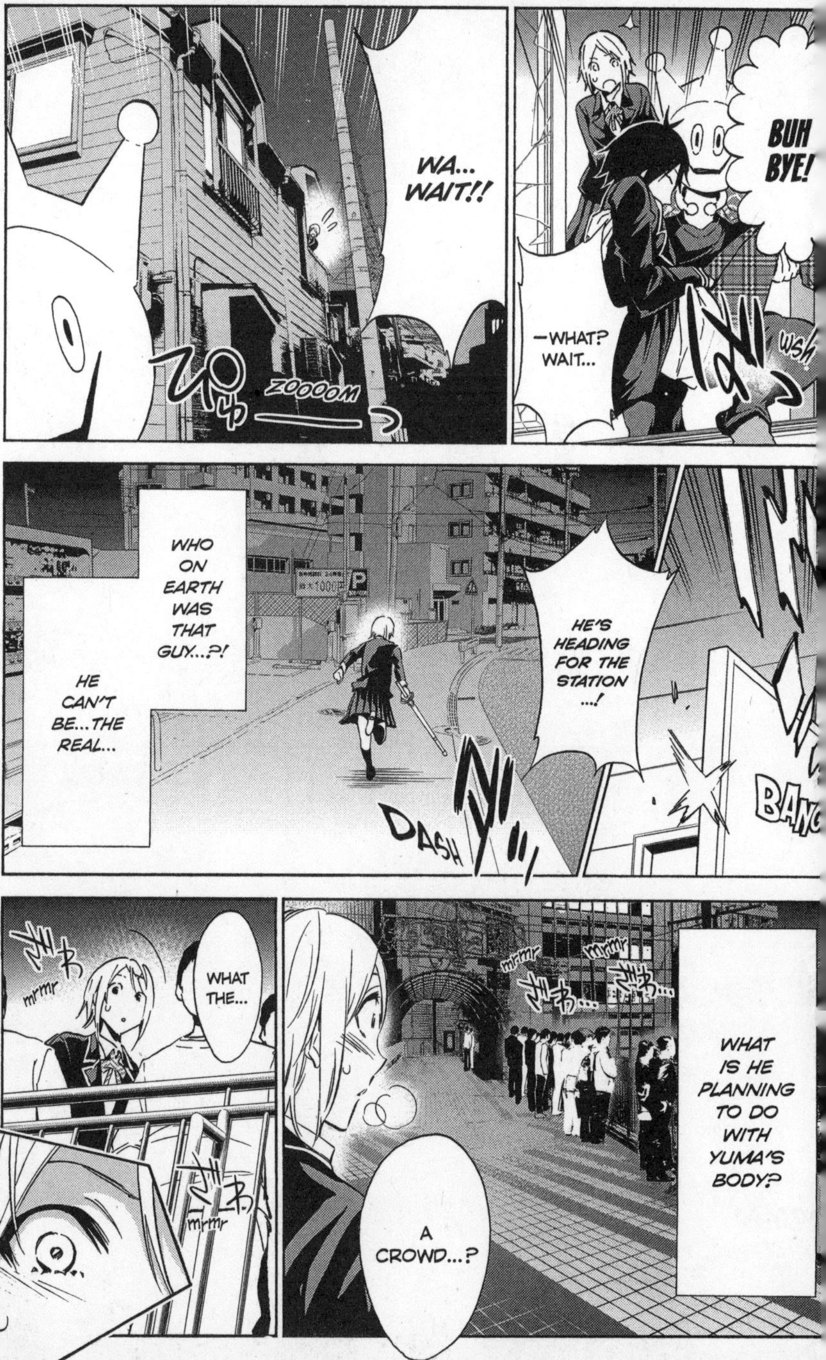
BUH BYE!
—WHAT? WAIT...
wsh
WA... WAIT!!
ZOOOOM
HE'S HEADING FOR THE STATION ...!
BANG
WHO ON EARTH WAS THAT GUY...?!
HE CAN'T BE...THE REAL...
DASH
WHAT IS HE PLANNING TO DO WITH YUMA'S BODY?
mrmr
mrmr
A CROWD...?
WHAT THE...
mrmr
mrmr

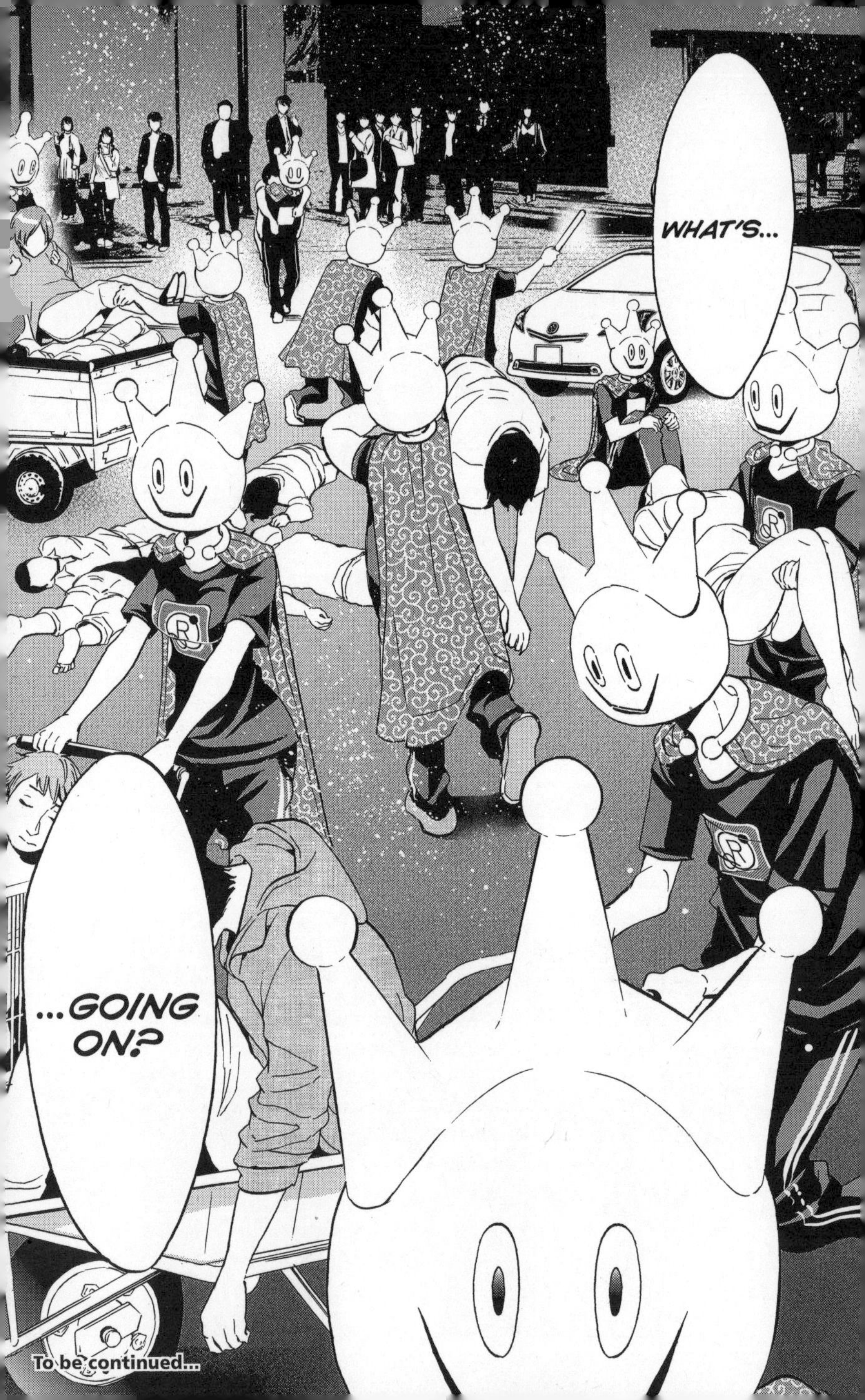
WHAT'S...
...GOING ON?
To be continued...

Artist:
SHIZUMU WATANABE

Twitter account: @shizumukun

It's the first time I've ever changed magazines for my serial publications. But this is the second time I've been published in a weekly magazine, so I thought "I can handle this!" But I underestimated just how much work it is. It's been pretty difficult (lol). I'll do my best to keep up with the speed of weekly publications!

Author:
OKUSHOU

Twitter account: @okushou

It's the third volume! The curtain rises on the second chapter!! What are the connections to the second volume?! For now we say goodbye to Ataru-kun and Koyori-chan, but no worries, they will definitely be back! So please stay tuned…!

REAL ACCOUNT

3

Shizumu Watanabe   Okushou

STAFF
Shotaro Kunitomo
Iyo Mori
Yushi Takayama
Kazuki Ishiyama

HELP STAFF
Mio Otsuka
Yosuke Kaneda
Yoneko Takamoto

EDITORS
Kazuhiko Otoguro
Sho Igarashi
Hideki Morooka
(Japanese GN)

JAPANESE COVER DESIGN
Tadashi Hisamochi
(HIVE)

I was going to do a bonus page, but it ended up being the staff credits...
Watanabe

REAL ACCOUNT

account 0: ONE DAY AFTER SCHOOL ~AVERAGE DAY

Okushou

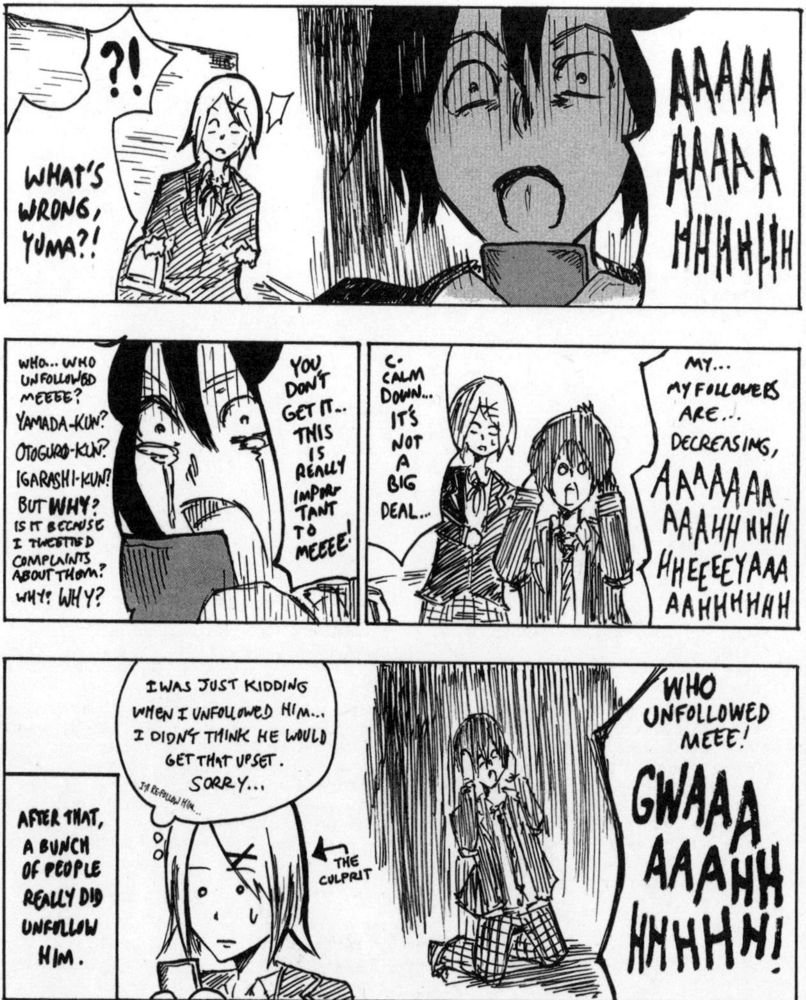
AAAAA AAAAA HHHHHH
?!
WHAT'S WRONG, YUMA?!
MY... MY FOLLOWERS ARE... DECREASING, AAAAAAA AAAHHHHH HHEEEEYAAA AAHHHHHHH
C-CALM DOWN... IT'S NOT A BIG DEAL...
YOU DON'T GET IT... THIS IS REALLY IMPORTANT TO MEEEE!
WHO... WHO UNFOLLOWED MEEEE? YAMADA-KUN? OTOGURO-KUN? IGARASHI-KUN? BUT WHY? IS IT BECAUSE I TWEETED COMPLAINTS ABOUT THEM? WHY? WHY?
WHO UNFOLLOWED MEEE!
GWAAAAAAHHHHHHH!
I WAS JUST KIDDING WHEN I UNFOLLOWED HIM... I DIDN'T THINK HE WOULD GET THAT UPSET. SORRY...
I'll RE-FOLLOW HIM...
THE CULPRIT
AFTER THAT, A BUNCH OF PEOPLE REALLY DID UNFOLLOW HIM.

END...?

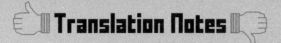

Translation Notes

PAGE 108

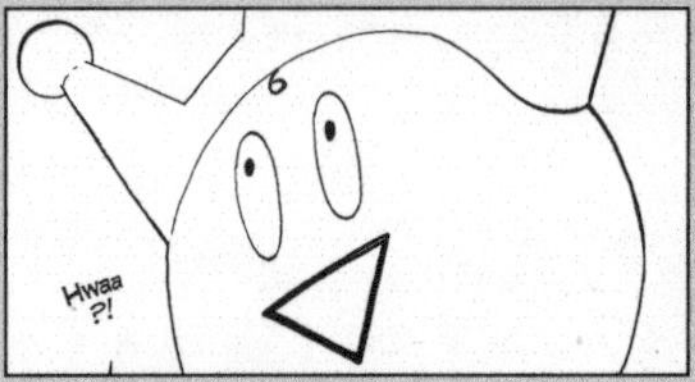

HWAA?!

Marble's puzzling reaction comes from a specific kao-emoji that gained notoriety in recent years on social media services like Twitter. The original kao-emoji is (´◁`)ﾊﾟｧ and it is meant to resemble a face with two hands palms-out followed by the expression "paa" which could be interpreted as the sound of a bubble bursting or a sort of sigh. So what does it actually mean? The truth is that there is no clear meaning to it. It is more or less regarded as an absurd expression—an answer when there's no real answer—and that is probably why Marble chose to make that face when questioned by the contestants.

PAGE 82

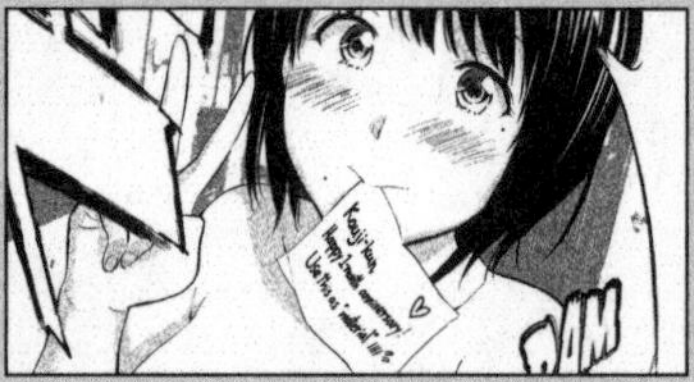

////

A symbol of three or four forward slashes following a statement is used to express one's cheeks blushing and thus denotes shyness or embarrassment. Though this has been used by Japanese netizens for a long time, its usage came into prominence starting around 2010 on sites like Twitter and 2chan.

PAGE 136, 151

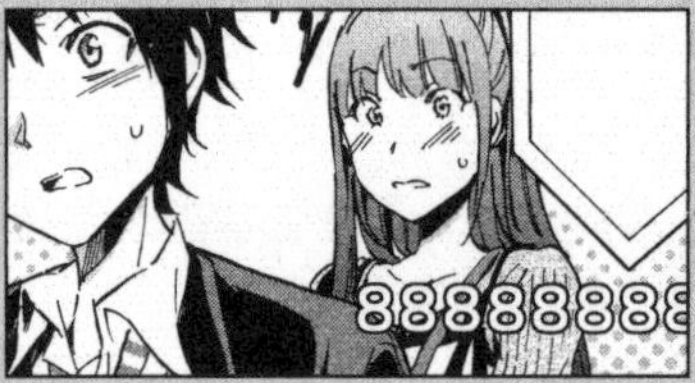

8888

8888 is Internet slang often used on social media services such as Twitter to indicate applause. The more 8s a user writes, the more they like the content they are commenting on. The reason for using 8 originates in the Japanese language itself. 8 is pronounced "*hachi*," and the onomatopoeia for clapping is "*pachi*." Since they are similar in sound, 8 (*hachi*) is written, but is read as "*pachi*." This form of wordplay, which is called *goroawase*, can often be seen in Japanese, but has an even greater presence in Japanese netspeak.

PAGE 134

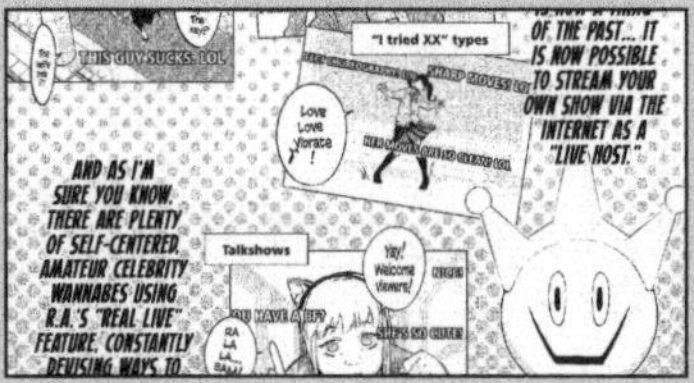

LIVE HOST

"Live Host" is more or less a direct translation of the Japanese term, *namanushi*, which has its origins in the Japanese streaming video service Nico Nico Douga. Nico Nico Douga is similar to YouTube, but separates itself with specific features, like the ability to place comments onto videos as they're playing. Live broadcasts are also a much bigger part of Nico Nico than its American equivalent, and so there are many terms specific to live broadcasts, like "Live Host."

PAGE 142

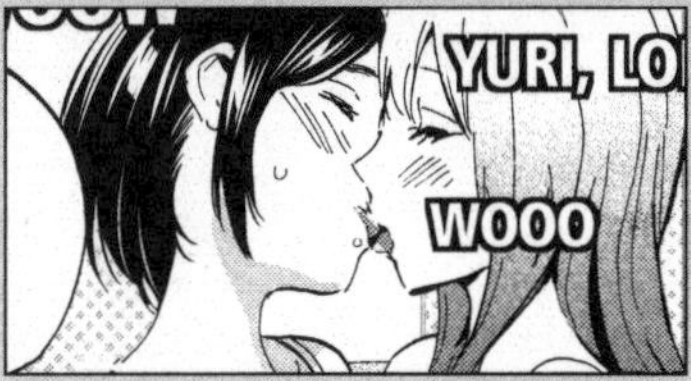
YURI, LO
WOOO

YURI

Yuri describes a genre of Japanese media that contains female homosexual content. It is also known by the term Girls' Love and is the counterpart to BL or *yaoi*, which features male homosexual content. In Japanese, the word "*yuri*" itself literally translates to "lily" and is said to have originated from the gay magazine *Barazoku* as a contrasting term to its "*bara*" (EN: Rose). The term *bara* also describes media featuring homosexual content, except with hyper-masculine men as highlighted characters, created by men for men, as opposed to *yaoi* which is primarily created by women for women.

PAGE 142

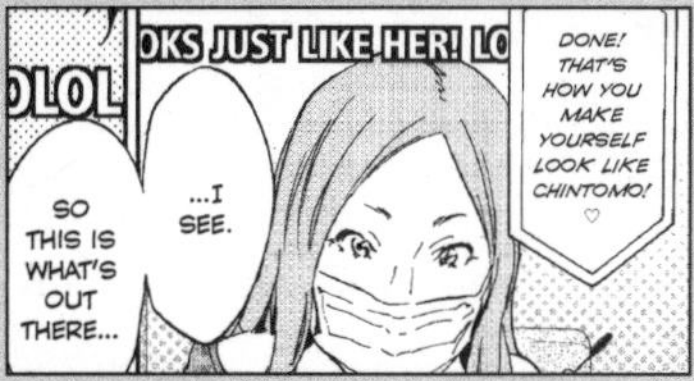
DONE! THAT'S HOW YOU MAKE YOURSELF LOOK LIKE CHINTOMO! ♡
OKS JUST LIKE HER! LO
...I SEE.
DLOL
SO THIS IS WHAT'S OUT THERE...

CHINTOMO AND MAKEUP TUTORIALS

Chintomo is a syllabic reversal of "Tomochin," the nickname of Tomomi Itano, a member of popular idol group AKB48. In this panel, the woman is hosting a stream of a makeup tutorial. In Japan, makeup tutorials on how to make yourself look like a celebrity are very popular. Using different shades of foundation, eye shadow, eyeliner, and other products, they are able to change the appearance of their face to look like a celebrity. They often use masks to hide their nose and mouth, features that are much harder to change.

PAGE 173

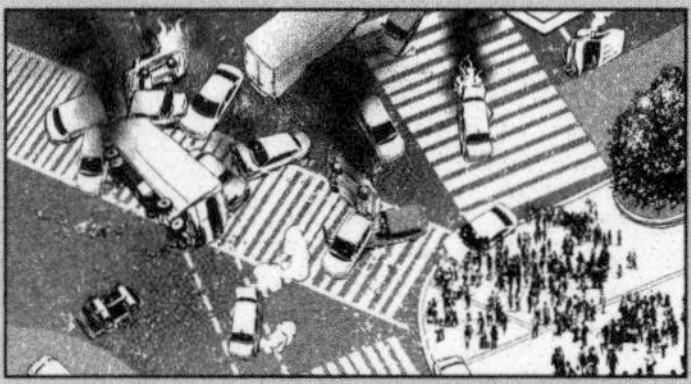

SHIBUYA SCRAMBLE CROSSING

A "scramble crossing" is an intersection that allows pedestrians from all different directions to cross while traffic is stopped. The most famous of these in Tokyo—if not in all of Japan —sits adjacent to Shibuya Station. Shibuya Station is one of the busiest stations in Japan and so this famous intersection constantly sees incredibly heavy foot traffic. It is often prominently displayed in Japanese media to represent scenes taking place in Shibuya, Tokyo, much like Times Square is used to represent New York City. It has also gained international fame, being featured in movies like *Lost in Translation*, and *The Fast and the Furious: Tokyo Drift*.

PAGE 156

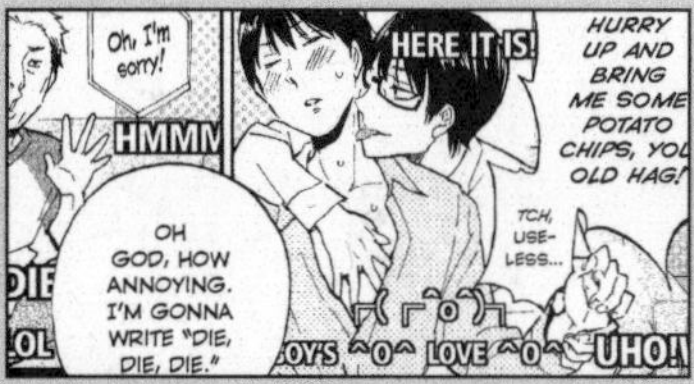
HURRY UP AND BRING ME SOME POTATO CHIPS, YOU OLD HAG!
HERE IT IS!
TCH, USE-LESS...
┌(┌ ^o^)┐
UHO!
Oh, I'm sorry!
HMMM
OH GOD, HOW ANNOYING. I'M GONNA WRITE "DIE, DIE, DIE."

┌(┌ ^o^)┐ (BL/HOMO EMOJI) AND UHO!

This particular emoji originated on Twitter as a meme for the purpose of mocking *fujoshi* (simply put, a female otaku who is primarily interested in manga portraying male-to-male sexuality). This emoji is supposed to depict a vaguely humanoid figure crawling along on all fours, with its mouth open saying, "homoooo." It's since been taken up by *fujoshi* for use in fanart and online postings.

Uho! also has links to *fujoshi* and is a comment typically used when two men get into a close, potentially steamy encounter. The full version of the term is "*Uho! Ii otoko!*" (EN: Ooh! Now that's a nice man!) and it comes from Junichi Yamakawa's *Kuso Miso Technique*, a one-shot manga originally published in the gay magazine *Barazoku*. Phrases from this manga like, "*Uho! Ii otoko!*" and "*Yaranaika?*" (EN: Wanna do it?) also became intensely popular parody memes on the Japanese-speaking internet and still elicit humorous reactions to this day.

a Silent Voice

"The word heartwarming was made for manga like this."
–Manga Bookshelf

"A harsh and biting social commentary... delivers in its depth of character and emotional strength." -Comics Bulletin

"A very powerful story about being different and the consequences of childhood bullying... Read it."
–Anime News Network

Shoya is a bully. When Shoko, a girl who can't hear, enters his elementary school class, she becomes their favorite target, and Shoya and his friends goad each other into devising new tortures for her. But the children's cruelty goes too far. Shoko is forced to leave the school, and Shoya ends up shouldering all the blame. Six years later, the two meet again. Can Shoya make up for his past mistakes, or is it too late?

Available now in print and digitally!

INUYASHIKI

A superhero like none you've ever seen, from the creator of "Gantz"!

ICHIRO INUYASHIKI IS DOWN ON HIS LUCK. HE LOOKS MUCH OLDER THAN HIS 58 YEARS, HIS CHILDREN DESPISE HIM, AND HIS WIFE THINKS HE'S A USELESS COWARD. SO WHEN HE'S DIAGNOSED WITH STOMACH CANCER AND GIVEN THREE MONTHS TO LIVE, IT SEEMS THE ONLY ONE WHO'LL MISS HIM IS HIS DOG.

THEN A BLINDING LIGHT FILLS THE SKY, AND THE OLD MAN IS KILLED... ONLY TO WAKE UP LATER IN A BODY HE ALMOST RECOGNIZES AS HIS OWN. CAN IT BE THAT ICHIRO INUYASHIKI IS NO LONGER HUMAN?

COMES IN EXTRA-LARGE EDITIONS WITH COLOR PAGES!

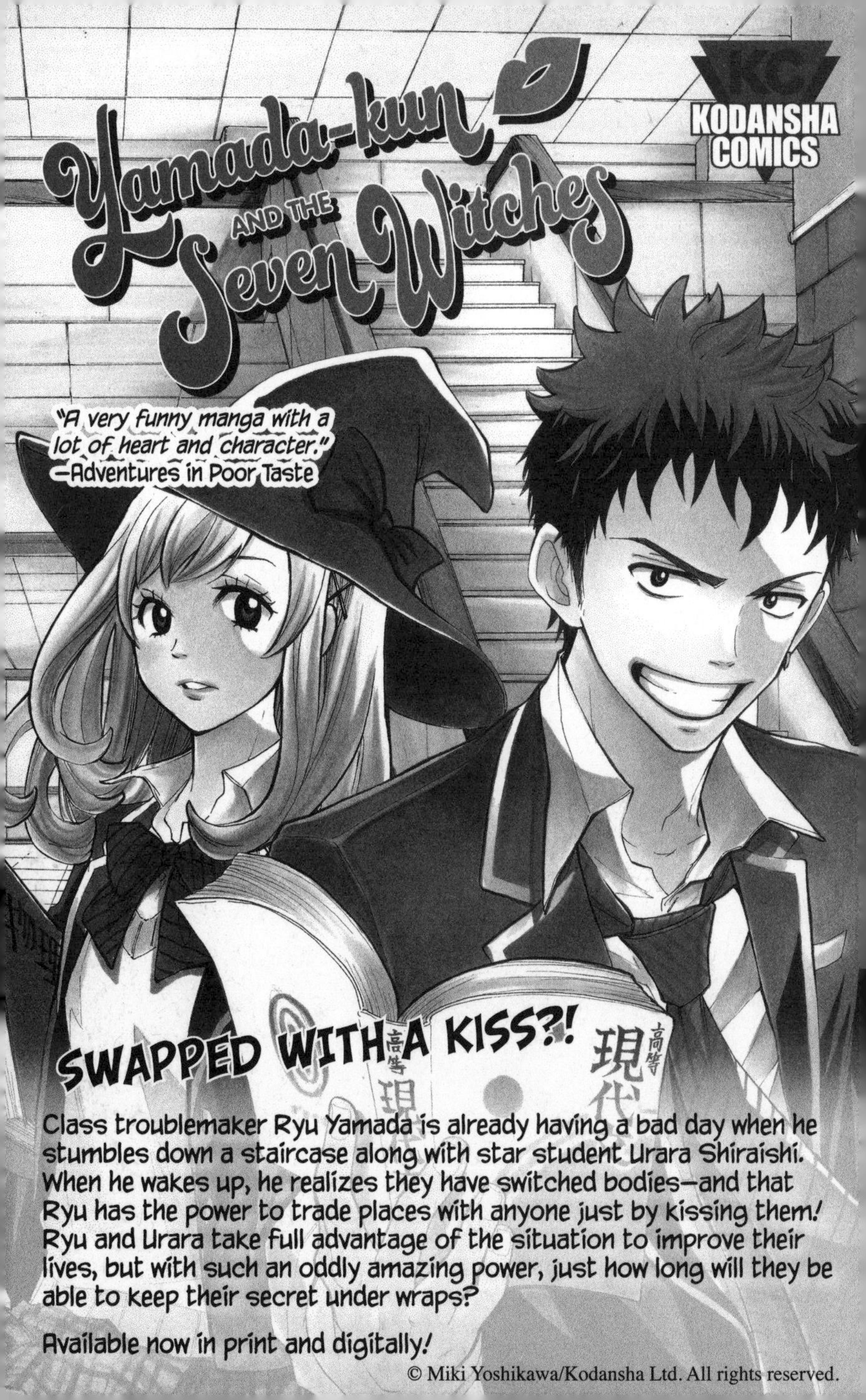
KODANSHA COMICS
Yamada-kun AND THE Seven Witches
"A very funny manga with a lot of heart and character."
—Adventures in Poor Taste
SWAPPED WITH A KISS?!
Class troublemaker Ryu Yamada is already having a bad day when he stumbles down a staircase along with star student Urara Shiraishi. When he wakes up, he realizes they have switched bodies—and that Ryu has the power to trade places with anyone just by kissing them! Ryu and Urara take full advantage of the situation to improve their lives, but with such an oddly amazing power, just how long will they be able to keep their secret under wraps?
Available now in print and digitally!
© Miki Yoshikawa/Kodansha Ltd. All rights reserved.

Real Account volume 3 is a work of fiction. Names, characters, places, and incidents are the products of the author's imagination or are used fictitiously. Any resemblance to actual events, locales, or persons, living or dead, is entirely coincidental.

A Kodansha Comics Trade Paperback Original.

Published in the United States by Kodansha Comics,
an imprint of Kodansha USA Publishing, LLC, New York.

Publication rights for this English edition arranged through Kodansha Ltd., Tokyo.

First published in Japan in 2015 by Kodansha Ltd., Tokyo, as *Real Account* volume 3.

ISBN 978-1-63236-236-0

Printed in the United States of America.

www.kodanshacomics.com

9 8 7 6 5 4 3 2 1

Translation: Claire Hallmark
Lettering: Evan Hayden and Jennifer Skarupa
Editing: Ajani Oloye
Kodansha Comics edition cover design: Phil Balsman